A CONCISE
HISTORY OF PAKISTAN

A CONCISE
HISTORY OF PAKISTAN

M. R. KAZIMI

OXFORD
UNIVERSITY PRESS

OXFORD
UNIVERSITY PRESS

Great Clarendon Street, Oxford OX2 6DP

Oxford University Press is a department of the University of Oxford.
It furthers the University's objective of excellence in research, scholarship,
and education by publishing worldwide in

Oxford New York

Auckland Cape Town Dar es Salaam Hong Kong Karachi
Kuala Lumpur Madrid Melbourne Mexico City Nairobi
New Delhi Shanghai Taipei Toronto

with offices in

Argentina Austria Brazil Chile Czech Republic France Greece
Guatemala Hungary Italy Japan Poland Portugal Singapore
South Korea Switzerland Turkey Ukraine Vietnam

Oxford is a registered trade mark of Oxford University Press
in the UK and in certain other countries

ISBN 978-0-19-547506-7

Typeset in Minion Pro
Printed in Pakistan by
Kagzi Printers, Karachi.
Published by
Ameena Saiyid, Oxford University Press
No. 38, Sector 15, Korangi Industrial Area, PO Box 8214
Karachi-74900, Pakistan.

For my grandson
Musi Reza Kazimi

Contents

PART VI
CONSTITUTIONAL HISTORY

PART VII
HISTORY OF THE INSTITUTIONS

PART VIII
DIPLOMATIC HISTORY

PART IX
ECONOMIC HISTORY

PART X
CULTURAL HISTORY

When the United States sought freedom from the British Empire, both the countries had a common religion, common language and common race. Today, no one, least of all, the British prime minister, questions the right of the United States to be independent. If the United States had continued as a British colony, they would not have had the resources or the inclination to side with Britain in the Second World War. The parallel between the American and Pakistani struggles has not totally been lost. A young Lyndon Baines Johnson wrote to congratulate the founder of Pakistan, Mohammad Ali Jinnah:

> Not only Pakistan is grateful for your accomplishment, but all people of the world, especially colonials. We in the Western Hemisphere salute you, and are also looking forward to the day of liberation from foreign yoke.[1]

Governments, unlike individuals, have to deal with exigencies, and if the British prime minister publicly hoped that partition was temporary, it was because the residual interests of Britain lay more with India than Pakistan. Such attitudes are understandable in politicians, they are not understandable in historians. Arnold Joseph Toynbee was perceptively loath to recognize the new country as a separate entity. In a small note called 'Pakistan as a Historian Sees Her', he commented:

> Yet the pace of the psyche's self-adjustment is so slow that, in AD 1947, the Muslim community in the Indian sub-continent decided that there was still not enough common ground between Muslims and Hindus to enable the two communities to be united under a single government.[2]

Toynbee who viewed history in terms of civilizations transcending nation states, mentioned only the challenges faced by Pakistan: 'If, in Pakistan, political allegiance were to be decided on lines of race or language, Pakistan would immediately fall to pieces'.[3] While this is intrinsically true, the fact remains that Toynbee saw greater differences within Pakistan, than between India and Pakistan. A historian of the standing of Toynbee was expected to grade historical developments on the basis of their impact on human rights and on human survival.

How these imperatives appeared in national perspective was grasped by Bertrand Russell. Writing letters to world leaders regarding the removal of Zulfikar Ali Bhutto as foreign minister, Russell made the following point:

> In Pakistan, the figure most closely identified with the creation of an independent foreign policy for Pakistan has been removed from office.[4]

At the centre of Z.A. Bhutto's national aspirations has been the issue of Kashmir. The present perception of the Kashmir issue is conditioned by the unipolar configuration, international terrorists, and the nuclearization of the belligerents. The historical coverage of the Kashmir issue is given in the main text, and I hope will contribute to a more realistic appraisal of a dispute that threatens world peace.

In the unipolar configuration, the Kashmir dispute is redundant and Pakistan itself seems expendable. Yet, the outbreak of the Second World War serves to show that the sacrifice of small countries like Poland or Czechoslovakia has not guaranteed peace. Apart from the issue of human rights, Kashmir serves as a reminder that had Russia not sold Alaska to the United States, it would not have lost the Cold War. Thus to argue that the dispute is settled because it has been prolonged is not convincing. As for international terrorism, it needs to be recognized that those organizing pogroms with the aid of state apparatus, are also terrorists.

There has also been an academic neglect in tracing the origins of Muslim militants. No effort has been directed towards studying the rise of the Kharijites, an early group which developed the doctrine of *Isti'rad*, that is the indiscriminate killing of all non-Kharijite Muslims who came their way. They killed the wives and children of those who crossed their path. It is due to this neglect that rage as a phenomenon remains unexplained. They were highly eulogized by the German historian Julius Wellhausen at the beginning of the twentieth century.[5] A re-appraisal is necessary, for it is their offshoots who have the greatest bearing on the third issue.

It is Pakistan which has accepted the UN resolutions on Kashmir; it was Pakistan which proposed that South Asia be a nuclear free zone, Pakistan had no means to respond to Indian nuclear tests in 1974, but before it responded to the 1998 tests, it sought as an alternative, a nuclear umbrella, which was rudely refused. In the main text there is mention of two caches of uranium having been stolen in India, by non-state actors. Non-state actors must be pursued wherever they are, for, the surest prescription for proliferation is discrimination.

Pakistan is, as I write, in the midst of a crisis. A transition to democratic rule is under way; but how sincere, and how complete, will be for future historians to record. But, it is a perennial lesson of history, a lesson not confined to Pakistan, that no matter how iron clad state terrorism may seem, it has the potential to implode. Obliterated from within a framework, bleeding wounds form an alternative vortex. This is how the sands of time keep shifting.

The assassination of Benazir Bhutto on 27 December 2007 is a tragic event which closes a chapter of history, at which point the present narrative should be allowed to conclude. The intervening imposition of emergency as well as its lifting, the setting of an election date, pale into insignificance. The shock and horror over this gruesome act, cut across the political divide, and united former antagonists. Benazir Bhutto had a presence and charisma which far transcended her present status as an opposition leader. The UNSC met and passed a unanimous resolution condemning the dastardly act. The assassin, still unidentified, was an anarchist by intent, if not an anarchist by creed. The news of the assassination was followed, understandably, by an outbreak of violence, in which innocent lives and precious property was lost. However, no one's grief can exceed the grief of her husband, Asif Ali Zardari, and her children, the eldest of whom, Bilawal, has succeeded his mother as Chairman of the PPP. Their dignity in grief is a ray of hope, for a nation which is desolate.

By offering a concise history of Pakistan, I am not unmindful of the suitability of writing a history of Asia, or even South Asia, as indeed, histories of France or Germany have not made superfluous European history as a discipline. The world has evolved different levels of historiography: universal, national, and local. Any one of them help the reader to arrive at an understanding of history, not possible at the other two levels.

The same can be said of the topic wise categories: Social history, Cultural history or Economic history. Since I have been schooled only in some categories, I had to fall back on my wife Dr Anjum Bano, Assistant Professor of Special Education at the University of Karachi, for the section on the history of Education; and to my daughter, an IBA student for the section on Economic history. It is only my extreme reluctance to lose political quarrels to them, that I refrain from naming them as co-authors. The faults that remain are, as they will be the first to tell you, mine alone. My son and daughter-in-law have helped me in diverse ways, especially by putting up with my grouchiness. I dedicate this book to my grandson, who not only made me take an optimistic view of events, but because it is children, who without any concern for rights or fairness, celebrate Independence Day with the utmost fervour. I need record the debt I owe Ms Ameena Saiyid, OBE, Managing Director of the Oxford University Press as also to Ms Ghousia Bano Ghofran Ali, Managing Editor, for their encouragement.

NOTES

1. Mehrunnisa Ali (ed.), *Jinnah on World Affairs*, Karachi: Pakistan Study Centre, University of Karachi, 2007, p. 521.
2. *Crescent and Green*, London: Cassell and Co., 1955, p. 3.
3. Ibid., p. 2.
4. Reproduced in Kausar Niazi, *Deedawar*, Lahore: Shaikh Ghulam Ali and Sons, 1977, pp. 112–118.
5. Julius Wellhausen, *The Religio-Political Factions in Early Islam*, tr. R.C. Ostle and S.M. Walzer, Amsterdam: North-Holland Publishing Co., 1975, pp. 41, 42.

PART I
ANCIENT AND
MEDIEVAL HISTORY

LAND AND PEOPLE

Pakistan enjoys several phenomenal features. It has the largest habitat of Green Turtles. It is home to Makli, the world's largest necropolis. In Ziarat, Pakistan has the world's largest juniper forest. It is home to the Blind Dolphin. It has in Sukkur, the world's largest man-made irrigation system. It has Tarbela, the world's largest, man-made, earth-filled dam. Pakistan also has the highest metalled road in the world: the Karakoram Highway/Khunjerab Pass.

Pakistan has Haleji, Asia's largest bird sanctuary; in Gilgit is Asia's longest suspension bridge. It has Bolan, Asia's longest railway tunnel, and is among the last refuge of the railway steam engine.

Another indication of Pakistan's prominence is that it has held at various times the world championship in four games: hockey, cricket, squash, and snooker.

LOCATION

Pakistan is located between 24° and 47° latitude North, and between longitudes 61° and 75.31° East. To Pakistan's east is India, to its west, Iran, and to its north-west, Afghanistan. In close proximity are China through Azad Kashmir, and across the Wakhan strip in Afghanistan lies Tajikistan. Pakistan's most strategic feature at present is the Makran coast, with the Gwadar sea port just across from the United Arab Emirates, which has sea access to Basra in Iraq.

CLIMATE AND TOPOGRAPHY

Few other countries offer such a sharp contrast between climates. In the north is Chitral, Gilgit, and Hunza where the highest mountains and snow-capped areas are located. In the south-east is the Thar desert. In the eastern half of Pakistan lies the Indus plain. The Balochistan area is a rugged and arid plateau. The North-West Frontier Province has a similar terrain but is relieved by three valleys.

AREA

Pakistan	796,096 sq. km.
Islamabad	906 sq. km.
Punjab	205,345 sq. km.
Sindh	140,914 sq. km.
North-West Frontier Province	74,521 sq. km.
Balochistan	347,190 sq. km.
Federally Administered Tribal Area	27,220 sq. km.

POPULATION

Total	165.8 million
Male	67,840,000
Female	62,739,000
Urban	42,458,000
Rural	88,121,000

POPULATION GROWTH   2.11%

LITERACY RATES

Total population	48.7% (2004 est.)
Male	61.7%
Female	35.2%

MANUFACTURING SECTOR

Growth for financial year (2004–5)	18%	
Automobile sector	30.1%	(*July–March)
Food, Beverages, and Tobacco	–2.7%	
Textile and Apparel	24.5%	
Paper and Board	4.2%	
Pharmaceutical	4%	
Electrical	54.9%	(*July–March)

AGRICULTURE

Agriculture accounts for 23 per cent of Pakistan's gross domestic product (GDP) and employs 42 per cent of its workforce.

MAJOR CROPS

1. Cotton accounts for 10.5 per cent of the value added to agriculture, and about 2.4 per cent to GDP. The production of cotton is estimated at 14,618 thousand bales for 2004–5.

2. Rice accounts for 5.7 per cent value added to agriculture. Production of rice in 2004–5 is provisionally estimated at 4991 thousand tons, which is 2.9 per cent higher than the previous year. Rice was cultivated on an area of 2503 thousand hectares showing an increase in acreage of 10.7 per cent over the previous year.
3. Sugarcane's share in value added agriculture and GDP are 3.6 per cent and 0.8 per cent respectively. Sugarcane was cultivated on an area of 947 thousand hectares while the size of the sugarcane crop was 45,316.
4. Wheat contributes 13.8 per cent to the value added to agriculture and 3.2 per cent to GDP. The size of the wheat crop is provisionally estimated at 21,109 thousand tons. Wheat was cultivated on an area of 8330 thousand hectares. Other major crops such as *bajra, jawar*, maize, and barley saw a slight decrease in production, while gram, tobacco, rapeseed and mustard showed an increase during 2004–5.

ENERGY

1. Gas: The balance recoverable reserves of natural gas were 30.13 trillion cubic feet as on 1 January 2005.
2. Petroleum: The balance recoverable reserves of crude oil have been estimated at 307.4 million barrels as on 1 January 2005.

Source: *Pakistan Economic Survey 2004–2005.*

PROFILE OF EARLY SOUTH ASIAN HISTORY

The land of ancient India is a peninsula, which means that it is surrounded on three sides by water. The fourth side, the north, is covered by high mountain ranges. This means that it is difficult to enter and to leave this land from this side. The difficulty of communication made the inhabitants inward-looking. Over time, this tendency became reinforced by religion. We are talking of the age when the Hindu religion dominated India. In Hindu society, if one crossed the sea, even to go from Keamari to Manora, one would lose one's caste. In those days caste was the sole means of identity, therefore few inhabitants ventured to cross the rough seas or the perilous mountains. This was the effect of the external boundaries.

Internally, distances were vast and travel unsafe because there were no roads, and there was also the danger of being attacked by wild animals or bitten by poisonous insects. The climate of one region, such as snow-bound Chitral, differed sharply from that of Tharparkar, a hot desert area. Just as the external boundaries gave a sense of unity, the internal topographical features pushed India towards diversity. The sense of unity was reinforced by religion: the sense of diversity promoted a rich and varied culture.

Since both unity and diversity had their basis in geography, both impulses were strong. Sometimes one tendency was uppermost, sometimes the other. We have seen since the Hindu period, how unity was identified with religion, and diversity with culture. These tendencies, moving towards, and away from unity, alternated.

Following the invasion of Alexander (327 BC), this rhythm manifested itself politically. Small local kingdoms and large paramount empires alternated. Small kingdoms gave way to the Maurya empire. When the Maurya empire disintegrated, small kingdoms took its place. This alternation we find continuing in the Muslim era. The Muslims conquered small Hindu kingdoms and ultimately the Delhi Sultanate was established. When the Delhi Sultanate disintegrated, the Bahmani kingdom, the Jaunpur kingdom, and the Bengal kingdom, were established.

These small kingdoms were succeeded by the Mughal empire which in turn gave way to the kingdoms of Awadh, Bengal, and Deccan.

This tendency was curbed under British rule. Being foreigners who retained links with their country of origin, they were not affected by these impulses as rulers with local roots were. Another factor was that the British themselves maintained two entities, British India and the princely states such as Kashmir and Hyderabad. Once the British withdrew, the divisive forces that had been held in abeyance reasserted themselves.

The partition of South Asia into India and Pakistan created two centres. By centre we mean the seats of political establishment which influenced the course of development over a large region. Since there were regional and provincial tendencies in both India (e.g. Andhra) and Pakistan (Bengal), a single strong centre in each country would be able to control both tendencies, over-centralization and regionalism. These are called respectively centripetal and centrifugal tendencies. We have already seen that the outside borders, reinforced by religion (firstly by Hinduism, then other religions), promoted a tendency for unity within the national frontiers. Since regional geography varies as stated from snow-bound areas like Chitral to deserts like Tharparkar, the languages and lifestyles which evolved in separate regions gave a varied complexion to culture within the same national frontiers. We can say that when the pull of religion was powerful, people favoured unity on that basis. This was witnessed in the creation of Pakistan. On the other hand, when the pull of culture was stronger, then the unity created by religion diminished as a force and cultural distinction led to regionalism.

For the present we must summarize briefly the phases through which our land has passed:

The cradle of world civilization is Balochistan. By 1954, Kile Ghul Mohammad was excavated to yield the remains of a Neolithic settlement. Initially the inhabitants of this dwelling were so primitive that they could not make pots, though later on they developed pottery of two distinctive styles: Zhob and Quetta. The script discovered at Kile Ghul Mohammad led Leslie Alcock to describe it as 'according to some scholars', the oldest alphabet in the world.[1]

Let us begin with the script. They were angular letters like A, T and V and were found inscribed on pots as single letters. This relates to the middle stage, as the development of pottery allows us to trace its evolution. The earliest pots were misshapen, thick and coarse. If the single letters were a primitive version of the alphabet, then, the developed version is yet to be discovered. Of the later two varieties, the earthenware discovered at Zhob had designs in black on a red background. The earthenware discovered at Quetta had a pale brown background. While Quetta ware had only geometric patterns, the Zhob ware had both geometrical forms and animal representations. In Kile Ghul Mohammad itself, the model of a house was discovered, the earliest in South Asia.[2] Female statuettes were also a feature of this dwelling. The people who occupied Damb Sadaat 4500 years ago are thought to have come from what is now called Quetta.

The discovery, about twenty years later, of Mehrgarh by Jean-Francois Jarrige proved far more momentous. Jarrige, on the basis of carbon testing dates this civilization from 9000 to 3500 BC. This makes Mehrgarh far older than the Egyptian and Mesopotamian civilizations. The Bolan River was close, because Jarrige asserts that Mehrgarh did not require any irrigation. The inhabitants used stone implements. The Swamp Deer was hunted, goats and sheep domesticated, barley and wheat were cultivated. Copper objects have been found, as have evidence of metal, ceramic and textile industries. The inhabitants buried their dead.[3]

The Mehrgarh populace built large mud brick halls as granaries. Their houses were large, containing many rooms. Mehrgarh has been linked to the succeeding Indus valley civilization because of common features like long blocks, sophisticated drain systems, canals and big water tanks. Thus the discovery of Mehrgarh also went to prove that the Indus valley civilization was indigenous, and did not originate in Mesopotamia as some archaeologists have speculated.

In between Mehrgarh and Moenjo Daro lies Kot Diji as a possible intermediary phase. Kot Diji and its subsidiary site at Rahman Dehri shows that the people could weave, produce pottery, as well as work at bronze and copper.

Both Moenjo Daro and Harappa, twin cities of the Indus Valley Civilization were riverside settlements, measuring three miles in circumference; both

Moenjo Daro and Harappa have two parts: the higher consisting of citadels, the lower consisting of small houses. The citadel at Harappa was built on a protective foundation with very high walls of burnt bricks. There are rectangular towers at intervals, especially at the corners. The imposing citadel at Moenjo Daro has a granary, a public bath, and dwellings consisting of many rooms. It is thought that they were the preserve of the rulers or the ruling class, which, from the available evidence, could have been either royal or religious. Architecture had reached the stage of the korbel arch.

In the twin cities, town planning is common to both parts, but the lower part shows uniformity. This uniformity, the smallness and sameness of the houses has led archaeologists to believe that this was a colony of the lower class, or, that a form of socialism was practiced. The houses consist of one of only two designs, both featuring two small rooms and a courtyard. The roads into which these houses open are symmetrical, geometrically planned roads, consisting of oblong blocks, measuring 400 yards in length 200 or 300 yards in width. There is a drainage system running alongside. The streets are unadorned. This leads Sir Mortimer Wheeler to conclude that: 'sameness, isolation, centralization are the abstract qualities of the Indus Civilization.[4]

This is the epitaph written on a silent and regimented populace, and until the Indus Script is deciphered, we must leave it in place. On the other hand, the fact that though Moenjo Daro had hunting implements, it had no weapons also speaks for itself. This inspired Faiz Ahmed Faiz to say:

> And their earthen lamps which shed no
> Light on the mysteries of human darkness
> The timelessness of the unicorn.

There are many seals bearing many types of representation, mostly of natural objects, but there is one type of seal which is enigmatic. These are seal representations of a three-faced deity with horns, and who is seen squatting with folded legs. The background varies. This figure bears resemblance to the later Hindu images of Shiva, the second member of the Hindu trinity. This so far appears to be the only possible link between the Indus Valley people and the Aryans who later occupied India.

What caused the destruction of the Indus Valley Civilization is debated. Either it was a natural calamity, or else invasion by the Aryans. With the coming of the Aryans we can trace the evolution of Hindustan, although this process has been questioned. According to Romila Thapar: 'The evolution of Hinduism is not a linear progression from a founder through an organizational system of sects branching off.'[5] She is partially correct in her view that the evolution of Hinduism was not linear, since the Hindu view of nature, and consequently of the supernatural was not linear.

In the Rig Veda pantheon (which we shall presently discuss) there is a deity known as Eka Deva or One God: 'The Vedic Aryans believed that the creation of the universe and the procreation of the human race were the result of a primeval sacrifice, the self immolation of a cosmic being.[6] Despite a superficial resemblance to the Big Bang theory, it is different, since it cannot be called creation *ex nihilo*, as the preceding period is described as between non-being and being. Apart from Eka Deva subsequently being identified with Indra, the next deity in the pantheon is Agni. It was worshipped as fire on earth, as lightning in the sky, and the sun in the celestial sphere. All these are pure and visible manifestations of nature. But despite showing Agni as the object of worship, the Rig Veda characterizes him as the chief priest, with the implication that the supernatural has a dimension beyond the celestial sphere.

In the later portion of the Rig Veda, a poet searches for the origin of creation, without mentioning any primeval sacrifice.

> Who really knows? Who shall here proclaim it?—whence came things to be, whence this creation. The gods are on this side, along with the creation. So then, whence it came to be?[7]

In other words, abstraction came after mythology. The progression is not linear, but then, it is also not chaotic, it is cyclic. This is not quite in tune with Romila Thapar's contention: 'The worship of icons was unthought of in Vedic religion, but the idol becomes significant feature of the Puranic religion.'[8] Thus while the progression is linear between the Vedas and the Puranas, as well as from abstraction to manifestation, but abstraction itself had not followed a linear progression.

But, what are the Vedas? The Vedas are four in number, Rig Veda, Sama Veda, Yajur Veda and the Atharva Veda. It is surmised that the Rig Veda was composed between 2000 to 1500 BC. Though the Samhita, a collection of 1028 hymns, was composed later than the other parts of the book, it forms an essential component of the Rig Veda. The Sama Veda was a textbook for rituals to be used by priests during the Sama sacrifice, the Sama being a sacred brew. The Yajur Veda was also a text for ritual purposes, but it extended to rituals beyond the Sama sacrifice. The Atharva Veda is made up of verses, incantations, charms against evil; and was composed much later than the preceding Veda.

The Vedas were followed by the Brahmanas, the Upanishads and the Sutras. The Brahmanas were basically an exegesis of the Samhita. The Upanishads area spiritual and mystical treatise. Upanishad means 'sitting at the Master's feet'. In its essence it is about the relation of the individual soul with the universal soul. It is here that we find the doctrine of the Transmigration of souls, the ultimate merger of the individual soul, spells liberation from the cycle of rebirth. This would be the matrix, not only of Hinduism, but Jainism and Buddhism as well. We give below only two glimpses of the Upanishads. The first is from the Mundaka Upanishad:

> Heavenly, formless is the Person
> He is without and within, unborn,
> Breathless, mindless, pure
> Higher than the high Imperishable.

This concept of god is not mythological; it is compatible with the monotheistic concept. Being unborn has a significance, because Hindu doctrine holds that the universe is eternal, not, in other words, born out of nothing. In the Svetasvatara Upanishad, there is a stanza which explains that knowing the One Supreme Person overcomes death:

> Higher than this is Brahma. The Supreme, the Great
> Hidden in all things, body by body
> The One embracer of the universe—
> By knowing him as Lord men become immortal.

The process of knowing here, is not confined to cognition, but is one of merger of the personal soul into the universal soul. In time the Hindu trinity came to consist of Brahma the creator, Vishnu the preserver and Shiva the destroyer. Distinguishable from Brahma is *Brahman* the universal soul, that is God, and the personal soul, called *Atman*. The soul suffers the consequences of action (*karma*) and according to the nature of deeds performed, is reborn again and again as a human being of either a higher or lower caste. If deeds committed in a lifetime are evil, the soul can find the body of even an animal. To exist is to suffer, and to seek salvation from suffering, the *atman* needs to perform deeds which enable it to escape rebirth by merging with the *Brahman*.

The Sutras were aphorisms, held by some scholars to be the earliest repositories of Indian philosophy. The Sutras require wide reading to yield meaning, since they are allusive and symbolic. It is rare to find a Sutra which is self-explanatory. This is intellectually a merit, but socially, it reflects the trend to make higher forms of knowledge inaccessible to the masses.

The Puranas became the text for the instruction of masses. They are eighteen in number, encompassing a wide range of subjects, mythology, philosophy, history and the laws. The oldest Purana dates to AD 400. Thus came about the dichotomy of Hindus worshipping the concept, and the Hindus worshipping idols. This was discernible even in the twentieth century. Mahatma Gandhi said that the Rama he worshipped was not the historical

Rama, the son of Dasharatha: 'The Rama whom I adore is God Himself, different from any historical Rama. He always was, is now, and will be forever, a God who was unborn and uncreated.'[9] Nevertheless, in carrying his political creed to the masses, Mahatma Gandhi alluded plainly to the mythology. Similarly, since his creed of non-violence was at odds with Krishna's exhortation to Arjuna, Gandhi interpreted the *Bhagavad Gita* symbolically:

> The battlefield setting of the Gita is allegorical, not historical... The human body is the true chariot, Arjuna the human mind and Krishna the Indwelling Guide... After exhorting repeatedly against anger and hatred in the Gita, why would Krishna ask for killing, a deed inseparable from anger or hatred?[10]

These allusions bring us to the Epic Age. There are two epics relating to ancient India, the *Mahabharata* and the *Ramayana*. The *Mahabharata* describes war between different tribes and factions, notably the battle of Kurukshetra between the Pandavas and Kauravas. The *Bhagavad Gita* referred to above, is a part of the *Mahabharata*. The *Ramayan* tells the story of Rama, the son of Raja Dasharatha, who was exiled for twelve years at the behest of his stepmother. The purity of Sita his bride, and the loyalty of Lakshman his brother have given a sacred aspect to a court intrigue. Rama's battle with Ravana, for the rescue of Sita is the episode which makes the *Ramayana* truly epic. Both Krishna and Rama are considered avatars or reincarnations of Vishnu.

With the Puranas, the forms of worship and the caste system became entrenched in Hindu society. Two successive creeds Jainism and Buddhism challenged the caste system, and practiced *ahimsa* or non-violence. Jainism remained confined to India but survives here though only as an unthreatening minority. Buddhism gained adherents in millions outside India, in the Far East and South East Asia, but in the country of its origin this creed too remains a minority. The main protagonists of the two religions, Mahavira and Siddhartha, were near contemporaries, and preached in the same region Magadha (modern Bihar).

Jain tradition holds that the first Tirthankara, Rikhav (aka Rishabhadev or Adinatha), lived around 6500 BC. Thus, Jainism would predate the coming of the Aryans. While it may not be possible to date the age of Rikhav with precision, but the possibility of his having lived in the pre-Aryan era lies in the similarity between Rikhav and the Hindu deity Shiva; both are symbolized by the Bull. Jain theology was codified orally by Indrabhuti Gautama, the direct disciple of Mahavira (Vardhamana) as Dvadasanga Sultan, but was committed to writing only a millennium after Mahavira.

The path to liberation under Jainism is called *Moksha Marg*. It consists of three jewels: correct faith, correct understanding, and correct conduct, and all three are interrelated. These jewels are universal, found in the ethical basis of all major religions. What is new are the Jain concepts of God, Universe and Time. God is not the creator of the universe, since the universe is considered uncreated and eternal, but God is defined as the souls that have been liberated. This would involve forging the plural into the singular, but it is not surprising that God should be identified with the soul, since Hinduism had already introduced the concepts of the individual soul (*atman*) and the universal soul (Brahman). The universe has always existed, according to the Jain doctrine, and shall always exist, but its nature lies in a state in between the real and imaginary. 'Both the spheres, of cognitive sensory soul, and non-cognitive and non-sensory matter exist.[11]

The Jain concept of time is also noteworthy: 'Time does not operate in the same way every where in the universe.'[12] These time zones correspond to real or imaginary parts of the universe. The universe is anthropologically conceived, that is, the universe is in the shape of a human being. Our world, in which we live, lies in the waist. This needs further inquiry, since the universe is considered eternal, but the origin of mankind is placed within time.

The life spans of Mahavira and Buddha overlapped, and the area where they carried out their mission is roughly the same. Indeed, Mahavira finds mention in Buddhist literature under the name Nigantha Nataputta. It is generally conceded that the figure of the first Tirthankara, Rikhav, because of belonging to remote antiquity, may have been legendary, but the four Buddhas are rarely mentioned together: Amitabha Buddha, Konakamana Buddha, Kalachakra Buddha and Shakyamuni, the prince of Kapilvastu. Amitabha is the celestial Buddha, Konakamana the ancient Buddha, and Kalachakra, the primordial Buddha. Hui Yuan, a Chinese monk bowed to Amitabha Buddha on 11 September AD 402. Ashoka doubled the size of the brick memorial to Konakamana Buddha in 254 BC, and Kalachakra Buddha was paid homage to by the present Dalai Lama at Budh Gaya in 1985. However, the scholar introducing these earliest figures to the present generation, seems not to believe in the historical existence of the three earlier Buddhas himself. His explanation is 'A nuanced account of Shakyamuni as founder must emphasize his relationship with other Buddhas, because, for Buddhists, Shakyamuni's non-uniqueness as Buddha is central to his status as founder.'[13]

Shakyamuni, Siddhartha, Gautama are the names by which the founder of Buddhism is known. There is another term Bodhisatta, which has acquired ambiguous shades of meaning, but it was first used in the sense of a previous incarnation of the Buddha. There is also the concept of a future Buddha, foretold by Gautama himself, and called Maitreya, who would, in the future, purify the world.[14] This is an eschatological concept not native to the soil of India. Gautama was a prince enjoying all earthly bounties, but he renounced all worldly pleasures when he encountered disease, old age, and death. He finally struck a middle path between hedonism and asceticism to gain *Nirvana* or Enlightenment. His four principles are the persistence of suffering, the root cause of suffering (that is existence), that suffering can be brought to an end (by ending the cycle of rebirth) and the measures to be taken to end suffering.

The question which arises is: how did Buddha reconcile his rejection of a Creator with acceptance of the conception of transmigration of souls? Both involving belief in the supernatural? Even the alleged Buddhist rejection of a Creator, contains a supernatural allusion. 'Brahma imagined himself to be the creator, when in fact the world came into existence as a result of natural causes.[15]

A.L. Basham, after citing a passage from Pitrputra Sanagama paraphrases it most lucidly:

> In an illusory world, rebirth is also illusory. The thing man craves, have no more reality than a dream, but he craves nevertheless, and hence his illusory ego is reborn in a new, but equally illusory body. Notice the importance of the last conscious thought before death, which plays a very decisive part in the nature of the rebirth.[16]

The metaphysical basis of Jainism and Buddhism may have been elusive, but their ethical basis is sound, and in a land where orthopraxy takes precedence over orthodoxy, its contribution to civilization is immense. In the meanwhile, the first kingdoms were making their appearance in the Magadha area. The first was the Shishunaga dynasty (600–317 BC) which had ten kings, out of which Bimbisara (528–500 BC) and his son Ajatasatru (500–475 BC) stand out. Bimbisara was fifth in the line of succession which means that it was midway through their rule that the Shishunaga dynasty was able to assert its power. Bimbisara built Rajagriha where the present day Rajgir is situated. Bimbisara began a series of conquests, and annexed a minor kingdom, that of Anga. Bimbisara renounced in 500 BC his crown in favour of his son, Ajatasatru, but this act of renunciation could not save him from being killed by his son. His rule was contested by the king of Kosala, the brother-in-law of Bimbisara. Ajatasatru not only defeated the king of Kosala, he reduced the entire territory between the Ganges and the Himalayas. Ajatasatru built the city of Pataliputra, modern day Patna. Pataliputra not only outstripped Rajgir but became the capital of the paramount power in India. All the other kings of this dynasty are known only in name, their deeds or achievements lie in obscurity. The last ruler Mahanandin was charged with patricide, and was deposed by his son Mahapadma Nanda. The Shishunaga finds mention in the Puranas. The Buddha is said have visited Bimbisara in 530 BC and had died towards the end of Ajatasatru's reign. In the same era, we find also the presence of small aristocratic republics like Vrijians and Mallas.[17] The principality of Sakya was also republican, and the name Shakyamuni for Siddhartha, denotes his descent from the Sakyas. In the light of this evidence, Siddhartha's father seems to have been a patriarch, and not actually the king of Kapilvastu. Hemchandra Raychaudhuri cites the Puranas to the effect that Mahapadma, the first of the Nandas was the destroyer of the Kshatriyas, the warrior cast. (The castle system is elaborated in a succeeding chapter.) The Nandas were able to found an extensive empire in Magadha before being supplanted by Chandragupta Maurya.

Since Magadha in the east, became the political centre of India, the insularity of the country became vulnerable from the west, as the Persian empire extended its borders to the banks of the Indus. Cyrus the Great (558–530 BC) the founder of the Persian empire annexed the territories of Afghanistan and Balochistan. Darius (521–486 BC) belonged to a second line of Achaemenian kings, and though no descendant of Cyrus, occupied the Persian throne and added the territory west of the Indus to his empire. Darius made this territory 'Hindush' the twentieth Satrapy (or province) of the Persian empire. From here Darius I realized an annual tribute of 360 talents of gold—indirect evidence of the prosperity of this region. One hundred and fifty years later when the Persian empire faced the invasion of Alexander the Macedonian, Darius III was able to raise a considerable number of soldiers for his defence. Thus, Alexander's invasion of Persia brought him to the bank of the Indus.

How Alexander's invasion became a catalyst which re-affirmed Indian nationhood has already been mentioned. Alexander, after his conquest of Iran, entered Afghanistan and probably entered South Asia from a pass in the Northern Areas. He secured an alliance with the king of Taxila and was able to advance to the Jhelum without resistance. Porus (also Raja Puru), king of the lands beyond, decided to resist. He had a large army of 50,000 to Alexander's 20,000. Porus had 200 elephants which were placed eight lines deep. Alexander was able to cross the cold and deep Beas before Porus could anticipate his move. He attacked the rear of the army of Porus and rained arrows on the elephants who stampeded and crushed their own forces. As always Alexander proved to be a better general, but found that his adversary had retained his royal dignity. When Alexander asked Porus, 'How would you like to be treated?' Porus's replied, 'Like a king'. Suitably impressed Alexander restored Porus's kingdom to him, for this would be his last victory. When he attempted further conquest, his war weary soldiers refused to advance beyond the Beas. Alexander sailed down the Indus and along the Mekran coast, eventually reaching the mouth of the Euphrates. Soon he would be dead and his empire would be divided among his generals.

During his advance, Alexander created the first world empire, and in retreat created the first Indian empire. Alexander's representative Philip was killed in a revolt led by Eudemos. Next Eudemos treacherously murdered Porus. Seleukos asserted the rule, but was defeated by Chandragupta Maurya (320–297 BC) Chandragupta was thus able to acquire territory extending from north India to Afghanistan. Chandragupta is said to have met Alexander, to seek his help in overthrowing the Nandas but nothing came out of this proposal. No meeting between their respective mentors, Aristotle and Kautilya is recorded. The cultural effects of Alexander's invasion would be long lasting. The defeat of Seleukos gave rise to central Asian principalities like Bactria situated between the Hindukush mountains and the Oxus River; and Parthia, situated south-east of the Caspian Sea. They achieved independence along the same time, i.e. *c.*250 BC. Ultimately, these movements would lead to the foundation of the Kushan empire.

Let us travel with Chandragupta Maurya to Pataliputra. His empire had been established by conquest, after the overthrow of the Nandas, Pataliputra became a city known far beyond South Asia, because of a Greek scribe, Megasthenes, and Buddhist missionaries. According to Jain tradition, Chandragupta Maurya became a Jain renouncing his kingdom, and became a mendicant. Little is known of his son Bindusara except that his title Amitragatha (the slayer of foes) shows that he continued the course of conquest, and could have extended the Mauryan empire to the south. Bindusara converted to the Ajivikas creed, another non-Brahmanic creed which Megasthenes mentions by the name of Sramanic. His son Ashoka, as the world knows, converted to Buddhism, and became Buddhism's greatest preacher taking Indian traditions far beyond its borders and leading to its eventual supremacy in East and South-East Asia.

The conversions of the Mauryan emperors to the creeds of the Jains, the Ajivikas and the Buddhists, leads Romila Thapar to observe that Sramanic creeds were prevalent in Magadha, therefore, exposure to them was not exposure to heterodoxy, but to current religious ideas.[18]

The pacifist policy of Ashoka, in some measure, led to the eventual decline of the Mauryas. Pushyamitra overthrew the last Mauryan and established the Sunga dynasty. Pushyamitra had heralded his accession by offering Ashwa Medha, the horse-sacrifice signifying the end of the non-violent creeds. Pushyamitra extended his boundaries to the Narbada in the south and successfully repulsed the invasion of Demetrius, the fourth king of Bactria. Little is known of the Sungas, and their successors, the Kanvas.

On the western borders, in the regions of Bactria, and Parthia, containing sizeable Greek colonies, we see a wave of migrations from Central Asia. The Sakas were pushed by the Yueh-Chi or Kushans, due to upheavals in China, and the Sakas then forced the Parthians to move. At Taxila the Yueh-Chi laid the foundations of the Kushan empire which straddled Central Asia and the Indus Valley. These constant invasions by Hellenic and Mongoloid people brought about a unique fusion. Many Bactrian coins rank with the finest in existence.[19] These cultural trends gave an impetus to Mahayana Buddhism, which allowed sculptural representation. Thus Buddism, an oriental creed received a Hellenic style in art. Gandhara, located between the Kunduz and the Indus rivers, was in the proximity of the roads traversing the known world, and thus gained a cosmopolitan character.

In 1913, Sir John Marshal discovered the Taxila site, where a university had flourished. In 2005 Muhammad Arif discovered Badalpur, near Haripur, which seems an extension of Taxila. However, in contrast to Taxila, Badalpur had mud plasters on both sides of a wall. This site held numerous metal objects, large and small, ranging from gold to iron. Also discovered was a building complex of eight cells, which housed Buddhist monks. Fortunately, the western side main entrance is still intact.[20]

The political and military side of this civilization was advanced by the Kushans. The first ruler was known as Miaos (or Heraos). He had to defeat four related tribes to make himself king. Next to gain prominence was Kadphises I who ousted the Parthians. His successor Kadphises II conquered Taxila. It was he who caused Roman gold to flow into his kingdom. In time the third ruler Kanishka would charge cess over the trade and fill the royal coffers with gold. In Kanishka's time the Kushan kingdom expanded. Bordered by Iran on the west, to the north beyond the Pamir plateau, in the east by the confluence of the Yamuna and Chambal rivers and the Malva plateau in the south. It was under Kanishka that Buddhism acquired a new sect and he built the Buddhist tower at Peshawar. 'Excavations at Mat near Mathura have disclosed a life-size statue of the great king.'[21] The language used in the Kushan empire was Bactrian from where the Kharoshti script evolved. Newly discovered sites of the Bactrian language are still opening up the secrets of the Kushan dynasty.[22]

The Kushan empire was politically strong, economically rich and culturally diverse, but it could not withstand the onslaught of the Sassanid dynasty of Persia. In the first year of his reign (AD 240) Shapur I captured Peshawar and extended his writ to the Khyber Pass. The death of Shapur I in AD 271 provided a brief respite, but when Shapur II came of age, the Kushans suffered a massive defeat. Neither the Persian reconquest nor the rise of the Guptas to the east ended the misery of the Kushan empire, for another people from Central Asia, the White Huns conquered the region in AD 465. They had a long rule, for the White Huns under Toramana were able to defeat the last of the Guptas. The tables were turned, when the successor of Toramana, known as Mihirkula was defeated by the ruler of Malwa, Yasodharman, forcing Mihirkula to seek refuge in Kashmir.

The Gupta dynasty was the first, if not the only paramount power in India to have been Hindu. Six centuries separate the Guptas from the Mauryas, when a vibrant civilization flourished. By the time the Guptas came, Sanskrit had passed from common usage and had become the preserve of the priests. It is remarkable that a language which was revived produced masterpieces. Kalidasa embellished the Gupta age and produced magna opera like *Shakuntala* and *Meghdoot*, which are world classics.

Chandragupta I, the founder of the dynasty was married to a princess of the Lichavi line, and from this position was able to secure his kingdom. His becoming the King of Kings thereafter was due only to his own ability. Although his reign was short, about six years, he extended his territories beyond the Ganges up to Allahabad. These conquests were carried forward by his son Samudragupta (AD 326–327) up to the mountains of Nepal in the north, and the Bay of Bengal in the east. He then turned south and west, taking Khandesh and Maharashtra. It was on his return from these conquests that Samudragupta performed the Ashwameda, symbolising the revival of Hinduism.

Samudragupta, besides being a poet himself, gathered to his court men of talent and learning. His successor Chandragupta II (AD 375–413) passed into lore as the legendary Vikramaditya, and gathered around him Nine Gems, individuals embodying the talent and the genius of his age. His conquests took his territory forward to Gujarat from Maharashtra, and secured for him the Kathiawar sea coast. Little has been recorded about the last two rulers. From the fact that Kumaragupta (AD 412–455) had held the horse sacrifice, it is deduced that he was militarily and politically, a powerful ruler. His son Skandagupta (AD 455–480) went down before the White Hun invasion.

Because the Gupta empire marked a state revival of Hinduism, its contribution to the flowering of South Asian culture has come in for criticism by revisionist historians. D.D. Kosambi is supported by Romila Thapar in his comment: 'Far from the Guptas reviving nationalism, it was nationalism which revived the Guptas.'[23] It remains unclear under what structure could nationalism make the Guptas its instrument. Moreover, this judgement presumes that nationalism was a force that was stronger than the rulers were. Even if this is so, then religion must be included as a vital ingredient of that nationalism. If this comment is supposed to mean that the Guptas acquired their role only retrospectively, it is an argument that cannot be seriously advanced, since the very fact that the Guptas passed into lore and legend, and were undoubtedly the patrons of great literature, their importance as a factor in the unfolding history of South Asia cannot be discounted.

According to the pattern of South Asian history, the upheaval caused by the inroads of the White Huns brought about a hiatus of fragmentation, before another paramount power, in the present case the empire of

Harshavardhan could emerge. Harshavardhan had inherited the kingdom of Thanesar which lay between the Sutlej and Yamuna. Rajyavardhan the elder brother of Harsha was killed by the Raja of Malwa, who had abducted the princess of Thaneswar, the daughter of the Raja of Kannauj. The Raja of Gaur who participated in the murder of Rajyavardhan was defeated and his kingdom was overrun. Harsha now became the Raja of Kannauj. The frontiers of the old Gupta empire were restored. Harshavardhan was also a wise and benevolent administrator. Farmers were taxed, about one-sixth of the produce. Here was a network of roads, and state-run rest houses, which provided food and medical aid to travellers. In the schools of the empire both Brahmin and Buddhist teachers were employed.

Harshavardhan was a worshipper of Shiva initially but later converted to Buddhism, yet his conversion brought about no intolerance. Harsha was advised by a Brahmin called Bana, who wrote an account of his patron's reign. Bana decried the cynical formulations of Kautilya in the *Arthashastra*. Harshavardhan was himself a scholar and a litterateur. He has left a book of grammar and some plays, one of which *Nagananda* has been translated into English and won acclaim as a world classic. Harsha's empire, built on his personal efforts crumbled when he died at the age of 57.

It was while Harshavardhan was ruling in India that Muhammad the Messenger of God (PBUH) and his progeny, appeared in Arabia. By the time of Harsha's death, Muslim warriors had conquered Afghanistan. We can now properly turn to the theme of Islam in South Asia.

Pre-Historic Partition

It has been sometimes asserted that the territories west and east of the Indus have always constituted two countries, and that the religious divide of 1947 was merely incidental. In our preamble, we identified the geographical forces of both unity and diversity, from which it follows that diversity by itself, is not proof of nationhood. The theory that the Indus has been an international frontier has been attributed to Kaniz Fatima Yousuf and Syed Qudratullah Fatimi, but developed into a treatise by Aitzaz Ahsan. This author, a celebrity, disarms readers at the outset by saying that he has not examined all trends, nor analyzed every historical event or fact.[1]

Such a candid and courteous entrant is deserving of full attention, and, if in the process we have to test, not a hypothesis by random sampling, but to determine the universe itself; the contention is well worth probing. Aitzaz Ahsan argues that the *Ramayana* and the *Mahabharata* overlapped. The earliest hymns of the Vedas were composed *c.*1400 BC. The Rig Veda itself from 1500 to 1200 BC. The *Mahabharata* was composed around 900 BC. The *Arthaveda* came later, between 900 to 500 BC. There is no evidence as to where the Vedas were composed. Since they were not composed together in time, the greater probability is that they were not composed together in space (p. iv). Similarly, to depict the over shadowing of Indra by Krishna as graduation from pastoral life to agrarian production (p. 43) is most arbitrary. The very size of the granaries in the citadels indicates that the Indus civilization was agrarian. Aitzaz Ahsan himself concedes: 'The Arabs had very little agriculture; Indus had (it seems) never been without it' (p. 91).

As compared to the east-west difference, the north-south differences are sharper: music and linguistics have different modes; different voice scales. Reportedly, their interpretation of the *Ramayana* also differs. The evidence for the Indus man is slighter than the Indus land. Defiance of imperial authority is not a localized trait; no essential difference exists between Dulla Bhatti and Mangal Pandey.

Notes

1. Aitzaz Ahsan, *The Indus Saga and the Making of Pakistan*, Karachi: Oxford University Press, 1996, pp. 11, 12. The page numbers in brackets refer to this book.
2. Sir Mortimer Wheeler, 'Pakistan Four Thousand Years Ago,' in *Crescent and Green*, London: Cassell and Company, 1995, p. 17.
3. Ibid., p. 19.

NOTES

1. Leslie Alcock, 'The Oldest Baluchistan', in *Crescent and Green*, London, Cassell, 1995, p. 39.
2. Ibid., p. 44.
3. *Dawn*, Karachi, 14 July 2006.
4. Sir Mortimer Wheeler, 'Pakistan: Four Thousand Years Ago', in *Crescent and Green*, op. cit., p. 21.
5. Romila Thapar, *Interpreting Early India*, New Delhi: Oxford University Press, 1992, p. 68. Ainslie T. Embree (ed.), *Sources of Indian Tradition*, New York: Columbia University Press, 1998, p. 8.
6. Ainslie T. Embree (ed.), *Sources of Indian Tradition*, New York: Columbia University Press, 1998, p. 8.
7. Ibid., p. 21.
8. Romila Thapar, op. cit., p. 69.
9. Rajmohan Gandhi, *Mohandas*, New Delhi: Penguin/Viking, 2006, p. 581.
10. Ibid., p. 299.
11. John E. Court, *Jains in the World*, New York: Oxford University Press, 2001, p. 18.
12. Ibid., p. 21.
13. Richard S. Cohen, 'Shakyamuni: Buddhism's Founder in Ten Acts', in *The Rivers of Paradise: Moses, Buddha, Confucius, Jesus, and Muhammad as Religious Founders*, David Noel Freedman and Michael J. McClymond (eds.), Grand Rapids, MI: Wm. B. Eerdmans Publishing Company, 2000, p. 133.
14. Ainslie T. Embree (ed.), *Sources of Indian Tradition*, New York: Columbia University Press, 1998, p. 155.
15. Ibid.
16. Ibid., 175.
17. Hemchandra Raychaudhuri, *Political History of Ancient India: From the Accession of Parikshit to the Extinction of the Gupta Dynasty*, New Delhi: Oxford University Press, 2006, p. 169 (Calcutta, 1923).
18. Romila Thapar, *Cultural Pasts:* Essays in Early Indian History, New Delhi: Oxford University Press, 2000, p. 423.
19. Tamara Talbot Rice, *Ancient Arts of Central Asia*, New York and Washington DC: Frederick A. Praeger, 1965, p. 138.
20. Mahmood Zaman, 'Badalpur', *Dawn Gallery*, Karachi, 4 November 2006.
21. H.C. Ray Chaudhuri, op. cit., p. 421.
22. B.N. Mukherjee, Commentary on ibid., p. 717.
23. Romila Thapar, *History and Beyond*, New Delhi: Oxford University Press, 2000, p. 108.

CHAPTER 1

MUSLIM SOCIETY IN SOUTH ASIA

The Arabs came to India as traders long before they came as invaders. Arab seafaring brought traders and even settlers to the west coast of India. It was a one-sided process. Indians could not go to Arabia, for if they crossed the sea, they would lose their caste. Some Indians were forcibly taken to Iraq by the Sassanid rulers of Iran but, this cannot count as a trend. The Coromandel Coast was called 'Ma'bar' by the Arabs, which means 'crossing'. These Arabs established colonies on the west coast of India. When Arabs converted to Islam, these colonies became the outposts of Islam in India. At first there was little resistance to the Arab settlers. Pandya kings employed Muslims as ministers and ambassadors. Thus, some Muslims were given more importance than Buddhists or Jains.

CONQUEST

A change in relations came about because of the Arab invasion of Sindh and Multan in AD 711. Even then a complete change in relations seems not to have taken place. The Labbes, a west Indian Muslim tribe, claimed to be the descendants of the Hashimites who sought refuge here from Hajjaj bin Yusuf, and it was Hajjaj bin Yusuf who, as the eastern viceroy of the caliph, organized the invasion of Sindh.

The Arab invasion of Sindh was not an isolated event; it was part of a wave of conquests which included Spain and central Asia. The reasons for the invasion of Sindh must be seen within this framework. It is quite possible, as the sources tell us, that pirates off the coast of Makran invited the wrath of Hajjaj by kidnapping and looting passengers on their way to Basra from Lanka. It is more probable that Raja Dahir, the ruler of Sindh, was right in pleading that the pirates were beyond his jurisdiction and he could not be held responsible for their crimes. It is also true that, after the conquest of Sindh, no chastisement of the pirates seems to have occurred. The conquest of Sindh proved to be a momentous event. It is not surprising, therefore, that Hajjaj bin Yusuf, who is considered a villain by the chroniclers of Islamic history, has been portrayed as a hero in Indo-Muslim history.

The image of Mohammad bin Qasim, the conqueror, is different. He is rightly regarded as a hero because he was victorious, whereas his two predecessors, Budhail and Ubeydullah, battle-worn veterans, were defeated and killed. Mohammad bin Qasim was a youth of seventeen. His skill, his courage and his boldness in psychological warfare (such as bringing down the red flag at Debul) all combined to make him a hero. In addition, the imprisonment and execution of this conqueror by his own people, and his evocative poem written in prison made him a legend. Mohammad bin Qasim's execution, like his conquest, was part of a general policy exercised by a caliph and not directed against an individual. All the conquerors under Walid I: Musa bin Nusayr, Tariq bin Ziyad (Spain) Quteiba bin Muslim (central Asia) and Mohammad bin Qasim (Sindh) were punished by his successor, Suleiman.

In time, small Arab kingdoms arose in Sindh and became part of the fragmented entity that India was, when Jaipal, the Hindu Shahi ruler of Kabul and Waihind, made a pre-emptive attack on the domain of Piritigin (also known as Pirai), the ruler of Ghazni, setting-off the second series of Muslim conquests led by Sultan Mahmud. Almost two centuries later, Sultan Moizuddin Ghuri and his lieutenants, Qutbuddin Aibek and Ikhtiaruddin Khalji, conquered north India as far as Bengal. Sultan Alauddin Khalji carried Muslim arms to south India in 1296, and two centuries later Babur, the Timurid prince, invaded India to found the Mughal dynasty. These conquests had long-lasting social consequences. The invasions of Timur, Nadir Shah, and Ahmad Shah Abdali remained intrusions and were regarded as catastrophes by both Hindus and Muslims.

CONVERSION

The Muslims ruled over the whole of India, but a Muslim majority emerged only in the north-west and north-east; the rest of the country retained its Hindu majority. This impels us to ask why Islam spread more in certain parts of India than in others. Many reasons have been advanced to explain this phenomenon. Many reasons have been advanced also to explain why any Hindus at all converted to Islam. The commonly advanced reason is that since Islam is an egalitarian religion, Hindus of the lower castes converted to Islam to escape from the tyranny and humiliation shown to them by higher caste Hindus.

This simple explanation does not take into account all the factors. If it were merely a question of escaping the caste system, then Buddhism was at hand. Buddhism was an Indian religion which had challenged the caste system, and the Arabs had liberated Buddhists, so Hindus adopting Buddhism could freely adhere to their creed with a minimum adjustment in theology; Buddha had already been hailed as an avatar of Vishnu. The reasons for the quick spread of Islam west of the Indus and to a lesser extent east of the Indus are many and complex. Richard M. Eaton, who has advanced new explanations for the conversions, admits, 'Clearly, this is a complex phenomenon involving a number of distinguishable processes, some which did not concern conversion at all'.[1]

Who was responsible for the spread of Islam and the assimilation of local elements into its fold, is a debatable issue. Therefore, we must probe the clues that history provides us. There are examples to show that when the choice was free, Hindus adopted Islam. Tara Chand relates, on the authority of Vincent, that there were so many Arabs on the Malabar Coast that the people had adopted the Arab religion (probably Sabean). Now whether Arab settlers followed the Sabean or the Pagan religion, the very fact that Indians were receptive to a foreign religion without coercion, is a factor which must be taken into account. When the Arabs themselves converted to Islam, there is every likelihood that the Indians, who had embraced the earlier religion of the Arabs, also embraced Islam.

Sabeans are star worshippers; pagans are idol worshippers having a closer affinity with the Hindus. The Hindus who converted to Islam could have, instead, followed the more sophisticated idol worship of the Hindus, as had the reconverts from Buddhism. Richard M. Eaton argues:

> A glance at the geographical distribution of Muslims in the subcontinent reveals an inverse relationship between the degree of Muslim political penetration and the degree of conversion to Islam ...those regions of the most dramatic conversion of the population, such as eastern Bengal or western Punjab lay on the fringes of Indo-Muslim rule, whereas the heartland of the rule, the upper Gangetic Plain, saw a much lower incidence of conversion.[2]

Dismissing outright the contention that conversion was forcible, Eaton ascribes it to the influence of living *qazis* and buried saints, arguing that the shrines of the saints who had died, exercised a greater hold on the population than a living saint.

There is much to support Eaton's contention. The sultan could vanquish the raja, but he could not vanquish the *sadhu*. To meet the Indian people at the spiritual level, a Sufi was needed. As we shall see, Khwaja Moinuddin Chishti could enter the domain of Prithviraj Chauhan before Moizuddin Ghuri. Then again, we may challenge Eaton's contention with regard to western Punjab because of its proximity to North-West Frontier and Balochistan, where migration and not conversion had created a Muslim majority; but we cannot challenge it with regard to East Bengal.

The sword of the sultan was double-edged. It created the political space for conversion and simultaneously created ill-will among the Hindus, not a sentiment inducive to a change of religion. Richard Eaton has further argued that Muslim rulers desecrated only royal temples and idols as a form of political vengeance, and did not desecrate the temples of the Hindu commoner.[3] It is doubtful whether the Hindu of the Sultanate period could distinguish between political and religious motives. It is true however that the Delhi sultans resisted the fanatical urgings of ulema to at least humiliate Hindus if they could not kill them.

These urgings were clearly against the injunctions of Islam. The ulema who did not understand this were temperamentally incapable of spreading Islam. Recently, even some western historians have drawn attention to the following verses of the Holy Quran:

> There is no compulsion in religion (Q2:256).
> And if thy Lord willed, all who are in the earth would have believed together. Wouldst thou [Muhammad] compel men until they are believers? (Q10:99).

ASSIMILATION

Assimilation took the shape of Hindus and Muslims borrowing from each other's festivals and rituals. This took place even though intermarriage and interdining were taboo. Even now in Pakistan, excepting for the *nikah*, marriage ceremonies like wearing *sehras* and playing music are of Hindu origin; by and large Muslims borrowed rituals and customs, while Hindus borrowed from the creed.

NOTES

1. Richard M. Eaton, 'Approaches to the Study of Conversion to Islam in India' in *Approaches to Islam in Religious Studies,* Richard C. Martin (ed.), Tuscon: University of Arizona Press, 1985, p. 122.
2. Ibid., pp. 107–08.
3. Richard M. Eaton, *Essays on Islam and Indian History,* New Delhi: Oxford University Press, 2000, p. 110 ff.

CHAPTER 2

A COMPARISON OF MUSLIM AND HINDU SOCIETY

Hindu society and Muslim society were different in many ways, but in one respect they were similar. Both had their value system grounded in religion, and both believed that their respective religions, Hinduism and Islam were a complete code of life, not merely a set of rituals.

Hindus were governed by their religion in two ways. Firstly, Hindu society was structured on the basis of castes. Secondly, all the phases of a Hindu's life were governed by his creed. It prescribed until what age a person may play, between which ages a person must study, how on attaining manhood, he should earn his livelihood, and how, on reaching middle age, he should retire from active life:

Brahmacharya	celibate education
Grihastha	domestic life
Vanaprastha	retirement
Sanyasa	ascetic search for divine life

Some traits of Hindu society became ingrained after a long evolution, particularly those regarding women. Child marriage came to be favoured, monogamy was generally practised, remarriage for widows was forbidden, as *sati*, the burning of wives on the funeral pyres of their husbands, was considered meritorious. Vegetarianism was practised, most probably due to the influence of the Jains and Buddhists since we hear that Ashoka had banned eating the flesh of animals.

The Hindus became vegetarians, and venerated cows as a symbol of their mother. This difference became the main cause of conflict between Hindus and Muslims, as Muslims were meat eaters and heartily relished beef.

The Muslims belonged to different racial backgrounds; they were descendants of the conquerors, the Arabs, Turco-Afghans and Mughals. Others were converts or descendants of people having converted to Islam from Hinduism. Islam prescribed an egalitarian social order in which piety, and not descent, would be the standard of excellence and closeness to God. This provided for greater social mobility than in Hinduism. A low-caste Muslim could attain the highest office. This was witnessed when, following the Ghurid invasion a number of slaves ascended the throne in Delhi. It needs to be emphasized however that Muslim society was not absolutely egalitarian and there were class differences. There was one great difference. The Hindu caste system was prescribed by religion, whereas class consciousness among Muslims in India was not. This was the reason that, although social barriers existed among Muslims, they could be surmounted, whereas in Hindu society the caste system could not.

THE FOUR MAJOR HINDU CASTES

1. *Brahmin* The priest class
2. *Kshatriya* The warrior class
3. *Vaishya* The merchant class
4. *Shudra* The menial class

The caste system evolved over time. The Brahmins and Kshatriyas contested each other's claim to be the highest caste. Caste was determined by profession. Once a family adopted a profession it was confined to it for all time to come. Castes were also determined on the basis of *Varna*, that is colour, and there were many sub-castes also. There were differences on the basis of creeds, for example between those who gave greater regard to Vishnu or to Shiva, but this difference did not create fissures in Hindu society.

The Hindus were polytheists—worshippers of many gods. It is true that polytheism was interpreted by various savants at different levels. Not only some Hindus, but a Muslim like Amir Khusro defended some features of the Hindu creed. Moreover, Hindus were idol-worshippers. This led to a head-on clash between the Muslims and the Hindus, after Mohammad bin Qasim brought down the red flag over the temple of Debul.

Jainism and Buddhism had defied Hinduism, especially the caste system, but after a protracted military and spiritual struggle, Jainism practically became a Hindu sect and Buddhism, while it spread over a vast expanse of Asia, became almost obliterated from India, the country of its origin. Hindus conceded that Gautama Buddha was an avatar of Vishnu, and by this means Buddhists were assimilated back into the fold of Hinduism. Such an assimilation for the Muslims seemed impossible due to their belief. It was in this light that K.M. Pannikar made his now famous observation that the Muslims brought about a vertical division in Indian society.[1] Previously, Indian society had been divided horizontally on the basis of caste.

When two societies are so different, it is difficult for one to influence the other. We must recognize at the outset that the impact of Islam on Hindu society was limited in scope. As Tara Chand has said:

> The new ruler was master of the immediate lands, within striking distance of his cavalry encampment; the petty land holder with his retinue was safe within his mud castle and defied the sovereign power.[2]

In other words, as Muneera Haeri also says, 'Muslim rule was centred around the cities. Hindus were concentrated in the villages and remote areas.' This is the reason why, except for a change in the language, Hindu society re-emerged almost intact, when Muslim rule showed the first sign of decline.[3]

Nevertheless, Hindus and Muslims shared the same land and inevitably there were some areas, especially in the cultural sphere, where Muslims were able to influence Hindu society. This influence was spread over a long period of time and confined to certain aspects of life but on the whole it culminated in transforming Hindu society.

MUSIC

Of all the arts, it was in music that Hindus and Muslims had the greatest compatibility. True, their approach was different. For Hindus, music was a sacred art to be performed in temples. Barring the devotional music of the Sufis, Muslims had a secular approach to music. Acharya Brahaspati says that the Hindu *gram moorchana paduti* gave way to the *muqam* music of Irani origin. That this transition was smooth was due to the fact that both Indian and Middle Eastern music were influenced by Hellenic music. Lal Khan Bakhshi has given a very long list of Middle Eastern and Indian compositions which were adopted into the raga form. A short list of Middle Eastern airs, on the left, and Indian, on the right, is given below:

1. *Shuba-e-Mukhalif*	*Ramkali*
2. *Eraq*	*Bhairawn*
3. *Qandhari Eraq*	*Malkauns*
4. *Nishapur Nihawand*	*Bilawal*
5. *Zangula Chahargah*	*Asawari*
6. *Nawa*	*Jaijaiwanti*
7. *Saghir*	*Eman Kalyan*

The Muslim contribution to Hindu music was personified in the figure of Amir Khusro (1253–1325) who is credited with adopting a system called *Indraprashta matt*. Khusro composed new ragas grafting them on ancient *thaats*, the master melodies on which ragas are based, such as *Eman* on *Kalyan*. Khusro was hailed as a Nayak, one proficient in the theory and practice of present and past music. He contributed equally to the evolution of folk music and *qawwali*, devotional Sufi music. He is also credited with inventing, among other instruments, the *sitar*. Amir Khusro was a great poet in Persian, but for his folk and devotional music he used the local language.

The next major figure in the development of classical music was Husain Shah Sharqi (1458–1505) the last ruler of Jaunpur. He composed ragas including *Gaud Shyam, Husaini Todi, Jaunpuri,* and *Asawari,* among a host of others. According to Abdul Halim, Sultan Husain Sharqi's greatest innovation was the evolution of *Khyal* in which ascension and decsension of the raga is less gradual. To bring about an alternative to the ancient and stately *Dhrupad* mode could be best effected by a Muslim and a ruler. *Khyal* was less rigid and more lively, the result of taking classical music away from the confines of the temple.

The flowering of music took place under Akbar (1556–1605) the great Mughal emperor. His court musician Mian Tansen was hailed by Abul Fazl as the greatest musician in a thousand years. He is credited with the composition of *Mian ki Todi, Mian ki Malhar, Darbari Kangra* and a host of *ragas.* Tansen was a great vocalist but the pandits hailed him only as a *Gandharv,* one proficient in the practice, but not the theory of music. Tansen was a disciple of Sheikh Ghous Gwaliori, and his elder contemporary, the shadowy Baiju Bawra, was the disciple of Sheikh Adnan Jaunpuri. His compositions include *Megh Malhar* and *Goud Sarang.* Baiju Bawra, like Khusro, was hailed as a Naik.

Music received patronage from the Mughals, but a further loosening of classical norms took place in the court of Awadh, where *Thumri* and *Dadra,* the faster forms of music evolved. *Thumri* is a shorter form with inflections and arias figuring more frequently than in *Khyal. Dadra* was a still more lively and faster mode. A single raga, for example *Bhairwin,* can be sung in the form of *Dhrupad, Khyal, Thumri* or *Dadra.* The composition does not change, the beat, the inflections and frequency of notes marks the change.

PAINTING

Hindu painting is seen at its best in the Ajanta caves. These wall paintings are a mixture of frescos and tempera and cover all the major themes, both religious and secular, of ancient India. The Muslim contribution was mostly miniatures, small-scale paintings on paper, to fill either folios or to illustrate books. There is literary evidence that Hindus painted miniatures and Muslims of the Sultanate period produced wall paintings, but the evidence has not survived. It is on the basis of surviving specimens that we note that the evolution of Hindu art and Muslim art was largely based on murals and miniatures respectively.

However, there was one conceptual difference which can be asserted: in ancient India, Shankar Acharya ruled that portraits should conform to traditional norms, and to render faithfully human features was wrong in principle.[4] Under the Mughals, faithful rendering became the requirement. Although Hindus had separate myths from Muslims, both drew upon them, but here also there was a difference between the religious and secular approach, and once they had done with illustrating the *Dastan-i-Amir Hamza* under Akbar, the Mughals, especially under Jehangir, forced painting towards authentic representation in order to preserve scenes for their pleasure as well as for their value as records.

In painting, Muslim influence came about through cooperation. Hindus and Muslims were employed by the same patron to illustrate the same manuscript. Later, again under Jehangir, a single illustration would be painted by different artists; one was responsible for tracing the outline, another would apply the colour, the third would shade the drapes, a fourth the background, another would design the margin and yet another would do the calligraphy. Persian calligraphy was more flowing and cursive than the *Nagri* script, which was angular and in blocks, and therefore did not integrate with the flow of the brush like the *Nastalique* Persian script.

The specialists, according to their flair, were trained in each aspect of art. Daswant, schooled under Abdus Samad, was the earliest artist to gain prominence. Other Hindu artists of natural talent followed and it is no wonder that, when the Rajput school of painting emerged, it was heavily influenced by the Mughals. The Mughal emperors had portraits painted of their Rajput grandees such as Man Singh, and this further eased the transition. Compared to music, Muslim influence in painting came rather late, and both the Bazar Mughal and the later degenerated and vulgar versions, were overtaken by the influence the British came to exercise over both Hindu and Muslim painters. Since influence came through cooperation, Muslim artists also painted Hindu themes, most notably Abdur Rahman Chughtai who, before he illustrated the poetry of Ghalib and Iqbal, had painted scenes from Hindu mythology.

ARCHITECTURE

In architecture, unlike in art, there was no close collaboration. Muslims designed appropriated pillars from Hindu monuments while the lower strata of masons were Hindus. Unlike in painting, Hindus were not entrusted with design or planning.

Architecture is governed by the purpose or function of a monument, the building material available, and the climate of the region. Tara Chand characterizes Muslim architecture as conditioned by vast deserts, and Hindu architecture as conditioned by lush and green plains.[5] This is borne out by the fact that except for in the arid areas of Sindh and Balochistan, the glazed tiles used by Muslims in Iran and Central Asia could not flourish in Indian plains.

Mosques and temples were not entirely different. Both had open courts surrounded by colonnades or chambers (although this is truer of Jain than

Hindu temples). The main difference was that temples had dim chambers and sparsely lit passages, while mosques were characterised by clarity and openness to light and air. The most visible difference was that temples had pyramidical spires with a small dome on top, which was either circular or polygonal. Mosques had domes standing on squinches, devices necessary to place round structures on a square base.

Tara Chand has summarised the mutual influence of Hindu–Muslim architecture by saying that 'the simple severity of the Muslim architecture was toned down and the plastic exuberance of the Hindu architecture was restrained'.[6]

The monument he uses to illustrate Muslim influence is the Kantanagar Temple built in Bengal between 1704 and 1722: 'It has three storeys and above the third rises the central tower with its pyramidical spire. The first two storeys have four octagonal towers at the corner'. This has a distinct resemblance to mosques in India. 'The whole surface is covered with terracotta but no figure sculpture is seen anywhere.' Divesting any part of a temple of sculpted figures is due solely to Muslim influence.

Since Hindus do not bury their dead, the appearance of Hindu mausolea in the seventeenth century is another manifestation of Muslim influence. The mausoleum of Bir Singh Deva at Orchha is typical: A large square block with two massive towers and a dome. The facade has three arches in the middle with no sculpture or decoration. In other words, the Muslims had an impact on Hindu architecture at the height of their power, but Muslim influence was limited in scope.

LITERATURE

The Muslim influence on Hindu literature was again the result of intermingling. Ever since Amir Khusro had composed poetry in both Persian and the early Hindi of his times, this tendency had been marked. Thus we see Abdur Rahim Khan-e-Khanan as a great poet of Hindi, and Chandra Bhan Brahmin an important poet of Persian. Muslim rulers patronized local languages. Dinesh Chandra Sen says that if the Hindu kings had continued to enjoy influence, Bengali would never have become a court language. This could be true of other regional languages also.

BHAKTI MOVEMENT

We began by noting that Islam and Hinduism were poles apart and that the assimilation of Islam by the Hindu religion was not possible. It is now necessary to inquire whether or not, in the development of Hindu sects under Muslim rule, Islamic concepts played any role, and if so, whether that role was extensive or limited. Tara Chand asserts that Siddharis and Virasaivas were largely influenced by Islam. This may be true, but the influence of Islam seems neither to have been conscious nor pervasive. There is the example of Lingayats, a sect founded by Basava which worshipped one god (Para Siva). Lingayats had many practices similar to those of Islam, for example, they believed that a bride's consent was imperative for marriage, child marriage was considered wrong, and the remarriage of widows was allowed. They practised burial, not cremation.

On the other hand, Lingayats were emphatic that there should be no sacrifice, no fasts, no feasts and no pilgrimage, all of which are essential to the practice of Islam. Lingayat beliefs had a mystical bias since they considered love as the first creation of God.

It is from this belief that it is possible to trace the origin of Bhakti to the *Bhagavad Gita* where it is mentioned as a major path to salvation. Bhakti means faithful devotion. Later, another leader, Ramanuja, (*c.*1025–1137) defined Bhakti as intense long meditation and devotion to God. As Stanley Wolpert states, 'the central tenet of Bhakti became love of God.' It is at this point that reformist Hinduism and mystical Islam meet, for the Sufi calls love for God real love and love for creatures temporal love. Another resemblance is in the concept of monism, *Hama Oost,* Every thing is He, or the doctrine of *Wahdat-ul-Wajood*—monism—or unity of existence. We know the Muslim shades of this concept, let us now see it in the creed of Shankara (*c.*780–820).

> God was one and there was no other besides him. God was the only reality, all else was illusion. He was without attributes or qualities. He was not a thinking or knowing being, but thought or knowledge itself.

Why Bhakti first appeared in the south is not clear. It could be because Muslim conquest was more recent there or because Islam had not penetrated as deep in the south as it had in the north of India. Whatever the cause, there were sincere seekers after truth and they went beyond Hindu orthodoxy towards Hindu mysticism.

The love of God is a sentiment, and a most powerful outlet of sentiment is poetry. In poetry Muslims tolerate and even enjoy sayings which do not conform to belief. It was quite natural then that the most celebrated exponent of the Bhakti movement was a poet called Kabir Das (*c.*1425–1492).

Kabir was first a disciple of Ramananda, who brought the message of Ramanuja to north India, Kabir was a disciple subsequently of Muslim Sufis, beginning with Shaikh Taqi of Manikpur. In his *dohas* or Hindi couplets, Kabir preached the importance of love and decried formal and ritualistic creed. Kabir did not recognize either caste or the four divisions of life as prescribed by Hinduism and refused to recognize the six schools of Hindu philosophy. Kabir refused to consider those aspects of Muslim and Hindu religion which were opposed to each other. *Bhakti*, or love, was the overriding essence of religion. When he preached at Benares he offended both Hindus and Muslims, but when he died at Maghar, both Hindus and Muslims claimed his body.

NOTES

1. K.M. Pannikar, *A Survey of Indian History*, Bombay: National Information and Publications, 1947, p. 286.
2. Tara Chand, *Influence of Islam on Indian Culture*, Allahabad: The Indian Press, 1946, p. 136.
3. Munira Haeri, *The Chishtis*, Karachi: Oxford University Press, 2000, p. 29.
4. Ghulam Abbas Moulvi, *Hindustani Musavvari Ka Irtiqa* (Urdu), Bombay: Published by author, 1942, p. 10.
5. Tara Chand, op. cit., p. 240.
6. Ibid., p. 243.

A MIR KHUSRO (b. Patiali, 1253–d. Delhi, 1325) was the disciple of a saint, and the courtier of five kings. He excelled in Indian music and Persian poetry—the most admired accomplishments of the Hindu and Muslim nobility. His mysticism engendered an eclectic outlook. He marked the coming of age of a distinct Indo-Muslim culture; and personified as no other genius did, the spirit of his age.

Orphaned at a tender age, Amir Khusro came under the care of his maternal grandfather. He saw his grandfather apportion a corner of his house to a then unknown and penurious mystic, who would later become a centre of attraction under the name of Shaikh Nizam-ud-din Auliya (1244–1325). The young boy, himself a dependent, saw his maternal uncle expel the mystic.[1] Amir Khusro's veneration for Nizam-ud-din Auliya became the hallmark of his life; and the inspiration for both his poetry and music. Amir Khusro dedicated his music to the mystic, just as he dedicated his poems to the kings who patronized him.

In 1280, Prince Muhammad, the son of Sultan Ghyasuddin Balban, invited Amir Khusro and Amir Hasan Sijzi (both poets, both friends and both devotees of Nizam-ud-din Auliya) to his court. Prince Muhammad manned the outpost against the Mongol menace, and in the course of an invasion, in 1285, laid down his life. Amir Khusro poured out his heart while composing the elegy of the Martyred Prince; and the bereaved Sultan found the elegy to be an expression of his own grief and frittered his stern and austere life away. From then on, Khusro's presence at the court of Delhi was assured.

Khusro not only became the poet laureate, but also the court historian. He wrote one account, *Khazain ul Futuh* (1312) in prose, but all others were in verse. A commissioned work was *Qiran us Sa'dain* (1288) which described the meeting between Sultan Moizuddin Kayqubad and his father, Bughra Khan, the Governor of Bengal. *Deval Rani/Khizar Khan* (1320) was completed after the couple's deposition, hence, it remained not only a romantic tale, but also became a social commentary. *Tughluq Nama* (1324) describes the foul murders of the children of the Khaliji household by the usurper, Khusro Khan. Unfortunately, this mature product of his poetic genius fell into comparative oblivion, and hence could not influence forcefully the Indian style (*Sabk-i-Hindi*). This mode was ascribed to Khusro's predecessor, Masud Sa'd Salman (d.1121) and came to be characterized by conceits, involved expressions, metaphors and unnecessary ornamentation.

According to the eminent literary critic, Syed Mumtaz Husain, Khusro provided a stylistic bridge between the two Shiraz luminaries, Sa'di and Hafiz.

Hailed as a Nayak of classical music, Khusro is credited with the founding of *Indraprashta matt*—a genre and mode—as well as grave and deep *ragas* like *Shudh Bilawal, Shudh Kalyan and Aiman Kalyan*. His contribution extended to devotional music, like *qawwali*, as well as folk music, which contained his proto-Hindi lyrics. Today, all three types retain their popularity. A number of musical instruments are said to be his inventions, notably, the sitar. A great deal of this information is shrouded in legend, but Zoe Ansari has discovered an anonymous manuscript, titled *Ghunyat ul Mayna* (1375), which apart from being an expository text, contains illustrations of the musical instruments played in the age of Khusro.[2]

Being a courtier of both Sultan and Saint was a trait which could be reconciled only by a genius of his calibre. In *Nuh Siphir* (1315), the masterpiece dedicated to Qutbuddin Mubarak Shah, Amir Khusro includes verses praising Nizam-ud-din Auliya, knowing fully well that his royal patron disliked his spiritual mentor. Khusro approached the Hindu creed sympathetically, even trying to reconcile idolatry with monotheism. Only the Mongols who killed his favourite prince, and had held him captive, aroused the satirist in him. Amir Khusro did not simply reflect the virtues of his age; he contributed to each of them.

NOTES

1. Khaliq Ahmed Nizami, *The Life and Times of Shaikh Nizam-ud-din Auliya*, New Delhi: Oxford University Press, 2007, pp. 28 and 29.
2. Zoe Ansari, *Khusro ka Zahni Safar*, New Delhi: Anjuman Taraqqi-i-Urdu, 1988/1977, p. 88.

THE ROLE OF THE ULEMA AND THE SUFIS

Islam is both a spiritual and a social religion. The ulema are the guardians of the Law—the *sharia*. The Sufis showed more concern for the spiritual side of Islam. In early Islamic history there was no distinction between the state and the church, and the ruler himself was the guardian of the law. However, by the time Muslim rule was established in India, the Sultan appointed a *Shaikhul Islam,* usually a renowned *alim* or scholar, who was given charge of the religious affairs of the kingdom.

THE ORIGIN OF ULEMA

Ulema is the plural of *alim*, the Arabic word for religious scholar. Every Muslim is expected to know the law and act accordingly. However, even in early Islam, Companions of the Holy Prophet (PBUH) were appointed Imams to lead the prayers, and as Qazis or judges to rule according to the *Shariah*. As specialization took hold, religious functionaries became distinct in society. The emergence of ulema as a class has a sanction in the following verse of the Holy Quran: [And the believers should not all go out to fight. Of every troop of them, a party only should go forth, that they (who are left behind) may gain sound knowledge in religion, and that they may warn their folk when they return to them, so that they may beware. (9:122)'.]

The Sufi was not connected with the court, but was the centre of his devotees. This was his distinctive feature. In Sufism (Islamic mysticism) the role of the Shaikh, or spiritual guide was vital. Since the Shaikh was expected to intercede with God on behalf of his followers, therefore, obedience to one's Shaikh is most heavily prescribed in Sufism. The chain connecting the Shaikh with his disciples is called a *silsila* or order.

What distinguishes the Sufi from the *alim* is the former's belief in the doctrine of *Wahdat-ul-Wujood*, monism, or the unity of creation. According to this set of beliefs, nothing exists apart from God. It follows therefore, that all that exists *is* God. Since man obviously cannot be God, some Sufis hold that the existence of human beings was unreal—an illusion—*maya*.

Muslim Revivalism was complicated by this factor: the reformers who defied kings and struggled for the restoration of orthodoxy were ideologically Sufis. This is further elaborated in the section on Mujaddid Alf Thani.

THE ORIGIN OF SUFIS

The word *Sufi* is derived from *Safa*, meaning purity in Arabic. *Sufis* are mystics who aim for a closer union with God. A dimension to this desire was added when they subscribed to the doctrine of monism, called *Wahdat-ul-Wujood*. The term *Wahdat-ul-Wujood* was coined by Sadruddin Qunavi to describe his teacher Ibn Arabi's theory written in Arabic—*Hama Oost* in Persian. This doctrine is explained in the main text. If all is God, then the union of man's soul with God becomes desirable and attainable. However, monism is a later development. The earliest historical figure to be identified as a *sufi* was Hasan al Basri (d. AD 728) reputedly a disciple of the Imam and Caliph Ali bin abi Talib. It was the figure of Ali which encouraged *sufis* to be called *wali* (plural *awlia*). As a consequence, *sufis* and disciples could invoke the verses of the Holy Quran in which this term was used. Although the term has greater meaning, it is sometimes translated as 'friend'. Thus *waliullah* would be translated in this verse as: 'Lo! verily the friends of Allah are (those) on whom fear (cometh) not, nor do they grieve.' (Q10:62).

Sufis practiced what was almost asceticism, living the lives of hermits and founding *khanqahs* or monasteries where their disciples gathered and spread their message. This life style had a particular appeal for Hindus, who were drawn to the *sufis*. *Sufi* saints allowed *sama* or devotional music which induced ecstacy.

Data Ganj Bakhsh (Syed Ali Hujveri, b. Ghazni *c*. AD 1007–d. Lahore AD 1072) was the first spiritual guide to leave an impression on north India. He came to Lahore from Ghazni with Sultan Masud. Previously he had visited Sultan Mahmud's court infrequently, most probably to participate in religious polemics. He had to leave his books behind in Ghazni, but once he arrived in Lahore (*c*.1039), he proved to be a source of spiritual eminence. He is said to have converted Rai Raju and his companions to Islam and gradually expanded his circle to include more devotees. His book, *Kashful Mahjub*, which is in circulation even today, is the only source which gives the list of the Data's books (which did not survive) and the authentic details of his life. As Qazi Javed has noted, '*Kashful Mahjub* is not a Sufi book usually and commonly written, but a treatise which represents a complete mystical system of thought'.[1]

Data Ganj Bakhsh did not favour neglecting the demands of orthodoxy and observance of compulsory prayers and fasting, although he preferred attainment of internal bliss to compliance with formal obligations.

During the lifetime of Data Ganj Bakhsh, Lahore was a small town in comparison to Multan. It was due to the spiritual grace provided by Data Ganj Bakhsh that Lahore grew in importance. Although he lived in seclusion, Data Ganj Bakhsh was the first Sufi to have a formative influence on Indo-Muslim society.

Khwaja Gharib Nawaz (Syed Muinuddin Ajmeri, b. Chisht AD 1141–d. Ajmer AD 1236) hailed from Sanjaristan in Seistan, became the disciple of Hazrat Uthman Haruni and received spiritual favours from Ibrahim Qalandar. He was orphaned at an early age and, impressed by the spiritual powers of Ibrahim Qalandar, gave up all his property. He performed the pilgrimage to Makkah and Medina. Some historians, notably Juzjani, say that he entered Ajmer as a soldier in the army of Sultan Moizuddin Ghuri. Chishti sources say that he preceded the Ghurid army and settled in Ajmer.

He is said to have converted seven hundred Hindus to Islam in Delhi before settling down in Ajmer. According to the Khwaja, love was the guiding principle behind creation, and he gave precedence to acts of kindness and charity over rituals. If a destitute person came to him, he would leave optional prayers to help him. This earned him the title of Gharib Nawaz, one who favours the poor. Khwaja Gharib Nawaz is one of the few Sufi saints whose marital life has been recorded.

He chose to remain in Ajmer even after it had lost its central position. He would teach the precepts of Islam to anyone who wished to convert and he initiated the seekers of spiritual elevation into the secrets of mystic love. It was his love for humanity which won him so many adherents, both in his lifetime and after his death.

The Chishtia order had the greatest influence on the masses but ultimately came into conflict with the Delhi Sultans who resented a parallel seat of authority, despite it being devoid of worldliness or political pretensions. Hazrat Farid Ganj-i-Shakar (b. Kahowal AD 1175–d. Delhi *c.*1265) made it his conscious policy to maintain a distance between his monastery and the royal court, but his successors, Hazrat Nizamuddin Auliya (b. Badayun AD 1238–d. Delhi AD 1324) and Khwaja Naseeruddin Chiragh-i-Dehli (b. Awadh AD 1277–d. Delhi AD 1356) incurred the wrath of the Tughluq Sultans. Sultan Ghiasuddin Tughluq had ordered Nizamuddin Auliya to leave Delhi before he returned from Bengal. However, the Sultan was killed before he could re-enter Delhi. Sultan Muhammad bin Tughluq tortured Hazrat Chiragh-i-Dehli into becoming his personal attendant. After his death, the saint is said to have favoured Sultan Feroz Tughluq's accession to the throne, but there is no evidence that he ever received any favour from Sultan Feroz Tughluq. Hazrat Chiragh-i-Dehli did not appoint any successor and the glory of the Chishti order ended with him.

There were two other orders that affected Indo-Muslim society: the Suharwardi and the Naqshbandi.

Shaikh Bahauddin Zakaria (b. Kotkrur 1182–d. Multan 1262) belonged to the Suharwardi order and had visited Hazrat Shahabuddin Suhrawardy in Baghdad. Shahabuddin was the most prominent saint of this order after its founder, Shaikh Najeebuddin. On Bahauddin's return to Multan, the city became one of the spiritual capitals of India. Bahauddin had favoured Iltutmish against the local claimant Nasiruddin Qabacha, and was made to suffer for it. However, when Iltutmish defeated Qabacha, Bahauddin was able to pursue his spiritual goals and spread his message and purify the souls of his followers through the teachings of the Holy Prophet (PBUH).

MUJADDID AND THE MUGHALS

Mujaddid Alf Thani (Shaikh Ahmad Sirhindi, b. Sirhind AD 1564–d. AD 1624). So far we have been recounting the services of the saints of the era of the Delhi Sultanate. By and large these Sultans were ideologically, if not factually, subservient to the caliphs and considered their domain part of the Muslim world. They were succeeded by the Mughal emperors who did not recognize the Ottoman Sultans as caliphs. They were inward looking and took a number of steps to conciliate the Hindu majority of India.

The most popular account of the relations between the Mujaddid and the Mughals states that Akbar was an infidel, Mujaddid Alf Thani opposed his un-Islamic policies, and was imprisoned because he refused to perform *sajda* or prostrate himself before Emperor Jehangir. It is further stated that Emperor Aurangzeb, who ruled from AD 1659 to 1707, was a firm adherent of Mujaddid Alf Thani and followed his policy of imposing orthodoxy. There is some truth in the first two statements, the last two are false.

THE MILLENIAL MOVEMENT

To understand the activities of both the Mujaddid and Akbar we must recall that they took place against the background of the *Alfi Tahreek,* or millenial movement. As the first thousand years of the *Hijri* era were drawing to a close, many religious movements were formed, based on a popular Hadith that after every thousand years there shall appear a person who shall renew the faith by reforming the practices prevailing in Muslim societies. This reformer was projected as a Mahdi, a guide. Exaggerated claims were made about the spiritual status of the expected reformers and many claimants came forward and started movements to confuse the common and pious Muslims of that time. Among them was Mahmud of Pasakhwan (d. AD 1492) who led the Nuqtawi Movement in Iran. They believed that the atom, or dot (*nuqta*), was the essence of the universe which was eternal and not created by any being. There is evidence that Abul Fazl and Faizi, courtiers of Akbar, were influenced by this movement.[2]

In India, Syed Muhammad of Jaunpur (b. Jaunpur AD–1443 d. Farah AD 1504) claimed to be the promised Mahdi and founded a movement whose main tenet was *Zikr,* a constant repetition of the names of God. Many features of this sect were considered innovations by the orthodox ulema.

Akbar the Great Mughal (Jalaluddin Muhammad, b. Umerkot 1542–d. Agra 1606) was an intelligent but illiterate member of a highly learned family. Such an unusual combination exposed Akbar to scepticism and eclecticism; that is doubting orthodox beliefs, and being quite prepared to borrow from other religions. It is true that from 1580 onwards Akbar walked a path which led him further and further away from Islam, but as the recent writings of Iqtidar Alam Khan indicate, we cannot simply summarize the religious policy of Akbar, we have to understand it chronologically.

Akbar abolished pilgrimage tax on Hindus	1562
Akbar abolished *jizya*	1564
Akbar proclaimed the conquest of Chitor as a victory of Islam over Hinduism, and destroyed temples	1568
Akbar suppressed Shias of Bilgram	1572
Akbar suppressed Mahdavis in Gujarat	1573
Akbar changed the name of Prayag to Allahabad	1574
Akbar reimposed *jizya*	1575
Infallibility Decree or *Mahzar* gives Akbar authority, but subject to the Holy Quran	1578
Din-i-Ilahi allegedly proclaimed	1581
Akbar protests to Abdullah Uzbek that he is a Muslim and is falsely reviled by ulema	1586
Akbar resumes Muslim prayers, reverts to orthodoxy	1601–1605

Some doubts have been expressed by S.M. Ikram as to whether Akbar actually promulgated *Din-i-Ilahi* as contemporary evidence is slim. This is, however, immaterial since his act of worshipping the sun was patently un-Islamic, therefore one Mulla Yazdi ruled that Akbar had become an apostate. Akbar had Mulla Yazdi killed. It is this factor which complicates the issue: Akbar insisted that he was a Muslim although his conduct and creed were un-Islamic. Yet Khwaja Shirazi and Sharif Amuli called Akbar the Renewer of the Millennium, exactly what the Mujaddid was called.

THE CREED OF MUJADDID ALF THANI

Even if we consider that Akbar was an apostate, it does not naturally follow that Shaikh Ahmad Sirhindi was orthodox. It was not his refusal to prostrate himself before Jehangir that caused the emperor to imprison him, but his claim to spiritual excellence over even the first caliph, Abu Bakr (RA), who, moreover, was the fountainhead of the Naqshbandi order. Ishtiaq Husain Qureshi described in muted terms Mujaddid Alf Thani's self-esteem and its consequences:

He attained the conviction that he held a very high position in the hierarchy of Muslim saints and that he was to bring about a renaissance of Islam. When he made his vision public, he incurred the criticism of several contemporaries of great eminence and also the wrath of the Emperor Jehangir, who imprisoned him for what he considered extravagant claims likely to cause mischief. The shaikh however, was not deterred from his work, nor was he ready to withdraw his claims.[3]

Among the contemporaries of great eminence mentioned by I.H. Qureshi was Abdul Haq Muhaddith Dehlavi. It is doubtful that Mujaddid was punished for not prostrating himself before Jehangir. It must be kept in mind that *sajda*, or prostration before the emperor, was not a Mughal innovation. It was Sultan Ghyasuddin Balban who initiated this practice.[4] Even the Chisthti mystics favoured this practice. Nizamuddin Auliya allowed it and it was only Chiragh-i-Dehli who forbade it.[5]

It is also claimed that the orthodox Islamic policies pursued by Aurangzeb were due to the influence of Mujaddid Alf Thani. This is not true as Aurangzeb had actually banned the works of Mujaddid Alf Thani, as pointed out by Yohanan Friedmann. On the contrary Dara Shikoh, who was the rival of Aurangzeb, had high regard for Mujaddid Alf Thani and mentions him with great reverence in his book *Safinat-ul-Aulia*.

As in the case of Akbar, so in the case of Sirhindi, we must view his thoughts chronologically. In his youth, when Mujaddid perceived that Akbar was not according due respect to the station of prophethood, he wrote *Athbat-un-Nubuwwa,* (Affirmation of Prophethood). In spite of criticisms, Mujaddid Alf Thani became the champion of orthodoxy in Islam and was responsible for curbing the trend towards Hindu-Muslim integration as seen in the Bhakti Movement. According to Ishtiaq Husain Qureshi, the main achievement of the Mujaddid was his ideological opposition to heterodox sufism in India:

> The cornerstone of his philosophy was the rejection of monism.... It is on the rejection of monism that Shaikh Ahmad Sirhindi's claim for being the Mujaddid of his age is based.[6]

Actually Mujaddid did not reject monism in its entirety, as it would have forced him to renounce Sufism altogether. He wished to reform, not to reject, monism. He sharply differed with Ibn Arabi (1165–1240) on this point but still respected him. What the Mujaddid did was to reject *ontological monism*, that is, *Wahdat-ul-Wajood*, or *Hama Oost*. He opted instead, for *phenomenological monism*, that is *Wahdat-as-Shuhood* or *Hamaaz Oost*. This means that 'all creation is not one, but that God is separate from what he has created, though all that he has created is one'.

Mujaddid Alf Thani was the most prominent person of the Mughal period to emphasize the difference between the Hindus and Muslims and to prevent an intermingling of their creeds. Since this is a question of attitudes it is important to know that he had no influence over Mohammad Ali Jinnah the founder of Pakistan, but had a profound influence over Maulana Abul Kalam Azad, the nationalist and Congress leader who termed the creation of Pakistan a tragedy.[7]

MUJADDID AND THE MYSTICS

In order to comprehend fully the mission and personality of Mujaddid Alf Thani we need to recall that he worked within the framework of mysticism. This, in turn, requires that we study his thoughts in relation to the thoughts of Ibn Arabi, (1165–1240), where he accepted, and where he rejected or where he modified the views of Ibn Arabi. This interaction was not as simple as his Puritanism. The ethical side of mysticism is simple, because it is behavioural. A Sufi lives as spiritual a life as possible without becoming a hermit or an ascetic (since Islam forbids it) and devotes himself to prayers to gain personal closeness to God.

The metaphysical side is complicated. It involves the introduction of concepts which were not present in the original doctrines of Islam. These concepts dealt with the nature of the universe: how it came into being, and how God is seen as the only reality, and whatever he created, as an illusion. Although such concepts interfered with the reformist mission of Mujaddid Alf Thani, he had perforce to deal with the views Ibn Arabi introduced in the cosmology of Islam. Ibn Arabi's doctrine of Oneness of Existence does not mean that all existence is one, but that only God exists and His creation does not exist. This was the concept which impelled Mansur al-Hallaj to proclaim 'An-al-haq' (I am the Truth). A creature's identification with God was held to be blasphemous, and consequently Hallaj was executed.

Hallaj was answered across the land and time by Rene Descartes (1590–1650) who said *Cogito Ergo Sum* (I think, therefore I am). Hallaj submerged his consciousness in the sea of existence while Descartes held his consciousness afloat. It is only at their starting point that they are divergent. Otherwise, this is where the *Wahdat-ul-Wajood* of the East meets with the pantheism of the West. It was Baruch de Spinoza (1632–1677) who took pantheism one step further. Spinoza resembles Ibn Arabi in an important respect when he speaks of the Divine: 'I hold that God is the immanent, and not the extraneous cause of all things. I say All is in God; all lives and moves in God.'[8] Spinoza holds that the process of nature and God are one.[9] He, however, clarified that' he did not mean that God and nature—i.e. a mass of corporal matter—are one and the same.[10] However Spinoza's clarification is not easy to reconcile with his basic contention, just quoted above. Similarly, Mujaddid's modification of

Ibn Arabi's views is unable to remove his doctrines from the basic fabric of monism.

This modification of Ibn Arabi's views, the shift from *Wahdat-ul-Wajood* to *Wahdat-as-Shuhood* was affected first by Ala ad-Dawla as-Simnani (1261–1336). Mujaddid merely applied Simnani's criticism to his own milieu. Simnani accused Ibn Arabi of idolizing a verb. Ibn Arabi faced opposition from Ibn Taymiyyah (1263–1328) who held that such a view would absolve mankind of moral responsibility for its deeds. Syed Abul Ala Maududi (1963–1979) focused more on the self-esteem of Mujaddid and Shah Waliullah (see Chapter 5).

> I cannot help saying, irrespective of what the world might say, that it is certainly one of the wrong actions on the part of these two sages to personally proclaim of their being mujaddid, and to repeatedly explain this viewpoint on the basis of divine revelations and inspirations.[11]

Equivalent terms: *Wahdat-ul-Wajood, Hama Oost,* Unity of Being. Ontological monism, oneness of existence and pantheism. *Wahdat-as-Shuhood, Hamaaz Oost,* Unity of creation and phenomenological monism.

SHEIKH ABDUL HAQ MUHADDITH DEHLAVI (1551–1642)

Like Mujaddid Alf Thani, Shaikh Abdul Haq was also a pupil of Hazrat Baqibillah and like him was also concerned that the Millenial Movement was making Muslims oblivious to the pivotal position of the Holy Prophet (PBUH) with regard to both the spiritual and mystical domain. To this end he wrote a book called the *Madarij-un-Nubuwwa* and questioned even Mujaddid Alf Thani in this regard. Shaikh Abdul Haq received his education in Makkah from Syed Ali Muttaqui, who convinced him that he was needed in India.

In India, Shaikh Abdul Haq concerned himself with the duties an emperor is enjoined with, regarding the Sharia and protection of the faith. He wrote *Nuranniya-i-Sultania* addressed to Jehangir. One tradition relates that Jehangir exiled him to Kabul. On his return, in the reign of Shahjehan (1592–1666), he wrote a monograph consisting of forty Ahadith on the rules of conduct for a good ruler. The science of Hadith, which he had learnt at Makkah, defined his ability and his role. About his historical role Aziz Ahmad writes: 'From him begins the Indian Muslim tradition of the scholarship of Hadith, which was to culminate in the works of Waliullah and the Ahl-i-Hadith of the late nineteenth century'.[12]

NOTES

1. Qazi Javed, *Barr-e-Saghir Mein Muslim Fikr ka Irtiqa*, (Urdu), Lahore: Nigarishat, 1986, p. 10.
2. A.F.M. Abu Bakr Siddiqui, 'Maktubat Imam Rabbani' in *Islamic Studies* (ed.) Zafar Ishaq Ansari et al., Islamabad, vol. 28, Summer 1989, p. 143.
3. Ishtiaq Husain Qureshi, *The Muslim Community of the Indo-Pakistan Subcontinent*, Karachi: BCCT, University of Karachi, 2nd ed., 1999, p. 169.
4. Aziz Ahmad, *Islamic Culture in the Indian Environment*, London: Oxford University Press, 1964. Reprinted, Delhi, Oxford University Press, 1999, p. 170.
5. Munira Haeri, *The Chishtis*, Karachi: Oxford University Press, 2000, p. 165.
6. Yohanan Freidmann, *Shaykh Ahmad Sirhindi*, New Delhi: Oxford University Press, 2000, p. 94.
7. Abul Kalam Azad, *India Wins Freedom*, Complete Edition, London: Sangam, 1988, passim.
8. Will Durant, *Outlines of Philosophy*, London: Ernest Benn, 1962, p. 159.
9. Ibid., p. 152.
10. Ibid., p. 160.
11. Syed Abul Ala Maududi, *Tajdid-o-Ihya-i-Deen*, Lahore, 1952, cited in Saiyid Athar Abbas Rizvi, *Shah Waliullah and his Times*, Canberra: Ma'rifat, 1980, p. 220.
12. Aziz Ahmad, op. cit., p. 190.

Table 3.1: The Theoretical Relation of Mujaddid to Ibn Arabi

Orthodox Ulema	Ibn Arabi	Mujaddid Alf Thani
1. The universe has a real and external existence	1. The universe does not have a real existence. It is imaginary. Ghalib has explained this concept in the following verses: (When nobody exists except You, Then, o God, what is this clamour?) (Asad! Do not be taken in by the deception of being. The whole world is encircled by the snare of imagination)	1. God Himself created the universe as imaginary. Thus, the universe has no external existence. The existence of the universe is not as real as the existence of God. Unless the Creator and His creatures are not separate, reward and punishment shall remain without justification. Mujaddid reasons that the most unique attribute of God is existence. If we consider the Universe to be as real as God, then, this will be a form of association (*Shirk*).
2. The universe was created *ex nihilo*, i.e. from nothing. The Holy Quran says: When he decrees a thing, He but says to it 'Be', and it is (2: 111). The Quran has two terms. *Khalq*: Creation, for mankind; *Amr*: Command, for the soul.	2. The universe is the shadow of God, who is Perfect and Absolute. It exists only in the knowledge of God. It has no external existence.	2. The Universe is imaginary, but to a degree it is eternal.
3. God is Un-dependant, Who has not begotten, and Has not been Begotten (Q112:2-4)	3. Between God that is the Absolute Entity and the world of mankind, there are six stages, which Ibn Arabi calls the *Tanazzulat-i-Sitta*. The first stage is the Reality of Muhammad, and in the second stage are *Ae'an-i-Thabita* (Fixed Prototypes of Things)	3. The Reality of Muhammad is less than the Reality of Ka'ba. (Mujaddid considers the reality of the Prophet (PBUH) to be separate from his person, which he holds to be superior to the Ka'ba)
4. This belief does not exist.	4. The six stages which are between God and the world of mankind are all the shadows or the radiance of the attributes of God.	4. These six stages are not the radiance of the attributes of God, but the negation of the attributions of God. This does not mean negation in the normal sense, but this, that God puts the shadow of His attributes on non-existent things and they become beings. Some beings, among whom Satan is the most prominent, acquire existence from non-existence; and (eventually) become good from evil. According to Ibn Arabi, the object of God is not to obliterate evil, but to transform it.

THE SIX DESCENTS

Tanazzulat-i-Sitta

1. God—The Absolute Being: According to Ibn Arabi, there existed only One Reality. This Reality however had two aspects; the Essence (*haq*), the unknowable Being, and the phenomenal world (*khalq*), which had a multiplicity of appearances. The phenomenal world is a mirror or shadow of the Absolute Being. This aspect can be explained, only through symbols.
2. The Reality of Muhammad (PBUH).
3. The sphere of Angels or the sphere of souls.
4. The sphere of similitude. This stage connects the sphere of souls to the sphere of bodies.
5. The sphere of *nasoot*. This is the sphere of bodies in the ideal or conceptual state. From this state proceeds the manifestation of the world of bodies (*ajsam*).
6. The sphere of mankind: Mankind was a mirror which needed polishing in order to become a worthy reflection of the Divine Being.

CHAPTER 4

THE FALL OF THE MUSLIMS AND THE ESTABLISHMENT OF BRITISH RULE

The decline of the Mughal empire led to the downfall of Muslim society in South Asia. Historians differ on the causes that led to the decline but are agreed that the decline followed the death of Aurangzeb (AD 1707). It is said that the successors of Aurangzeb were inefficient and weak, therefore they could not protect the empire from either the Hindu Marathas or the Muslim governors of Bengal, Awadh and Deccan. It is nevertheless strange that all the rulers from Babur to Aurangzeb were strong in intellect and character, and all the rulers from Bahadur Shah I (1707–1712) to Bahadur Shah II (1775–1862) were weak and incapable. Thus impersonal forces should be examined. The structure of society and the events which led to the decline were the wars of succession which began with Jehangir's revolt against his father Akbar.

The structure of the Mughal empire was agrarian. Akbar and his successors had imposed a system called the Mansabdari system. Beginning with Akbar's prime minister, Abul Fazl, no historian has been able to explain adequately the intricacies of the Mansabdari system. Only one thing is apparent, that the hereditary nature of land ownership gave way to lifelong ownership. Jagirdars refused to return their jagirs at the end of Aurangzeb's reign. In the feudal system, land or its revenues were allotted so that troops could be maintained and these troops, when called upon by the king or governor, joined the state armies during war. These troops, in normal times, were maintained to collect the *lagân* or land cess and protect the estate from attacks by outsiders. The produce of the land was needed to pay the soldiers, and the soldiers were needed to protect the produce. This balance was upset by the wars of succession.

When there was war between king and prince, as in the case of Akbar and Jehangir, or between royal brothers, such as the sons of Jehangir or the sons of Shahjehan, loyalties were divided and the holder of one estate would attack the holder of another estate. One of the two estates would be destroyed. As the wars of succession continued there ultimately came a stage when there was no produce to pay the soldiers and no soldiers to protect the crop. This was the vicious circle which replaced the balance of the golden age.

Salaries were often in arrears and if a landlord died without paying them, the soldiers would not allow his funeral prayers to be held. Only if the inheritors were able or willing to pay off the soldiers with jewellery or any other form of wealth, were the funeral prayers performed, otherwise the deceased would suffer the indignity of being buried without religious rites. At one point a landlord told the troops that he could not pay their salaries. They had his permission to loot and plunder the countryside and keep all of the loot except the gold. This measure tore apart the fabric of society.

Soldiers with swords and horses went from estate to estate, raja to raja and nawab to nawab in search of employment. The soldiers had already mortgaged their shields to feed their children. At a new estate they would be paid some salary initially, but thereafter payment was stopped. Soldiers were thus uprooted from their original estates and became a floating armed population, further destabilizing society.

Apart from soldiers of fortune there were the *Pindaris*, the terrorists of that age. Disenchanted with continuous misery, these were mostly the dregs of society, whether Hindu or Muslim, and out of pure greed or meanness they attacked people savagely. The *Pindaris* had their hideouts in forests or caves, and emerged to attack the villages or settlements they thought could yield loot. Often, when by hard work and perseverance, cultivators managed to make an economic recovery, the *Pindaris* used to attack them with a vengeance that defied description. Thus the decline was sustained.

How did the British take advantage of the Muslim decline? The Europeans, especially the British and the French, set up factories processing goods to be sent back to Europe. Like the native estates, these factories also needed protection, so they began to hire Indian soldiers. Since the source of its wealth or strength lay outside India, the British East India Company was able to offer the best terms to the best soldiers. Handsome salaries were paid regularly. Soldiers employed by the East India Company were given arms and ammunition as well as fodder for their horses. The British were superior to the Indians in almost all aspects, except that they lacked manpower. By recruiting the best Indian soldiers, the British overcame this disability. In the battle of Plassey Lord Clive could bring an army against Nawab Sirajuddaulah which consisted mainly of Indian, not British soldiers. The East India Company, as the name implies, was a trading company. It saw an opportunity to acquire political power in India because of the anarchy which prevailed there.

K.M. Pannikar has described the war between the Mughals and the British as a battle between an elephant and a whale. The Mughals were masters of the land; they neglected to build a navy; only Sher Shah Suri with his vision centred on Bengal and not on Delhi, had set out to build a navy capable of warding off European sea-farers. His rule was far too short and the Mughals did not build on his work. In those days, naval power was as decisive as air power is today, therefore the British had the military edge over the Mughals.

It is true that there was a conspiracy at the Battle of Plassey in 1757. Mir Jafar and his cohorts betrayed Sirajuddaula on the battlefield, but in the battle of Buxar, 1764, there was no betrayal and there was no disunity. The Mughal king, the nawab of Murshidabad and the nawab of Awadh had combined forces, but were still defeated by the British, who won because of their superior arms and strategy. As at Plassey, so at Buxar, the British army consisted of a majority of Indian troops. Better training and modern strategy were making the difference, not racial characteristics.

Thus far we have been determining how the British defeated the Indians. One sentence only about how Lord Clive, the British commander, was able to outstrip J.F. Dupleix, the French commander. Dupleix was a very capable man but, unlike Clive, he forgot the commercial side of his mission. Clive, even at the height of war, never neglected trade, and kept on making profits while Dupleix found the war expensive.

There was one other cause of the Muslim decline, recently propounded by Karen Leonard.[1] She implies that the causes of decline did not pertain only to agriculture but extended to banking. She differentiates between moneylenders who gave money to landlords on interest, and the bankers who not only advanced loans but received deposits and dealt with *hundis*. Karen Leonard asserts that by 1750 there were bankers who actually managed to collect land revenue 'The amount of interest set and the securities demanded by bankers were more critical economic conditions than the revenue demand fixed by a territorial ruler'.[2] These banking firms turned down requests for loans made by Aurangzeb and Farrukhsiar but advanced loans to the East India Company. When the East India Company became prosperous, it took over the tasks of revenue collection and advancing loans from banking firms. In two strokes the decline set in: banking firms directed revenue from the Mughals to the British and after 1750 the British displaced the banking firms.

Karen Leonard claims that these financial shifts explain the decline of the Mughals and the rise of the British in economic terms, emphasizing processes rather than events or individuals.[3] Our historians nevertheless give greater importance to events and individuals. The roles of Akbar and Aurangzeb are contrasted and discussed by British, Muslim and Hindu historians alike.

AKBAR AND AURANGZEB

There is a tendency to compare and contrast the roles of Akbar and Aurangzeb. The basic premise is that Akbar was responsible for consolidating the Mughal Empire by conciliating the Hindus, while Aurangzeb was responsible for its decline by alienating them. Akbar became the symbol of tolerance and Aurangzeb became the symbol of bigotry. This image has been reinforced by British historians.[4]

The matter is not so simple. Akbar was a most attractive personality but his treatment of his mentor, Bairam Khan, did not do him credit. Aurangzeb is blamed for killing his brothers and imprisoning his father (Shahjehan). It is forgotten that in wars of succession only the survivor was the king therefore, only the king was the survivor.

As far as their religious policies are concerned, we have mentioned (see Mujaddid and the Mughals) that Akbar did not gain the adherence of the Rajputs by conciliating them, but by his conquest of Chittor which he publicly proclaimed to be a victory of Islam over Hinduism. On that occasion Akbar broke idols and desecrated temples, behaving no differently from Mahmud of Ghazni. The decline of the Mughals is supposed to have been caused when Aurangzeb broke idols and desecrated temples, but as Jnan Chandra pointed out, while Aurangzeb indisputably broke some idols and desecrated temples, he also built and supported others by royal grant.[5]

Aurangzeb is accused of alienating Hindus by reimposing *jizya*. Here again the facts have not been carefully sifted. We have already seen that at one stage Akbar had reimposed *jizya* (1575). It is, however, not recognized that Aurangzeb reimposed *jizya* after Shivaji's insurrection. It is also alleged that Aurangzeb invaded Bijapur and Golconda because their kings were Shias, but Aurangzeb had a large number of Shia commanders. When asked to appoint one Sunni Bakhshi, Aurangzeb replied: 'What connections have wordly affairs with religion? And what rights have administrative works to meddle with bigotry. For you is your religion for me is mine. If this rule were established it would be my duty to expirtate all rajas and their followers.'[6] It can easily be deduced that the motives of Aurangzeb were imperial, not sectarian.

The emperor was able to annex the kingdoms of Bijapur and Golconda, and he was able to defeat, capture and execute Shambhaji, Shivaji's son, in 1689, but these victories were not decisive. The Marathas rallied under Tarabai and by the beginning of the nineteenth century were entrenched in Delhi. Chin Qilich Khan (Asif Jah) founded an independent kingdom in the Deccan in 1724. The real cause of decline was Aurangzeb's presence in the Deccan from 1681 to his death in 1707. We can recall here Muhammad Habib's comment on Sultan Muhammad bin Tughluq's decision to shift the capital from Delhi to Deogir, 'The south could not be ruled from Delhi, but equally the north could not be ruled from Deogir.'[7] This long absence from the capital contributed to the decline to a large extent. Secondly, Aurangzeb's son could succeed him only when he himself was old, and then he did not last for more than five years.

Ishtiaq Husain Qureshi speaks of the ideological compulsion of a minority ruling over a majority. He argues that it was wrong to give concessions to the majority. At a later point in history the British were to apply the same argument. The contrast between Akbar and Aurangzeb was sharp with regard to their temperaments, but in the end it was their imperial, rather than religious policy, that had long-term effects.

NADIR SHAH

The collapse of the agrarian system led to the proliferation of soldiers of fortune and to the emergence of the *Pindaris* which rendered society chaotic. Conditions were appalling but with stable and strong rulership they were still reversible. However, when Nadir Shah of Iran invaded India in 1738 and sacked Delhi, the loss of life and property was staggering and the process of decline became irreversible. The people of Delhi constituted the intellectual capital of India and the imperial Mughal treasury could have financed recovery in the outlying provinces. Nadir Shah killed and pillaged indiscriminately and apart from taking the peacock throne and the Kohinoor diamond and other valuables amounting to forty crores of rupees, he also emptied the royal stables of horses and elephants.

The people were still staggering under this calamity when, from around 1756 onwards, Ahmad Shah Abdali (1722–1772) of Afghanistan began his raids. He is historically prominent as the Muslim king who defeated the Marathas in 1761 but his earlier raids caused great devastation. Mirza Sauda in poetry,[8] and Mir Taqi Mir in prose,[9] have described the ravages brought about by his raids.

In 1761, Ahmad Shah Abdali, at the invitation of Shah Waliullah (see Chapter 5), fought the Marathas in the Third Battle of Panipat. The Marathas were defeated and suffered a great setback and the leader, Balaji Baji Rao, died broken-hearted. The defeat of the Marathas could have led to the revival and resurgence of Muslim rule in India, but this did not happen because four years earlier, the British under Lord Clive had defeated Nawab Sirajuddaulah at the Battle of Plassey (1757) and the foundation for British rule in India was already laid.

NOTES

1. Karen Leonard, 'The Great Firm Theory of the Decline of the Mughal Empire' in Muzaffar Alam and Sanjay Subhramanyam (eds.), *The Mughal State*, New Delhi: Oxford University Press, 2000, pp. 398–418.
2. Ibid., p. 407.
3. Ibid., p. 417.
4. James H. Gense, *A History of India*, Madras: Macmillan, 1957, pp. 195–6.

5. Jnan Chandra, 'Aurangzeb's Endowments', *Journal of the Pakistan Historical Society,* Karachi, 1959, Vol. VII, pp. 99–100.
6. Satish Chandra, *Parties and Politics at the Mughal Court,* Aligarh: Peoples Publishing House, 1959, p. 9.
7. M. Habib, 'Muhammad bin Tughluq'. *Politics and Society during the Early Medieval Period,* New Delhi: Peoples Publishing House, 1981, p. 276.
8. Mirza Muhammad Rafi Sauda, *Kulliyat-i-Sauda,* Abdul Bari Aasi (ed.), Lucknow, 1932, Vol. I, pp. 367–81.
9. Mir Taqi Mir, *Zikr-i-Mir* (tr. and ed.) C.M. Naim, New Delhi: Oxford University Press, 1999, pp. 77ff.

PART II
HISTORY OF MUSLIM REVIVAL MOVEMENTS

CHAPTER 5

SHAH WALIULLAH (1703–1762)

Shah Waliullah was the first reformer to appear during the period of Muslim decline. Hitherto, kings and governors had dominated the public life of the Muslim community, but the leadership now passed to this intellectual figure, who was both an *alim* and a Sufi, and had made it his life's mission to reverse the trend of Muslim decline. He realized that the Muslim community had to be emancipated both militarily and morally. Militarily and politically the Maratha power was the threat. To this end he wrote to Ahmad Shah Abdali to remind him of his duty as a Muslim king to liberate the Muslim community, and the result was the Maratha defeat in the Third Battle of Panipat in 1761.

Shah Waliullah was one of the few ulema who realized that war was the lesser *jihad* and the greater *jihad* was against the temptations facing one's own soul. Therefore, the greater and longer part of his mission was to effect a moral reform of his community. Shah Waliullah was the first major figure to analyse the causes of Muslim decline and to suggest remedies. In his description of the rise and fall of societies he shows his familiarity with the philosophy of history propounded by Ibn Khaldun, illustrating how civilizations rise and fall.

His guiding principles of reform were *adl* and *tawazun,* justice and balance; therefore Shah Waliullah was in favour of an equitable distribution of wealth in society. The concentration of wealth in one class leads to wasteful spending at one level and extreme deprivation at the other. He found it objectionable for anyone to be a burden on society; he wanted every individual to be productive and yet he laid great stress on moral constraints. Wealth he said should be acquired only by honest and ethical means.

Shah Waliullah forbade the adoption of Hindu customs for two reasons. First, he believed a beleaguered minority needed to assert its distinctive identity. Participating in *diwali,* which meant lighting lamps and exploding fireworks, or lighting lamps and fireworks on the Muslim festival of *Shab-i-Barat* were to be avoided. There were many customs taken from Hindus, such as *sehra* and music during marriage and even on minor occasions, that led Muslims to extravagance and ultimately, to debt.

He gave central importance to *fiqh,* or jurisprudence, because he felt that deviation from Islamic norms had led the Muslim community into decline.

This deviation he attributed to lack of direct access to the meaning of the Holy Quran. He took the bold step of translating the Holy Quran into Persian. By translating the Holy Quran, Shah Waliullah sought to curb the influence of the ulema as a class, and for this reason he also favoured *ijtihad* over *taqlid*. Usually *ijtihad* is called innovation and *taqlid* is called imitation. Shah Waliullah explained that these concepts in jurisprudence are not so simple. According to him *ijtihad* 'is an exhaustive endeavour to understand the derivative principles of canon law'—in other words a jurist must strive hard to find the Quranic and Sunnic principles which must be applied to new situations and problems.

In arriving at this conclusion, Shah Waliullah was aided by his upbringing and his education in Makkah. His father, Shah Abdur Rahim, was a renowned scholar, who founded the Madrassa-i-Rahimiyah where Shah Waliullah studied and taught. During his pilgrimage he also visited Medina, where he studied under Shaikh Abu Tahir Muhammad bin Ibrahim and Shaikh Sulayman Maghribi.

One of the most important steps he took was towards conciliation between sects and approaches. He realized the necessity of Muslim solidarity, and was able to achieve this because he had humanistic concepts of worship. Ishtiaq Husain Qureshi has pointed out that Shah Waliullah believed what God has revealed is beneficial for mankind:

> God is not a tyrant revelling in getting himself obeyed; such a conception is unworthy and erroneous. In His great mercy He has shown the way which leads to mundane and spiritual well-being and progress![1]

Shah Waliullah detailed the benefits to be gained from such obligations as prayers, alms-giving (*zakat*) and fasting. Although Shah Waliullah was a zealous guardian of Muslim identity, he said that force cannot compel people to accept Islam. The *mujtahid* should persuade people to accept Islam by such means that they should freely adopt it and stand by it even when the *mujtahid* was in no position to impose his belief.[2]

Therefore, he set upon his task of reconciliation with sincerity. First of all he tried to reconcile both strands of sufism. He maintained that both the *Wahdat-ul-Wajood* of Ibn Arabi and the *Wahdat-as-Shuhood* of Mujaddid Alf Thani were correct and that there was no meaningful difference between them. In the next stage he said that all the Sufi orders consist of *Tariqat* (or spiritual path) and all *Tariqat* is subordinate to *Shariat* (religious law). This was also the main platform of his reformist movement, as it was under the cover of sufism that a number of practices, threatening morality had crept into Muslim society. He further tried to reconcile the Sunnis and the Shias.

He wrote a book, *Izalatul Khifa,* disputing their beliefs, but at the same time he vehemently declared that the Shias were within the pale of Islam.

Shah Waliullah's philosophy of life is contained in his most famous book *Hujjat ullah al Baligha.* No other book of the eighteenth century has had such a profound effect on the Muslims of South Asia. Shah Waliullah, because of his learning and piety, commanded the respect of kings. It is not merely that Ahmad Shah Abdali responded to the request of Shah Waliullah to face the Marathas on the field of Panipat. What is important is that Ahmad Shah Abdali heeded Shah Waliullah's warning against tyrannising and terrorising Muslims as had been his habit in all his earlier expeditions.

NOTES

1. Ishtiaq Husain Qureshi, *The Muslim Community of the Indo-Pakistan Subcontinent,* Karachi: BCCT, University of Karachi, Reprint, 1999, p. 213.
2. Ibid., p. 67.

CHAPTER 6

THE JIHAD MOVEMENT

Shah Waliullah was able to defeat the Marathas by invoking the help of Ahmad Shah Abdali, the ruler of Afghanistan. When Maharaja Ranjit Singh established his kingdom over the Punjab and the Frontier, the political landscape had changed. Sayyid Ahmad Barelvi, (1786–1831), the leader of the Mujahideen, had met the Maratha grandee, Maharaja Daulat Rao Scindia at Gwalior in 1828. Sayyid Ahmad Barelvi gave Sindhia an assurance that, if successful, the Mujahideen would help restore power to the Marathas, and actively sought his help.

The problem of the position of the Sikhs straddling the route from Afghanistan to India, took precedence in their reckoning to those of the growing power of the British and the teeming majority of the Hindus. The mission of Shah Waliullah gave rise, in the following generation, to the Jehadi movement. Sayyid Ahmad Barelvi, with the active cooperation of Shah Ismail Shahid (d.1831), Shah Waliullah's grandson, set out against the Sikhs.

The movement of the Mujahideen has sometimes been called the Wahhabi Movement because of its puritan and strict monotheistic character, but this is a misnomer because, in spite of some resemblance in their outlook the two movements were not identical. The basic tenets of Sayyid Ahmad Barelvi are enshrined in his book *Siratul Mustaqim* (1818) which had as its main theme the denunciation of *bida't* or innovations which beset Indo-Muslim society: He decried:

1. The use of disrespectful or blasphemous words for God—which were uttered by poets and mystics in ecstasy.
2. Monism, pantheism or any form of *Wahdat-ul-Wajood*. This put him apart ideologically from Shah Waliullah.
3. Any disputation against fate or predestination being a part of the Sharia is most objectionable, as Sayyid Ahmad Barelvi held predestination to be a fundamental Islamic doctrine.
4. Excessive adulation of one's spiritual guide or *murshid*.
5. Offering food to saints and ancestors (*nazr niaz*) as polytheism (*shirk*).
6. The belief that holy personages could intercede with God on behalf of other mortals; a Muslim should appeal to God directly.

Sayyid Ahmad Barelvi's mission was mistakenly identified with the Wahhabi Movement because he had drawn inspiration directly from Makkah. Setting out for Hajj, Sayyid Ahmad Barelvi reached Makkah in May 1822 and returned to his native town, Rae-Bareli, in April 1824. Both on his way to Arabia and on his way back Sayyid Ahmad had stopped at Patna, in Bihar (the ancient Patliputra) and made it his organizational base. This is the reason why Patna became the centre of Jihadi activities after the martyrdom of Sayyid Ahmad Barelvi.

For his main mission, to dislodge the Sikh kingdom of the Punjab, Sayyid Ahmad Barelvi set out from Tonk and, to avoid a direct route, he traversed the deserts of Sindh and Rajputana to reach Peshawar in 1826. Sayyid Ahmad Barelvi's mission was directed against the Sikhs, but his reformist zeal extended to the Muslims of the frontier region, most of whom regarded his zeal as excessive, therefore he had to face both the Sikhs and the local Muslim chieftains.

The course of his battles with the Sikhs started with the battle of Akora on 20 December 1826, in which five hundred Sikhs lost their lives. In the battle of Saidu the Mujahideen suffered a set back when Muslim tribal leaders were enticed away from the battlefield by the Sikh commander, Budh Singh. After the victory at Hund in August 1829, Sayyid Ahmad told a local Muslim commander that he reposed his faith in God, not in canons. The friction with frontier tribal leaders continued and Sayyid Ahmad was finally able to secure his base, Peshawar, in the battle of Mayar (1830).

A major reversal suffered by the Mujahideen was at the battle of Phuleria. After gaining this victory, Maharaja Ranjit Singh sued for peace. He offered the Mujahideen territory on one side of the Indus river and revenue from the other side. Sayyid Ahmad Barelvi turned down this tempting offer as it went against his mission. The struggle of the Mujahideen reached its culmination at the Battle of Balakote (8 May 1831). When the battle began, the Mujahideen allowed the Sikhs, under Kunwar Sher Singh, to climb up to their position. The Sayyid's strategy was to attack the Sikhs at the foothills when they were headed towards the hilltop. This strategy failed because the Mujahideen lost contact with each other. Dispersed into small groups they were surrounded by the Sikhs and cut down. Among the martyrs were Sayyid Ahmad Barelvi and Shah Ismail. Both these warriors have been known as *Shahids* since that fateful day.

Although the Mujahideen movement ended in destruction, it did not end in failure. The Mujahideen had upheld their principles against all odds and temptations. They left behind a nucleus of Muslim armed resistance which is still active. Another effect of the Mujahideen Movement was to save Sindh from Sikh ambitions. Maharaja Ranjit Singh had extracted tribute from the chieftains of Sindh, but after seeing the ferocity of the battle, they desisted from further adventures.

Sayyid Ahmad had decided to frame a system of leadership because the Mujahideen were ruled by local chieftains during the war. This would impose discipline without detracting from the chieftain's sense of independence. In 1827, Sayyid Ahmad Barelvi was proclaimed the Imam. According to Qeyamuddin Ahmad, this concept: 'envisages the coexistence of the secular authority of the Sultan and the religious authority of the Imam. The former was to function under the general supervision of the latter'.[1] This system could not evolve because the Mujahideen lost political power. However this dualism seems to have resurfaced in contemporary Iran where Khamenei deputises for the Imam and President Khatami is the political leader.

. Why did the movement of the Mujahideen fail to dislodge the Sikhs? Firstly the Muslim chieftains of the North-West Frontier considered the Mujahideen to be fanatics and did not subscribe to the harsh system of beliefs they found in *Siratul Mustaqim*. The Mujahideen were able to mollify the Marathas, and elude the British but were unable to unite the Muslims. As Qeyamuddin Ahmad admits:

> If one were to judge by the yardstick of battles fought, there was more fighting between the tribal Muslim chief than between him and the forces of the Sikh darbar.[2]

The struggle of the Mujahideen lasted a full five years and, seen in that perspective, it was quite admirable.

NOTES

1. Qeyamuddin Ahmad, *The Wahhabi Movement in India*, second edition, New Delhi: Manohar, 1994, p. 67.
2. Ibid., p. 301.

CHAPTER 7

TITU MIR (1782–1832)

With the rise of Titu Mir (Mir Nisar Ali) the reformist and emancipatory zeal of the Muslims shifted to rural Bengal and the grievances of the Muslims became economic rather than military. Titu Mir is supposed to have met Sayyid Ahmad Barelvi at Makkah, either in 1819 or 1822. Whether Titu Mir actually became a disciple of Barelvi is hard to determine, but there is little doubt that his religious ideas were quite in keeping with those of Sayyid Ahmad Barelvi. In Bengal there was a class of Muslims called *Sabiqui* who clung to old customs, including idolatrous customs such as propitiating the Hindu goddess Sitala Devi on the outbreak of smallpox. Titu Mir, like Sayyid Ahmad, was against such concepts of intercession by saints and pilgrimage to tombs of saints. In addition, he was opposed to the observance of Muharram. Muinuddin Ahmad Khan is of the opinion that since the nawabs of Murshidabad were Shiites, *Muharram* came to have great significance for the Sunni population of Bengal. Bengali literature developed many forms devoted to the tragedy of Karbala, like *puthis* and *zarigans*. The making of *tazias* and taking them out in Muharram processions was objected to by Titu Mir, and this was the first tension encountered by his followers. The second tension was caused when Titu Mir ordered his followers to keep away from Muslims who did not accept his reforms.

However, Titu Mir's movement was not the result of sectarian dissension, but of the exploitation of the Muslim peasantry by both the Hindu *zamindars* and the British indigo planters. This, unfortunately, was not only an adverse economic equation but an adverse social equation. When Lord Cornwallis imposed Permanent Settlement in 1793, he was ending the temporary settlement or ownership of land. To secure ownership under the new Permanent Settlement, large sums of money were demanded which most of the old Muslim landowners were unable to pay. Their Hindu menials, such as agents and accountants, on the other hand, collected money and multiplied it by advancing loans on interest. In most cases, Muslim landlords became subjugated to their former Hindu employees.

Apart from this antagonism, Hindu *zamindars* began charging tax to spend on expressly Hindu rituals and festivals. These taxes included *Durga Vritti* and *Shrudhi Vritti*. Quite apart from the unaffordable nature of such taxes, the puritan persuasion of Titu Mir's followers prevented them from paying such taxes to their landlords or *zamindars*. In retaliation Hindu *zamindars* began taxing Muslim cultivators for the beards they grew and the mosques they built. Attempts to collect such taxes from Poorna and Sarfarazpur, led to violence.

Meanwhile, the European indigo planters appeared on the scene and became another source of exploitation. Muslim cultivators wanted to grow rice and other grains, but European (mostly British) planters found the export of indigo to be most lucrative and forced the cultivators to reserve their most fertile land for indigo.[1] They forcibly advanced about two-and-a-half rupees for the cultivation of indigo. If a farmer or cultivator refused, the planter would take away his cattle and starve them until the cultivator relented. Once he accepted the advance, he could never repay the debt due to the corruption of the police, and would forever be under the yoke of the planter. Only Titu Mir and his followers had the courage to resist this double exploitation. The economic exploitation reinforced feelings of Muslim identity and popularised reforms.

Titu Mir made Narkulbaria, a village in twenty-four parganas (a district next to Calcutta), his headquarters. From here he prevented the collection of cess from Sarfarazpur, which resulted in a riot in which people were killed and a mosque was burnt. In retaliation, the followers of Titu Mir attacked Poorna (1831). In the riots which ensued a temple was defiled, and a Brahmin and a Christian were killed. The British realized that the movement was no mere insurgency; it had deep social and economic implications for British rule and the social order they had imposed. Accordingly, one Alexander, an employee of the Government Salt Agency was ordered to advance from Barasat to Narkulbaria on 18 March 1832. In the fighting that ensued, Titu Mir was killed while fighting gallantly.

NOTE

1. Muinuddin Ahmad Khan, *Fara'idi Movement*, Karachi: Pakistan Historical Society, 1965, p. cxi.

CHAPTER 8

THE FARAIDI MOVEMENT

The Faraidi Movement centred in rural East Bengal was an organized religious movement which set up most successfully an hierarchical system of control. It was a militant movement which met violence with violence and succeeded in both religious and social reform. The leaders of the Faraidi Movement, Haji Shariatullah (1781–1840) and his son Dudhu Mian/Mohsinuddin Ahmad (1819–1862), responded to the same challenges of Hindu *zamindars* and British indigo planters as Titu Mir had, but avoided outright confrontation with the British. Some scholars have tried to emphasize the difference between the movements of Titu Mir and Haji Shariatullah but their similarities are more apparent. It is said that Dudhu, on his way to Haj, had met and paid his respects to Titu Mir. There were certain doctrinal differences between Titu Mir and the Faraidis, but there was only twelve years' difference between the two movements, the first centred in West Bengal while the second was focused in East Bengal. To their Hindu and British adversaries their resemblance was more apparent than their differences.

The religious tenets of the Faraidis were different from those of Titu Mir and the Jehadis, only in the sense that in jurisprudence the Faraidis were strict Hanafis and believed in *taqlid* rather than *ijtihad*. They were called Faraidis because they gave primacy to the five basic pillars of Islam, including *Kalma,* prayers, fasting, *hajj* and *zakat*. They wished to return to the pristine purity of Islam and waged a war against what they termed was *bida't* (innovation) and *shirk* (polytheism). This meant that they actively opposed Muharram observances such as processions, *tazias*, and dirges on the tragedy of Karbala like *zarigan* and *puthis*. As with other reformers, they considered visiting the graves of saints and seeking their intercession with God to be polytheism. They were also against un-Islamic rituals and customs during marriage and other ceremonies. The *zamindars*, who were mostly Hindu, (for the reasons discussed in the chapter on Titu Mir), had imposed as many as thirty-two Hindu religious cess on Muslim peasants including *Shrudhi Vritti* and *Durga Vritti*. In retaliation, the Hindu *zamindars* subjected the Faraidis to different types of torture and imposed the *beard tax*. It should be noted that the Faraidis insisted on cow slaughter on *Id-ul-Azha*, because, in the words of Muinuddin Ahmad Khan, 'it was less expensive and more convenient in Bengal'.[1] The Faraidis differed from other reformers in insisting that under

British rule congregational prayers like those on Fridays and the two *Ids* could not be held. Scholars have insisted that unlike Titu Mir, the Faraidi leaders, succeeded in keeping their movements away from politics. This is true only to the extent that they avoided armed reprisals by the British, but their doctrinal position, that congregational prayers were not allowed in Dar-ul-Harb, the domain of war as they characterised British rule, was undeniably a political stance.

Apart from propagating their beliefs, the Faraidis were successful in communal organization and imposed a system of control and interaction which they called a 'khilafat' system. The head, next to the *ustad* (Dudhu Miyan) were the *Uparasta khalifas,* next to them were the *superintendent khalifa,* followed by the *village khalifa,* who was in charge of around three hundred families. Thus a whole network was at the disposal of the Faraidis, making it easier to combat the *zamindars.* In addition, they had a *panchayat* system where disputes were settled. Muslims were discouraged from approaching the British judiciary. However, if they were summoned by the courts they had to attend, as did Dudhu Miyan who himself faced a number of cases filed by *zamindars* or planters.

One positive action they took was to combat the caste system within the Muslims' own professions or even the professions of their forefathers which had led to discrimination and segregation. Even fishmongering was looked down upon. The Faraidis abolished this evil and social organization helped in inculcating egalitarian values. Since the Faraidi leadership, like Titu Mir's family, came from the lower middle class, class parity was all the more necessary.

Such a radical class movement invited the hostility of the vested interests of the Hindu *zamindars* and British plantation owners. However, it should be noted that this situation did not pertain to the rest of India. In neighbouring Bihar the Muslim landlords were quite prominent and they had Hindu tenants. Some Muslim landlords were licentious but they were not tyrannnical like the *zamindars* in Bengal.

Haji Shariatullah was in and out of police custody, because of his resistance to the *zamindars'* oppression, and his insistence on cow slaughter, but he was never convicted. During the leadership of Dudhu Miyan, the incidence of confrontation increased. During the lifetime of Haji Shariatullah, Dudhu Miyan had raised a cadre of club-wielding men, who used their blunt instruments to combat the hirelings of the landlords and planters.

Since the Faraidis were organized, the *zamindars* took strong and sweeping measures to suppress them. They inflicted various forms of torture, of which the least was sprinkling of chilli powder on their beards, to prevent their tenants joining the Faraidis. In retaliation, Dudhu Miyan led his club-bearing men in two major encounters against *zamindars.* The first was against the

Shiqdar of Kanaipur in 1841. In this case, merely a show of strength was sufficient. The Shiqdar agreed to cease torture and exempted Muslim tenants from cess intended to fund Hindu festivals.

During the following year, Dudhu Miyan led a campaign against the prominent landlord Joynarain Ghosh. According to the police who investigated this incident, the landlords had degraded their tenants, including the females. The Faraidis attacked the landlord and carried off his younger brother, Maddan Narayan Ghosh. Subsequently, Maddan Narayan was cut to pieces and his body buried under the river bed of Padma. The Faraidis next turned their attention to an indigo planter, Anderson, who had attacked Dudhu Miyan's house, killed four watchmen, severely wounded others and stole one-and-a-half lakh of rupees. On 5 December 1846, the Faraidis killed Anderson's agent, Kanjhi Lal. Dudhu Miyan was convicted of murder by the lower court, but the appellant court, the *Dewani Adalat*, acquitted him because his presence at the site was not proved. The British kept a watch on him and during the 1857 War of Independence, he was placed under 'protective custody'. On 24 September 1862, Dudhu Miyan died peacefully at his Dhaka residence. His grave has been declared a historical site. All reformist movements were eventually overtaken by the events of 1857.

NOTE

1. Muinuddin Ahmad Khan, *Faraidi Movement*, Karachi: Pakistan Historical Society, 1965, p. 17.

The War of Independence of 1857 was the last attempt to dislodge the British by force of arms. This attempt failed, but in the process all the parties committed and suffered great atrocities. Since these events affected the fortunes of all the three communities involved, it must be considered a key point in history. Whether it should be considered a Sepoy Mutiny, as the British called it before 1947, or the First War of Independence as most South Asians called it after 1947, is still the subject of debate. During the centennial celebrations in 1957, two eminent Indian historians, Surinder Nath Sen and Ramesh Chandra Majumdar, were of the view that events were not as widespread as to be called a national struggle, nor so constricted as to be called a mere Sepoy Mutiny.

However, the question cannot be settled merely by invoking the magnitude of the events because they were governed by opportunity. The Punjab and the Deccan did not support the uprising, but they made attempts to join the War. The NWFP was not insensitive to the crisis and attempts to rebel were made by sepoys at Nowshera and Mardan on 21 and 22 May 1857. In the Punjab, Jullundhar revolutionaries marched to Delhi, and in the Deccan there was partial mutiny at Aurangabad on 13 June 1857.

Although both Hindus and Muslims participated and suffered, the Muslims were singled out for punishment, because of a misconception, shared by all three communities: Muslims were bitter because they had lost power to the British while the Hindus were lukewarm because they had only suffered a change of masters. The point was that the British had to struggle more against the Marathas than the Mughals to gain power in India. This misconception spread to the British because the mutineers had made the last Mughal ruler, Bahadur Shah Zafar, the titular head of their movement. The mutineers asserted the legitimacy of the Mughal empire to counteract the claims made by the British East India Company and both Hindus and Muslims were united in pursuing this course. This was an ideological stand involving an acceptance of Muslims as insiders as against the British who were considered to be, and conducted themselves as, outsiders. The proclamation by the mutineers, among whom the Hindus were in majority, of Bahadur Shah II as the emperor of India shows that the two communities were not just fighting a common enemy but were struggling for a common cause. During the mutiny, Hindus and Muslims forgot their differences, and in the aftermath of 1857 neither community can be blamed for bringing about disunity. Their unity did not last as not all Indians were united in the cause of dislodging the British.

Just as the battle of Plassey was won with a majority of Indian soldiers,[1] the Sepoy Mutiny was overcome with the help of Indian allies. Maharashtrian and Sikh soldiers joined in suppressing the mutineers in Awadh and Rohilkhand.[2] The transformation of Sepoy attitudes which took place between 1757 and 1857 was the cause of the mutiny.

CAUSES

The causes of the mutiny were political, economic and religious. Although sepoys had joined the British they had not forgotten patriotism. In 1806, sepoys at Vellore (South India) showed visible sympathy for Tipu Sultan. In 1824, sepoys in Barrackpure (Bengal) refused to serve in the campaign against Burma because perquisites for past services were not being offered.[3] The British underestimated the effects of this and were unprepared for the magnitude of the outbreak of hostility. The annexation by the British of Awadh in 1856, added to the unrest. The steps the East India Company took were insufficient to prevent a rising but aroused suspicion. The number of British troops was increased and the artillery kept away from the sepoys.

Wittingly or unwittingly, the social reforms that the British favoured, the abolition of *sati*, abolition of child marriage and provision for the remarriage of widows aroused suspicions that the British intended to spread Christianity by force. This impression was further strengthened by an act passed by the viceroy, Lord Canning, in 1850, which allowed converts to other religions to inherit the property of their Hindu or Muslim parents or ancestors. The sepoys were made to sign contracts that they would not refuse to cross seas, and would remove their earrings while in uniform.

The induction of greased cartridges for the regulation Enfield rifles triggered the mutiny. Soldiers were required to bite the cartridge before loading, and it was widely rumoured that these cartridges were smeared with the fat of pigs and cows, so that both Hindus and Muslims were defiled. The East India Company denied these rumours, and cancelled the provision of biting the bullet, but suspicions had been so widely aroused that these measures came too late. This was coupled with the fact that, over the century, British high-handedness had increased.

The Sepoys noted that the salary and emoluments of Europeans were higher than theirs. Another cause of disaffection was the system of pensions and land grants for invalid soldiers or survivors of those slain. The Company maintained detailed records of sepoy families, and on this basis had the right to determine the heirs entitled to a pension. This was Lord Dalhousie's

'Doctrine of Lapse' according to which no adopted heir could inherit in the absence of true issues. This was a cause of discontent, 'which eventually culminated in the mutiny—rebellion of 1857'.[4]

EVENTS

On 22 January 1857, sepoys stationed at Dum Dum showed their unease about the Enfield cartridges. The discontent simmered from January to March and broke out at Barrackpur and Behrampur. Sepoys then tried to communicate with their colleagues in other cantonments by sending lotus flowers as a symbolic message asking fellow troopers to rise up. Civilians communicated through *chappatis* (a flat bread).

The mutiny proper began at Meerut on 10 May 1857. Sepoys overpowered their officers, and indulged in arson and killing of European inhabitants. The mutineers marched to Delhi and on 11 May 1857, proclaimed a reluctant Bahadur Shah Zafar as the emperor of India. This step was taken to prove that the rebels had legitimate power in the land whereas the East India Company was an outright usurper. The mutineers established their rule at Delhi, forcing all European survivors to take refuge in Karnal. On 16 May, fifty European prisoners, including women and small children, were massacred in Delhi.

The mutineers moved quickly and ruthlessly but neglected to cut the telegraph wires. This alerted loyal forces far sooner than the rebels had anticipated. On 4 July 1857, Europeans were massacred at Rampur. The Lucknow residency had also been besieged and on the same day, Sir Henry Lawrence, the chief commissioner of Awadh succumbed to his wounds. Meanwhile, the common people of Rohilkhand, Awadh and Bihar joined the mutineers. Agricultural tax was excessive and the money-lenders rapacious, therefore both landlords and peasants had been seething with disaffection. At the same time, it should be noted that the sepoys lost the sympathy of the common people when they started taking revenge on the infirm, women and children among the British.

The tide turned against the rebels in July. On 16 July 1857, Nana Sahib, one of the main leaders, was defeated at Fatehpur. In retaliation he ordered all 'Bengali babus' to be apprehended. On 16 August 1857, Nana Sahib was again defeated at Bithur. On 28 May 1859 the Nana Sahib was reported to be at Butwal, with Hazrat Mahal, the Begum of Awadh, who had taken up arms against the British. On 20 April 1859, Nana Sahib sent a message to Queen Victoria hoping to be reconciled with the British but was unsuccessful. He reportedly died in Nepal sometime in September 1859.

As early as 1857, the British captured Bahadur Shah II at Delhi, killed two of his sons and a grandson, and sent their severed heads to the king for breakfast. This was on 22 September 1857 and two days later the Lucknow

Residency was relieved by General Havelock. Two prominent British generals were killed along with six hundred Englishmen.

In 1858, Lakshmi Bai, the Rani of Jhansi, declared war against the British. Early in April, Jhansi was stormed and sacked but the Rani escaped. On 1 June the Rani of Jhansi, along with Tatya Tope, Rao Sahib and the Nawab of Banda succeeded in capturing Gwalior. On 17 June the Rani of Jhansi was killed in battle. Another revolutionary, Mahbub Khan, was hanged at Aligarh on the same day. Later, Tatya Tope was captured and hanged on 18 April 1859.

Not all events can be recounted here, but one aspect is apparent: this was an uprising in which both Hindus and Muslims participated. It was a deliberate policy of the British to blame the Muslims for playing the leading part, being convinced that they were the main leaders because the British had seized power from them. In their view Hazrat Mahal of Awadh proved to be more heroic than either her husband, the deposed Wajid Ali Shah, or even Bahadur Shah II who at one stage was more concerned with protocol than independence.

CAUSES OF FAILURE

If we examine the reasons for the failure of the mutiny, we can see that firstly the revolutionaries had not been able to plan or synchronize their uprising. Naturally their means of communication, were not safe and reliable and, being clandestine, were also not very effective. Secondly, the Sikhs and the Marathas with whom the British had fought wars, sided with the British in attacking the rebels. The problem of lack of manpower, the one weakness of the British, was solved by the Sikhs and Marathas and the soldiers of the Nizam of Deccan who also came to the rescue of the British. Great valour and, at the same time, great bestiality was shown on both sides. Had Bakht Khan not been deserted while defending Delhi, the rebels would have given a better account of themselves. In the end, access to the ports and to ammunition secured victory for the British.

Nevertheless, it had been a close call for the British. A reappraisal of their rule in India was thought necessary, and though there was a widespread call for revenge, the viceroy, Lord Canning, adopted a policy of conciliation.

THE EFFECTS

Queen Victoria was a constitutional monarch and was guided by parliament. The events of the mutiny pained her, and she did not take a one-sided view. The prime minister also decided that it was an opportune moment to end the constitutional anomaly of a trading company conducting the trial of a king (Bahadur Shah II) for treason. The first casualty of the 1857 revolt was the

East India Company itself. The British Crown abolished the Company's rule and governed India directly. It was officially recognized that it was Lord Dalhousie's Doctrine of Lapse, (which provided for the annexation of a state if the ruler did not have a direct heir) which was the cause of the revolt. Lord Canning toured India, and assured all princes that the British had no wish for further acquisitions. Thus about five hundred states, including Kashmir and Hyderabad, were left out of British India and formed separate autonomous entities. They recognized Britain as the paramount power, ceded defence and foreign affairs to Britain but in internal matters they were quite free, having only to accommodate a British officer, 'the Resident'. J.H. Gense explains,

> That during the rising most of the states ruled by Indian princes had proved exceptionally loyal; so that it was better to have a laudatory prince than an annexed state.[5]

An Imperial Legislative Council was formed in British India and a number of princes were admitted to the council.

NOTES

1. Nirad C. Chaudhurie, *Clive of India*, Bombay: Jaico Press, 1977, p. 269.
2. Burton Stein, *A History of India*, New Delhi: Oxford University Press, 2001, p. 226.
3. Ibid.
4. Seema Alavi, *The Sepoy and the Company*, New Delhi: Oxford University Press, 1999, p. 9.
5. James H. Gense, *History of India*, Madras: Macmillan, 1957, p. 374.

IFTIKHAR-UN-NISA; HAZRAT MAHAL (b. Awadh, *c.* 1825–d. Nepal, 1879). She was a dancing girl who caught the eye of the king, Wajid Ali Shah. She entered the royal harem, and on the birth of her son, Birjis Qadar, she was granted the status of queen. In the upheaval of 1857, defending the honour of her nation, she emerged as a natural leader of men. She had the charisma to galvanize both the nobility and the masses, who had taken the 7 February 1856 annexation of Awadh lying down. Not conversant with the arts of war herself, she commanded brave and experienced generals, like Raja Jai Lal Singh which is another indication of the communal harmony fostered by British expansionism.

As a first step, she had her twelve-year-old son, Birjis Qadar, crowned king of Awadh (July 1857). Wajid Ali Shah was somewhat taken aback by this supersedence of his position, but Bahadur Shah II ratified this investiture. It was taken for granted that Hazrat Mahal would rule in the name of her son. The siege of Lucknow was efficiently organized, and left an indelible imprint on British memory. When the British rallied, the desertions were mainly from the nobility. Hazrat Mahal confiscated the property of Raja Man Singh, who after initially siding with Awadh, went over to the British.

When the British inflicted reverses, Hazrat Mahal held court, and after recounting the treason of Sikh militias, and the rajas loyal to the British, she exhorted her subjects: 'The whole army is in Lucknow, but it is without courage. Why does it not attack Alumbagh [where the British had regrouped]? Is it waiting for the English to be reinforced and Lucknow to be surrounded?'[1] She lost the Battle of Musabagh, despite the great courage and gallantry displayed by her troops, but she did not lose heart. She emerged as a politician through tumultuous events—the first in South Asia after the ancient Chanakya. This was most evident in her rejoinder to the proclamation of Queen Victoria, on 1 November 1858, ending the rule of the East India Company. The proclamation provided an opening to end the uprising.

In her counter proclamation, issued on the next day, Hazrat Mahal said that the British were not to be trusted. She reiterated that the British never forgive a fault, be it great or small. 'What is the use of accepting the idea that the company is dead, and that now the Queen rules; when the laws, settlements and judicial are all unchanged?' She went on to give details of when and where the British had broken pacts and treaties. Citing Queen Victoria's intention of rebuilding India, Hazrat Mahal issued her rebuttals. 'It is worthy of little reflection that they have promised Indians no better employment than making rocks and digging canals.'[2]

Unlike the Rani of Jhansi, who was born to a father learned and cultured, and respected for his attachment to the Peshwa's house, Hazrat Mahal originally belonged to a profession responsible for the streak of frivolity pervading Awadh culture; therefore historians, not without malice, mention the men in her life. The first is Mammu Khan, her pre-marital paramour, and adviser after her assumption of the throne. She finally dismissed Mammu Khan for cowardice. Mammu Khan surrendered to the British, but was, nevertheless, hanged, tragically vindicating the presentiments of his queen. The second man was, of course, her husband, Wajid Ali Shah (b. Lucknow, 30 July 1822–d. Calcutta, 21 September 1887)—who has been painted heavily as a debauched sensualist—but, who, nevertheless, displayed courage. Even his antagonist, Major-General Outram, wrote, 'I am told that his conduct at the time of annexation astonished our officers; that is, it was characterized by dignity and propriety.'

At the outbreak of the Mutiny, Wajid Ali Shah was placed under custody at Fort William. He consistently refused to sign a treaty legitimizing the annexation of his kingdom.[3] The British perceived negative opposition and passive resistance in him, which they would later encounter manifold under Gandhi. The third man was Maulvi Sikander Shah, of Faizabad; he had come on stage as a rival because of his military expertise. He came under her service but they lost the battle of Nawabganj together. She retreated into Nepal, where she died in 1879. It was a sign of the times that the maulvi could not replace the courtesan.

Notes

1. P.J.O. Taylor (ed.), *A Companion to the Mutiny of 1857*, Delhi: Oxford University Press, 1996, p. 42.
2. Ibid., p. 273.
3. Ibid., also see Mirza Ali Azhar, *King Wajid Ali Shah of Awadh*, Karachi: Royal Book Company, 1982, Vol. I, p. 463.

Chapter 10

The Educational Movements

Sir Syed and Aligarh

The first Indian reaction to the failure of the 1857 uprising was the realization that it was not possible to dislodge British rule by force of arms. The second was to seek the causes of British superiority, and the third was to prescribe modern education as the remedy for political decline. The quest for exploring non-military means of emancipation led to reform in religious thought and to the adoption of western scientific education.

The trail blazer was Raja Ram Mohan Roy (1772–1833), who called for a reform of Hindu religion. He claimed he was returning Hinduism to ancient Vedic purity (just as the Muslim revivalists aimed at restoring Islam to the purity of the early or right-guided caliphate). In practice, Raja Ram Mohan Roy favoured belief in one god (monotheism), repeal of the caste system, the abolition of *sati* and child marriage, and recommended the remarriage of widows. He formed an organization called the Brahmo Samaj which, though influential in the intellectual circles of Bengal, caused it and the creed of Raja Ram Mohan Roy in general to be cast outside the pale of Hinduism. In truth, his creed came closer to Christianity and Islam than to Hinduism at is was practised. The Bengali intelligentsia was discerning and while it rejected the prescriptions of Raja Ram Mohan Roy, it heeded his advice to adopt western education and to qualify for service under the British.

The reaction of Sir Syed Ahmad Khan (1817–1898) to the trauma of 1857 was similar to that of Ram Mohan Roy and ran into similar difficulties. Sir Syed tried to modernize Muslim belief. He sought a natural explanation for every phenomenon and denied the incidence of miracles recounted in the Holy Quran and Hadith. He said every law is according to nature and that there can be no contradiction between the work of God and the word of God. Every belief had to be subordinate to science. No wonder then that he too was branded a heretic. This was, in fact, also a great psychological reaction because, in his youth, Sir Syed had written a pamphlet to 'prove' that the sun revolved around the earth! In the midst of all these controversies, Sir Syed published a refutation of Sir William Muir's *Life of Mahomet*, a scurrilous attack on the Holy Prophet (PBUH) and moreover carried his inquiry to the western side by subjecting the Bible to theological scrutiny. This represents the first aspect of Sir Syed's contribution.

The second aspect was political. He had saved British lives at Bijnor in 1857, therefore there was a hard core of Englishmen who paid attention to what he said. Sir Syed wrote a number of pamphlets and books, the most prominent among them being *The Causes of the Indian Revolt,* which he sent to the members of the British Parliament. To a great many, whose arrogance had increased by their success in 1857, this book, in itself constituted treason, but others, as reflective of 1857 as the Indians, gave it their serious attention.

There were two main strands in the writings of Sir Syed Ahmad: first, to explain that Muslims were not obliged, by their belief, to oppose British rule. In the second strand he maintained that the main cause of the 1857 uprising was the absolute lack of communication between the British and the natives, between the rulers and the ruled. Sir Syed said that had there been any means of bringing Indian aspirations to the notice of the British, the 1857 war would not have erupted.

The last observation, it is said, led Allen Octavio Hume (1829–1915), to lay the foundation of the Indian National Congress (1885) as a forum for forming Indian aspirations and airing them. However, Sir Syed emerged as the foremost critic of the Congress. It is important to recall the circumstances under which the Congress was founded; it had a British president (Hume) and the blessings of the British. Sir Syed could have been expected to go along with it, but he did not. As Aziz Ahmad has explained, at first Sir Syed remained silent, but he spoke out in 1887 when a Muslim, Badruddin Tyabji, was elected as the Congress president.

Earlier, Sir Syed had not taken a separatist stance, but in 1867, just ten years after the mutiny, a language controversy between Hindi and Urdu arose, when Hindus said Hindi should replace Urdu as the language of instruction and of the courts. Hindi was the language of the majority but the Muslim elite regarded Urdu as representative of the joint Indo-Muslim culture, therefore this demand came as a shock to them. Both an Indian and a Pakistani historian, Tara Chand and Farman Fatehpuri have concurred that the Muslim reaction to Hindi was conditioned by the fact that Hindi had not naturally evolved as a language; the British through Fort William College, Calcutta, patronised *Prem Sagar* by Laloo Lalji to create deliberately a Sanskritized version of Hindi which was different from the spoken language.

The result of this cultural shock was that Sir Syed, who had previously said that India was a bride with one Hindu eye and one Muslim eye, now said that Hindus and Muslims were separate nations. He said that if the British withdrew, Muslims would not share power with the Hindus but would lead a life of subjugation. With these presentiments Sir Syed opposed Muslim participation in the Indian National Congress. He forecast that despite being favoured by the British, the Congress was a political party and at some juncture it could come into conflict with the British; if the Muslims participated in it, they would again face punishment as they had after 1857. His fears were justified as even Pandit Jawaharlal Nehru has written that Muslims suffered more than Hindus after 1857.

Sir Syed had the example of Raja Ram Mohan Roy before him, and knew fully well that his own religious views were considered heretical, therefore he consciously sought to separate his religious outlook from his educational reforms. It was to this end that he inducted the services of Shibli Nomani (1857–1914) to teach Islamic studies at Aligarh.

Sir Syed's first venture was to open a school at Muradabad, in 1858 just one year after the mutiny. Sir Syed had embarked on his career of imparting western education while the mutiny was still in the news. The next step was to establish a translation society at Ghazipur, in January 1864. Later it was renamed the Scientific Society because its purpose was to translate scientific literature into Urdu. It was in Aligarh that Sir Syed gave expression to his main ambition in education. In 1866 he founded the *Aligarh Institute Gazette* a magazine devoted to the cultural needs of Muslims having an English education. Also at Aligarh, Sir Syed started a primary school on 24 May 1875, Queen Victoria's birthday, and on 1 January 1877 the viceroy, Lord Lytton, laid the foundation stone of the college. The All-India Muhammadan Educational Conference was founded at Aligarh in 1866, a society which held its sessions all over the country and was the means of spreading the spirit and the message of Aligarh to all corners of the country. It was the All-Indian Muslim Educational Conference (as it was later known) that proved to be the parent body of the All-India Muslim League in 1906.

It was twenty-two years after Sir Syed's death, in 1920, that Aligarh College was raised to the status of a university. Lord Macaulay, the great historian, had favoured the spread of western education in India, with English as the medium of instruction, but to get conservative Indians to accept this was quite another matter. Raja Mohan Roy persuaded the Hindus and Sir Syed Ahmad Khan persuaded the Muslims. It was only due to their efforts that Hindus and Muslims began to *demand* from the British the fruits of a modern western education.

Sir Syed held communal and class interests supreme and did not favour modern education being imparted to the lower classes. He also did not favour emancipation of Muslim women. These criticisms have substance, but if one considers the progress that western education made due to Sir Syed's efforts, one realizes the extent of Sir Syed's contribution to the Indo-Muslim renaissance. Peter Hardy offers an objective appraisal of Sir Syed's movement:

What Aligarh did was to produce a class of Muslim leaders with a footing in both western and Islamic culture, at ease both in British and Muslim society and endowed with a consciousness of their claims to be the aristocracy of the country as much in British as in Mughal times.[1]

It was this last-named trait which gave the Muslim community the morale necessary to voice the demand for Pakistan. The Quaid-i-Azam was to call the Muslim University, Aligarh, his arsenal. Two heads of the new Pakistani state, the first prime minister, Liaquat Ali Khan and the second president, Mohammad Ayub Khan, were graduates of the Muslim University, Aligarh.

Deoband

Sir Syed had been inspired not only by Lord Macaulay, but by Shah Waliullah as well. Sir Syed's mission was to preserve the future of the Muslim community. There were conservative elements, opposed to him, who were anxious to ensure the religious identity of the community, and the premier traditional institution where this need was nurtured was at the Darul Uloom at Deoband. Aligarh was considered loyal to the British, Deoband, hostile. Aligarh worked against the Congress, Deoband did not favour separatism. Aligarh and Deoband were to exercise profound influences on the Muslim mind from opposite directions.

Deoband lies in the Saharanpur district of United Provinces. The Darul Uloom (seminary) began as a small *maktab*, (a primary school where the three R's are taught). It was founded on 30 May 1867 by Maulana Fazlur Rahman, the father of Maulana Shabbir Ahmad Usmani, and Maulana Zulfiqar Ali, the father of Shaikh-ul-Hind, Maulana Mahmud-ul-Hasan. Later, the Darul Uloom was run by Maulana Muhammad Qasim Nanotwi (1832–1880) and Maulana Rashid Ahmad Gangohi (1828–1905).

Since Aligarh was founded to further the material progress of the Muslims, the ulema of Deoband pointedly illustrated their reliance on the bounty of Allah by refusing to plan ahead, and therefore refused all grants and sources of fixed income. Neither the government nor rich patrons were allowed to contribute to the funding of the Darul Uloom. Apart from showing their reliance on God for their day to day sustenance, by refusing large grants they preserved their intellectual and ideological freedom. In spite of such strict screening of funds, the buildings of the seminary were completed in good time through small donations from the people. At the end of the first year, seventy-eight students had enrolled. Today it is the largest seminary after the Al Azhar University in Cairo. It is a residential university and students from all over the world study there.

The seminary of Deoband follows essentially the syllabus of the Madrassa-i-Rahimia founded by the father of Shah Waliullah, where Shah Waliullah himself and his sons, Shah Abdul Aziz (1746–1824) and Shah Abdul Qadir (d.1813) had taught. The syllabus was consequently traditional, Arabic including prosody and rhetoric, logic, indirectly obtained from the Greeks, *Kalam* (religious discourse), jurisprudence, Quranic exegesis, Hadith and its subordinate disciplines and, somewhat suprisingly, *tibb* or traditional medicine. Urdu was the medium of instruction. The students were trained in very few vocations and the result was that the graduates of Deoband spread out all over the country to seek positions in mosques and madrassas. It was this practice that made Deoband not the name of a seminary, but the name of a creed.

This creed was derived from the Mujahideen, the followers of Sayyid Ahmad Barelvi, Titu Mir and Haji Shariatullah. They forbade belief in the intercession of saints, and prescribed limits beyond which adulation of the Holy Prophet (PBUH) himself transgressed the concept of *tauhid* (or monotheism). Visiting the graves of saints and Sufis was forbidden as was *nazr* and *niaz* (religious food offerings) and of course *azadari* in Muharram was forbidden.

Maulana Qasim Nanotvi wrote a book, *Tasfiyya-al-Aquaid,* to counteract and refute the religious thought of Sir Syed Ahmad Khan. In this work he asserted that reason was subordinate to Hadith. The Deobandis held that that 'which God commands is good, rather than God commands what is good'.[2] The ulema of Deoband wrote tracts against Judaism, Christianity and Hinduism and carried out a jihad against Qadianis. On the political plane, the ulema of Deoband, especially Maulana Rashid Ahmad Gangohi, issued a *fatwa* that it was permissible to associate with the Congress under certain circumstances, but under no condition was it possible to cooperate with Aligarh. In the twentieth century Deoband continued its relations with Congress and opposed the Muslim League. This did not prevent the Congress government of independent India from closing down the Deoband seminary. The ban was brief, but it was a sad comment on the political stance of Deoband. Of the prominent ulema of Deoband, only Allama Shabbir Ahmad Usmani (1885–1949) was a supporter of the Pakistan Movement.

MADRASSA MANZAR-I-ISLAM, BARELVI

The Deobandis and Barelvis are the two major denominations of Sunni Islam in South Asia. The Deobandi persuasion was the successor of all the revivalist movements beginning with Shah Waliullah. Although Sayyid Ahmad Barelvi, Titu Mir and Haji Shariatullah did not identify themselves with the creed or movement of Shaikh Muhammad bin Abdul Wahhab (1703–1792) there was nevertheless sufficient resemblance for the British to label all South Asian revivalist movements of Sunni Islam as Wahhabi, though it did not represent the majority of Sunni Muslims—who were shocked by the Wahhabi desecration of holy tombs in Madina and its attack on Karbala. To the Sunni Muslims with Sufi tendencies, who venerated Sufi saints and who flocked to the tombs of the Sufis, the revivalism of Deoband was sacrilege. They believed in offering *fateha* for the departed and believed in the intercession of saints and other holy personages for the salvation of their souls. Ever since Shah Ismail Shahid had published *Taqviat-ul-Iman* there had arisen a tendency to decentralize the love and veneration for the Holy Prophet (PBUH) in the revivalist creeds. To correct this, Maulana Ahmad Reza Khan of Barelvi (1856–1921) made his appearance. He founded the Madrassa Manzar-ul-Islam in his home town. Ahmad Reza Khan was a spellbinding orator and a good poet, writing *na'ats* in praise of the Holy Prophet (PBUH) and other holy personages of Islam.

He believed in the *Qadiri Silsila* and believed that Shaikh Abdur Qadir Jilani was at the apex of spiritual authority, below the Holy Prophet (PBUH). Ahmad Reza Khan believed in the intercessory power of the Holy Prophet (PBUH) and the venerated Sufi saints. He had a high regard for the Syeds. Usha Sanyal sums up his mission: 'In all he did or wrote, love of the Prophet was the motivating factor.'[3]

Of all madrassa founders, Ahmad Reza Khan was the only one to expound the Two-Nation theory. This is contained in his book *Al Hujjat al Motmainna*. As such Ahmed Reza Khan can also be considered one of the spiritual founders of Pakistan.

NADVAT-UL-ULEMA, LUCKNOW

There were many concerned dignitaries within the Muslim community who felt that Deoband and Aligarh represented two opposite poles; Deoband was concerned only with the hereafter, while Aligarh was concerned only with the worldly. They felt that a balance had to be struck and for this purpose, an institution which cared for both the spiritual and temporal concerns of the Muslims should be set up.

The proposal to found the Nadvat-ul-Ulema was floated in Kanpur by Maulana Muhammad Ali Mongeri in 1892. It received an impetus when Maulana Abdul Hye joined the Nadva and undertook a tour of Bareli and Fatehpur to seek support for this institution, and on 2 September 1898 Nadvat-ul-Ulema was transferred to Lucknow.

A new life was infused into the Nadva, when Shibli Nomani joined it after the death of Sir Syed. His celebrity shed lustre on Nadvat-ul-Ulema. Shibli Nomani had been a protégé of Sir Syed but, over the years, he felt that Sir Syed had become more loyalist and communal than the circumstances warranted. His background of traditional Arabic education and his exposure to modern education at Aligarh made him the most suitable person to head Nadvat-ul-Ulema, but this was only in theory. In practice, and in spite of the stated purpose of founding the Nadva, Shibli faced resistance from a group of his colleagues led by Safdar Yar Jung when he tried to introduce a minimum of English and science into the Nadva syllabus.

Later, when Maulvi Abdul Karim challenged Shibli's concept of *jihad* in an article, Shibli dismissed him from service. At this, a storm of protest was raised and Shibli had to leave the Nadva. When asked what the achievement of the Nadva had been, he replied that the production of a scholar like Syed Suleman Nadvi alone justified the establishment of the Nadva. However, Syed Suleman Nadvi was not alone; a galaxy of scholars like Riyasat Ali Nadvi, Najeeb Ashraf Nadvi, Abdul Hye Nadvi, Muzzafaruddin Nadvi, and Abul Hasan Nadvi were among the ulema produced by the Nadva. They excelled in historiography, literary criticism and theology. Shibli's successor and official biographer, Maulana Syed Suleman Nadvi, was also a pupil of Maulana Ashraf Ali Thanvi, the renowned *alim* from Deoband. Due to his influence, the Nadva began to lean more towards Deoband than towards Aligarh. Shibli's impact on his first generation of disciples was limited, but he was able to influence considerably the second generation. This was no mean achievement.

ANJUMAN HIMAYAT-E-ISLAM

The Anjuman Himayat-e-Islam was founded against the backdrop of Christian missionary activity in the Punjab. It was not a policy of the British Raj to convert the natives to Christianity, but missionaries, mostly European, were engaged in converting the poorer section of society. Another challenge came from the Arya Samaj who had made it their mission to reconvert to Hinduism the descendants of those who had converted to Islam. The Anjuman represented a beleaguered minority when it was formed. The initiative to found a society to support Islam and prevent conversion was taken by Qazi Khalifa Hameed ud Din, scion of a noble family of Lahore. The Anjuman was founded on 24 September 1884. The other office bearers were Maulvi Ghulamullah Qasuri (honorary secretary) Munshi Chiragh Din and Munshi Pir Bakhsh (joint secretaries) and Munshi Abdur Rahim Khan (treasurer).

By the end of December 1885, there were 600 members. Their office was set up in the *Haveli* of Sikander Khan. The Anjuman raised its funds in a novel manner; every member would put a handful of wheat flour in an earthern vessel every day. The volunteers would collect this flour and go from door to door selling the flour for one-and-a-half rupees. In this way the Anjuman raised Rs 754 per month but spent only Rs 344.

There were four aims of the Anjuman as determined by the founders: to counter the propagation of Christain missionaries and Arya Samajists, to preserve Islamic values, to spread religious and modern education to the youth of the community, and to further social and cultural development. The last aim was taken very seriously. The Anjuman not only founded educational institutions for boys and girls but also for adults. It founded orphanages and shelters for women. It founded seven boys' schools, two girls' schools and also the famous Islamia College which became no less an 'arsenal' than Aligarh during the Pakistan Movement. Muslim politics in the Punjab took many turns, but it was the Anjuman Himayat-e-Islam which gave the Muslim cause its constant attention.

Only after the Anjuman had established its credentials by collecting funds from its own members, did the rulers of the princely states, like the nizam of Hyderabad, the amir of Bahawalpur, the nawabs of Bhopal and Rampur, start sending their contributions. King Habibullah of Afghanistan had the Habibiya Hall of Islamia College built. One feature of the Anjuman was to have its annual sessions presided over by literary luminaries such as Sir Syed Ahmad Khan, Maulana Shibli Nomani, and Maulana Zafar Ali Khan. However, the most distinguished personage was Allama Iqbal. Allama Iqbal had stopped reciting at the *Mushairas*, but recited his long poems from 1903 onwards. The first such poem was *Nala-e-Yateem* (The Lament of an Orphan). Copies of Allama Iqbal's poems were sold on the spot, thereby generating more funds.

Other dignitaries who served the Anjuman as presidents were Sir Muhammad Shafi, Nawab Sir Zulfiqar Ali Khan, Sir Abdul Qadir and Sir Fazl-i-Hussain. They ensured not only quality education for Muslims, but also performed social and political services when the political forces of Punjab such as the Unionist government, were hostile. It was the students of Islamia College who brought Jinnah safely to Minto Park in a procession for the historic Lahore session in the very tense atmosphere created by the Khaksars. It was in the grounds of Islamia College that Jinnah hoisted what was to become the national flag of Pakistan, and it was the students of Islamia College who canvassed for the votes which brought Punjab—the very province whose adherence was most vital to the creation of Pakistan—to the Muslim League. This was the institution that brought together the services of Allama Iqbal and Mohammad Ali Jinnah.

SINDH MADRESSATUL ISLAM, KARACHI

Sindh was the first province to demand separation on the basis of its Muslim majority, and the first province to call for separate Hindu and Muslim federations. Sindh's assembly was the first to demand partition, and Sindh's premier institution, the Sindh Madressatul Islam, was the *alma mater* of the founder of Pakistan. All these achievements were made possible by the founding of the Sindh Madressa.

Sindh Madressa owed its existence to the efforts and vision of a great benefactor, Hasan Ali Effendi (1830–1895). He conferred directly with Sir Syed when he went to Aligarh to admit his children. Sir Syed was impressed by this devoted man and advised him not to be content with founding a school but to aim at establishing a college and a university too. Hasan Ali Effendi also came into contact with Syed Amir Ali, and it was under the auspices of the National Muhammadan Association, that the Sindh Madressa was formed.

Hasan Ali Effendi opened the Sindh Madressa on 1 September 1885 and had it formally inaugurated by the viceroy, Lord Dufferin, on 14 November 1887. Not only did Sindh Madressa spread education and political awareness throughout Sindh, it also produced the most illustrious students including the Quaid-i-Azam Mohammad Ali Jinnah, Sir Shahnawaz Bhutto, Sir Ghulam Hussain Hidayatullah, Haji Sir Abdullah Haroon, Dr Umar Muhammad Daudpota, Dr I.I. Kazi and a host of other luminaries.

The Sindh Madressa body, also founded, one after the other, the S.M. Science College, S.M. Arts and Commerce College and S.M. Law College, institutions which had luminaries among their faculty and students. Sindh was known as *Babul Islam*, the gate of Islam in India, and this gate was opened for the emancipation and the glory of Pakistan by the students of Sindh Madressatul Islam, Karachi.

Islamia College, Peshawar

Like the Punjab, the NWFP also had an association called the Anjuman Himayat-e-Islam that founded an institution which grew to be Islamia College, Peshawar. Over time it became the University of Peshawar. In 1890, Babu Haider Thakedar and Mian Abdul Karim set up the Anjuman. An Englishman, George Roos-Keppel (d.1919) collaborated with Nawab Sahibzada Abdul Qayyum and according to Sir Olaf Caroe:

> Together they created the Islamia College, now grown into the University of Peshawar. That is their joint and visible monument, the tribute to their foresight and wisdom. No man who was not great, whose imagination did not soar, would have founded a great place of learning on the very margin of the cultivated land, overlooked by the black jaws of Khaibar, open maybe to raiders, on the very site of the furious battle between Akbar Khan and Hari Singh.[5]

This vision infused life into the intellectual and cultural body of the Pathans. In the 1940s, Islamia College had a very distinguished and effective principal, Sir Ian Dixon Scott, who later, as a member of the viceroy's staff, was to contribute to the uplift of this institution. It is a matter of significance that the founder of Pakistan chose Sindh Madressa, Karachi, Islamia College,

Peshawar, and Muslim University, Aligarh to bequeath his personal wealth in recognition of their contribution to the Pakistan Movement.

Notes

1. Peter Hardy, *The Muslims of British India,* Cambridge University Press, 1972, Reprint, New Delhi, 1998, p. 103.
2. Ibid., p. 171.
3. Usha Sanyal, 'Pir, Shaikh and Prophet' in T.N. Madan (ed.), *Muslim Communities of South Asia,* New Delhi: Manohar, 1995, p. 442.
4. Olaf Caroe, *The Pathans,* London: Macmillan, 1965, p. 424.

PART III

HISTORY OF THE POLITICAL STRUGGLE

Chapter 11

The Political Aspects of the Aligarh Movement

Political activity began at the turn of the twentieth century. When Urdu was curtailed, Muslims formed the Urdu Defence Association on 2 May 1900 at Aligarh. The next stage was the Partition of Bengal on 16 October 1905 at Calcutta (now Kolkata), which led to violent Hindu protests. As a reaction, the conservative section of Muslims formed the Simla Deputation on 1 October 1906, while the radical element established the All-India Muslim League on 30 December 1906 at Dhaka.

The Muslim community of India had developed its centre at Aligarh in the aftermath of the 1857 uprising. Only two years after the death of their leader, Sir Syed Ahmad Khan, the Muslims of the United Provinces received a cultural setback with the introduction of Hindi by the British in 1900. Since the use of Urdu had been actually banned in Bihar, the UP Muslims were alarmed. Although Sir Syed had warned Muslims against political activity against the British, the resurgence of the Hindi-Urdu conflict forced the Muslims to disregard his advice: after all, it was the 1867 Hindi-Urdu conflict which had originally led Sir Syed to formulate his Two-Nation theory. Muslims began to organize themselves politically and to protest against the official decision. Nawab Mohsinul Mulk, the new secretary of Aligarh College, organized the Urdu Defence Association on 2 May 1900.

Urdu had replaced Persian as the official language in 1837. Thirty years later the Hindi-Urdu conflict broke out. Four years later, on 7 November 1871 at Muzaffarpur, the Lt. Governor of Bihar, G. Campbell banned the use of Urdu in offices and schools. On 13 May 1872, the Muslims organized a public protest at Aligarh followed by a meeting on 18 August 1872 in Lucknow.

These activities invited the wrath of Sir Anthony McDonnell, the Lt. Governor of UP. He had moved the Hindi resolution and, feeling that he had been defied, forced Mohsinul Mulk to resign from the Urdu Defence Association. These measures politicalized the Muslims even more. In October 1901, a meeting of Muslim notables was called at the Lucknow residence of Hamid Ali Khan. It was here that the Mohammadan Political Association was formed.

THE PARTITION OF BENGAL

The earliest associations that the Muslims had formed were in Calcutta. On 31 January 1856, the Mohammadan Association, with Fazlur Rahman as president and Mohammad Mazhar as secretary was founded. The Mohammadan Literary Society was founded in 1863 by Nawab Abdul Latif. The first open political body was established in 1878 by Syed Amir Ali, called the National Mohammadan Association. It was in Bengal that the British had first established themselves, and built their own capital city, Calcutta, which led the rest of India in adopting western education, manners and fashions.

It should be noted that political activity as such was a British importation. The native rule for centuries had been autocratic; what passed for politics was intrigues and conspiracies. The democratic ideals of Europe came along with western education. Politics as a public activity began with the founding of the Indian National Congress with official encouragement by a British president, Allen Octavio Hume. But in 1905 Lord Curzon, the viceroy, was exasperated with the Congress.

Bengal was a large, thickly populated area and Calcutta had to administer not only British India but the Bengal presidency itself. Lord Curzon, for reasons of facilitating administration, divided Bengal into two parts, West and East. To East Bengal was added Assam. Although both parts of Bengal were to be under British rule, the creation of a new province in the east led to sharp Hindu protest.

Bengal was a Muslim majority area but the Muslims seemed not to be aware of this, because in West Bengal, where Calcutta was located, there was a concentration of Hindus. Muslim rule under the nawabs of Murshidabad practically ended in 1757 and in the 1857 upheaval the vestige of Muslim revivalist movements like those of Titu Mir and the Faraidi had been wiped out.

The reason why there was such a hue and cry was that West Bengal became predominantly Hindu and East Bengal predominantly Muslim. The Hindu reaction was visibly religious. The protest meeting on 16 October 1905, the day the partition took effect, was organized at the Kali temple. The protest was swiftly and efficiently arranged because the vested interests of the professional classes were in danger.

The professional classes in the main cities grew as the result of western education. These classes were led by lawyers. During the Hindi-Urdu controversy of 1900 it was noted that most of the leaders from both sides had been lawyers. Knowing the law of their masters they could plead for their clients in the courts and for their country in the assemblies. They had large incomes and an independent status, therefore they could afford to enter the political arena. Lawyers practised in the chief court in Calcutta which had its jurisdiction over all of Bengal, thus they had clients throughout Bengal.

Next came the doctors who were highly educated and, since they could cure a number of diseases that traditionally trained *hakims* or *veds* could not, they were highly regarded. Sometimes the doctor would be the only educated person in an entire village, therefore his opinion, even on political matters, carried weight. Third in line were the professors of Calcutta University. Though they were employed by the government and were not allowed to participate in political activities, they enjoyed an autonomous status and could influence students indirectly. When Sir Ashutosh Mukherji became vice-chancellor of Calcutta University, he prescribed Lord Byron's poem *The Childe Harold* in the syllabus. This poem filled the students with revolutionary fervour.

Following partition, the new Muslim majority province of East Bengal and Assam threatened the wealth and influence of the professional classes. The new province would have a new chief court, a new medical college hospital and a new university, all located in Dhaka. The Calcutta lawyers would lose half their briefs, and the Dhaka lawyers would gain them along with the money and influence. The doctors of Calcutta would lose half their patients who would, for reasons of convenience and economy, seek doctors and hospitals closer at hand. Doctors from the region would have greater opportunities for education and practice. The University of Dhaka would cater to students not able to obtain admission in Calcutta, and teaching posts would go to local people.

Because of the lead the Hindus had in all three professions, all the new posts and opportunities would initially go to them. But they saw all the implications and looked ahead. Dominance in Calcutta, in undivided Bengal, seemed to them the more secure policy. The people of Bengal were united by language but divided by religion. At that juncture religion became the over riding sentiment, and the Kali temple in Calcutta became the starting point of agitation against partition.

The Indian National Congress, thoroughly disliked by Curzon, was still under the control of the moderates led by Gopal Krishna Gokhale (1866–1915). But a radical group supporting the protest sprang up led by Bal Gangadhar Tilak (1856–1920), and Lala Lajpat Rai (1865–1928).

LEADERS OF THE AGITATION

1. Surinder Nath Bannerjee (1848–1925)
2. Jatindra Mohan Tagore (1831–1908)
3. Narendra Nath Sen (1843–1911)
4. Motilal Ghose (1847–1922)
5. Bipin Chandra Pal (1858–1932)

Very early in the term of the new province, its lieutenant governor, Sir Bampflyde Fuller (1854–1935), was forced to resign. He had been dealing with the agitation firmly and was widely considered pro-Muslim and was indeed looked up to by the Muslims whom the partition had benefited. Fuller had disaffiliated two schools in Serajgunj because their students had taken part in the agitation. This was disallowed by Lord Minto (1847–1914) the new viceroy, and Fuller resigned. The Muslims of Bengal mourned the removal of Fuller just as the Muslims of UP had rejoiced over the retirement of McDonnell. It seems that, rather than adopting a policy of 'Divide and Rule', British functionaries were themselves divided into pro-Hindu and pro-Muslim groups. Fuller's resignation was seen with foreboding by Bengal Muslims. They had been encouraged by policy statements of the British that the partition of Bengal was a settled issue. Sir Bampflyde Fuller's resignation showed that this resolve could weaken.

The resolve was broken because the agitation was marked by violence. This violence was uninhibited, it was directed against the highest dignitaries and not confined to India. Sir Curzon Wyllie, political secretary to John Morley, secretary of state, was killed in London on 1 July 1909. Two successive viceroys were attacked along with their wives, but survived. Lord and Lady Minto were attacked in Ahmadabad on 13 November 1909. After the partition was annulled, on 23 December 1912, Lord and Lady Hardinge were attacked in Delhi; Lord Hardinge survived but was severely injured.

In Bihar, a public prosecutor and a deputy superintendent of police were assassinated. A judge in Muzaffarpur escaped when he was attacked but a European lady and her daughter were killed. Trains and telegraph lines were a constant target of terrorism. Three attempts to derail trains were recorded and twelve attempts were made to bomb them.

As a result of these activities, two groups of Muslim politicians emerged. One, centred in Bengal, grateful for the creation of the Muslim province of East Bengal and Assam, was concerned to see that it was not undone. Another group, centred mostly in UP, realizing that the British, exasperated with the Hindus, might be sympathetic to their plight, decided to approach Viceroy Lord Minto at his summer residence at Simla.

THE SIMLA DEPUTATION

The Simla Deputation that called on Viceroy Lord Minto, on 1 October 1906, was led by Sir Aga Khan III. The Aga Khan was chosen with the confidence that the British would listen to him. As secretary of the Aligarh College, Mohsinul Mulk was the successor of Sir Syed and it was expected that the Muslim community would listen to him. Mohsinul Mulk had to incur a personal loan of Rs 2000 from Kings and Kings Company. The memorial was drafted by Nawab Imadul Mulk (1844–1926) and was signed by 1,461,183 Muslims. The deputation stressed that the Muslims were a large and distinct community in India and formed at least one-fifth of the total Indian population. They said their importance should not be measured only by their population, but by their cultural and historical role. They mentioned that Muslims had been the rulers of India barely a century before.

Their four demands were for separate electorates for Muslims, weightage, a larger share in government service, and the status of a university for Aligarh College.

In his reply, Lord Minto expressed profound sympathy for the Muslims especially their plea that their importance extended beyond their numbers. He mentioned that the partition of Bengal was a settled issue, although the deputation did not directly mention this. He did not mention any other demand, for example giving more government and judicial posts to Muslims or elevating the Aligarh College to the status of a university.

Contrary to the general impression, Lord Minto did not accept any of the demands of the delegates. He was sympathetic but did not commit himself to any step whatsoever.

THE DEMANDS OF THE SIMLA DEPUTATION

1. *Separate electorates.* This meant that Muslim voters would be registered separately from the Hindus and would vote only for Muslim candidates. The candidates could be independent or belong to any party.
2. *Weightage.* This meant that minorities would be given more representation than their population proportion. For example, the Muslims of UP were 13 per cent of the population; they would get 20 per cent representation.
3. *Government and Judicial Service.* This was the most sought after employment. It brought handsome salaries, power, and influence in society at large. People adopted western education mainly to qualify for such posts. Appointments as judges were even more prestigious. Judges were supposed to judge impartially between the government and the people. They enjoyed an autonomous status which even English officers had to respect.
4. *Aligarh* was the nerve centre of the Muslim political revival. As long as the college was subordinate to a university for examinations and award of degrees, it could not freely prescribe its own syllabus or award post-graduate degrees. The college acquired university status in 1920.

The demands for separate electorates was based on practical considerations. The Muslims of Bengal, who comprised more than 50 per cent of Indian Muslims, had a little over 10 per cent representation in provincial councils.[1]

The demand for separate electorates was not achieved at Simla, but was the means by which the demand for Pakistan was ultimately achieved. Two years later, on 27 November 1908, Lord Morley (1838–1923), the secretary of state for India, suggested a new system for Muslim representation: reservation, but not separate electorates. Lord Minto did not object to the new scheme and the Muslims began to display anxiety. The honorary secretary of the Muslim League, Syed Hasan Bilgrami, commented that under Morley's scheme, all the Muslim votes of a constituency would be insufficient to elect the candidate of their choice. The reservation of seats would only ensure that the Hindus could elect any Muslim they nominated. When Muslims raised a storm of protest, Morley said in effect that there could be separate electorates but no weightage. Still later, after Syed Hasan Bilgrami and Syed Amir Ali had applied pressure, Morley conceded separate electorates at all levels. Bilgrami had argued on 23 February 1909 in parliament, that separate electorates were already practised in some constituencies; the Muslims only wanted the law to be applied all over India. It was the deputation which met Morley on 23 February 1909 in London that made separate electorates a part of the constitution in 1909 [see Chapter 12].

THE CONSPIRACY THEORY

It is often alleged that the Simla Deputation was a British conspiracy to subvert the movement for Indian independence. The Simla Deputation was called by the viceroy following the announcement of the acceptance of separate electorates which divided the Hindus and Muslims, it was alleged.

Fuller's departure caused discomfiture to Muslims. Mohsinul Mulk wrote to A.J. Archbold, principal of Aligarh College to ask if Lord Minto would receive a delegation of Muslims. Archbold contacted the viceroy's secretary, Dunlop Smith, in Simla who, after using persuasion, replied to Mohsinul Mulk that a delegation would be welcome. Archbold's reply was quoted but Mohsinul Mulk's letter was suppressed to create an impression that the initiative came through Archbold. While insisting that a conspiracy existed, Peter Hardy wrote that, 'The members of the Simla Deputation knew in advance that they would not, to say the least, meet with a hostile reception from Lord Minto, and that this preknowledge powerfully influenced the requests they made and the manner in which they made them'.

Francis Robinson, on the other hand refutes this argument by observing that, 'Yet in October 1906 Minto promised and intended to promise nothing except sympathy'.[2] The correspondence between Morley and Minto also confirms that the initiative had not come from the British, nor did the Muslims gain anything from sending this deputation. It has assumed importance only because it was seen as a step leading to the foundation of the Muslim League.

NOTES

1. R.A. Zakaria, *Muslims of India 1885–1905*, London University Thesis, 1948, p. 155.
2. Francis Robinson, *Separatism Among Indian Muslims*, Delhi: Oxford University Press, 1994, p. 147.

Chapter 12

The Formation of the
All-India Muslim League, 1906

Background

Political parties are the gift of British rule in India. Britain has a constitutional monarchy which means that the actual conduct of government is not carried out by the monarch but by elected members of parliament. When the British decided to introduce into India their own system of education they were also introducing their concept of democracy. They did not introduce their political practices and concepts because they had conquered India by force of arms and naturally wished to rule autocratically. In Britain, on the other hand, there were statesmen who forced the East India Company to act responsibly and respect the human rights of the conquered people. This can be illustrated by a brief summary of the Acts in the constitutional history of India on page 83. These were not constitutions in the normal sense, because a constitution contains the terms according to which a people wish to live together. Since these were imposed by foreign rulers these Acts did not have this feature. A constitution is also a law which is the basis of all other laws.

When Sir Syed Ahmad Khan analysed the causes of the 'Indian Revolt' of 1857, he stressed that the uprising took place because there was no communication, no contacts, between the British and Indian races. The only way known to the British for removing this barrier between the ruler and the ruled was parliamentary democracy run by political parties. People who shared similar opinions about public matters, came together and formed political parties. These parties participated in elections and sought votes on the basis of their programmes. Whichever party secured a majority in parliament formed the government. It was up to the people to retain or reject the party in power during the next elections.

The Indian National Congress

It was with the object to have representative institutions that the British actively sponsored the formation of the Indian National Congress at Bombay (now Mumbai) in 1885. Its first president was an Englishman, Allen Octavio

Hume. Gokhale was later to admit that without British patronage, the Congress would not have been successful. The Bengal Councils Act which practically introduced the principle of self-government came seven years after the formation of the Congress, in 1892.

With British support and Indian participation, the Congress would have been the most natural means to attain self-government. This did come about, but not as fully as expected for two reasons.

DEMOCRACY SUITABLE TO INDIA

The first reason was that the British wished to transfer power gradually, not completely and not immediately. The second reason was that Sir Syed, who had himself advocated communication between the British and the Indians, challenged the representative character of the Congress, saying that it did not represent the Muslims. In 1887, Sir Syed publicly asked Muslims not to join the Congress. Since the Hindi-Urdu conflict of 1867, he had asserted that Hindus and Muslims, were different nations. The Congress would represent the majority community, the Hindus; and Muslim representation would be by default as the Muslims were outnumbered four to one and were unable to secure adequate representation.

When Sir Syed told the Muslims not to join the Congress, he also discouraged them from joining or forming any political party. He explained that it was in the nature of political parties to confront the government sooner or later. Some Muslims, knowing that the British were themselves patronizing the Congress, found this hard to believe. But it was true, and within twenty years of its founding, Lord Curzon had become totally alienated from the Congress, so much so that the very concept of a political party became distasteful to the British. This is how it came about that the Congress, which was founded by the British, was seen by them as being hostile, while the All-India Muslim League, which was formed against the wishes of the government, came to be seen as pro-British.

WHO FOUNDED THE MUSLIM LEAGUE?

It is generally assumed that the same leaders of the Simla Deputation also founded the All-India Muslim League (AIML). This is far from true. It was mentioned earlier that the conservative section of Muslims led the Simla Deputation, while the radical, that is the more revolutionary and extreme, section of Muslims formed the AIML. The interests of both sections, conservative, led by Aga Khan III and Nawab Mohsinul Mulk, and the radical section led by Nawabs Viqarul Mulk (1841–1917) and Saleemullah (1884–1915) were similar but not identical.

The Muslims of Bengal, led by Saleemullah, the nawab of Dacca (now Dhaka) were concerned mainly that the partition of Bengal should not be undone. Sir Bampflyde Fuller's removal had sounded a warning bell and Bengali Muslims were apprehensive that the British might yield to violence. The leaders of the Simla Deputation had made no direct mention of Bengal's partition. The Muslims from minority provinces were concerned mostly with separate electorates. The nawab of Dhaka was not present in Simla and Sir Aga Khan was not present in Dhaka. The Aga Khan was of the opinion that the issue of forming a political party should be left to a future generation of Muslims. The annual session of the All-India Muslim Education Conference was to be held at Dhaka in December. The secretary of the conference, Mohsinul Mulk, who was also the secretary of the Simla Deputation, wrote an article in the *Aligarh Institute Gazette* forbidding any political discussion at Dhaka. The delegates to the Muslim Educational Conference completely disregarded Mohsinul Mulk's article and founded the AIML at Dhaka on 30 December 1906. Nawab Viqarul Mulk presided. The British, who were averse to the creation of a new party, were given the excuse that if Muslim youth were not given a political party of their own, they would flock to the Congress. However, when the aims and objectives, rules and regulations of the party were being framed, the older generation gained the upper hand. *From Consultation to Confrontation* is the title Matiur Rahman gives to his book covering these events.[1]

In retrospect, the anxiety or anger of the British over the formation of a new political party seems to have been somewhat exaggerated; but it seemed very real then. The aims and objects of the AIML were therefore expressed in terms of abject loyalty. No doubt, some members felt the need to placate the British so that the partition of Bengal would last. For some, this may have been only a stratagem to overcome British disapproval by showing their loyalty. Both factions felt the need to show unity and the above stated objectives were adopted. Being pro-British was one criticism that the AIML faced, the other was that the party was an elite organization, not representative of the people. In 1906, this was quite true.

The main development following the foundation of the AIML was the passage of the Morley-Minto Reforms, or India Councils Act 1909. The demand for separate electorates was finally accepted in these Reforms. From the notes on the Simla Deputation, it is evident that Lord Minto had not actually accepted the Muslim demand, and that the honorary secretary of the Muslim League, Syed Hasan Bilgrami, had to struggle to have it accepted in London. In the end it took three years from the placing of the demand to its acceptance. In his presidential address to the first AIML session in Karachi in 1907, Sir Adamjee Peerbhoy (1845–1913) admitted that the viceroy had made no commitment. Lord Minto himself wired Morley on

2 May 1909 that: 'If interpreted literally that would involve separate Muslim electorates within the various electorates proposed.... This is manifestly impractical and has never been suggested.'

Seven months later Morley wrote to Minto saying that his reply to the Simla Deputation had first raised the hopes of the Muslims. Perhaps it was the intention of the Viceroy to convey this impression but to offer nothing concrete.

AIMS AND OBJECTIVES OF THE ALL-INDIA MUSLIM LEAGUE (AIML) 1906

a) To promote among Musalmans of India, the feeling of loyalty to the British Government and remove any misconceptions that may arise as to the intention of the Government with regard to any of its measures.
b) To protect and advance the political rights and interests of the Musalmans of India and to represent their needs and aspirations to the Government.
c) To prevent the rise among the Musalmans of India of any feeling of hostility towards other communities without prejudice to the other objects of the League.

PROFILE OF THE AIML

The membership of the All-India Muslim League was limited to 400 members. Members had to be over 25 years of age, as well as:
• literate in an Indian language,
• have an annual income of more than Rs 500,
• be able to pay Rs 25 as entry fees, and
• Rs 25 as an annual subscription.

REVISED AIMS AND OBJECTS OF THE AIML 1912

1. To maintain and promote among the people of India feelings of loyalty to the British Crown.
2. To protect and advance the political and other rights of the Muslims of India.
3. Without detriment to the pregoing objectives, to attain under the aegis of the British Crown, a system of self-government suitable to India through constitutional means.

NOTE

1. Matiur Rahman, *From Consultation to Confrontation*, London: Luzac, 1970.

 GOPAL KRISHNA GOKHALE (b. Kotluk, 9 May 1866–d. Poona, 19 February 1915). By caste, Mahatma Gokhale was a Chitpavan Brahmin. He opted for the teaching profession and joined the New English School, Poona, at a salary of Rs 35, in January 1885. The following year he was appointed lecturer at Ferguson College, Poona. He caught the attention of the eminent leader, Mahadev Govind Ranade, who put social reform ahead of political emancipation. Ranade appointed him the secretary of Saranjinik Sabha. Later in 1897, Ranade sent Gokhale to London to appear before the Lord Welby Commission on Indian Expenditure. Gokhale entered electoral politics in 1899, becoming a member of the Bombay Council, and in 1901, he was elected to the Imperial Legislative Council.

It was as a parliamentarian that Gokhale excelled. Lord Curzon, who had grown impatient of the Congress, was unflinching in his praise for its leader. Ten years after he had left India, within a month of Gokhale's death, Lord Curzon recalled that he had never met a man of any nationality more gifted with parliamentary capacities. 'Mr Gokhale would have obtained a position of distinction in any parliament in the world, (16 March 1915).

This was no ordinary praise: parliamentary practice was introduced to India by Britain, and excellence as a legislator meant that the white man was finding a native capable of self-government. Other leaders of India had received high praise, but no other received it universally.

The phrase 'ambassador for Hindu Muslim unity', for M.A. Jinnah, had been picked up by Mrs Sarojini Naidu, from Gopal Krishna Gokhale. However, Gokhale realized how daunting the task was. When Mrs Sarojini Naidu expressed her opinion that Hindu-Muslim unity would be achieved in five years; Gokhale replied, 'Child, you are a poet, but you hope too much. It will not come in your lifetime or mine. But keep your faith and work if you can.'[1]

Two English sympathizers of Congress, William Wedderben and Henry Cotton sent Gokhale to appear before parliamentary candidates, in London. The other delegates were Surinder Nath Bannerjee, Mohammad Ali Jinnah and Lala Lajpat Rai. This was the highest quality of leadership, to inspire a whole generation of leaders to work together. Another Congress delegation, of whom Jinnah was the spokesman, urged that one third of the members of the India Council be elected by Indian legislators. Gopal Krishna Gokhale had deliberated that, 'The India of the future could not now be only a Hindu India or a Muhammaden India; it must be compounded of all the elements which existed in India-Hindu, Muhammaden, Parsee, Christian, and aye, the Englishman who adopted India as his country.'[2]

For ensuring communal harmony, Gokhale put greater responsibilities on the Hindus:

'They had the advantage of numbers, education and wealth. It was their duty to understand the genuine fears of the Muslim minority, and to treat it with tact and forbearance.'[3] The advice Gokhale gave Muslims was also sound: 'You must remember that the British, who love patriotism and liberty, cannot but despise you. There may be small favours, but when a certain limit is reached, you too will not be allowed to go further.'[4]

He was honoured for his sincerity. In Lucknow, he was feted separately by Nawab Mohsinul Mulk, and the Maharaja of Mahmudabad. 'At Aligarh, the Muslim youth unhorsed his carriage and pulled it through the streets to the College Hall, amidst shouts of 'Gokhale Zindabad.'[5] Unfortunately, Gokhale died at 48, an early age for a statesman, while all the politicians of the succeeding generation reached their three score and ten. Even his distant hopes for unity vanished in the coming years.

NOTES

1. B.R. Nanda, *Gokhale, Gandhi and the Nehrus*, London: George Allen and Unwin, 1974, p. 17.
2. B.R. Nanda, *Gokhale*, Delhi: Oxford University Press, 1977, p. 442.
3. Ibid., p. 341.
4. Ibid.
5. Ibid., p. 339.

CHAPTER 13

THE LUCKNOW PACT, 1916

The period from the Delhi Durbar in 1911 to the Nehru Report of 1928 is seen as one of Hindu-Muslim cooperation. The Lucknow Pact, the Khilafat Movement, the Delhi Muslim Proposals and the Simon Commission all came about during this period.

DELHI DURBAR, 1911

The King of England was the emperor of India. For most of his Indian subjects however, he was a distant and awe inspiring figure. Only King George V visited India. He held court at Delhi. *Durbar* being the Indian word for Court, his presence was recalled as the Delhi Durbar.

King George V used this ceremonial occasion to make two announcements: that the partition of Bengal was annulled and that the capital would be shifted from Calcutta to Delhi. The British had repeatedly called the partition of Bengal a 'settled issue' but within six years it was undone. A common reaction was that the result of this reversal would be for Indians to think that agitation was the only way to change British decisions and that just their word was not reliable.

This was also the reaction of Indian Muslims. The partition of Bengal had so far been the only British decision which had benefited the Muslims. It was to uphold this decision that Dhaka was chosen as the venue for the formation of the All-India Muslim League (AIML). The announcement that the capital would be shifted to Delhi, the old Muslim capital, made no impression because it was considered to be an empty gesture.

Violence had forced the British to undo the partition of Bengal. This gave rise to a slogan, 'No bombs, no boons'. The shock led Muslims to a major policy reconsideration. Fortunately there were some Muslim Congress-men for whom the independence of India was the primary goal, and communal safeguards were secondary. These politicians had previously refused to join the Muslim League, because they thought it pro-British. Most prominent of these leaders were Sir Wazir Hasan (1874–1947), Maulana Mohammad Ali Jauhar (1878–1931), Maulana Abul Kalam Azad (1888–1958) and Mohammad Ali Jinnah (1876–1948). These leaders helped Wazir Hasan, the honorary secretary of the Muslim League to change the party's creed, transforming it from a loyalist to a revolutionary party.

These were far-reaching changes. Allegiance to the British Crown instead of the British *government* implied a vast constitutional difference. Allegiance to the British Crown meant that Indians would be self-governing like other dominions of the British Commonwealth such as Canada and Australia. The provision for self-government 'suitable to India' meant that a joint freedom struggle would still be based on separate electorates. Thus some difficulties remained in the way of Hindu–Muslim cooperation since not only Hindus but some prominent Muslim leaders including Mohammad Ali Jinnah and Liaquat Ali Khan had spoken against separate electorates. These leaders were able to create goodwill which enabled Hindu–Muslim cooperation to last from the Delhi Durbar in 1911 to the Nehru Report in 1928.

LUCKNOW PACT, 1916

The era of Hindu–Muslim harmony overlapped with the duration of the First World War (1914–1918). This cooperation was formalized by a pact midway through the war which was to be the high point of Hindu–Muslim rapprochement. The leaders who effected it were Mohammad Ali Jinnah and Wazir Hasan on one side and Ambica Charan Mazumdar (1851–1922) and Bal Gangadhar Tilak (1856–1920) on the other. The pact which was signed in Lucknow on 30 December 1916, provided for a joint struggle against British rule and attainment of representative government in India. The Congress, in view of the changed creed of the Muslim League, agreed to both separate electorates and weightage.

For the Congress it was an achievement that the Muslim League would be a partner and not a rival in the freedom struggle. For the Muslim League, Congress support for separate electorates and weightage was of equal importance. It is true that the British had finally accepted these demands under the Morley-Minto Reforms, but Congress support was more reassuring. The partition of Bengal and its annulment had shown that whatever the British gave, they could take back under Hindu pressure.

Within the Muslim community however, the Lucknow Pact did not enjoy equal popularity. In the Muslim majority provinces of the Punjab and Bengal it caused resentment.

There was a general agreement over separate electorates. We have seen how, despite being in a majority in Bengal, Muslims were not a majority in the council. Weightage was also producing the same result. In the minority provinces of UP for example, Muslims constituted 14 per cent of the population, but were given 30 per cent representation. In Madras, Muslims made up less than 7 per cent of the population but were given 15 per cent representation. This enhancement did not bring any concrete benefits as the Muslims were a minority, and they remained a minority. In return the Bengali Muslims surrendered 25 per cent, and in Punjab 10 per cent of their entitlement. This reduced the Muslim majority to a minority and proved detrimental to the Muslims.

Weightage was tied to separate electorates, and separate electorates was desired by all Muslims. This disadvantage was not immediately apparent as the Congress agreed to extend this principle to the Punjab and Central Provinces where it had not been imposed by the British.

On the larger Indian stage, the Lucknow Pact actually marked a culmination and not a new beginning. By signing the Lucknow Pact, Jinnah was playing the role of 'Ambassador of Hindu-Muslim Unity'. This phrase was first coined for Jinnah by Gopal Krishna Gokhale and given currency by Sarojini Naidu (1878–1949). Jinnah could play this role because, at that time, he enjoyed equal eminence in both the Congress and the Muslim League.

However, this phase did not last because a year earlier, in 1915, Gopal Krishna Gokhale had died and Mohandas Karamchand Gandhi (1869–1948) had returned to India. Gandhi was present in Lucknow when the Lucknow Pact was signed, but had 'no high opinion of it'. The pact had the approval of Congress, but since it lacked endorsement by Gandhi, this instrument of Hindu-Muslim cooperation did not last long.

CHAPTER 14

THE KHILAFAT MOVEMENT, 1918–1924

The Muslims of India had an emotional attachment to the Khilafat (Caliphate). Powerful sultans were proud to receive investitures from the caliphs of Cairo who were little more than prisoners of the Egyptian sultan. In the twentieth century, this attachment took on a different aspect: the Muslims of India, deprived of power themselves, looked up to the Ottoman caliphate as the only surviving symbol of Muslim glory.

For most of British rule in India, Britain and Turkey were allies. This partly helped to reconcile Muslims to British rule. During the First World War, there was a complete reversal of alliances; Turkey became an ally of Germany against Britain and when Germany lost the war, it was proposed that the Ottoman caliphate be deprived of all its territories. This caused an uproar among the Indian Muslims, and when the Treaty of Sèvres was imposed, the protest became organized.

THE ROLES OF GANDHI AND JINNAH

The events in the Middle East caused some dramatic and permanent changes in Indian politics. Towards the end of the war, the British had badly needed Indian cooperation. Tilak and Jinnah withheld cooperation until the British allowed Indian soldiers to be commissioned into the army. Stanley Wolpert states that Gandhi frustrated them by offering the viceroy, Lord Chelmsford unconditional support. When the war ended, Gandhi joined the Muslim agitation over the Khilafat.

Jinnah, on the other hand, discouraged discussion of the Khilafat issue in the AIML Council but was overruled. Jinnah wrote to Gandhi, warning him against raising the religious sentiments of the masses, but Gandhi would not agree even though the religious sentiments would be those of Muslims and not Hindus. Above all, Jinnah wanted both the Congress and the Muslim League to concentrate on Indian issues. This caused him and the Muslim League to be sidelined exactly at the time when Hindu-Muslim unity was touching new heights.

The leaders of the Khilafat Movement, as a gesture of goodwill, agreed not to slaughter cows because cows are sacred to the Hindus. For the first time a large number of leaders, mostly from the ulema class, came forward to join the Khilafat Movement.

THE EVENTS

The Khilafat Committee was formed on 20 March 1919 in Bombay. As a follow-up, the All-India Khilafat Conference was founded on 23 November 1919, in Delhi, with 300 members. The following day, Gandhi was elected leader of the joint Hindu-Muslim Committee. On the same day, Hasrat Mohani moved a resolution calling for a progressive boycott of European goods. The resolution was passed by a majority, but was opposed by Gandhi personally.

Later, however, Gandhi supported the same resolution and started a Non-Cooperation Movement. First in Calcutta and then in the Nagpur Congress session of 1920, a seven-point resolution was passed. When Jinnah opposed the resolution he was shouted down, and as a consequence he resigned from the Congress.

NON-COOPERATION

In principle, Jinnah supported some form of non-cooperation but was against extreme and impractical measures. He agreed with the provisions which called for surrendering titles given by the British, refusal to attend official *durbars* or to serve in Mesopotamia (Iraq). What he opposed was the boycott of schools, colleges, and law courts and the boycott of foreign goods. Jinnah said these measures would only harm Indians as they had no replacements for these goods and services.

The high point of the movement was the trial of the Ali Brothers at Khaliqdeena Hall in Karachi. After their arrest, and in front of thousands of their compatriots, their mother Bi Amman made her appearance, rallying women folk to join the movement.

THE END OF THE MOVEMENT

This movement, because of its fervour, had a fair chance of success since the British had been weakened by the First World War, but the following external factors brought it to an end:

1. **The Moplah's Uprising of August 1921:** Taking national liberation to mean social liberation, the Muslim Moplahs of Malabar set upon their Hindu landlords, killing and looting them. This damaged both Hindu-Muslim relations and Gandhi's creed of non-violence. However, leaders from both sides controlled the extent of the damage.

2. **The Chauri Chaura Incident of 5 February 1923:** Police fired on unarmed protesters in the village of Chauri Chaura. In retaliation twenty-two policemen were rounded up and burnt to death. Terming this act as an end to non-violence, Gandhi called off his Non-Cooperation Movement leaving the Khilafat cause in the lurch.
3. **The Abolition of the Caliphate—October 1924:** The grand national assembly of Turkey itself abolished the office of caliph or khalifa. One leader of the Khilafat Movement, Maulana Abul Kalam Azad, agreed with the Turkish decision and advised Indian Muslims to leave Turkey to its own fate and to concentrate on matters closer to home. Thus, what Jinnah said at the beginning of the Khilafat Movement, Azad conceded at its end.

RESULTS OF THE MOVEMENT

Among the negative results of the movement the greatest disaster was the Hijrat Movement when Maulana Jauhar asked Muslims to migrate to Afghanistan in February 1921, but Afghanistan closed its borders. Many Muslims who had sold their property cheaply were ruined while many others died.

Secondly, Dr Saifuddin Kitchlew and some other Khilafat leaders spoke out against the Lucknow Pact, saying that it was unnecessary since Hindu-Muslim amity would last forever. In this, they were joined by Hindu leaders. Thus separate electorates, the only political victory gained by the Muslims, became controversial.

Finally, the All-India Muslim League was weakened.

However, all the above negative aspects were counterbalanced by the experience gained in mass agitation: organising processions, conducting strikes and going to jail. Had such a cadre not been available to the Muslim League in the years following 1940, the struggle for Pakistan would have been impossible.

THE LEADERS OF THE KHILAFAT MOVEMENT

1. Haji Jan Mohammad Chotani (1873–1932)
2. Maulana Abdul Bari (1878–1926)
3. Maulana Shaukat Ali (1873–1938)
4. Maulana Mohammad Ali Jauhar (1878–1931)
5. Maulana Abul Kalam Azad (1888–1958)
6. Dr Saifuddin Kitchlew (1888–1963)
7. Maulana Hasrat Mohani (1881–1951)

CHITTARANJAN DAS (b. Calcutta, 5 November 1870–d. Darjeeling, 16 June 1925), fondly called '*Deshbandhu*' (friend of the nation) by his followers, was a poet and lawyer, before he was a politician. He graduated from Presidency College, Calcutta, in 1890, and was called to the Bar from the Inner Temple, in 1892. The books he authored were *Malancha, Mala, Kishor Kishori* and *Antaryyami*. Being a contemporary of Rabindranath Tagore and Sarat Chandra Chatterji, he needed to have extraordinary literary merit merely to gain recognition. His reputation as a lawyer was made in 1908, when he conducted the defence of Sri Aurobindo Ghosh, then editor of *Bande Mataram* (however, as a lawyer he was outstripped by his brother, P.R. Das).

C.R. Das came into contact with M.K. Gandhi, in 1919, during the Khilafat/ Non-cooperation Movement. For his part, he was arrested by the British—not alone, but along with his wife, sister and son. He called a successful meeting at the Calcutta Town Hall, to protest against the Rowlatt Act. He strongly denounced the Montagu-Chelmsford Reforms: 'Wholly inadequate, unsatisfactory, disappointing.'[1] During the Non-cooperation Movement, he initially opposed Mahatma Gandhi's resolution, but ultimately, at the 1920 Nagpur session of the Indian National Congress, he supported it.

Two years later, however, in 1922, along with Pandit Motilal Nehru, he founded the Swaraj Party. They favoured council entry—a move that Mahatma Gandhi opposed. It was because of this association that Jawaharlal Nehru could observe C.R. Das closely.

'Mr Das, in spite of being a lawyer, was a poet and had a poet's emotional outlook. He is reputed to have written fine poetry in Bengali. He was an orator, and he had a religious temperament.'[2]

It was precisely this religious temperament which endeared C.R. Das to the Muslims. Magnanimity and sacrifice were the two guiding principles of his faith. He did not profess to be secular. He clearly said: 'I am not a Brahmo. I am a Hindu, and I claim to be a sincere Hindu...My point of view is the Hindu point of view.'[3]

C.R. Das said that Hindu-Muslim unity was vital for Swaraj.[4] This was commonplace. What was lofty in his perception was his credo: 'Life is certainly greater than dogma and logic, and I want you to be men—whole men—who will obey none but the will of God.'[5]

C.R. Das became the first mayor of Calcutta, and gave effect to the Bengal Pact.

This gave Muslims representation in the Bengal council on the basis of their population, with separate electorates, even in places where they formed the majority. They would have 60 per cent in local bodies; 55 per cent of government posts. There was to be no interference with cow killing for sacrificial purpose. No law relating to cow killing for food was to be taken up. Cow killing was to be carried out in a manner as not to wound the feelings of Hindus![6] C.R. Das had stood the Faraidi Movement on its heads. To his opponents, C.R. Das replied: 'You can delete the Bengal Pact from the resolution, but you cannot delete Bengal from the Indian National Congress'.[7] The pact resulted in C.R. Das winning the November 1923 Council elections.

Concessions only whet the appetite, but generosity overwhelms. The reverence which C.R. Das received from H.S. Suhrawardy, Maulana Abul Kalam Azad and even Chaudhry Mohammad Ali shows that C.R. Das had touched their hearts with his nature, and not just his proposals.

NOTES

1. S.R. Bakshi, *C.R. Das Congress and Swaraj*, New Delhi: Anmol Publications, 199, p. 3.
2. Jawaharlal Nehru, *An Autobiography*, Delhi, 1962, pp. 10, 105 ff.
3. S.R. Bakshi, op. cit., p. 20.
4. Ibid., p. 15.
5. Ibid.
6. Ibid., p. 13.
7. Ibid., p. 14.

CHAPTER 15

FROM DELHI MUSLIM PROPOSALS TO QUAID-I-AZAM'S FOURTEEN POINTS, 1927–1929

DELHI MUSLIM PROPOSALS, 1927

The Lucknow Pact had contained the first constitutional proposals put forward jointly by Hindus and Muslims. Since it was based on separate electorates, which had become controversial during the Khilafat Movement, a new constitutional formula was required to replace it. The Muslim League had lost its appeal by this time and the Congress had not fared much better. Srinavasa Iyengar, the Congress president found that his party had become ineffectual in the Indian legislative assembly. He approached Jinnah in the hope that cooperation between the two parties might speed up the process of liberation. Jinnah responded by convening a meeting of thirty Muslim notables on 20 March 1927 in Delhi. Briefly stated, the following proposals were formulated:

1. Sindh should be separated from Bombay and form a new province.
2. Reforms should be introduced in NWFP and Balochistan, making them full provinces.
3. Weightage for Hindu minorities in Muslim provinces should be equal to weightage given to Muslim minorities in Hindu provinces.
4. In the central legislature there should be a one-third representation of Muslims.

In return for these provisions Muslims would agree to joint electorates. A two-thirds majority being traditionally required for any constitutional amendment, a one-third majority at the centre was sufficient for safeguarding arrangements within the provinces.

These proposals presuppose a federal form of government in which the maximum number of subjects (e.g. finance, education etc.) would be vested in the provinces. In a unitary form of government, the centre would have overriding control of the provinces. Muslims wanted power concentrated in the provinces where they would have access to it rather than at the centre where they had no access. Hindus would have no serious objections because traditionally the key federal areas such as defence, foreign affairs and communications would, for the time being, be controlled by the British. Six Muslim provinces, out of a total of thirteen, while Muslims constituted one-fifth of the population, would be a very favourable arrangement.

Replacing separate electorates with joint electorates meant that the distribution of power between Hindus and Muslims would be aggregate and not watertight. It would provide a healthy atmosphere for the economic and cultural progress of Muslims. There was a feeling of relief when the Congress, in its 15 May Bombay session, accepted the Delhi Muslim Proposals. The Congress ratified its acceptance of the proposals in its 30 December 1927 Madras meeting. Apparently India was now securely set on the path to freedom. Only the absence of Gandhi from the Madras Congress provides a hint of what the future held.

Two factors impeded the culmination of this process of reconciliation. First was the opposition of the Mahasabha, the fundamentalist Hindu party. The Hindu Mahasabha had accepted only the renunciation of separate electorates and rejected all the other clauses of the proposals (23 March). However, those members of the Hindu Mahasabha who were also members of the Congress did not raise any objection in the Congress sessions.

The Congress was aware of this opposition, but guided by Iyengar and Motilal Nehru, it stayed firm. At one stage they even offered a concession not contained in the original proposals: 'No bill or resolution on any communal matter would be passed or even considered if three-fourths of the concerned community were opposed to it.'

The Hindu Mahasabha carried out insidious propaganda against Motilal Nehru saying that he was a beef-eater. In the end, he had to yield to this propaganda.

The second factor was British opposition; the Simon Commission was appointed to supplant the new Congress–Muslim League proposals.

THE SIMON COMMISSION, 1927

A new constitution to replace the Montagu–Chelmsford Reforms had been demanded by political parties and discussed within official circles well before the Delhi Muslim Proposals were formulated, yet the timing of the announcement on 8 November 1927, that an Indian Statutory Commission had been set up, was disruptive.

Statute means law passed by a legislature, and a statutory commission means a body set up by a statute. An Indian Statutory Commission was formed to review the prevailing Government of India Act 1919. It was due in 1929 but was advanced by two years. This commission was called the Simon Commission after its chairman, Sir John Simon (1873–1954).

Since no Indian was included in the commission, the majority of Indian leaders and parties boycotted its proceedings. An All-India Leaders Manifesto issued on 16 November 1927 plainly stated this position. Among the signatories of this manifesto were Jinnah and Sir Tej Bahadur Sapru (1875–1949).

The Madras Congress of December 1927 took three interconnected decisions: (i) to ratify the Delhi Muslim Proposals (ii) to boycott the Simon Commission, and (iii) to set up an All-Parties Committee under Pandit Motilal Nehru to draft a constitution for India. All three steps were positive in nature and had they been acted upon in unison and harmony they would have led to a free and united India.

The All-India Muslim League, in contrast, was a house divided. Its president, Sir Mohammad Shafi (1869–1932) was in favour of cooperating with the Simon Commission, while its honorary secretary, Dr Saifuddin Kitchlew, was firmly in favour of boycott. This caused a rift in the Muslim League on 11 December 1927. Sir Mohammad Shafi had with him as honorary secretary and associate secretary Allama Sir Mohammad Iqbal and Maulana Hasrat Mohani, both revolutionary poets, the latter of the fire-brand variety. This was a notable alliance since Hasrat looked down upon even dominion status and insisted on full independence. He was expected to side with Kitchlew, but sided with Shafi instead.

Kitchlew, the original honorary secretary, had with him as president first Sir Mohammad Yaqub (1879–1942) and then M.A. Jinnah. Sir Mohammad Shafi presided over the session of the Muslim League in Lahore from 30 December 1927 to 1 January 1928. Sir Mohammad Yaqub presided over his faction's session at Calcutta from 31 December 1927 to 1 January 1928.

The Simon Commission visited India twice; (i) from February to March 1928 and (ii) October 1928 to April 1929. The members included Clement Atlee, the future prime minister of Britain who saw for himself the intensity of the boycott when he landed in Bombay on 3 February 1928. Leaders from the Muslim aristocracy such as the maharaja of Mahmudabad (1879–1931) and Sir Abdur Rahim (1867–1947) had become banner-carrying protesters shouting 'Simon Go Back'.

Why did the Muslim aristocracy of the Punjab side with the Simon Commission and go against the political mood of the country? To please their British masters? The answer is not that simple. The group, represented by Shafi, had advised the viceroy, Lord Irwin, that the time was opportune to appoint a statutory commission and it was at this group's repeated insistence that the Simon Commission was kept all white.

The Shafi Group, as David Page has established, was supporting its own scheme, not its masters'. This faction influenced the viceroy through Sir Malcolm Hailey (1872–1969), governor of the Punjab. They took the stance that the induction of Indians in the commission would encourage Indian representation in the central government in New Delhi while the Punjab Muslim aristocracy, having its leverage in the provincial power structure, was not willing to weaken it by having to defer to Indians at the centre instead of to the British. How they chose to clothe their objectives was to tell the viceroy that provincial administrations were closer to the Indian people than the central administration which the viceroy governed.

Lord Birkenhead, the secretary of state who had infuriated Jinnah by stating on 24 November 1927 that the induction of Indians would create divisions, did not himself believe in this argument. Unknown to the public, Lord Birkenhead had tried to convince Lord Irwin of the folly of excluding Indians from the commission, first as far back as August 1926 and then again in March 1927.

Jinnah, unaware of Birkenhead's actual opinion took his rebuff personally and undertook to produce an agreed constitution for the Indians, by the Indians. Jinnah was confident that since a basic constitutional agreement already existed under the Delhi Muslim Proposals, all that the Congress and Muslim League would have to do was to supply the details, to answer Birkenhead's challenge. For Jinnah, national pride came before personal prestige. He forgot his humiliation at the 1920 Nagpur Congress and preferred a split in the Muslim League to leaving the Congress in the lurch. During the time Jinnah led the agitation, Gandhi adopted a low profile.

When the recommendations of the Simon Commission were published, they were strongly biased towards empowering the provinces. The provinces would decide what form the federation would take at the centre. Against this background, the Simon Commission recommended that provincial boundaries be redrawn. Various objections were raised against the separation of Sindh and reforms in the NWFP and Balochistan.

The unkindest cut was the recommendation that at the centre, separate electorates be replaced progressively with proportional representation. In the Punjab, separate electorates which would ensure a Muslim majority were rejected. This naturally caused a chorus of protests led by Allama Iqbal. The Simon Commission's recommendations were never implemented and, therefore, it never served its constitutional purpose, but it served the political purpose of derailing the Hindu–Muslim joint struggle.

THE NEHRU REPORT, 1928

The Nehru Report was the first attempt by the Indians to frame a constitution for themselves. Previously they were limited to trying to influence or modify British imposed constitutions. In view of the challenge given by Lord Birkenhead, the 1927 Madras Congress appointed a committee under Pandit

Motilal Nehru to frame a constitution. In the same session, his son Pandit Jawaharlal Nehru had moved a resolution calling not for a dominion status but for complete independence. Gandhi considered this an extreme and impractical demand. It seems from the direction the Nehru Committee took, that the younger Nehru was forcing the hand of both his mentor Gandhi and his father Motilal. According to David Page:

> The determination of the author to face the problem and solve it, his condemnation of communal organizations for not wanting to change the existing structure of society, and his faith that in a free India political parties would be formed on an economic basis, all smack strongly of Jawaharlal and not his father.[1]

This midway change in policy reflects a change in personalities. Motilal was harassed by Hindu Mahasabha propaganda, not Jawaharlal. He caused the committee to resile from the Delhi Muslim Proposals not due so much to communal considerations as to a liberal outlook which considered communal safeguards out of date.

RECOMMENDATIONS OF THE NEHRU REPORT

According to the recommendations of the Nehru Report the new central governments were to control all departments without reserving any for the British. A governor-general and a prime minister would be appointed by the king. A six member cabinet would be appointed by the governor-general but recommended by the prime minister. This system would be repeated in the provinces with governors and chief ministers.

The new features were that (i) the cabinets would be responsible not to their appointing authorities but to their respective assemblies which (ii) would be elected by direct adult franchise.

The distribution of responsibilities between the centre and provinces suggested that the form of government would not be federal. This meant undercutting the very basis of the Delhi Muslim Proposals. As for the creation of new provinces, only conditional support was given to the separation of Sindh. Balochistan would have the same status as the NWFP, which would remain the same, lower than that of a full province, without governor or legislature.

CONSIDERATION OF THE NEHRU REPORT

When the All-Parties Committee met at Lucknow on 28 August 1928, it was apparent that of all the safeguards for minorities that had earlier been agreed upon, not a trace remained. Jinnah suffered a blow when his close friend, the maharaja of Mahmudabad, and his closest disciple, M.C. Chagla, signed the

Nehru Report. Abul Kalam Azad tried unsuccessfully in Calcutta to obtain a majority in favour of the Nehru Report from within the Muslim League.

At a larger All-Parties Conference, called on 22 December 1928, it was principally Jinnah who prevented the Muslim League from accepting the Nehru Report. As a politician, Jinnah was an idealist, but as a lawyer he was prudent. He was in favour of written guarantees not vague expressions of goodwill. Thus the era of Hindu-Muslim détente was over.

THE FOURTEEN POINTS, 1929

The efforts at Hindu-Muslim reconciliation which began with the Delhi Durbar in 1911 ended with the publication of the Nehru Report in 1928. The All-India Muslim League, which had split over cooperation with the Simon Commission, was reunited. The original body led by Sir Mohammad Shafi was for cooperation and against giving up separate electorates. The group led by Jinnah had been against cooperation with the Simon Commission and in favour of joint electorates with some guarantees in exchange. Jinnah tried to move a three point amendment to the Nehru Report. The points were:

(i)   One-third representation of Muslims in the central assembly,
(ii) Muslim majority in Bengal and the Punjab be maintained on the actual population ratio for ten years, and,
(iii) The provinces should have residuary powers, which meant a federal and not a unitary scheme.

All three amendments were turned down by the All-Parties Conference even though they demanded considerably less than the Delhi Muslim Proposals. The reunited Muslim League, under Jinnah's leadership issued the Fourteen Points as the basis of any future constitution for India. The Delhi Muslim Proposals had been an alternative to separate electorates. The Fourteen Points emerged as the Delhi Muslim Proposals in addition to separate electorates. They were:

1. The form of the future constitution should be federal, with the residuary powers vested in the provinces.
2. A uniform measure of autonomy shall be granted to all provinces.
3. All legislatures in the country and other elected bodies shall be constituted on the definite principle of adequate and effective representation of minorities in every province without reducing the majority in any province to a minority or even equality.
4. In the central legislature, Mussalman representation shall not be less than one-third.

5. Representation of communal groups shall continue to be by means of separate electorates as at present, provided it shall be open to any community at any time to abandon its separate electorate in favour of joint electorate.
6. Any territorial re-distribution that might at any time be necessary shall not in any way affect the Muslim majority in the Punjab, Bengal and the NWF Province.
7. Full religious liberty, i.e. liberty of belief, worship and observance, propaganda, association and education, shall be guaranteed to all communities.
8. No bill or resolution or any part thereof shall be passed in any legislature or any other elected body if three-fourths of the members of any community in that particular body oppose such a bill, resolution or part thereof on the ground that it would be injurious to the interests of that community or in the alternative, such other method is devised as may be found feasible and practicable to deal with such cases.
9. Sindh should be separated from the Bombay presidency.
10. Reforms should be introduced in the NWF Province and Balochistan on the same footing as in other provinces.
11. Provision should be made in the constitution, giving Muslims an adequate share along with the other Indians in all the services of the state and in local self-governing bodies.
12. The constitution should embody adequate safeguards for the protection of Muslim culture and for the protection and promotion of Muslim education, language, religion, personal laws and Muslim charitable institutions and for their due share in the grants-in-aid given by the state and by local self-governing bodies.
13. No cabinet, either central or provincial, should be formed without there being a provision of at least one-third Muslim ministers.
14. No change shall be made in the constitution by the central legislature except with the concurrence of the states constituting the Indian federation.

These demands formed the basis of negotiation by Muslims in the Round Table Conferences, but they were overshadowed by the demand of Allama Sir Mohammad Iqbal.

NOTE

1. David Page, *Prelude to Partition*, Karachi: Oxford University Press, 1987, p. 172.

MOHANDAS KARAMCHAND GANDHI (b. Porbandar, 2 October 1869–d. New Delhi, 30 January 1948) lived for the emancipation of India and died for the survival of Pakistan. Described by two eminent historians[1] as the greatest Indian after Gautama Buddha, Mahatma Gandhi was—by any criterion—a most remarkable man. To the West, with its notion of India as a land of maharajas, tigers and the rope trick, this 'half naked *faquir*' acquired a mystical aspect—a Hollywood film bringing this image to a climax. Unfortunately, the vacillations of this great man brought about results contrary to his aims. Gandhi's role in the Khilafat Movement led Gail Minault to describe him as: 'This "simple" man who was the most complex character imaginable, and treated them as their own, though he had had an advantaged youth, a foreign education and a career away from India.'[2]

Gandhi's mindset was medieval, his schemes were visionary, and his strategies whimsical, yet there had to be a wellspring from where the intense and widespread influence he exercised, proceeded. Whatever his personal limitations, his political stature was gigantic. Stanley Wolpert has closed in on the main feature of Gandhi's genius; his greatest and elemental contribution to the awakening of India: 'He equated cotton spinning with his own quest to see God face to face.'[3] This alone among all other items of his protest and boycott was neither impractical nor medieval; its economic and social potential being immense.

That said, we have to inquire whether his vision and his approach were a reliable basis for communities seeking emancipation. Gandhi's interaction with the Depressed/Dalit castes provides a precedent. As early as 1915, Gandhi had lodged three low caste inmates in his *ashram*, being undeterred by the threats of the upper castes. But when, on 17 August 1932, Ramsay Macdonald announced separate electorates for the depressed castes, Gandhi was outraged. A mystified British premier wrote to Gandhi that since the Communal Award had doubled low caste votes, he had expected Gandhi to approve, rather than to undertake a fast. Gandhi's reply was that the depressed castes must be emancipated by their oppressors—and not by the British. Instead of separate electorates, Gandhi offered double reservation of untouchable seats. This resulted in the untouchables losing each and every seat in the next elections. Gandhi was verbally contrite but offered no practical remedy; leaving them ultimately to face caste wars and riots.

This, in essence, was Gandhi's approach to the Muslim problem, and this is what the Muslims rejected, much to the chagrin of those who would judge India in the light of her professions, not her actions. However, in contrast to his conduct towards the depressed castes, Gandhi tried to make amends to the Muslims. His last interaction with Jinnah was that of concurrence; they both desired a united Bengal, independent of India and Pakistan. In this, Gandhi was frustrated by Jawaharlal Nehru. When Nehru withheld Pakistan's share of her financial assets, Gandhi undertook a fast until death to make India release the funds. This in turn led a Hindu fanatic Nathuram Godse to assassinate him. Only ten days earlier,

Gandhi had refused police protection, saying that if he had to die by an assassin's hand, he must do so without anger or fear.[4]

For three days all the programmes of Radio Pakistan were dedicated to his memory. These bulletins consisted of the descriptions of the tragic events, statements by Jinnah and Liaquat, and provincial heads. The next day's transmission opened with Gandhi's favourite *bhajan*, 'Raghupati Raghav Raja Ram' followed by other *bhajans*. The third day's transmission covered condolence meetings in Lahore.[5] Pandit Nehru was moved enough to say that the best programmes on the Mahatma, were done by Radio Pakistan.[6]

NOTES

1. Stanley Wolpert, *Gandhi's Passion: The Life and Legacy of Mahatma Gandhi*, New York: Oxford University Press, 2001, p. 263; Michael Brecher, *Nehru: A Political Biography*, London: Oxford University Press, 1959, New Delhi, Reprint, 2004, p. 387.
2. Gail Minault, *The Khilafat Movement*, New Delhi: Oxford University Press, 1999, p. 124.
3. Stanley Wolpert, op. cit., p. 124.
4. Michael Brecher, op. cit., p. 384.
5. *Dawn*, Karachi, 12 February 1948.
6. Sabeeh Mohsin, *Dastan Kahte Kahte*, Karachi: Maktabai-i-Jamal, 2006, p. 49.

CHAPTER 16

ALLAMA IQBAL'S ALLAHABAD ADDRESS, 1930: IQBAL AND THE IDEOLOGY OF PAKISTAN

The most often quoted passage from Iqbal's presidential address to the 1930 Allahabad session of the All-India Muslim League is:

> I would like to see the Punjab, North-West Frontier Province, Sindh and Balochistan amalgamated into a single State. Self-government within the British Empire, or without the British Empire, the formation of a consolidated North-West Indian Muslim State appears to me the final destiny of Muslims, at least of North India.

This is substantially as Pakistan emerged and how it presently exists. These words of Allama Iqbal promoted for the first time, from the platform of the All-India Muslim League, the idea of a separate Muslim state in India.

Two aspects need attention. Firstly, this address is not the sum total of Iqbal's contribution to the Pakistan Movement. Secondly, in this Allahabad address Iqbal was proposing both long-term and short-term solutions. The following passages from the Allahabad address also deserve to be considered: 'The life of Islam as a cultural force in this country very largely depends on its centralization in a specified territory.'

He went on to emphasize that his demand was 'actuated by a genuine desire for free development, which is practically impossible under the type of unitary government contemplated by the nationalist Hindu politicians with a view to secure permanent communal dominance in the whole of India'. Iqbal further underlined that 'The problem of India is international, not national.'

This address is an important landmark in the Pakistan Movement but it should also be realized that Iqbal's entire life and work was a contribution to the Pakistan Movement. To begin with, Iqbal's poetry, both Urdu and Persian, struck the most responsive cord of Indo-Muslim consciousness. We cannot separate the message from the style in Iqbal's poetry as both were inspired by the same zeal. Apart from his poetry, Iqbal wrote a number of articles and essays intended to reform Muslim society and give it a clear political direction. In 1904, he wrote an article on national life, pin-pointing the aspects that needed reform. In 1909 he wrote on 'Islam as a Moral and Political Ideal'. In 1910, he addressed the students of Aligarh on their patriotic duty. In 1931, he delivered his lectures on *The Reconstruction of Religious Thought in Islam* where he stated that the concept of Islam is bound up with majesty, which has the state as its manifestation. Finally in his letter to M.A. Jinnah dated 21 June 1937, Iqbal wrote:

> A separate federation of Muslim provinces, reformed on the lines I have suggested above, is the only course by which we can secure a peaceful India and save Muslims from the domination of non-Muslims. Why should not the Muslims of North-West and Bengal be considered as nations entitled to self-determination, just as other nations in India and outside India are?

Iqbal's Allahabad address has an added importance because it was a public statement from a representative platform. All the leaders of the Pakistan Movement, Quaid-i-Azam Mohammad Ali Jinnah, Nawabzada Liaquat Ali Khan and the Raja of Mahmudabad had publicly acknowledged the contribution of Iqbal even before Independence in 1947.

IQBAL AND HIS IDEOLOGY

Shaikh Mohammad Iqbal was born in Sialkot on 9 November 1877. He was educated in his home town, Government College, Lahore, and Trinity College, Cambridge. He passed his Bar examinations from London, and obtained his PhD from Munich University. He became a professor at Government College and later practised law before the Punjab High Court. Iqbal was briefly honorary secretary of the All-India Muslim League and a member of the Punjab legislative council. He was knighted in 1922.

Iqbal earned international acclaim as a poet in both Urdu and Persian. Very few poets who have written on philosophic themes in a grand style like Iqbal have become a favourite of the masses. Iqbal died in Lahore on 21 April 1938 after having published poetic collections in Persian and Urdu, as well as prose-works in English. He was also a literary critic, having written a tract in English on the Indo-Persian poet Bedil Azimabadi.

THE PHILOSOPHY OF ALLAMA IQBAL

The philosophy of Allama Iqbal is contained in both his Urdu and Persian poetry as well as in his English prose. It is very difficult to summarize his philosophy as it is very complex. However, the high points of his metaphysics have a bearing on his political thought and are summarized here.

1. The central concept of Iqbal's philosophy is *Khudi*. In English it can be translated as *Self* or *Ego*. Unlike its general meaning, *Khudi* in Iqbal's philosophy does not mean pride. It means *self awareness* and *loftiness of character*. Iqbal's concept of *Khudi* is partly a reaction to the traditional creeds where the *Self* is a mere delusion of the mind. In Islamic mysticism as well as Hindu and Buddhist philosophy, *self-negation* is the dominant trend.

   Khudi is not merely personal, but is divided into three basic realities (a) *Unique Self*, that is God (b) *Creative Self*, that is man (c) and *Larger Self*, that is society. According to Iqbal, a harmonious working of man and society produces a durable human civilization, which fulfils the purpose of God.

2. It follows, as Iqbal stated in Allahabad, that religion is not the private affair of an individual.

3. For both science and religion the way to pure objectivity lies through the purification of experience.

4. Because Iqbal's concept of the larger self is social, he makes a distinction between spirituality—*Ruhaniyat* and monasticism—*Rahbaniat*.

5. The reconstruction of Muslim society is possible only through democracy.

6. An Islamic state is based on social contract; therefore, non-Muslims have nothing to fear in an Islamic state.

7. Belief in Monotheism, the One-ness of God, brings about three values in human society; liberty, equality and stability.

8. Iqbal's concept of Islam is bound up with Majesty (or power). If majesty is the objective of Islam, its manifestation is the state.

9. God does not give different principles for different nations but chooses a certain nation and trains it spiritually to make it a model for other nations and thus gives universal rules for human society.

10. The state is the territorial specification of Islam.

11. Religious experience is a state of feeling with a cognitive aspect.

12. Thought is not a principle which organizes and integrates its material from the outside, but is a potency which is formative of the very being of its material.

13. Iqbal holds that there are potential types of consciousness lying close to human consciousness. These have the ability of imparting life-giving and knowledge-giving experience. These concepts of consciousness, Iqbal derived from Mujaddid Alf Thani who describes three stages, *Ruh* or Soul, *Sirr-i-Khafi*, the lesser mystery and *Sirr-i-Ikhfa* the greater mystery. In this sense, it is possible that religion can become the source of a higher experience.

14. In this manner, Islam is socially, morally and spiritually rewarding. This is why Iqbal stresses the need of cultural independence more than economic independence. This is the ideological aspect of Iqbal's demand for a separate Muslim state, different from the political aspect which was shaped by the attitude of the Hindu majority and British autocracy towards the Muslims as a minority.

THE SOCIAL CONTRACT THEORY

This was a theory designed to replace the theory of the Divine Rights of Kings. The thinkers who preceded the French Revolution 1789 had begun to advance theories which spoke of the sovereignty of the people. Among these theorists, the most prominent were Thomas Hobbes (1588–1679), John Locke (1632–1704) and Jean-Jacques Rousseau (1712–1778).

According to Thomas Hobbes nature was a state of perpetual strife because people were governed by (1) competition (2) distrust and (3) glory. These traits are inherent in human nature, but are redeemed by Reason. Reason leads all citizens to make a contract with one another. Every person gave up his/her right to govern him/herself, provided other people did likewise. Thus, citizens made a contract among themselves to delegate their authority to the ruler. The ruler himself was not a party to the contract, therefore, his actions could not be questioned. Although Hobbes held the ruler to be above the social contract, he negated the Divine Right of Kings and upheld the will of the people as the basis of the King's authority.

Historically, speaking, such a contract was never actually signed. Its signing is hypothetical and a supposition. Hobbes was fascinated by Geometry in which a theorem begins with one supposition and leads to another.

John Locke maintained that the state of nature was benign and peaceful, not of conflict or disorder, yet it was unsatisfactory because there was no judge or common authority to interpret the laws of nature. Locke emphasized that one man's freedom stopped where it could injure another man's freedom. Hence, freedom in political society is freedom under law. Locke said men enter into society to preserve their property. Individuals surrendered their natural rights to a properly elected ruler, so that the ruler may protect their remaining rights. In an advance over Hobbes, Locke held that the ruler was also party to the contract, and therefore answerable to the people. The people could resist, even change their ruler.

Jean-Jacques Rousseau said, 'Man was born free, but is everywhere in chains.' Nature was paradise, but with the growth of population, complications and problems arose, therefore people contracted among themselves to create a civil society. Society secured the freedom of individuals. Since each gave himself to all, he gives himself to none. (They all become an abstraction.) There is gained the equivalent of what is lost, with greater power to protect what is left.

According to Rousseau, the contract was not one between the people and the ruler, it was among the people themselves, and sovereignty belonged to the General Will, which can be expressed in an assembly. The ruler is a mere agent of the people. General Will is not the sum total of all selfish or particular wills. Rousseau objected to delegation of power at all, as sovereignty cannot be surrendered. Rousseau claimed that the General Will emanates from the community as a whole, so sovereignty must reside in it.

The Social Contract Theory as we have seen, passed through an evolutionary process. When Iqbal assured minorities of an Islamic state of their rights, he was announcing that there would be no Divine Right for the sultan. Rousseau did not equate General Will with Majority Will, therefore, the rights of the minorities would remain inalienable.

CHAUDHRY RAHMAT ALI (b. Balachaur, Hoshiarpur [East Punjab], 16 November 1897–d. Cambridge, UK, 3 February 1951) did his MA from Cambridge in 1940, and was called to the Bar from the Middle Temple in 1943. Ten years earlier, on 28 January 1933, he published *Now or Never*. Later in the same year, he published *What Does the Pakistan National Movement Stand For?* Thus, the word 'Pakistan' was coined by Chaudhry Rahmat Ali. He introduced this name in a pamphlet called *Now or Never*. He explained the composition of the word in the following manner:

> Pakistan is both a Persian and Urdu word. It is composed of letters taken from the names of all our homelands—'Indian' and 'Asian'. That is Panjab, Afghania [North-West Frontier Province] Kashmir. Iran, Sindh (including Kutch and Kathiawar) Tukharistan, Afghanistan and Balochistan. It means the land of the Paks—the spiritually pure and clean. It symbolizes the religious beliefs and ethnical stocks of our people and it stands for all the territorial constituents of our original Fatherland.

His pamphlet was launched from the platform of an association the Pakistan National Movement that he had founded the same year. Chaudhry Rahmat Ali urged Muslim delegates at the Round Table Conference not to recognize the Indian Union. Jinnah had then called Pakistan an impossible dream.

The British Parliament and Hindu organizations took Chaudhry Rahmat Ali's proposal far more seriously than Jinnah had done. On the same day as *Now or Never* was issued, the British Parliament took notice of what it termed the testimonial of Chaudhry Rahmat Ali and his associates, and the following August, a Joint Parliamentary Select Committee queried a number of Muslim leaders about their views on a separate Muslim State.

The reaction of Hindu organizations was quite sharp. Mahr Chand Khanna of the Hindu Conference declared Rahmat Ali's proposal 'dangerous'. In 1935, Chaudhry Rahmat Ali published another pamphlet, calling for the separation of Pakistan, just as Burma was being separated from India and by 1937 the *Encyclopedia of Islam* had featured Chaudhry Rahmat Ali and his scheme for Pakistan.

Chaudhry Rahmat Ali was a very sincere and devoted servant of the Muslim community, however, his scheme for Muslim separatism was impractical. Apart from Pakistan, in which he wished to include Lucknow, Delhi and Aligarh, he named the second entity 'Bang-i-Islam' comprising Bengal and Assam. This at least had an overall Muslim majority, the third entity was to be Usmanistan, the domain of Usman Ali Khan, Nizam of Hyderabad, who ruled over a Hindu majority state.

When Jinnah and the Muslim League accepted the 3 June Plan Chaudhry Rahmat Ali broke out in invective. He accused Jinnah of shattering the foundations of Muslim nationhood and sabotaging the future of 100 million Muslims living in India. He called the creation of Pakistan 'the blackest and the bloodiest treachery in our history!'[1]

Chaudhry Rahmat Ali has an indelible place in our history. His demand loomed so large in the Hindu and British imagination that even though the Lahore Resolution had not mentioned Pakistan by name, the press designated it as the 'Pakistan' resolution, and later M.A. Jinnah thanked them for this name. The disappointment that Chaudhry Rahmat Ali felt was severe but his outburst was most intemperate. Jinnah had not actively wanted a divided Punjab and Bengal, he had himself termed such a Pakistan, 'truncated and moth-eaten', but when an ideal solution is not forthcoming, the next best solution has to be accepted. Since Chaudhry Rahmat Ali was a very zealous votary of setting up a Muslim state, he was deeply disappointed that the Pakistan which emerged fell far short of the Pakistan he proposed. Still, he should be remembered with gratitude for giving Pakistan its name.

NOTE

1. Khalid Hasan, 'The Quaid's Detractor,' *The News International*, Karachi, 14 April 1998.

CHAPTER 17

THE ROUND TABLE CONFERENCES 1930–1932

RTC: FIRST SESSION—21 NOVEMBER 1930 TO 19 JANUARY 1931

The Round Table Conferences were held partially to support the Simon Commission, and partially to meet the objection that it contained no Indian members. A series of Round Table Conferences (RTCs) were held between 1930 to 1932. The first session was opened by King George V in London on 10 November 1930. A fifty-eight member Indian delegation led by Aga Khan III representing diverse interests; Muslims, liberals and the Chamber of Princes was present. Only the Congress, the largest political party of India, was absent. During this session, a Federal Structure Subcommittee was formed under Lord Sankey. The communal question could not be resolved. Edward Thomson, on the prompting of some quarters he did not name, proposed that the communal question be submitted to the arbitration of three members, one Hindu, one Muslim and one British. Thomson also observed that the younger Muslims were not as communal as the older. This remark was resented by the Muslim delegates and this proposal found no favour.

At the conclusion of the first session, 19 January 1931, the British Prime Minister Ramsay Macdonald (1866–1937) made the commitment that if the Indian legislature was formed on the basis of a federation, the British would recognize the principle that the executive would be responsible to the legislature. During this session, the princes gave their assent to joining a federation.

Meanwhile in India, both the Congress and the Muslim League were voicing their demands. It was during this session that Sir Muhammad Iqbal delivered his Allahabad address. Motilal Nehru demanded full dominion status by 31 December 1931; his son Jawaharlal Nehru demanded full independence. On 5 April 1930 Gandhi broke the Salt Law, heralding another Civil Disobedience Movement.

RTC: SECOND SESSION—7 SEPTEMBER TO 1 DECEMBER 1931

This session saw Sir Muhammad Iqbal and Pandit Madan Mohan Malaviya as new delegates with Mohandas Karamchand Gandhi as the sole representative of the Congress. Communal differences could not be resolved despite the initial conciliatory gestures of Gandhi. Liberals like Sir Chimanlal Setalvad, Vitthal Bhai Patel, Sir Srinavasa Shastri and Sir Tej Bahadur Sapru were in favour of a settlement but Mahasabhaites like Madan Mohan Malaviya were not. At the first RTC session a formulation by M.A. Jinnah had been vetoed by M.R. Jaykar (1873–1959) of the Mahasabha party. Gandhi had to announce to Sir Muhammad Shafi on 8 October that his mediatory efforts had failed and that he had his limits. In this session the princes withdrew their assent to join a federation. The role of Jinnah was described as 'unique'. According to a British journal:

> The Hindus thought he was a Muslim communalist, the Muslims took him to be pro-Hindu, the princes deemed him to be too democratic, the British considered him to be a rabid extremist—with the result that he was everywhere but nowhere. None wanted him.

This is a correct assessment and is also ironic because it was Jinnah who had originally written to Macdonald on 19 June 1929 that only a conference of Indian delegates in London could break the political impasse. Since Jinnah was denied a leading role, the efforts of the Muslim delegates became ineffective. Allama Iqbal disagreed with Sir Akbar Hyderi during the RTC and on his return to India criticized the role of the Muslim delegates as well as the British government.

The Depressed Classes (Untouchable Hindus), led by Dr Bhimrao Ramji Ambedkar (1891–1956), had asked for separate electorates like the Muslims. Gandhi asked the Muslim delegates to oppose this demand. The Muslims agreed to abide by any agreement reached between Gandhi and Ambedkar, but said that they could not reasonably oppose the extension of the same right they had claimed for themselves.

RTC: THIRD SESSION—17 NOVEMBER TO 24 DECEMBER 1932

This session of the conference was almost inconsequential; only the White Paper embodying recommendations of all three sessions was of consequence. Gandhi and Jinnah were both absent. There was a change of viceroy and Lord Willingdon, who had succeeded Lord Irwin, had Gandhi arrested. The Gandhi–Irwin Pact was undone and the Congress started another Civil Disobedience Movement. Jinnah was not invited to this session because he had accused Lord Sankey, chairman of the Federal Structure Subcommittee, of partiality. He explained that his insistence on the Fourteen Points were the reason for his exclusion from this RTC session.

GANDHI—IRWIN PACT, 5 MARCH 1931

Since the Congress was the largest political party in India, the Viceroy, Lord Irwin sought to break the deadlock. He released Mahatma Gandhi and for four days (17, 18, 19 and 27 February 1931) he held talks with him. The result of these talks were the Gandhi–Irwin Pact. The provisions of this Pact were that the British would:

> Release all prisoners, withdraw notifications declaring certain associations unlawful, withdraw all prosecutions relating to non-violent offences; would allow Congress peaceful picketing to persuade people to buy only Indian goods.

The Congress would discontinue its Civil Disobedience Movement and participate in the RTC.

THE COMMUNAL AWARD, 16 AUGUST 1932

The Communal Award issued by the British was the consequence of the failure of the Indian delegates to solve their problem themselves. The British Prime Minister Ramsay Macdonald had said, on the final day of the Second RTC session:

> His Majesty's Government would have to settle for you, not only your problems of representation, but also to decide, as wisely and justly as possible, what checks and balances the constitution is to contain to protect minorities from an unrestricted and tyrannical use of the democratic principle expressing itself solely through majority power.

Macdonald followed this principle in the Award he announced. For Muslims both separate electorates and weightages were retained. However, this was not an unmixed blessing. In Hindu majority provinces, Hindus would retain their majority in their legislatures; but because of the weightage given to Muslims in Hindu majority provinces, the Muslim majority of Bengal and the Punjab was reduced to a minority. This was a carry over from the Lucknow Pact 1916 but it was generally harmful. The weightage given to Muslims did not reduce Hindus in any province to a minority, but in Punjab, where Muslims were 57 per cent, they were given 49 per cent representation. In Bengal, a 55 per cent Muslim population was given 48 per cent representation. However, in practical terms and indirectly, the Muslim majority was in force because they were elected through the special seats reserved for landlord, labour and university constituencies.

Sikhs were also given weightage, to which provision no community raised any serious objection. Under the Poona Pact this principle was first given to the Untouchables and then withdrawn.

THE POONA PACT

Mahatma Gandhi had advocated for a long time, the rights of the Depressed Classes (Untouchables). When Ramsay Macdonald announced in his Communal Award, separate electorates for them, Gandhi was outraged. He said he was against statutory separation of the Depressed Classes. If the British emancipated them, Gandhi explained, the work of Hindu reformers would be undone. Gandhi undertook a fast unto death for the removal of this redressal. B.R. Ambedkar, in a meeting held at Poona, was forced to agree to Gandhi's terms which were double reservation of Untouchable seats, that is, a form of weightage, instead of separate electorates. When under this arrangement the Untouchables were defeated on each and every seat they contested during the Kanpur Municipal elections, Gandhi admitted that statutory separation of the Untouchables was fit 'punishment' for upper class selfishness. However, he did not withdraw his demand nor did he undertake a fast to undo the harm he had done to the Untouchables.

THE WHITE PAPER, 17 MARCH 1933

As stated above, the White Paper contained the recommendations of all three sessions of the RTC. Most of them were embodied in the Government of India Act 1935 after much debate and deliberation. It was first considered by a select committee of the British parliament made up of sixteen members from the House of Lords, and sixteen members from the House of Commons. There were in addition twenty assessors from British India and seven from the Princely States. Among them were five Muslims led by the Aga Khan. The committee reported to parliament on 22 November 1934. Its recommendations were approved by the House of Commons on 12 December, and the House of Lords on 18 December 1934. After a final reading, it received the Royal Assent on 4 August 1935.

JAWAHARLAL NEHRU (b. Allahabad, 14 November 1889–d. New Delhi, 27 May 1964) was a Kashmiri Brahmin by lineage, an agnostic by belief, and an aristocrat by upbringing. As one of his admirers remarked shortly before independence, '[Nehru] is explosive in speech, disciplined in action, impulsive in gestures, deliberate in judgement, revolutionary in aim, conservative in loyalty, reckless of personal safety, cautious about matters affecting Indian welfare'.[1]

If we refuse to bicker about the mutual incompatibility of these stated qualities, we must admit that they mark out greatness in his makeup. Alas, Nehru lacked the humility which underscored greatness. In the words of his latest biographer, Nehru 'interiorized this complex sense of superiority'.[2] Another chronicler has been more explicit: 'A little greater humility, a little less certainty of righteousness, might conceivably have saved their ideal of a united India'.[3]

This trait may have sprung from Jawaharlal's psychological reserve regarding his father, Motilal. Michael Brecher, one of Nehru's earliest biographers, commented that 'respect and affection were there, but Motilal Nehru could not draw out his son's emotional response to the same extent or in the same way as the Mahatma'.[4]

Judith Brown, who approached Nehru after her momentous study of Gandhi, has noted, 'As his attitude sharpened, he became increasingly critical of his father's political stance, and this created tension between them'.[5]

Now Mohammad Ali Jinnah, a friend of his real father, but a rival of his political mentor became the focus of Nehru's ire. How close Motilal and Mohammad Ali had been can be glimpsed from one of Jinnah's speeches: 'Will you bring Motilal Nehru to bow before the throne at Viceregal Lodge? What has Pandit Motilal Nehru been doing in the Assembly? Has he not been cooperating with you? Have you no eyes, have you no ears, have you no brains?'[6]

Jinnah was chiding the British for being unable to discern policy from posture. His exasperation went unnoticed by not only the Viceroy, but by Motilal's son. Even after a rift with Jinnah, Motilal remarked: 'We can afford to fight like Kilkenny cats and still be friends'.[7] Once, when Jawaharlal Nehru, as Secretary of the Congress, offended a Muslim League delegation, Motilal rushed to conciliate Jinnah. Soon after Motilal's death, Jawaharlal Nehru referred to 'my dear friend Mohammad Ali Jinnah'.[8] To describe one's father's friend as one's own went against the grain of Indian culture, and did not bode well for the future.

In the ultimate analysis, Nehru's sophistication overcame his pragmatism. When, despite a tacit electoral understanding, Nehru forbade Govind Ballabh Pant from bringing the Muslim League into the 1937 UP cabinet, he did not characterize it as a communal or even religious party, but as a 'small' party. His next decision was to sabotage the Cabinet Mission plan. Latter day apologists have justified Nehru's 10 July 1946 press conference on the ground that acceptance would have led to the creation of Pakistan. Certainly, this defence would have been justified had Nehru's refusal prevented the emergence of Pakistan. Nehru spurned Jinnah's demand for a corridor between West and East Pakistan, even though it was accompanied with an offer of common defence—a step that would have prevented the nuclearization of Pakistan.

More inexplicably, Nehru turned down President Ayub Khan's offer of a common defence against China—not pausing to reflect how his acceptance would have isolated Pakistan. Shortly after, Nehru was cheered by a nostalgic Pakistani crowd when he came to sign the Indus Water Treaty (1960). When Nehru died, Inder Malhotra reported from Pakistan, that the grief was sincere.

NOTES

1. Michael Brecher, *Nehru: A Political Biography*, London: Oxford University Press, 1959; Delhi: Oxford University Press, reprint, 2004, p. 596.
2. Judith Brown, *Nehru: A Political Life*, New Delhi: Oxford University Press, 2004, p. 36.
3. H.V. Hodson, *The Great Divide: Britain–India–Pakistan*, Karachi: Oxford University Press, 1989, p. 182.
4. Michael Brecher, op. cit., pp. 608–09.
5. Judith Brown, op. cit., p. 39.
6. Ian Bryant Wells, *Ambassador of Hindu–Muslim Unity: Jinnah's Early Politics*, Delhi: Permanent Black, 2005, p. 157.
7. Ibid., p. 138.
8. Ibid., p. 144.

CHAPTER 18

THE GOVERNMENT OF INDIA ACT 1935

The constitutional history of India began with British rule. Before British rule, there were only monarchies under whom the rights or obligations of the subjects were not defined. When British rule began, there started a struggle between the unscrupulous and rapacious East India Company and the liberal and idealistic ruling classes of Britain. Even though the parties kept changing, the policy towards India remained contentious. Following the RTCs there began a tug of war, with the Congress demanding swift and complete transfer of power, and members of the British Conservative Party led by Winston Churchill, who were strongly opposed to Home Rule in India. The British Labour Party sympathised with the Congress Party and joined it in its boycott of the third RTC. The Muslim League also wanted Home Rule but with safeguards so that the transfer of power would not simply result in a change of masters.

A constitution is normally the set of conditions according to which a people agree to live with each other, as well as the basic law, which is the source of all other laws. The various Acts of the British parliament which determined how India was to be governed, was not a set of rules freely arrived at by the people, because the rules were imposed from above, by outsiders.

However, these Acts were constitutions in the sense that they were the basic law in India which became the source of subsequent legislation. Under both definitions a constitution determines the structure and nature of government and lays down how power is to be shared by the different segments of society. A constitution is easy to propose, and also easy to impose, if the concerned population is homogenous; that is, if the people follow one religion, belong to one race, speak one language and have a common culture. This was not the case in India. Apart from Hindus and Muslims, there were Sikhs, Christians, Parsis, Buddhists and Jains. Ethnically they were descended from Aryan, Dravidian, Mongol and aboriginal races. The variety in climate created a variety in culture, causing diversity in food, clothing, language, and the arts. These taken together, made reaching a constitutional agreement a daunting task in India.

There was another entity, not normally found in other countries; this was the princely states. When the British conquered India, they annexed some territories, leaving some rajas and nawabs holding territories ceded by them to the British under different treaties. This made them constitutionally the vassals of the British crown as all matters of defence, external affairs and communications were given under British control. In all other matters these rulers exercised freedom. Their subjects enjoyed even fewer human rights than the citizens of the British-ruled provinces. There were many princely states some as large as Kashmir and some as small as Porbandar. Half of the Indian population lived in these princely states. They were not contiguous, therefore they formed a Chamber of Princes to represent their interests collectively.

Under the Government of India (GOI) Act of 1935, the British wanted both the provinces and princely states to come together under a federation. The British themselves had a unitary form of government with one parliament and one government.

At the first RTC the princes had shown their willingness to join the federation, but later they changed their minds because of the fear of losing their wealth and privileges. Their fears were not unfounded. The Congress did not wish to join the federation because it preferred a unitary system since the British were witholding most of the power. Liaquat Ali Khan explained the Muslim League's stand: 'Inadequate safeguards for the Muslims is an additional grievance of the Musalmans to other fundamental objections to the scheme (1935 Act) namely that it does not give any real power and control in vital matters to the Federal Legislature or the Minister that may be appointed'. The GOI Act 1935 had shifted dyarchy from the provinces to the centre. Some subjects were transferred to Indians who were responsible to their legislatures and some were reserved for British officials responsible to no one. This dyarchy had been introduced in the provinces through the GOI Act 1919 and had proved unpopular. It was proposed to remove dyarchy from the provinces and introduce it in the centre; therefore the Congress and Muslim League were willing to work on the provincial part of the 1935 Act but not on the federal part.

This decision had two consequences, one immediate and one long-term. The immediate consequence of the 1935 Act was that in 1937 elections were held for provincial legislatures, but not for the federal legislature (which had until then been held under the 1919 Act). The long-term consequence was, as H.V. Hodson states, that both India and Pakistan adopted the GOI Act of 1935 as their basic law before promulgating their respective constitutions.

While all parties condemned the federal part, the AIML led by M.A. Jinnah, expressed willingness to work 'the scheme of provincial autonomy for what it was worth.'

Therefore, elections were held only for provincial legislatures in 1937.

Main Features of Government of India Act 1935

(a) Federal Part:
Reserved federal executive was to be constituted of a governor-general and a council of ministers. The following portfolios would be described as reserved: defence, foreign affairs, tribal area affairs and ecclesiastical affairs that is administration of Christian churches. Transferred were: education, finance, home, law, railways, commerce, industries and labour.

A bicameral legislature was proposed. The upper house known as the Council of State was to consist of 250 members. The lower house to be known as the House of Assembly was to consist of 375 members.

(b) Provincial Part:
Dyarchy was removed and a measure of autonomy was introduced; the governor except in the case of 'special responsibility', was to act on the advice of the elected chief minister.

Six provinces, i.e. Bengal, Bihar, Assam, UP, Bombay and Madras had bicameral legislatures. The upper house was known as the Legislative Council and the lower house was called the Legislative Assembly.

In the remaining five provinces only the lower house existed.

Three new provinces were created. NWFP was made a full-fledged province with a legislative assembly and a governor. The same condition applied to Sindh which was separated from Bombay, and Orissa which was separated from Bihar.

(c) A federal court was to be set up to decide disputes between the federal government and provincial governments.

(d) The Council of the Secretary of State (or India Council) was abolished.

CHAPTER 19

THE 1937 ELECTIONS AND CONGRESS RULE

The 1937 elections were the first broad-based elections in which the representative status of political parties was tested. The tone of the campaign was set by Jawaharlal Nehru's statement that 'there were only two parties in India, the British and the Congress, all the others must line up'. To this the Quaid-i-Azam rejoined: 'I refuse to line up with the Congress. There is a third party in this country and that is the Muslims. We are not going to be dictated to by any one.' (Calcutta, 8 January 1937) However, when the elections were held, the Congress won and the Muslim League lost, though under separate electorates the Muslim League had to face only Muslim voters.

The Muslim League could win only 104 out of 489 Muslim seats. The position of the Muslim League was worst in the Muslim majority provinces. In NWFP, the pro-Congress Khudai Khidmatgars won by a large margin. In the Hindu majority provinces the Muslim League had a respectable win only in UP and Bombay. In UP out of 66 Muslim seats AIML won 27 and in Bombay, out of 30 Muslim seats it won 20.

The Congress had won less than half the general votes; 711 out of 1585, but its results were still better, and the distribution of seats allowed it to form the government in 7 out of 11 provinces in India.

CAUSES OF THE AIML FAILURE

There were three main reasons for the defeat of the All-India Muslim League in the 1937 elections:

1. The Muslim League had suffered a setback during the Khilafat Movement. Since this was an emotional issue for the Muslims, they set aside political considerations and came out against the British, under the Congress. Muslims sidelined Jinnah and the Muslim League to join Gandhi and the Khilafat cause. Although the Khilafat could not be saved, this trend of bypassing the AIML could not be completely reversed.
2. Since elections were held only for provincial legislatures and provincial autonomy was the most attractive feature of the GOI Act 1935, regional and provincial tendencies surfaced in Muslim parties. Even Sir Khwaja Nazimuddin, who was to become the second governor-general and second

prime minister of Pakistan stated on 30 July 1936 that no All-India party could select proper candidates from rural areas.

Provincial parties like the Unionists in Punjab and the Muslim United Parties of Sindh, Bengal and Bihar were proving more popular.

3. The organization of a party, especially during elections, is the responsibility of the honorary secretary. On 12 April 1936, Liaquat Ali Khan was first elected honorary secretary of the AIML and on 11 November 1936 he resigned from the AIML Parliamentary Board, and stood as an independent candidate. The combination of all these factors contributed to the defeat of the AIML in 1937.

MUSLIM LEAGUE EXPECTATIONS

The Congress had won sufficient seats in UP and Bombay to form a government, yet the AIML insisted that it should be included in the government and given representation in the cabinet. It did not believe that it would have to sit as the opposition. What was the basis for the Muslim League making this extraordinary demand, which was particularly strong in the UP?

One reason was that the manifestos of the Congress and Muslim League in social and economic terms were compatible. The Congress wanted abolition of *zamindari*. The Muslim League was not in favour of outright abolition but was strongly in favour of land reforms.

A second reason was that in UP, the Congress and Muslim League had a tacit understanding against the National Agriculturist Party, a party sponsored and favoured by the British and representing the landlord class. Fearing the influence of the Royal party, both Congress and the Muslim League opposed it. This agreement lasted beyond the general elections. Rafi Ahmad Qidwai, the main Congress candidate in the Muslim list had lost the elections. He was elected in a by-election when the Muslim League agreed not to put up any candidate against him.

Thirdly, during the period between the elections and the assumption of ministries by the Congress, the Muslim League sided with the Congress and refused all British offers of ministries. The 1935 Act had vested special responsibility in the governor according to which he could over-rule the ministry, therefore, the Congress, despite winning the elections, refused to assume office unless this condition was removed.

Meanwhile, a minority government backed by the British was formed by the Nawab of Chatari. He offered ministries to Muslim League members including Liaquat Ali Khan. If the Muslim League had cooperated with the National Agriculturist Party, the Congress could have been made to sit as the opposition. However, the Muslim League refused all offers and Liaquat Ali

Khan stated that to form a minority government, one not supported by the majority of members, was undemocratic, and in principle, the Muslim League would not support it. In expectation of having their members included in the UP cabinet, by the Congress, the Muslim League refused British offers to join the government. On the refusal of Congress to include them the Muslim League reacted with bitterness.

MUSLIMS UNDER CONGRESS RULE

The Congress ministries alienated the Muslims of their provinces by their conduct. Some practices were symbolic; Muslims resented the singing of the song *Vande Mataram* taken from Bankim Chandar Chatterji's virulently anti-Muslim novel *Anand Math*. Moreover, Muslim schoolboys had to salute Gandhi's portrait and Hindi replaced Urdu in schools. Other features were far more threatening. In UP, Hindu–Muslim riots doubled in number. This was put down to Congress neglect or connivance because incidents of armed robbery had increased by 70 per cent and those of murder had gone up by 30 per cent.

It must be recalled that because of separate electorates, Muslim League candidates had been defeated by Muslim voters, not Hindu voters. It was because of the Congress's attitude that the Muslims began to regret having caused the defeat of the Muslim League. The Muslim League published three reports about Congress misrule. The 'Pirpur Report' covered UP, the 'Sharif Report' covered Bihar, and the 'Fazlul Haq Report' covered the Congress rule in general.

Foreign writers called these reports Muslim League propaganda. It is not explained why Muslims should believe the propaganda of a party they had themselves recently rejected at the polls. Moreover, recently published correspondence between Jinnah and Liaquat (2003) shows that both leaders were initially reluctant to blame the Congress. Only when the evidence mounted, did they blame the Congress.

REVIVAL OF THE MUSLIM LEAGUE

The Muslims, not only of minority provinces, but of majority provinces like Bengal and Punjab, came to the realization that if this was the behaviour of the Hindu majority while the British still controlled the central government, what would be their conduct if the British withdrew and the Congress controlled the centre as well?

AIML LUCKNOW SESSION: 15 TO 18 OCTOBER 1937

This meeting was organized by the treasurer of the Muslim League, the Raja of Mahmudabad (1914–1973). Besides paying the expenses of the session from his own purse (Rs 30 lakhs), he toured the nearby districts of Agra and Muzaffarnagar inviting every Muslim to attend the session and led Jinnah's carriage procession when he arrived. It took the procession four hours to cover a distance of three miles. In his welcome address, the Raja of Mahmudabad stated 'We are here not to follow history, but to create it'.

The Muslim premiers of the Punjab, Bengal and Assam, Sir Sikandar Hayat, Fazlul Haq and Sir Muhammad Saadullah, attended the 1937 Lucknow session. In their provinces they and their parties prevailed over the Muslim League, but now they closed ranks. They wanted the Muslim League, not the Congress to represent them at the centre. In early 1937, the Muslim League was in decline; in October 1937 it was resurgent and only because, as Jinnah said at the Lucknow session 'the Congress have shown their hand that Hindustan is for the Hindus'.

DAY OF DELIVERANCE

The Second World War broke out on 3 September 1939. The same day, Lord Linlithgow announced that India was also at war. The Congress protested that they were not consulted. On 15 September 1939 the Congress said that India would not participate in the war unless the British accepted the principle of full and immediate independence for India. This the British refused but offered instead full dominion status at the end of the war. On 22 September the Congress resigned all its ministries.

Even after such a bitter experience, M.A. Jinnah first offered terms to the Congress rather than to the British. He asked for Muslim League–Congress coalitions in the provinces, an end to anti-Muslim moves and acceptance of the principle that no legislation affecting the Muslims would be passed unless two-thirds of Muslim members voted for it. Only when the Congress did not respond did Jinnah go ahead with a programme to observe 22 December 1939, as a 'day of deliverance' from Congress rule.

At this juncture the Congress president, Jawaharlal Nehru, approached Jinnah saying that he had asked the British to express their war aims, agree to Indian independence and the right to frame its own constitution—'as the Muslim League has the same declared object there should be no difference of opinion about them'. Nehru expressed these sentiments when Congress ministers had already resigned, and not when the ministries were being formed in 1937 or even when Jinnah had recently made an offer of cooperation.

On 22 December 1939, Muslims rejoiced over their deliverance and what is more, were joined by small non-Muslim parties as well. The Congress had made a strategic mistake by resigning. The British were relieved that they would be able to fight the war with Indian soldiers and resources but without any hindrance from the Congress. This gave an opening to the Muslim League to consolidate their political gains.

 RAJA OF MAHMUDABAD, MUHAMMAD AMIR AHMAD KHAN (b. Mahmudabad, 1914–d. London, 1973) The raja of Mahmudabad was the third of the triumvirate which created Pakistan. As treasurer he ranked immediately after the president and honorary secretary of the AIML. A prince who would be pauper, he sacrificed his fabulous wealth for the cause of Pakistan, and on the success of his mission, refused to partake of its fruits and retired from politics. He was the only member of the AIML hierarchy to undergo ideological stress. He personified the transition from movement-oriented to state-oriented politics in Pakistan.

The raja of Mahmudabad's endeavours towards the establishment of Pakistan consisted mainly of financing and organizing the movement. We have already mentioned, under the 1937 Lucknow session, the contributions made by the raja. This session was only the beginning. According to Chaudhry Khaliquzzaman, the raja opened his purse strings to meet election expenses—whatever the amount.[1] The raja's efforts reversed the 1937 defeat by winning 86 per cent of the seats in the by-elections. Apart from elections, the raja's recorded contributions were to *Dawn*. All these efforts won him the appreciation of the Quaid-i-Azam who hosted, in Bombay, the largest ever dinner of his life, inviting 400 guests to honour the raja of Mahmudabad. 'The raja of Mahmudabad, although young in age' Jinnah told his guests, 'is a great man in wisdom and capacity'.[2] This was a momentous tribute, but it unfortunately marked the point from where the tide ebbed.

Although he held the largest estates in UP, he led an abstemious life, following the precepts of the holy personages of Islam. Another outcome of his religious idealism was his espousal of an Islamic state. It was this idealism which would cause him ideological stress. On 28 July 1940, he wrote to the Quaid-i-Azam: 'When I say an Islamic state, I do not mean a Muslim state.'[3] According to Isha'at Habibullah, when the raja reiterated his stand in Jinnah's presence, Jinnah responded:

> Did you realize that there are over seventy sects and differences of opinion regarding the Islamic faith, and if what the raja was suggesting was to be followed, the consequences would be a struggle of religious opinion from the very inception of the State leading to its very dissolution…[4]

Jinnah's objection to an Islamic state was not ideological but empirical, but it was only in 1970, that the raja wrote that Jinnah had been right and he had been wrong.[5] Apart from the issue of an Islamic state, the raja wished Jinnah to bide his time, and not accept the partition of Bengal and Punjab. When the raja went to NWFP, buying up arms in the aftermath of the 1946 riots, Jinnah reprimanded him sharply. No wonder that the raja had refused to go to Karachi on 14 August 1947, in spite of being in Hyderabad (Sindh). In all three issues—his insistence on an Islamic state, his insistence that Jinnah risk the creation of Pakistan to prevent bifurcation of provinces, and taking recourse to violence during the riots—Jinnah was right and the raja was wrong. This did not detract from the emotional crises the raja underwent. On 16 December 1943, the raja had written to Jinnah: 'But I have nobody except you whom I regard in place of my father and the prodigal son in trouble returns only to his father'.[6] In 1947, the son was prodigal and there was no father to return to. The only meeting that the raja had with Jinnah after independence was when he was forcibly made to disembark, at Karachi. The scene was stormy but the governor-general exercised restraint: 'Amir! You have no idea of the situation here, I am surrounded by traitors. I cannot entrust the fate of Pakistan to them'.[7]

The raja came to Pakistan after a decade, in 1957, and left again after ten years, in 1967, when he was asked to show his passport. Within that decade, he shunned offers of high office given by Presidents Iskander Mirza, Ayub Khan and Yahya Khan. He also refused to build up a constituency. In a Karachi public meeting, on 19 March 1958, he told the *muhajir* audience that they—and not Bengalis or Punjabis—were responsible for the spread of racial prejudice.[8] When Princess Abida Sultaan visited him when he was on his London deathbed, he recalled bitterly that he was being cared for by the very British against whom he had struggled.

NOTES

1. Chaudhry Khaliquzzaman, *Pathway to Pakistan*, Lahore: Longman, 1961, p. 159.
2. Shaiq Ahmad Usmani (ed.), *Asr-i-Jadid*, Calcutta, 24 January 1938.
3. Rizwan Ahmad Collection, Baitul Hikmat, Hamdard, p. 74.
4. Isha'at Habibullah, Autobiography, unpublished typescript, pp. 108–9.
5. Raja of Mahmudabad, 'Some Memories', in Mushirul Hasan (ed.), *India's Partition: Process, Strategy and Mobilization*, Delhi: Oxford University Press, 1994, p. 426.
6. Shamsul Hasan Collection.
7. Dr Afzal Iqbal, 'The Young and Fiery Raja of Mahmudabad', *Dawn*, 11 November 1983.
8. *Imroze*, 20 March 1958.

Part IV
History of the Pakistan Movement

CHAPTER 20

THE LAHORE RESOLUTION 1940 TO THE 1945 ELECTIONS

The 1937 elections were the lowest point for the Muslim League. The 1937 Lucknow session was the highest point of resurgence. The attendance of the premiers of Muslim majority provinces where the Muslim League had lost, showed that the damage had been controlled, and the Muslim League was on its way to success. Between 1937 and 1942, the Muslim League had won 46 out of 56 seats in by-elections.

The reason behind this resurgence is not simply that the Muslims felt that they had to unite to face the prospects of a central government headed not by the British, but by the Congress, as could easily be forseen, but also because the Lahore Resolution gave Muslims, as Khalid B. Sayeed states, 'a clear aim and direction'.[1] It meant that Muslims had forsaken seeking guarantees for themselves as a minority and now asserted their rights as a separate nation. In constitutional terms it meant that the Muslims would not be subject to the law of the land, as all minorities are, but to international law. Under international law, being smaller in numbers than the Hindu population or in occupied territory did not matter; Hindus and Muslims would form equal sovereign states.

There are a number of individuals who were already thinking along these lines. Dr Syed Abdul Latif of the Deccan put forward a scheme in 1939, proposing four zones for Muslims in India. Professors Syed Zafarul Hasan and M. Afzal Qadri of the Aligarh University proposed three federations: one each in the north-west and north-east, and one centred in Hyderabad Deccan. However, no scheme which envisaged the creation of a Muslim entity over areas where Muslims were in a minority could be seriously considered.

It was the Sindh Muslim League which, on 10 October 1938, adopted a resolution moved by Sir Abdullah Haroon which called for a division of India into two federations, Hindu and Muslim. G.M. Sayed said Hindus and Muslims were two separate nations. On 25 March 1939 at Meerut, Liaquat Ali Khan voiced his preference for division. Less than a year later, the (AIML) held its historic session at Lahore.

THE TWO-NATION THEORY

The Lahore session is noted for the formal adoption of the Two-Nation theory by the (AIML). Presiding over the session, M.A. Jinnah said:

> The Hindus and Muslims belong to two different religious philosophies, social customs, literatures. They neither intermarry or interdine, and indeed they belong to two different civilizations which are based on conflicting ideas and conceptions.

The theory raised a storm of controversy. The first question was, is Jinnah sincere in formulating this theory? Durga Das, a journalist, asked Jinnah in Lahore whether Pakistan was a serious demand or merely a bargaining stance. The reason behind such speculation was that firstly, early in his career Jinnah had opposed separate electorates and was called 'Ambassador of Hindu–Muslim Unity' by Gopal Krishna Gokhale. Secondly, on achieving the goal set by the Lahore Resolution, Jinnah partially weakened the Two-Nation theory; on 11 August 1947 he said:

> You may belong to any religion or caste or creed-that has nothing to do with the business of the State…we are all starting with this fundamental principle that we are all citizens and equal citizens of one State.

Thus the Two-Nation theory was an intermediary position adopted by Jinnah. He was careful to emphasize that the Two-Nation theory was held also by some Hindus, notably Lala Lajpat Rai. The differences Jinnah pointed out between Hindus and Muslims, were, and are, real. The question is whether they were capable of political integration despite these fundamental differences.

The question that needs to be answered is, why did Jinnah formulate the Two-Nation theory in 1940 and discard it in 1947.

Here we have to study the essence of the Two-Nation theory. Not only Lala Lajpat Rai but other Hindu leaders had elaborated this theory. Gandhi, while inspecting the extremist Rashtriya Swayamsevak Sangh (RSS) camp in Wardha, had supported their creed by saying: 'Every community is entitled, indeed bound to organize itself, if it is to live as a separate entity'.[2] Of course he did not forsee then that a few years later the RSS would bring his life to its violent end. Even Jawaharlal Nehru inadvertently upheld the Two-Nation theory when Bengali nationalism made a bid to assert itself in 1947. Therefore, we have to examine whether the Two-Nation theory was valid as an instrument of partition or not.

The Two-Nation theory in India was put forward to protect a minority from a majority. In Pakistan the same Two-Nation theory would encroach on the rights of the minorities. This can be explained by a single example. The Muslims, being a minority in India, struggled to achieve separate electorates. Without these, they felt that their voice would not be heard. In Pakistan, General Ziaul Haq imposed separate electorates against the wishes of the minority. The minorities struggled to have this provision removed because they felt that separate electorates were marginalizing them and because of this provision they were unable to make their voice heard.

Therefore, the essence of political emancipation is securing measures for survival, the essence is not any theory. The religious parties in Pakistan have held that since Partition had been achieved by separate electorates, it should be retained, whether the minorities demand it or not.

A resolution was moved on 23 March 1940 at Lahore by Maulvi Abul Kassem Fazlul Haq who represented Bengal, a Muslim majority province, and was seconded by Chaudhry Khaliquzzaman representing UP, a Muslim minority province. It was this resolution of the AIML which was responsible for the creation of Pakistan.

The main resolution stated:

No constitutional plan would be workable in this country or acceptable to the Muslims unless it is designed on the following basic principles, viz., that geographically contiguous units are demarcated into regions which should be so constituted with such territorial adjustments as may be necessary, that the areas in which the Muslims are numerically in a majority, as in the north-western and eastern zones of India, should be grouped to constitute 'Independent states' in which the constituent units shall be autonomous and sovereign.

The text of the resolution is ambiguous. The name Pakistan is not mentioned. The areas which were to constitute the state demanded by the Muslim League are not mentioned by name, nor are they clearly demarcated. By using the word 'states' (in the plural) it is not clear whether Pakistan would consist of one state or more. Furthermore, 'autonomous' and 'sovereign' are not equal terms; states can be autonomous without being sovereign. whether this ambiguity was inadvertent or deliberate is also not clear.

Whatever the ambiguity, it definitely rules out a unitary state and points to a federal state. Even Fazlul Haq, as a politician, and Khaliquzzaman, as a historian proved to be revisionists. Fazlul Haq, as governor of East Bengal, and Khaliquzzaman in *Pathway to Pakistan,*[3] later expressed their reservations about Pakistan as a country and as a solution to the communal problem in India. The reality is discussed under the Cabinet Mission Plan.

Jinnah cleared some of the ambiguity in an interview with the Associate Press of America. He said that Pakistan was to be a democratic federal state comprising the existing provinces of the North-West Frontier, Balochistan, Sindh and Punjab in the west and Bengal and Assam in the east. From 1940 onwards, the Muslim League observed 23 March as Pakistan Day. The Muslim League had now introduced a new factor in the politics of India at a time when the British were fighting for survival in the Second World War.

THE CRIPPS MISSION 1942

The Second World War was determining every move of the British. On its part, the Congress had realized its mistake in resigning from provincial ministries. Being in office would have been tactically beneficial to the Congress at a time when they thought British rule would collapse before the Japanese onslaught which had taken Singapore and Burma (now Myanmar) and which was bombing Calcutta. The British were relieved that the Congress was not there to hinder their war efforts, but their ally, the United States of America, insisted that Britain enlist the active cooperation of Indian politicians. President Franklin Delano Roosevelt (1882–1945) expressed this view personally to Winston Churchill, the British prime minister, and the result was that Churchill had to send Sir Stafford Cripps (1889–1952) to India to seek a solution which would induct the political leadership of India into the war effort.

Sir Stafford Cripps had been the British ambassador to the USSR and was widely credited with bringing the USSR into the war on the side of Britain and against Germany. He was a socialist, a member of the Labour Party and a personal friend of Jawaharlal Nehru, the Congress leader. The president of the United States wanted Cripps to succeed in enlisting the Congress and Muslim League cooperation, while the British prime minister prayed that he would not.

The outcome of the Cripps Mission has become controversial. Some say that Cripps initially assured the Congress that they could enter the Viceroy's Executive Council which, by convention though not by constitution (GOI Act 1935), would be a cabinet, or a quasi-cabinet in the phrase of Sir Reginald Coupland. According to this version, Lord Linlithgow, the viceroy, complained of being sidetracked and Cripps had to modify his offer which the Congress then rejected. At one stage Cripps had assured Nehru that he would not let any British official, no matter how high, hold up an agreement; an obvious reference to the viceroy.

There was much bickering over whether an Indian or a British representative would exercise control over the conduct of war. A draft declaration was officially endorsed by Winston Churchill on 11 March 1942. Cripps declared on 29 March, that as soon as the war ended, an elected body would be charged with framing a new constitution for India. Cripps offered dominion status to India after the war with the option to leave the British Commonwealth. The Congress turned down the proposal and wanted immediate power. *Roy's*

Weekly described the Cripps offer as a 'post-dated check on a crashing bank', a comment popularly but wrongly attributed to Gandhi.

At one stage Cripps wondered why Nehru did not understand that even if he brought the Congress into government without changing the Constitution, as a 'quasi-cabinet' the viceroy would not be able to override it. It is reasonable to infer that the real reason behind the Congress's refusal was the non-accession clause. Peter Clarke, who has had access to the private papers of Sir Stafford Cripps, does not think so, and there was actually a Congress resolution which said that the Congress committee would not force any territorial unit to remain in India against 'their declared and established will'. However, during a private discussion which Cripps had with Maulana Azad and Nehru, it surfaced that the Congress leaders were contemplating a Pakistan which could secede five or ten years hence. The Congress was demanding immediate powers from the British and offering deferred (or delayed) power to the Muslim League. In 1946 the Congress was prepared to offer the Muslims even less.

The non-accession clause of the Cripps offer meant that provinces which wished to remain outside the proposed Union of India could do so, and if the non-acceding units wished to form a union of their own, this union would be at par with the Union of India; a constitutional and roundabout way of saying that the British would concede Pakistan. M.A. Jinnah thanked Cripps for recognizing the principle of Pakistan, but still did not accept the Cripps offer because the non-acceding provinces would have to vote in a joint electorate system, and not through separate electorates. Thus, for different reasons, both the Congress and the Muslim League turned down the Cripps offer.

THE QUIT INDIA MOVEMENT 1942

Since great expectations had been initially raised by Sir Stafford Cripps, the disappointment was deep. Cripps had made his offer in the expectation that the Congress and the Muslim League would cooperate in Britain's war against Germany. Gandhi persuaded the Congress to adopt a Quit India Resolution. At first Nehru and Sardar Patel resisted but finally agreed with Gandhi.

In the Muslim League, the Quit India Movement was fanning differences of opinion in the working committee. The Raja of Mahmudabad and G.M. Syed moved a resolution calling for the Muslim League to join the Quit India Movement. Ultimately, the Raja of Mahmudabad abstained and only G.M. Syed voted for the resolution. It must be mentioned that the Quit India Movement had created an emotional crisis. Police had fired upon students in Allahabad, Nehru's home town, and Hindu students appealed to their Muslim classmates to join them. However, Jinnah did not want participation in the Quit India Movement and instead coined the slogan 'Divide and Quit.'

Why the Muslim League chose to remain aloof from the Quit India Movement is a question often asked. Jinnah viewed the Quit India Movement with suspicion, considering it a Congress effort to force the British to transfer power only to the Congress, thereby leaving the Muslim League in the lurch. His suspicion was based on past experience. Jinnah recalled how, during the First World War, when he had opposed cooperation with the British, it had been Gandhi who had thwarted him by extending unconditional cooperation to the British. In 1918, Gandhi had written to Jinnah that independence would soon be achieved if their party became a recruiting agency for the British army. Jinnah had not understood Gandhi's logic then, and he did not understand his motives in 1942. While speaking on the war efforts, Jinnah recalled Gandhi's phrase, saying that: 'I could not play the role of a recruiting sergeant'. However, he added that the Muslim League was not non-cooperating. In other words, the non-cooperation of Gandhi was active, Jinnah's non-cooperation was passive. He said he could give the British much more trouble than Congress but the result of that would be either a change of masters or the fragmentation of India. He meant that if the British quit, the advancing Japanese would take over India, or some parts would fall as Burma (now Myanmar) and Singapore had. Even now Jinnah was showing concern for the unity of India but he opposed the Quit India Movement because he thought it was meant to pressurize the British into handing over power to the Congress alone leaving the Muslim League high and dry.

The British eventually subdued the Quit India Movement, the Japanese advance on India was halted, and the war ended in victory for the British and their allies.

SIMLA CONFERENCE AND THE 1945 ELECTIONS

In 1943, the British Prime Minister Winston Churchill replaced Viceroy Lord Linlithgow and appointed the Commander-in-Chief, Lord Wavell in his place. Churchill had expected that, being a military man, Lord Wavell would take no political initiative but the new viceroy, a conscientious man, made an attempt to break the political deadlock in the country by installing an interim government representative of Indian political parties. In his scheme, the viceroy and the commander-in-chief would continue to be British while all the members of the Viceroy's Executive Council would be Indian.

Unlike at the time of the Cripps offer, the Congress did not raise any objection to the conduct of war being directed by the British. The viceroy made it clear that this arrangement would last as long as the war with the

Japanese continued. The interim government would function under the existing constitution, i.e. GOI Act 1935.

The viceroy broadcast his proposals on 14 June 1945, simultaneously announcing the release of Gandhi and other Congress leaders. The Simla Conference opened on 25 June, and on 14 July Lord Wavell announced its failure apportioning the blame to himself. The Conference had actually failed because M.A. Jinnah, as president of the AIML, had said that since his party was the sole spokesman for the Indian Muslims, no other political party had the right to nominate any Muslim to the Viceroy's Executive Council. This contention was unacceptable to the Congress and the viceroy and thus the Conference failed and no interim government could be nominated.

Objectively the stand of the Muslim League could not be upheld in the light of its dismal performance in the 1937 elections. Before the AIML delegation left Simla, it called for fresh elections. These were held in December 1945 and January 1946. In the elections to the (central) Indian Legislative Assembly, the AIML secured all 30 Muslim seats. In the elections to the various provincial assemblies it won 446 out of a total of 495 Muslim seats. Thus the claim the AIML made in Simla, that it was the sole spokesman of Indian Muslims, was vindicated.

NOTES

1. Khalid bin Sayeed, *Pakistan: The Formative Phase*, Karachi: OUP, 1978, pp. 179, 197.
2. *Young India*, 6 January 1929.
3. Chaudhry Khaliquzzaman, *Pathway to Pakistan*, Lahore: Longman, 1961.

A BUL KASSEM FAZUL HAQ (b. Barisal, 1873–d. Dacca, 1962) moved the 23 March 1940 Resolution which culminated in the creation of Pakistan. In 1954, he stated at a Calcutta meeting that he could not understand the *raison d être* of Pakistan.[1] In 1916, he had fervently advocated the Lucknow Pact, although weightage to the Hindus would make Muslim majority precarious in Bengal, and in 1931, he opposed it. In 1918, Fazlul Haq became president of the all India Muslim League; and in 1941, he resigned from it. In 1939, he denounced Shyama Prasad Mookerji as being communal minded. In 1941, he included Mookerji in his Bengal cabinet. Thus, Fazlul Haq had a vacillating disposition and in consequence, suffered the most checkered career in the political history of South Asia. He also sometimes got what he had given. In 1954, he was denounced as a traitor for his Calcutta statement, and in 1956 he was appointed Pakistan's Minister of Interior.

Behind all these political moves was a most charismatic personality. He was the exemplar of the indigenous Bengali elite; intellectually exasperating, he had a heart of gold. He helped anyone who approached him, not hesitating to incur heavy debts in order to succor the needy. It was this trait which shone brightly amidst the ruins of his political career. Also, his volatile personality presented a spectacle rarely witnessed in the political arena. A case in point is the manner in which his Krishak Sramik Party, by ousting the rival Muslim United Party provided a reopening to the Muslim League in Bengal. According to M.A.H. Ispahani, he had briefed Fazlul Haq minutely on how to disrupt the All Bengal United Muslim Conference of August 1936. As the plan unfolded, Fazlul Haq reacted first with suspicion, then with disbelief and finally with amusement. According to the script, immediately after the Muslim United meeting, Fazlul Haq, head of the rival Krishak Sramik started to address the meeting:

> As expected, shouts from the dais were first heard calling upon him to sit down and to shut up. The more he was reprimanded, the more he insisted on speaking at the top of his voice. These shouts and counter-shouts made the conduct of serious business impossible. Appeal for silence was made, and I addressed the gathering with words to this effect:
>
> That as a dispute had unfortunately arisen, it was necessary that it be resolved and for that purpose that a neutral person of national status, namely Mr Mohammad Ali Jinnah, be invited to Calcutta immediately.[2]

In Pakistan, all his appointments, barring one, were provincial. As advocate general, chief minister, and governor during the crucial Language Movement, Fazlul Haq had remained uncommitted. That is why he did not enjoy the measure of success H.S. Suhrawardy enjoyed, even though it was brief. Fazlul Haq has also suffered for not having an influential biographer: Shaista Ikramullah wrote about the life of her cousin Huseyn Shaheed Suhrawardy, but she scarcely mentions that Fazlul Haq was her uncle. Her father and Fazlul Haq had married sisters.[3]

NOTES

1. H.S. Suhrawardy, *Memoirs*, Dhaka: The University Press, 1987, p. 86.
2. M.A.H. Ispahani, *Quaid-e-Azam Jinnah as I Knew Him,* 3rd ed., Karachi: Royal Book Co., 1976, pp. 23–4.
3. Rajmohan Gandhi, *Eight Lives: A Study of the Hindu-Muslim Encounter*, New York: State University of New York Press, 1986, p. 190.

CHAPTER 21

THE CABINET MISSION PLAN, 1946

Against the background of unfolding events at the end of the Second World War, Britain, with the help of her Allies had won the war, but in the effort had lost her economic ascendancy, a section of her population and its imperialist sentiments. The Conservative Party led by Winston Churchill (1874–1965) still nurtured hopes of an empire and great power status; but was defeated in the 1945 elections.

The Labour government under the new Prime Minister, Clement Atlee, was more conscious of the economic plight of Britain, and also more sympathetic to the cause of Indian independence. They realised that they had to transfer power to India. The question was, to whom should power be transferred? Left to itself, the Labour Party would have transferred power to the Indian National Congress (INC) as the overall majority party, but the Conservative Party, especially its leader, were aware of the pledges the British had given to the minorities and the Chamber of Princes. Recognizing that Muslims numbered ninety million, Churchill held the opinion that the word 'minorities had no relevance or sense when applied to masses of human beings numbered in many scores of millions.' He was later to publicly state this in parliament. The Conservative Party was then in opposition, but in the strong two-party system the opposition was powerful, and in the House of Lords, the Conservative Party had greater influence.

The Viceroy, Lord Wavell, desired a united India because it would serve the residual strategic and commercial interests of Britain. The Congress had their own justifications for wanting India to remain united. Both, thus, disagreed with Jinnah. However, Wavell realized that the Congress did not represent Muslims, and wanted Muslims to be given safeguards in the future constitution. The Congress considered safeguards unnecessary. They wanted a unitary government with a strong centre. The viceroy felt that the Muslims would be better protected in a federal system with a weak centre. The viceroy's fair-mindedness was proving to be a hindrance in the transfer of power, therefore Clement Atlee agreed to send three members of his cabinet to India. They were to seek an agreement among the parties, and if no agreement was forthcoming, to transfer power on the terms demanded by the Congress. On 20 February 1946, M.A. Jinnah had disapproved the decision to send a Cabinet Mission to India, but cooperated with it nevertheless.

The Congress leaders M.K. Gandhi and Jawaharlal Nehru dominated the proceedings from the beginning. Gandhi had anticipated that the Cabinet Mission would ultimately produce a document and he extracted a commitment from Pethick-Lawrence that such a document should be in the nature of a recommendation and not an award which would be binding on the parties. Lord Pethick-Lawrence did not disclose this to Lord Wavell, nor to the Congress President, Maulana Azad, and the question of his confiding in M.A. Jinnah did not arise. There was confusion during the negotiations and the secret undertaking was revealed to King George VI only after the Cabinet Mission had failed.

According to Sir Penderel Moon (d.1987), the Cabinet Mission decided that the Muslim League was to be offered two options:

1. Pakistan—with six provinces, which would be part of a common union with India and without sovereignty.
2. A fully sovereign Pakistan with the partition of Bengal and Punjab. The Pakistani Punjab would not include Gurdaspur.

These two options were disclosed to M.A. Jinnah except the clause pertaining to Gurdaspur. He considered both options: a sovereign Pakistan, which would result in dividing the Muslim community; an autonomous Pakistan which would consist of six provinces, but which would keep the Muslim community intact within one country. The Cabinet Mission pressed this option on him and sent CGS General Sir Arthur Smith to convince him. Smith told Jinnah that Indian security would be endangered if the country was divided. Jinnah said both Pakistan and Hindustan could have a military pact when there was war with outside forces, but not during peace time.

Nevertheless, there are indications that the defence of South Asia weighed on him. It is worth recalling that during the Quit India Movement, Jinnah had said that he neither wanted a change of masters (i.e. the Japanese) nor the fragmentation of India. Perhaps this sentiment was stronger in him than he realized. There is a body of scholars, led by Ayesha Jalal, which holds that Hindu–Muslim parity within a united India was Jinnah's real demand. The Muslim provinces would be grouped together and derive maximum autonomy. However, Gandhi had let it be known to the Cabinet Mission on 8 May 1946 that he did not favour grouping, and parity was worse than a sovereign Pakistan.

Sir Stafford Cripps and Lord Pethick-Lawrence insisted that the acceptance of 'grouping' by the Congress, and the acceptance of a common Union of India by the Muslim League would be a fair basis for agreement between the two parties. Therefore, on 12 May 1946, the Muslim League sent its constitutional proposals conceding a union which would deal with defence and foreign affairs, but have no legislature and no powers of taxation. There would be a Pakistan group of provinces and a Hindustan group of provinces which would contribute voluntarily towards the expenditure of the union. Even such a vital concession by the Muslim League was not appreciated, and the Cabinet Mission published its own plan on 16 May 1946, in which the Muslim League proposals had been further diluted.

Thus it seems that the Cabinet Mission incorporated the essence but not the safeguards that the AIML had proposed four days earlier. After the Cabinet Mission Plan was published, Liaquat Ali Khan sent M.A. Jinnah, on 21 May 1946, some typed objections to it. Far from proving to be a stepping stone for Pakistan as the Muslim League leadership asserted, Liaquat Ali Khan argued that the Congress, as the majority party, would control the coercive apparatus of state, the armed forces and the police; it would not only physically prevent secession, but also wipe out the given safeguards. However, M.A. Jinnah favoured acceptance. M.A.H. Ispahani has revealed that the Cabinet Mission told the Muslim League that it would have to accept its 16 May 1946 plan without change or face the consequences, which were riots. It transpired that the Cabinet Mission was willing to let the Congress modify its plan. On 17 May, Mahatma Gandhi, in his journal the *Harijan,* wrote that there was 'no take it or leave it business about the Plan, and the provinces were free to reject the very idea of grouping'. This he could write because of the undertaking he had extracted from Lord Pethick-Lawrence. The Muslim League disregarded this editorial of Gandhi's, thinking that the British would uphold their own scheme, regardless of whatever anyone wrote.

On 6 June 1946, the AIML council voted to accept the Cabinet Mission Plan, saying that it could be a stepping stone to Pakistan. Jinnah later explained that the AIML had accepted it as it would give Muslims sufficient autonomy to develop economically and culturally.

THE CABINET MISSION PLAN, 16 MAY 1946

Three Tier Administration

Union   Provinces   Group A   Group B   Group C

There were two sections: (a) The Long-term Plan, according to which **provinces** would be grouped together.

Group A: would have all the Hindu majority provinces: Bombay, Madras, Bihar, UP, Orrisa and Central Province.

Group B: would consist of North-Western Muslim majority provinces: Sindh, Punjab, NWFP and Balochistan.

Group C: would consist of North-Eastern Muslim majority provinces: Bengal and Assam.

The groups would frame their own constitutions; what powers the provinces would decide to delegate to the groups would be determined by these constitutions. A constitution for the Union would be enacted at the next stage. A province could opt out of a group after the first elections under the new constitution were held, but not before.

The Union would have a legislature, powers of taxation and three subjects: Defence, Communications necessary for Defence, and Foreign Affairs.

THE DOCUMENTS ISSUED BY THE CABINET MISSION

The British Government issued four documents on framing the constitution and formation of the interim government in 1946.

1. The main and basic document was the **Cabinet Mission Plan**. It was also called the State Paper of 16 May 1946.
2. The 25 May 1946 Statement stated clearly that the grouping of provinces was necessary. The Congress had asserted that the grouping of provinces was not compulsory, and that a province could stay away from a group from the beginning. This statement was issued to contradict the Congress interpretation.
3. The 16 June 1946 Statement outlined the Short-term Plan, or the formation of an Interim Government. Paragraph 8 of this statement said that if one party refused to accept the Long-term plan of 16 May, the Interim Government would be formed by those parties which had accepted. This meant that if Congress did not accept, the Muslim League would be invited to join the Interim Government.
4. The 6 December 1946 Statement was issued from London. On 25 June 1946, the INC accepted the 16 May Plan but with its own interpretation. The Congress had said: 'While adhering to our views we accept your proposals, and are prepared to work them with a view to achieve our objective.'

Their 'views' were that grouping was not necessary and their objective was to form the Interim Government alone. In Lord Wavell's view this was not a genuine acceptance as it did not adhere to the 16 May or 25 May Statements. The Congress leaders said that it did not matter what the Cabinet delegation intended its Statement to mean, it only mattered what the Congress understood it to mean. The 6 December Statement contradicted the Congress position and upheld the AIML position that grouping was essential. The Congress said that this 'created a new situation.'

The Congress had always criticized the demand for Pakistan; it did not believe in dividing the country. M.A. Jinnah and the Muslim League had accepted the formula of 16 May 1946 according to which India was not to be divided. Instead, Hindu majority and Muslim majority provinces were grouped so that zonal sub federations were created. The Congress and Mahasabha ridiculed the AIML for its weakness and said that 'Mr Jinnah had come to his senses.' It is not known why they pushed the Muslim League after having gained a united India. Why did they object to the grouping of Muslim majority provinces when the Congress would dominate the Union? Another enigmatic question is, even if the Congress disliked grouping, why did they not wait for the British to leave before saying so?

The AIML was aware that the Congress did not like the grouping clause, but they thought that the British would uphold their Plan. However, on 10 July 1946, Jawaharlal Nehru told a Bombay press conference that the Congress did not accept grouping and was not bound by any agreement except that it had decided, for the moment, to enter the Constituent Assembly.

Now the AIML had no choice. All the safeguards it had accepted in lieu of a sovereign Pakistan were proving illusory. The AIML council reassembled at Bombay on 29 July 1946 and withdrew its acceptance of the Cabinet Mission Plan. It also announced Direct Action. There were two Muslim leaders of India, M.A. Jinnah, who wished to see India divided, and Abul Kalam Azad who wished to keep India united. Abul Kalam Azad has written a book called *India Wins Freedom* in which he calls the Cabinet Mission Plan a scheme that would have preserved the unity of India and still have solved the communal problem. He blames Nehru, not Jinnah, for wrecking the Plan. The latter's interpretation he accepted as correct. Jinnah had given united India a chance, but the Congress ruined that chance. In view of Azad's admission, it is wrong to imply that Jinnah and Azad held opposing views, because both had reached the same conclusion.

DIRECT ACTION

At the 29 July 1946 Bombay meeting, Jinnah had said that he was now bidding farewell to constitutional methods and calling for Direct Action. This came as a surprise to the Congress because Jawaharlal Nehru had written to Sir Stafford Cripps that the Muslim League was incapable of Direct Action.

At a press conference, Liaquat Ali Khan said that Direct Action meant any action against the law. The AIML fixed 16 August 1946 as Direct Action Day. All over India the day passed peacefully but in Calcutta, where Huseyn Shaheed Suhrawardy led the provincial government, a holiday was declared. This resulted in the Great Calcutta killings. When the viceroy visited Calcutta, he upbraided H.S. Suhrawardy for starting the Hindu–Muslim riots.

Suhrawardy politely told the viceroy to set up an inquiry committee under the Chief Justice, Sir Patrick Spens. This was done, and in his report the chief justice exonerated Suhrawardy, or the Muslims, of having started the riots. It was clear however, that once Hindus started the riots, the Muslims also retaliated most fiercely. As a result of the Calcutta riots, Muslims of Noakhali in East Bengal killed Hindus and the Noakhali riots spread to Bihar where the Muslims suffered most.

In the midst of this bloodshed, the Congress Party, formed the interim government on 2 September 1946. It was only on 26 October that the AIML bloc, led by Liaquat Ali Khan joined the Interim Government. Nehru's official designation was vice-president of the Viceroy's Executive Council, but he insisted on being called the prime minister of India although he had accepted office on the condition that the GOI Act 1935 be retained as the constitution for India. In the meantime, a parliamentary delegation from Britain led by Professor Robert Richards visited India, and on its return met with Clement Atlee and pressed him to accept the Pakistan issue.

Early in 1947, Congress members of the interim government insisted that the Muslim League members be expelled because they were not attending the Constituent Assembly of India which had started functioning in December 1946. Once again the question of whether the Congress had accepted the 16 May 1946 Cabinet Mission Plan came up. Congress had said that it accepted the Plan but would not accept the grouping clause. On 6 December, when both Congress and Muslim League leaders were in London, the British government conceded that the AIML interpretation of the Plan was correct; in other words grouping of provinces was an essential feature of the 16 May Plan and the Congress interpretation, that the Cabinet Mission Plan could be accepted without grouping, was wrong. Nevertheless, since the AIML had formally withdrawn its acceptance, the Congress said it had no right to remain in the government.

While participating in the interim government, Liaquat Ali Khan had taken the lead in the division of the armed forces. Lord Mountbatten who succeeded Lord Wavell as viceroy in 1947, had intended to divide the country without dividing the armed forces. He hoped to be the governor-general of both India and Pakistan, and by this method undo partition. Liaquat Ali Khan told Lord Mountbatten that Hindu officers of the Indian army were planning a coup, a development which would prevent partition. When Mountbatten did not believe Liaquat Ali Khan, Jinnah accompanied him to meet the viceroy and convinced him of the impending coup. Following this meeting, Mountbatten agreed to divide the army.

On 28 February, Liaquat Ali Khan, as finance member, presented the last budget of United India. He had imposed a business profit tax of 25 per cent on all profits exceeding Rs 100,000. Liaquat Ali Khan said he was following

Islamic principles by taxing the rich and providing relief to the poor. The people of India termed it the 'Poor Man's Budget'. Actually Liaquat had drawn up an anti-British budget, but because it hurt the rich of every community, the largest community, the Hindus, complained. Among the plutocrats who were being taxed were those who provided funds to the Congress. They were angry. There were many more rich Hindus than rich Muslims, but despite having a majority in the Indian Legislative Assembly, the Congress did not dare defeat the budget because they knew that there were many more poor Hindus than there were poor Muslims. Abul Kalam Azad has written that Sardar Vallabhbhai Patel was so annoyed with Liaquat's budget that he was willing to consider partition seriously. According to Hugh Tinker, Sardar Patel said that, 'If the Muslim League did not accept the Cabinet Mission Plan, then the Congress desired Partition'.

Eventually, the Congress agreed to the creation of Pakistan. Why the Congress preferred partition of the country rather than grouping of provinces is not clear unless we accept the view that the Congress thought that partition would be temporary. They thought that Pakistan without industries would not be economically viable and would collapse. Whatever the reason, Independence and Partition were to come about simultaneously under the 3 June Plan.

Maulana Abul Kalam Azad's (b. Khem Kharan, 1888,—d. New Delhi, 1958) real name was Mohyuddin Ahmad. Azad is the exemplar for those intellectuals who hold that the partition of India was a mistake, since it weakened India, as well as the Muslims of India. Such people think that if Abul Kalam Azad and not M.A. Jinnah had been followed, all bitterness and strife would have been avoided. Here we consider this line of argument.

Azad began his career as a journalist in Calcutta, editing *Nairang-i-Alam*, in 1900, and *Al-Misbah*, in 1901. Early in his life, Azad came under the influence of Sir Syed Ahmad Khan, and wrote a poem, in 1901, to commemorate the coronation of King Edward VII. He made his revolutionary impact with the launch of *Al-Hilal* (1912—1915). When the British closed it down, he launched *Al-Balagh* (1915–1916). These journals established him as a stylist of high repute, and his political commentaries began gaining him admirers. At around this time he joined Congress. His journalism saw him interned at Ranchi, from 8 July 1916 to 27 December 1919. On his release, Azad met Gandhi for the first time. During the same time, Azad made a bid to become Imam-ul-Hind. Maulana Abdul Bari said: 'Azad is ready to accept, I have no objection.' However his candidature did not find general acceptance. He then floated the idea of having an Amir-i-Hind. The CID report of 1 April 1920 stated that Azad wished for the position.[1]

Earlier in 1913, Azad had joined the Muslim League, and remained a member till 1929, and resigned only when his efforts to obtain a party majority in favour of the Nehru Report failed. Azad has suppressed mention of his membership of the Muslim League from both his memoirs *India Wins Freedom* and *Azad Ki Kahani, Azad Ki Zabani*.

In 1923, at the age of 35, Azad became the youngest president of the Indian National Congress. Azad was jailed from 1942 to 1945, for participating in the Quit India Movement. It was during deliberations over the Quit India Movement that Azad first ran afoul of Gandhi who called for his resignation for not supporting the Non-cooperation proposal. From then on his high profile presence in the Congress was only a façade. On 13 July 1942, Gandhi wrote to Nehru with regard to Azad: 'I do not understand him, nor does he understand me. We are drifting apart on the Hindu–Muslim question as well as on other questions. Therefore I suggest that the Maulana should relinquish Presidentship.'[2] Gandhi's assessment was correct, as he was taking Congress solicitude about Muslims at face value. During the visit of the Cabinet delegation, in 1946, Azad's solution to the communal problem coincided with that of the Muslim League: maximum autonomy to the provinces, with a centre having only defence, foreign affairs and communications; substantially what M.A. Jinnah had proposed on 12 May 1946. Azad wrote a letter to the Cabinet ministers embodying these proposals, but denied it to Gandhi while Gandhi held his letter in his hand.[3] Azad next wrote to say that the Congress would not nominate a Muslim to the interim government.[4] In this also, he exceeded his brief, and his undertaking was disowned by the Congress.

He was extricated from this imbroglio by Nehru, yet he unfairly singled out Nehru for denunciation for wrecking the Cabinet Mission plan on 10 July 1946. In *India Wins Freedom*, Azad passes over his own, and Gandhi's role in opposing the Cabinet Mission Plan.

After independence, Azad remained minister of education till his death. Thirty pages of his memoirs—that Azad had withheld for thirty years—were published, in 1988—the year of his birth centenary. As a religious scholar, Azad was both erudite and enlightened. His *Tarjuman-al-Quran* (1932 and 1936) was a landmark in exegesis. He enjoys an enviable position as an Urdu litterateur: his belle letters—written in the grand style, being highly esteemed. These are evident in *Tazkira* (1919) and *Ghubar-i-Khatir* (1946).

NOTES

1. G.I. Home Poll 180/1921, CID Report on Bihar *Ulama* Conference, 25, 26 June 1921 in David Page, *Prelude to Partition*.
2. Stanley Wolpert, *Gandhi's Passion*, New York: Oxford University Press, 2001, p. 203 vide Gandhi to Nehru dated 13 July 1942.
3. Sudhir Ghosh, *Gandhi's Emissary*, London: Cresset Press, 1967, p. 108.
4. Ibid., p. 167.

CHAPTER 22

THE PARTITION PLAN, 3 JUNE 1947

The 3 June 1947 Plan was announced simultaneously in the House of Lords, the House of Commons and at Viceregal House in New Delhi. It is also known as the Mountbatten Plan because it was announced by Lord Mounbatten, the last viceroy. M.A. Jinnah on behalf of the AIML, Jawaharlal Nehru on behalf of the INC and Sardar Baldev Singh, on behalf of the Sikh community followed the viceroy in speaking to the nation over the radio.

Under the 3 June Plan, the British would transfer power to two successor authorities, the Congress and the Muslim League, meaning in territorial terms the dominions of India and Pakistan, which would remain within the British Commonwealth. The 565 princely states in India included Kashmir and Kurwai which comprised a territory of 144 square miles. British paramountcy over them would not be transferred to the two dominions and consequently would lapse constitutionally. Thus the third option of remaining independent, and not joining either dominion was kept open for the princely states while it was denied to provinces, as in the case of Bengal.

The Indian Independence Act of 1947 received King George VI's assent on 18 June 1947. This Act expressly provided for the partition of Bengal and the Punjab. The Act also provided for the continuation of the GOI Act 1935 until such time as the two dominions framed their own constitutions. Until then the governor-general could adapt the GOI Act 1935 to suit the peculiar requirements of his dominion. The office of the secretary of state for India was abolished. Lord Listowel was the last secretary of state.

The Congress was the first to accept the 3 June Plan by demanding the partition of the Punjab and Bengal and in this indirect way they made known their agreement to the partition of India. Conversely, it was the partition of the two provinces which prevented the Muslim League from accepting the Plan immediately. Jinnah could concede only a personal and provisional nod of acceptance. Lord Mountbatten told Jinnah it would be impossible to hold the Plan until such time as the AIML council assembled. (He thought the Congress would retract, as it had from the Cabinet Mission Plan). Mountbatten, in this way threatened Jinnah with the permanent loss of Pakistan if he did not give an immediate and firm acceptance, but even this threat did not work. Lord Mountbatten then took it upon himself to speak for the AIML council and expressed his willingness to accept the blame if the AIML council did not ratify his Plan.

The partition of the provinces caused the 3 June Plan a rough passage in the AIML council. Prominent members said that the Plan should be rejected because the territory being offered was almost the same which was offered by C. Rajagopalachari in 1944. Maulana Hasrat Mohani protested the loudest and said that a truncated Pakistan should not be accepted. Jinnah replied that he had not accepted the Plan and that it was the AIML council's privilege to accept or reject it. He added however, that there could be no modification of the Plan, which had to be either completely accepted or completely rejected. Some members said the Muslims left behind in India would suffer, some members who would be left behind said that at least a section of Muslims would be free; Abdul Hamid of Assam was one of these. The most memorable words were spoken by Sir Ghulam Hussain Hidayatullah, the chief minister of Sindh:

> We will rapidly industrialize our country and provide a haven of refuge to Muslim traders and craftsmen who would choose to migrate to Sindh from the Muslim minority provinces. We have removed the consideration of Sindhi and non-Sindhi from our province and we will see that Sindh will soon progress far.

Abul Hashim, the general secretary of the Bengal Muslim League, was disappointed that the 3 June Plan did not provide for the independence of Bengal. At a later date the Congress wanted the provision of independence to be given to the NWFP, but Lord Mountbatten said that since the Congress had rejected that option in the case of Bengal, it could not be reintroduced in the case of the NWFP.

The AIML council session was held *in camera*. The AIML council accepted the 3 June Plan under protest and authorized its President M.A. Jinnah, to take 'further necessary action'. This was unacceptable to the Congress leaders, particularly Nehru and Sardar Patel, who wanted a clear-cut acceptance of the 3 June Plan before the Congress ratified it. Liaquat Ali Khan countered Sardar Patel by reminding him that after the AIML had accepted the Cabinet Mission Plan, the Congress had defeated them by proposing so many reservations that AIML had to withdraw its acceptance. Lord Mountbatten accepted undertakings from both the Congress and the AIML simultaneously. The AIML also undertook to term their acceptances 'a compromise settlement'. The stage was now set for the creation of Pakistan.

MAULANA HASRAT MOHANI (b. Mohan, Unnao district, UP, India, 1878–d. Lucknow, 1951) was the maverick and gadfly of the South Asian freedom struggle. He was an extremist in politics, a romantic in poetry, and an ascetic in character. By all criteria, Hasrat was a remarkable man, and had he been made of sterner stuff, his image would have been as well known as Mahatma Gandhi's. In the 1907 Surat session of the Congress, Hasrat proposed the policy which proved to be the precursor of non-violent protest. Of the three courses available, Hasrat said that we should not accept the humiliation of being beggars, neither should we risk violence, but rather we should take the path of defensive resistance. Hasrat also championed Bolshevism, refusing to accept that it was in conflict with Islam. He convened a session of the All-India Communist Party, at Kanpur, in 1925. When the Khilafat Movement began, Hasrat joined it fervently. On 23 November 1919, he moved a resolution calling for a progressive boycott of European goods. His resolution was passed over the opposition of Mahatma Gandhi and Seth Chotani. On 1 June 1920, at the Allahabad Khilafat Conference, Hasrat horrified non-Muslim delegates when he vowed to join any Afghan army, in order to drive the British from India. On 23 October 1921, at the Agra Provincial (Khilafat) Conference, Hasrat not only called for people to resign from the army and the police, but also for a declaration of complete freedom. On such occasions, Hasrat's stand was exasperating to the Congress, as indeed, it was to the Muslim League. Once, in 1942, when Hasrat was violently opposing the Cripps proposals, Miss Fatima Jinnah was infuriated. Jinnah pacified his sister by saying that Hasrat was incorruptible.

This attribute of Hasrat's remained unquestionable. Jinnah's tribute had come in the aftermath of severe political differences. When the Simon Commission was formed and the Muslim League was split, Hasrat sided with the pro-British faction of Sir Muhammad Shafi, rather than the anti-British faction of Jinnah. Hasrat later explained his conduct, by saying that he had wished for all Muslims to be united in one organization; and in the expectation that if the conservative element did not support complete independence, 'it will at least not dilute the demand by calling for dominion status'.

Hasrat's expectation that he would be able to prevail over the loyalist majority was unrealistic in view of his own conduct. Hasrat's editorial, on 25 February 1930, for the *Mustaqbil*, Kanpur, was quite uncalled for:

> As far as participation in the Round Table Conference and negotiating with the British is concerned…Jinnah, Shafi and [Sir Muhammad] Yaqub are capable. Hasrat will not be able to do this, and he will not interfere in this matter—on the condition, that in the matter of complete independence, they should also not interfere and should leave it to Hasrat, Muhammad Ali and Abul Kalam……

With all his concern for complete independence, there came a stage when Hasrat was willing to settle for even less than dominion status.[1] He was a man of principle;

he suffered rigorous imprisonment from 1910–1912, for not revealing that the anti-British articles included in his edited *Urdu-i-Mualla* were written by Syed Sulaiman Nadvi and Iqbal Ahmad Suhail. More terms in prison would follow. But Hasrat was like a Greek hero imbued with the defect of inconsistency. After taking the lead in promoting non-violent agitation, he proposed the use of violence in the joint Congress/Muslim League/Khilafat meeting, in December 1921. In mid-March 1922, Hasrat favoured dropping non-cooperation altogether. Inconsistency can be detected in all the great leaders of the freedom struggle, but the tragedy is that Hasrat's inconsistency was not anchored to any great political vision. Hasrat never lost his courage. In the Indian Parliament, he strongly criticized the invasion of Hyderabad.

The strong support Hasrat received from his wives, caused his lyrics to be as sweet as his political invectives were bitter. He performed the last of many *Hajjs*, in 1950, and in the following year faced death with complete composure.

NOTE

1. Ahmad Salim (ed.), *Hasrat Ki Syasat (The Politics of Hasrat)*, Karachi: Pakistan Study Centre, University of Karachi, 2000, p. 452.

CHAPTER 23

THE RADCLIFFE AWARD

Only one step remained before the British withdrew from the subcontinent. This was the demarcation of boundaries between India and Pakistan, running through the Punjab and Bengal, as well as the district of Sylhet in Assam. The terms of reference were drafted by the Congress, and sent to the viceroy on 12 June 1947. They were:

> The Boundary Commission is instructed to demarcate the boundaries of the two parts of the Punjab on the basis of ascertaining the contiguous majority areas of Muslims and non-Muslims. In doing so, it will also take into account other factors.

The same terms were repeated for Bengal with the word 'Bengal' being substituted for 'Punjab'.

The nominees to the commission were, two Congress and two Muslim League members of high judicial standing, under a chairman. The members for Punjab were Mr Justice Mehr Chand Mahajan, Mr Justice Teja Singh (Congress) and Mr Justice Din Mohammad and Mr Justice Mohammad Munir (Muslim League). The members for Bengal were Mr Justice Bijan Kumar Mukherji, Mr Justice C.C. Biswas (Congress), Mr Justice Saleh Muhammad Akram and Mr Justice S.A. Rahman (Muslim League). Sir Cyril Radcliffe was the chairman for both commissions.

Sir Cyril Radcliffe's name was first proposed by Lord Listowell, the secretary of state for India. It was then conveyed to the Congress and Muslim League by Lord Ismay, the chief of the viceroy's staff. When Lord Mountbatten first mentioned Radcliffe's name to Jinnah, he made a non-committal comment that he would need time to consider Radcliffe's nomination. Lord Ismay in his *Memoirs* asserts that Radcliffe's conduct was unassailable because he did not accept any payment for his work. This is contradicted in the *Transfer of Power Papers* which show that high fees were negotiated between Lord Listowell and Lord Jowitt. Radcliffe's awards became controversial when, in Punjab, Muslim majority areas Gurdaspur, Ferozepur and Zira were given to India. A series of documents has long been available to show that Radcliffe, almost at the last moment, departed from his judiciously considered award, under pressure from 'authorities in Delhi'.

With respect to Gurdaspur, which provided India an all-weather access to Kashmir, suggestions had been pouring in, *before* Lord Mountbatten's appointment as viceroy, more than a year before Partition. Vapal Panguni Menon (1899–1966) wrote to Lord Wavell on 17 July 1946 to stress the strategic importance of Gurdaspur to India. Menon next wrote to George Abell (private secretary to the viceroy) asking for Gurdaspur to be excluded from Pakistan.[1] Sir Penderel Moon revealed in 1973 that the Cabinet Mission proposed giving to Jinnah the Muslim majority areas of the Punjab *excluding* Gurdaspur.

On 4 June 1947, Lord Mountbatten told a press conference that the accession of Gurdaspur to Pakistan was unlikely. Not satisfied with this, Vengalil Krishna Menon (1897–1974) Nehru's confidant, wrote to Lord Mountbatten that Anglo–Indian relations would suffer if Pakistan was strengthened with the accession of Kashmir.[2] V. Krishna Menon had asked Mountbatten to destroy his letter, but Mountbatten chose to preserve it. On 17 June Nehru wrote to Mountbatten directly asking for Kashmir to be given to India. 'It is absurd to think that Pakistan would create trouble if this happens' reasoned Nehru. These letters which are still preserved, clearly prove that India's claim of obtaining an Instrument of Accession from the Maharaja of Kashmir was false. Alastair Lamb has shown such an Instrument does not exist. The reasons for the tribal incursion which India cited, was to save Muslims of Poonch from annihilation.

On 25 February 1948, Philip Noel Baker, secretary of state for common-wealth relations wrote to Prime Minister Clement Atlee that there was reason to believe that Radcliffe had altered his award after showing the first draft to 'authorities in Delhi'. Baker, in a hand-written paragraph sought Atlee's permission to 'warn' Sir Zafrullah Khan, Pakistan's foreign minister, from pursuing an inquiry regarding the role of Lord Mountbatten.[3] In spite of these sentiments Baker was dismissed by Atlee on Nehru's complaint that he was unsympathetic to India. Many years later he told Richard Symonds that he would write the true story of the Kashmir dispute, even if it meant going to jail.[4]

FEROZEPUR AND ZIRA

On 11 August, Chaudhry Mohammad Ali saw a map in Lord Ismay's study which showed Gurdaspur as part of India, but Ferozepur and Zira still as parts of Pakistan. Nehru and the Maharaja of Bikaner put pressure on Mountbatten to have this award withdrawn. With two strokes, the injustice to Pakistan was done and with this loss, Pakistan lost the control of its rivers.

THE ROLE OF H.C. BEAUMONT

H. Christopher Beaumont, private secretary to Radcliffe in 1947, issued a statement on 24 February 1992, that Radcliffe had altered the awards of Ferozepur and Zira at the last moment at the behest of Mountbatten. 'Grave discredit to both', said Beaumont. His own conduct during Partition caused Justice M. Munir to complain of Beaumont's pro India bias. Beaumont had tried to mislead Radcliffe into believing that there was no bridge on the river Beas which would allow Sikhs access to Amritsar from East Punjab.

The 9 August 1947 diary entry of W.H.J. Christie, P. Noel Baker's admission to Atlee in 1948 and H.C. Beaumont's confession of 1992 all confirm that the Radcliffe Awards were grossly unfair. Though termed unfair and even 'perverse' by Jinnah they were accepted because Pakistan was honour-bound to do so. There is no other document of the twentieth century that has caused more wars, repression and human misery than the Radcliffe Awards.

NOTES

1. On 23 January 1946 in S.M. Burke, and S.A.D. Qureshi, *The British Raj in India*, Karachi: Oxford University Press, 1995. Appendix B, p. 3.
2. Alastair Lamb, *Kashmir: A Disputed Legacy*, Karachi: Oxford University Press, 1992, p. 108.
3. S.M. Burke and S.A.D. Qureshi, op. cit., p. 562.
4. Richard Symonds, *In the Margins of Independence*, Karachi: Oxford University Press, 2001, p. 96.

CHAPTER 24

ROLE OF THE MAJORITY PROVINCES

Neither the role nor the aspirations of the Muslim majority provinces and the Muslim minority provinces were identical. The differences were nuanced but they were apparent. The Muslims in the provinces in which they were in a majority, and the Muslims in the provinces in which they were in a minority were situated separately, and since the beginning of their political struggle, this became noticeable. The Simla Deputation was inclined to the demands of the minority provinces, while the foundation of the All-India Muslim League (AIML) was geared to the aspirations of the majority provinces. In the 1916 Lucknow Pact, while the demand for Separate Electorates was common the demand for weightages was not equally shared. While weightages to Muslims in minority provinces, no matter how generous, did not affect their status materially, the reciprocal weightage provision in the majority provinces had the effect of reducing the Muslims of Bengal and Punjab to minorities.

On the issue of cooperating with the Simon Commission, the AIML split up with the original president Sir Mohammad Shafi favouring cooperation, the factional president Mohammad Ali Jinnah was leading the boycott. When Jinnah formulated the Delhi Muslim Proposals, majority provinces Muslims resisted the move to supersede Separate Electorates. When the trust placed by Jinnah on the Congress was belied in the shape of the Nehru Report, all Muslims came together under 14 points.

Provincial imperatives were strong during 1937 elections, and the AIML could show a presence in only two minority provinces, UP and Bombay. It was only in the 1937 Lucknow session of the AIML that leaders from the majority and minority provinces shared the same platform, having become uncomfortable at the prospect of Congress replacing the British at the centre. Even then, the Jinnah–Sikandar Pact proved to be a drag, and weakened Jinnah's bargaining position during the Second World War

Two nation theories had been floated by leaders both Hindu and Muslim, from time to time, but the empirical quotient derived only from the Muslim majority areas, the partition of Bengal in 1905 and the separation of Sindh in 1937. These territorial demarcations proved more convincing than verbal theories, and had the Punjab undergone a religious divide at the same time as the separation of Sindh, the borders would have been more equitably drawn, and would have been less contention than in 1947 when the dividing line provoked a holocaust.

Since one of the major problems besetting Pakistan at establishment, was the continuous influx of refugees having suffered pogroms in minority areas, the contribution of the Muslim majority provinces did not immediately impress itself on the historian. However, within the last two decades a number of works have appeared and the reader is enabled to view the contribution of the majority provinces more clearly.

Sindh has been called the gateway to Islam in South Asia, and has also proved to be the gateway to Pakistan. Sindh offered the greatest military resistance to the British and had always displayed battle ready defiance. In this preparedness, the Hurs, the followers of the Pirs of Pagara, formed the core. In 1826, the then Pir Pagaro Sibghatullah Shah Rashidi ordered the Hurs to aid the Mujahideen of Syed Ahmad Barelvi against the Sikhs. The Hurs as a permanently armed cadre was a constant thorn in the side of the British, and from the beginning of the Khilafat Movement to the Second World War the Hurs kept up a progressively increasingly armed resistance. Finally the movement of the Hurs had to be put down concertedly, the only military distraction the British suffered during the Second World War, when South Asian troops were fighting for the British in far off lands. In 1943 a nonchalant Pir Pagara was executed by the British. This created great resentment as Muslims compared this execution with the mild treatment of Gandhi, who had been in open rebellion since 1920.

The next momentous development, already covered, was the setting up of the Sindh Madressatul Islam in Karachi by Hasan Ali Effendi on 14 November 1887. The alumni of the Sindh Madressa constituted the cadre of political leaders—led by Jinnah which achieved partition. The first issue before these leaders was to secure the separation of Sindh from the Bombay presidency. Ironically this demand was first put forward from the platform of the Congress in 1913, as Hindu Sindhis at that time resented the dominance of their co-religionists in Bombay and Ahmadabad. It was only later, when the political atmosphere was charged with communalism, that this demand was taken over by the Muslim League, most pointedly in the Delhi Muslim Proposals and the Fourteen Points during the Round Table Conference. This objective was pursued with great persistence by Sir Shanawaz Bhutto. In the Government of India Act 1935 this demand was conceded. The separation was affected on 1 April 1936.

The Muslim League did not have a strong presence in the after math of the Sindh separation in 1937. Sindh Muslims like their counterparts in Bengal and Bihar had a number of small parties. On the eve of the 1937 elections, Jinnah was able to persuade only four politicians, all from urban Sindh to contest on the Muslim League tickets. In the 1 February 1937 elections there were upsets, and both stalwarts, Sir Shanawaz Bhutto and Sir Abdullah Haroon lost. Consequently, two ministries were formed, under Sir Ghulam Hussain Hidayatullah (March 1937 to March 1938) and Allah Bux (March 1938 to March 1940) which were dependant on Congress members for their majority.

It was during this period of exclusion that the Sindh Muslim League held a conference at Karachi (8 to 12 October 1938). Delegates from all over India attended including Jinnah, Liaquat and Mahmudabad. Resolution No. 5 proved to be the operative one, calling upon the All India Muslim League to devise a scheme of constitution under which Muslims may attain full independence. The Director, Intelligence Bureau characterized their resolution, on 16 November 1938 as going 'Further than the Pakistan scheme'. It was again during this session that Jinnah stated that he was proud to be a Sindhi, and also that he had been born in Sindh.[1]

In 1939 the communal polarization was accentuated by the Manzilgah Mosque controversy, an old monument at Sukkur, claimed by both Hindus and Muslims. This claim led to Muslim demonstrations against Allah Bux, and ultimately caused the fall of his ministry. It was their perception of the Congress attitude as communal that led leaders like G.M. Syed to resign from Congress and join the Muslim League. As adherent or adversary, G.M. Syed cast a long shadow over Muslim politics in Sindh. Concerned now over these developments, the Congress sent Abul Kalam Azad to negotiate a pact with Sindhis leaders which called for cooperation especially in the Sindh assembly.

The Azad pact was signed in November 1940 by G.M. Syed and M. Ayub Khuhro, but denounced by Hidayatullah. It was only on 22 October 1942, that Sir Ghulam Hussain Hidayatullah was able to form a full fledged Muslim League ministry in Sindh. This ministry lasted till independence, Hidayatullah's fortitude earning for him the ire of Jawaharlal Nehru. Most crucially, the Muslim League ministry remained intact while negotiations with the Cabinet Mission were in progress.

On 3 March 1943, G.M. Syed moved a resolution in the Sindh Assembly, endorsing the 23 March 1940 Lahore Resolution. Unfortunately, during a clash between the Sindh Muslim League Party and Ministry, Hidayatullah and Syed fell out. In the ensuing 1946 elections the Muslim League won 27 out of 35 seats in the Sindh Assembly. When a re-election was ordered the Muslim League seats increased to 34. On 24 June 1947 the vote for partition was won by 33 votes in favour and 20 votes against. The Speaker of the Sindh Assembly aptly remarked: 'Sindh has arrived at the portals of Pakistan first. Congratulations'.

The Punjab was the most indispensable province for Pakistan the most elusive, yet in the end suffering the most. Punjab held a member of advantages,

it had a canal system which made it the granary of India, a feud
subordinate to educational progress and the area which provided n.
soldiers. All these factors gave Punjab a predominant position. While 1
the Cabinet Mission Plan, Pandit Nehru had speculated that Sindh wou. .ot
like to be dominated by the Punjab. True to Nehru's fears the eastern half of
the Punjab which fell to India was divided into three provinces Punjab,
Haryana and Himachal Pradesh.

For a long time cultural cohesion translated into communal harmony. We
need to understand the process whereby the Unionist Party founded in 1923
by Sir Fazl-i-Hussain and Sir Chhotu Ram dominated Punjab politics till the
very eve of partition, and finally made place for the Muslim League after a
display of street power. In the elections of 1937 only two members of the
Punjab Assembly had been elected on the Muslim League ticket, Malik Barkat
Ali and Raja Ghazanfar Ali Khan, but the latter almost immediately defected
to the Unionist Party. In the elections of 1946, the situation changed
dramatically, the Muslim League winning 75 out of 86 seats we need to
understand the process whereby this transformation was effected.

Ian Talbot is the pre-eminent authority on pre-partition Punjab first
offered the solution that the Second World War transformed Jinnah's status,
and enabled him to dispense with Unionist backing.[2] This is hardly tenable
since the same war which enhanced Jinnah's status, enhanced the status of Sir
Sikandar Hayat, Chief Minister of the Punjab. Jinnah's position over the war
efforts were far more constricted than Sikandar's. When the Punjab body sent
in a requisition for a special meeting of the AIML Council to move a
resolution supporting the war efforts, both Jinnah and Liaquat balked. The
Raja of Mahmudabad was enlisted to counter this move; and in 1941 the
AIML expelled those of its members who joined the Viceroy's Defence
Council over its head.

The Unionist Party under both Fazl-i-Hussain and Sir Sikandar Hayat had
an uneasy relation with the Muslim League. The Unionist Party supported
not only communal harmony but also the British. After an acrimonious
relation with Jinnah stretching over decades, Fazl-i-Hussain wrote to him on
15 May 1934: 'Muslim India cannot afford to lose you. Men of clear vision,
independent judgment and strength of character are very few.'[3]

Yet, two years later Fazl-i-Hussain sent the same Jinnah empty-handed,
warning him to keep his fingers out of the Punjab pie. Sir Sikandar Hayat
under a pact with Jinnah allowed the Unionist Muslim members of the Punjab
legislatures, to form a Muslim League, so for all intents and purpose, the
Unionist Party doubled as the Muslim League in the Punjab, despite the
efforts of Iqbal, Malik Barkat Ali and Ashique Hussain Batalvi, to form a
provincial body independent of the Unionists. Why the Muslim League,
though being subordinate, remained so close to the surface, is explained by

Ian Talbot that the Unionist Party never achieved a mass base of political support. It owed its success in 1937 to strategic local factional alliances.[4]

There can be no other explanation for why the Muslims of Punjab demonstrated so violently against Sikandar Hayat during the 1940 Lahore Session of the AIML. The very fact that the AIML held it's most momentous session in the Punjab capital, refusing to be distracted by police violence on the Khaksars, is a strong indication of a strong local support. The following eye-witness account of Ashique Hussain Batalvi was endorsed by the Punjab governor in his secret report.

The people were listening quietly and calmly to Nawab Shahnawaz Khan Mamdot, who was presenting the address of welcome, but when he mentioned the efforts of Sir Sikandar Hayat in restoring the Badshahi Mosque.

> As soon as Sir Sikandar's name was mentioned, there was consternation from one end of the ground to the other. From all corners the cries came: We won't listen, 'don't take the name of Sir Sikandar' 'sit down' and 'shame shame'. Sir Sikandar... saw the demonstration of the people's unhappiness and anger with his own eyes he went out from the backdoor of the podium.[5]

The stage had been set for the Muslim League victory in the 1946 elections; it won 75 out of the 86 Muslim seats. Still, Sir Khizr Hayat Tiwana, who had succeeded Sikandar Hayat in 1942, who had only 18 seats out of 175 was called upon by the governor, Sir Bertrand Glancy to form the government. Muslim League volunteers, half of whom were ladies, led demonstrations, braved police brutalities and jail but succeeded in forcing the resignation of Sir Khizr Hayat on 2 March 1942.

Two days later the Sikhs demonstrated against the decision under the leadership of Master Tara Singh. Riots started in Amritsar spread to Rawalpindi and then the whole province was up in flames. The Sikhs presence in the Punjab was an element not found in other provinces. The treatment of the Sikhs by the Mughals had been savage, and it was natural that in the cauldron of 1947, the Sikhs veered towards the Hindus, brushing aside their affinities to the Muslims as a minority. The Muslim League had achieved power too late and after a very bitter struggle for the party to attempt reconciliation with the Sikhs.

This was the reason why, when the Muslim League leadership attempted an approach to the Sikhs leadership, it proved futile. M.A. Jinnah handed over a blank paper to the Maharaja and Dewan of Patiala to inscribe their conditions for accession to Pakistan. At the 17 August 1947 meeting, Liaquat Ali Khan asserted his right to speak for the Sikhs of Pakistan, just as Pandit Nehru was speaking on behalf of the Sikhs of India. The Muslim League wanted neither a homogeneous population, nor communal dislocation. The amorphous nature of the land and people admitted only of approximation, but the communal flareup of 1947 denied the Sikhs a balancing role. Even if Khalistan had emerged, it could have acted as a buffer state between India and Pakistan, and the upshot was that the people of Punjab had to go through fire and blood to achieve Pakistan.

NWFP is a nameless province inspiring nameless fear. Sir Olaf Caroe, a former governor of NWFP, in his defining work *The Pathans*, has devoted a whole chapter to Waziristan, by which he sought to characterize the whole region. 'No empire of which we have any record has ever succeeded in making subjects of the tribes of Waziristan.'[6]

Perhaps this was one of the reasons why the British delayed reforms in the NWFP. It was only through the logic and persistence of Lord Curzon that NWFP was separated from the Punjab on 9 November 1901 and made a Chief Commissioner's Province, that is, a province with no governor and no assemblies. The first demand that came forward was from the Arya Samaj. It was to re-amalgate the NWFP to the Punjab. When Lala Lajpat Rai came to inaugurate the Peshawar Arya Samaj School, he promised to support re-amalgation.[7]

Thus, despite the over whelming majority of Muslims, the NWFP was not entirely free of communal troubles, and Muslims could have seen that their majority status needed vigilance to be maintained. On 23 April 1930, Hindu-Muslim riots took place in Peshawar, but certainly communalism was not an issue as it was in the Hindu majority areas. The NWFP continued to progress, we have already mentioned the establishment of the Islamia College, Peshawar, through the efforts of three dedicated notables Roos-Keppel the Chief Commissioner, Sahibzada Sir Abdul Qayyum and Nawab Akbar Hoti, but it was only in 1932 that the NWFP was raised from a Chief Commissioner's to Governor's province, and under the GOI 1935 another instalment was received. Sir Abdul Qayyum became Minister of Transferred Subjects (see under Montagu-Chelmsford Reforms).

The Congress established itself firmly in the NWFP, strangely through religious means. Since the Khilafat and Non-Cooperation Movements were being run together by Mahatma Gandhi, the Congress inducted the Khudai Khidmatgars led by Khan Abdul Ghaffar Khan. They believed in non-violence, but the British did not. The British fired at unarmed Khudai Khidmatgars at Qissa Khawani Bazaar, Peshawar on 23 April 1930. This was the frontier version of the Jallianwala Bagh tragedy, but unlike in the Punjab a massacre did not have a sobering effect; it was followed by firing on unarmed protestors in a number of smaller frontier towns. The Khudai Khidmatgars had established a firm moral basis and it would have taken a party with utmost probity and efforts to dislodge it. Unfortunately, the

Muslim League government which had a brief tenure from 1943 to 1945 could not effect this.

The AIML established its presence in 1912, under Mian Abdul Aziz (barrister) but as the First World War erupted in 1914, the British promptly suppressed the AIML, and it disappeared. In October 1936, M.A. Jinnah had travelled to the NWFP but was not able to persuade any politician to contest elections on the Muslim League ticket. It was only in September 1937 that Sir Abdul Qayyum facilitated the foundation of the Frontier Muslim League, and during the following month, the Peshawar City Muslim League was established putting the party in a position of vantage.

The next step was placed forward, but proved unfortunate; when Sir Abdul Qayyum died (6 December 1937) Sardar Aurangzeb Khan (1892–1953) was chosen as his political heir. He had served as Sir Abdul Qayyum's secretary during the RTCs. He presided over the first session of the All-India States Muslim League on 23 March 1940 at Lahore.[8] Because of his prominence; he had to be persuaded to join the Muslim League. In 1939 he became leader of the opposition in the NWFP Assembly. Even when the Congress resigned in late 1939, the Muslim League under Sardar Aurangzeb Khan was unable to form a ministry, and governor's rule had to be resorted to. When ten Congress legislators were jailed on 25 May 1943, Aurangzeb was invited to form a ministry. Aurangzeb was able to win four more seats for the Muslim League in by-elections, but his position remained so fragile that he resorted to large-scale corruption.

It is true that the Muslim League was faction-ridden. Khan Bahadur Sadullah Khan was an inveterate rival of Aurangzeb, but the corruption and nepotism that he complained of to Jinnah was real. Large scale corruption meant large scale discontent, even within the ranks of the Muslim League. When Congress legislators were released from jail, it was natural that Aurangzeb faced a no-confidence movement. What was not natural that three members of the Muslim League, led by Sadullah Khan had voted against Aurangzeb. On 14 March 1945, Aurangzeb resigned.

The outgoing chief minister refuelled the charges against himself by offering the defence that 'Corruption started with Adam and will end on doomsday.'[9] Far from being a means of consolidating of the Muslim League, the Aurangzeb ministry had the opposite effect. In the elections of 1946, the Muslim League won only seventeen of the Muslim seats to the Congress figure of thirty. These results were contrary to the country-wide trend, but these results, conditioned by the corruption of the Muslim League did not prove to be stable. The visits by Pandit Nehru to the NWFP signalled a reverse in attitudes. As Maulana Abul Kalam Azad was later to recall: 'The actual position in 1946 was that the Khan brothers did not enjoy as much support in the Frontier as we in Delhi thought. When Jawaharlal reached Peshawar, this discovery came to him as an unpleasant shock.'[10]

Jawaharlal Nehru faced a hostile black flag waving demonstration at the Peshawar airport. The Khan brothers had themselves needed police protection, they were in no position to protect Nehru. On his way back from Landi Kotal, he had stones thrown at his car. The sentiments of the public had been made clear. On 28/29 April 1947 Lord Mountbatten, the new Viceroy arrived in the Frontier, and what he saw and heard convinced him that the results of 1946 no longer held.

A medical team from the NWFP had visited Bihar, and when they saw the riot stricken Muslims, the religious divide was brought home to them in a manner that the Muslim majority of their province had prevented than from seeing. Two months after Nehru's departure (December 1946), tribesmen attacked Hindus and Sikhs, uprooting them from Hazara. In the Referendum of 20 June 1947, Pakistan received 50.49 of the votes effectively doubling the AIML's performance since the 1946 electron. An explanation of this reversal is provided by Ian Talbot: 'The Muslim League's claims that the choice was either *Akhand* Hindustan or Pakistan, overnight look on a reality that had been missing during the earlier provincial elections.'[11]

To gauge the intensity of the feeling, we need to recount the efforts of the brave Pakhtun ladies who led the demonstrations against the Congress ministry. A delegation of the Zanana Muslim League led by Lady Nusrat Haroon arrived in Peshawar on 17 October 1945. Besides addressing public meeting in purdah they visited other cities of the province, especially Mardan, at the invitation of Begum Zari Sarfaraz. By early 1947 Zanana League offices had been opened in all urban centres.

On 14 April 1947, members of the Zanana Muslim League lay down on the railway tracks, the 58 Down Bombay Express did not stop, knocked down three women and injured 30 more. The AIML high command prevented them from risking their lives any further.[12] On 3 June 1947, Jinnah paid them tribute: 'I cannot but express my appreciation of the sufferings and sacrifices made by all the classes of Musalmans and particularly the great part the women of the Frontier played in the fight for our civil liberties.'[13]

Balochistan served as a reminder of the brief occupation of its territory by the Persian Empire. Balochistan was partitioned between the British and Persian empires in 1875. At the first opportunity that presented itself, Baloch people rebelled against the British, in 1914, siding with the Germans. This movement was crushed militarily by the British but initially the concern of Baloch leaders remained irredentist. Baloch sardars organized the Anjuman-i-Ittehad-i-Balochistan, and by the beginning of the Second World War, they held public meetings to demand the separation of Balochistan from British

India. This move naturally alarmed the Muslims of India, and they pleaded against such a move.

One year earlier, a young man Qazi Isa by name, met Jinnah in Bombay and was asked by him to establish the Muslim League in Balochistan. Qazi Isa first inducted Akhunzada Abdul Ali Khan, and thereafter the two of them toured the length and breadth of the vast province, establishing local branches. The Balochistan Muslim League held its first conference at Quetta on 10 and 11 June 1939. It was in this conference session that Qazi Isa was elected President. After holding forth on the poverty in his province, and the lack of educational opportunities, Qazi Isa declared: 'We are Muslims first, Baloch next, and Indians third.'[14]

The Balochistan League was affiliated to the AIML in September 1939. Speaking on that occasion Quaid-i-Azam said: 'About six months ago, I had commissioned Qazi Isa do the work. He has performed a great miracle in such a short time.'[15]

Thereafter the activities of Qazi Isa increased. He held a meeting at Quetta on 19 April 1940 to observe Muslim Independence Day. Four years later he published a booklet called *Balochistan: Case and Demand*. Qazi Isa had succeeded in setting the direction of Baloch Muslims to the East instead of the West. Since he had proved to be an effective orator, Jinnah sent him to NWFP at the time of the by-elections. Thereafter he was sent to Aligarh, where, contrary to his expectations, he discovered great affinity, and soon he became familiar to the students at Aligarh.

From 26 to 28 July 1940 the Annual Session of the Balochistan was held. Liaquat Ali Khan who presided said in his address: 'The British government has treated the province most unjustly, so much so that its parallel cannot be given any where else in India.'

Writing privately to Jinnah, Liaquat Ali Khan gave him a detailed report of the Conference, rueing the fact that Jinnah himself was not there:

> The Conference was a great success. There were large gatherings every night, and people stayed on till 2 o'clock in the morning at every meeting. It was encouraging to see what wonderful progress a backward province has made in such a short time. Of course the credit is due to the untiring zeal and enthusiasm of Isa.[16]

On 1 July 1943, the Balochistan Muslim League held a meeting to honour the Quaid-i-Azam. Jinnah spent two months in Balochistan. From 10 to 14 July, he was the guest of the Khan of Kalat. Jinnah paid another visit in September 1945 and addressed a number of meetings. In 1945 Nawab Mohammad Khan Jogezai of the AIML defeated Abdus Samad Achakzai of the Congress by 61 votes to 13.

In the Shahi Jirga that followed 54 members voted en bloc for Pakistan. The Jirga had been scheduled for 30 June 1947, but since an overwhelming number of members were present, the Shahi Jirga gave its verdict one day earlier. On 4 August 1947 Ahmad Yar Khan, the Khan of Kalat in the presence of Lord Mountbatten, M.A. Jinnah, Liaquat Ali Khan, Pandit Nehru, Sardar Patel and Sir Sultan Ahmad, Legal Remembrances of the Chamber of Princes, signed a stand still agreement with Pakistan. This agreement accepted Kalat as an independent state, with the privilege to decide whether British Balochistan would be part of Kalat or Pakistan. The allocation of subjects like Defence, Foreign Affairs, Communications and Currency were to be decided by mutual consultations.

Negotiations with Kalat were prolonged. On 17 March 1948, other Balochistan states, Lasbela, Kharan and Makran acceded to Pakistan. Being isolated, Kalat acceded to Pakistan on 28 March 1948, and its independent status ended. Only one aspect of Balochistan's services to Pakistan remain to be recalled. In his last tour, Children's Muslim Leagues were formed at Sibi and Loralai. Quaid-i-Azam had saluted them. Had he been alive the Quaid-i-Azam would salute the children today. It is they who celebrate Independence Day with great enthusiasm and patriotism.

NOTES

1. D.A. Pirzada, in M.A. Shaikh (ed.) *The Role of Sindh in the Creation of Pakistan*, Karachi: Sindh Madressatul Islam, 1998, p. 171. I am grateful to D.A. Pirzada for answering my queries.
2. Ian Talbot, *Provincial Politics and the Pakistan Movement*, Karachi: Oxford University Press, 1988, p. 91.
3. Ian Bryant Wells, *Ambassador of Hindu Muslim Unity*, New Delhi: Permanent Black, 2005, p. 235.
4. Ian Talbot, *Freedom's Cry*, Karachi: Oxford University Press, 1996, p. 84.
5. Ashique Husain Balalvi, *Our National Struggle January 1940 to December 1940*, Lahore: Altaf Husain, 1975, pp. 17, 18.
6. Olaf Caroe, *The Pathans*, London: Macmillan, 1965, pp. 390–91.
7. Himayatullah, 'Jinnah Muslim League and the Introduction of Reforms in the NWFP' in Riaz Ahmed (ed.) Papers Presented at the Three-Day International Conference on All India Muslim League, Islamabad: NIHCR 2006. Vol. I, p. 275.
8. Ahmad Saeed, *Muslim India*, Lahore: Institute of Pakistan Historical Research, 1997, p. 91.
9. Altaf Ullah, 'Sardar Mohammad Aurangzeb Khan', in Riaz Ahmad, op. cit., p. 18.
10. Abul Kalam Azad, *India Wins Freedom*, Calcutta: Orient Longmans, 1959, p. 171.
11. Ian Talbot, *Provincial Politics*, op. cit., p. 21.

12. Lal Baha Ali, in Riaz Ahmed, op. cit., vol. 11, p. 143.
13. Ibid., p. 145.
14. Inam ul Haq Kausar, Famous Personality of BML, Qazi Isa in Riaz Ahmed, op. cit., vol. 11, p. 12.
15. Ibid., p. 13.
16. Muhammad Reza Kazimi (ed.), *Jinnah-Liaquat Correspondence*, Karachi: Pakistan Study Centre, University of Karachi, 2003, p. 99.

PART V

POLITICAL HISTORY OF THE STATE

INTRODUCTION: IDEOLOGY OF PAKISTAN

In this section we shall first discuss the political developments resulting from the creation of Pakistan. Thereafter we shall discuss the Ideology.

On 14 August 1947, the Dominion of Pakistan came into existence. A movement had led to the establishment of a state. In a state, the rights and duties of citizens have to be defined, as their loyalty to the state. In the context of Pakistan it is important, at the outset, to learn what a state is, and what is the nature of its relations with the government and society.

The State: Political scientists hold that the state is a politically organized community, and government is its agency. Government is only one part or constituent of a state. The state is permanent, government is temporary. In democratic states people are asked to vote every five years or so. The people, by voting, either retain the government or change it. This change of government does not affect basic principles such as national security or territorial integrity.

The Government: The state is abstract, but government is concrete. A government has the following components: Executive, Legislature and Judiciary.

The Executive: The executive is headed by a President, or Prime Minister. It consists of the cabinet ministers, the bureaucracy and other officials. They implement the policies of the government. These policies either originate from the legislature or they originate from the government and are sanctioned by the legislature.

The Legislature: It is a body of members elected by the people to represent them primarily in their function of framing laws, but also to project their aspirations and protect their rights generally. Theoretically, the legislature can change the executive. Legislatures exist at the district, provincial and national levels. The national parliament is bicameral consisting of the National Assembly and the Senate

The Judiciary: Described collectively, the judiciary means the judges of a state. The judiciary exists at the district, provincial and national levels. The judiciary decides disputes between citizens or between citizens and government on criminal, civil or constitutional matters. There is also a *Shariat* Court which decides cases according to Islamic law.

Society is wider than the state. The state is territorial whilst society is not. The state is organized while society is not necessarily organized. The state has coercive forces while society has moral forces.

The above represent the basic concepts in the abstract. Whether they have remained the same in practice is explained in the following sections.

IDEOLOGY OF PAKISTAN

The term 'ideology' was coined by Antoine de Strutt de Tracy, during the French Revolution (1789). It meant a 'science of ideas'. Without making any direct reference to de Tracy, Justice Mohammad Munir explained that ideology is the science which deals with beliefs, notions and theories. These in turn have their origin in the fundamental assumptions held by a people. These ideas may be naturally acquired; sometimes they may be consciously spread.

The ideology of the French Revolution could be summed up as equality, fraternity and liberty. It overthrew the theory of the divine rights of kings. It also modified the still unfolding law of social contract. According to Charles E. Bressler, ideology refers to the collective or social consciousness of culture.[1] This is opposed to the material reality on which an experience is based. This means that though the ideology of Pakistan has been derived from the Two-Nation theory, it is not identical to it. In other words, the ideology of Pakistan is enshrined, not in the Lahore Resolution, but the Objectives Resolution.

This needs an explanation. An ideology is expressed in absolute, not relative terms. The Two-Nation theory is relative, because it depends on the existence of the 'other'—in our case, the Hindu majority of undivided India. If the Hindus did not exist—or if they existed as a minority—there would have been no need to propound the Two-Nation theory according to which Hindus and Muslims form different nations.

Islamic ideology means to order our individual and collective behaviour in accordance with the Islamic concepts of justice, morality, human rights, and tolerance. Human rights in Islam are an important component of its ideology. The rights of God and the rights of worshippers are clearly demarcated. There are sins against God, such as neglecting prayers, fasting, and pilgrimage. There are sins against human beings, such as killing them, stealing from them, and even backbiting—against which the holy Quran has passed the severest of strictures. Islamic ideology is a matter of personal conscience, but social behaviour.

IDEOLOGICAL HISTORY

The nature of Islamic ideology was hotly debated during the process of framing constitutions. The place of Islam in state polity was viewed differently by the Pakistan Muslim League, Pakistan National Congress and the Jama'at-i-Islami. It is undeniable that while religious majorities prefer an ideological state, religious minorities prefer a secular state. This was witnessed between 1937–1939, when Muslims objected to the Congress practices like the Wardha scheme of education, singing of the anti Muslim song, *Bande Matram*, and the practice of saluting the portrait of Gandhi. It is also undeniable that minorities sought mainly to safeguard human rights. If the majority guarantees freedom of conscience and belief, then, the ideology so practiced can be acceptable to minorities.

According to Jinnah, under Ideology we thought it proper to confine ourselves to the public speeches of the Quaid-i-Azam, however, in the testimony of the Raja of Mahmudabad[2] and Isha'at Habibullah, he had objected to Pakistan becoming an Islamic state,[3] on the ground that there were over seventy sects, and 'the consequences would be a struggle of religious opinion from the very inception of the state leading to its very dissolution'. What Mr Jinnah wanted was a 'Liberal Democratic State.'

It should be noted that Jinnah's objection to an Islamic state was not ideological, but empirical. There is one strand of ideology, on which—not only Jinnah and Mahmudabad—but the entire leadership of the Muslim League was in agreement, and that is, Islamic socialism.

ISLAMIC SOCIALISM

This concept had a long Middle Eastern pedigree, with its origins in the so-called fundamentalist circles with Syed Qutb, and Mustafa al Sibayi at its head. Syed Qutb had said, in 1948, that Islamic socialism avoided the pitfalls of Christianity's separation of religion and society, and those of communism's atheism.[4] 'Maulana Hasrat Mohani espoused Islamic Communism'—Quaid-i-Azam mentioned it as an ideal in Chittagong on 26 March 1948.[5] Liaquat Ali Khan projected it as state ideology. He said, at Lahore, on 3 September 1949: 'For us, there is only one 'ism'—Islamic Socialism.'[6] Miss Fatima Jinnah, while differing with Liaquat Ali Khan on a number of issues, agreed with him on the issue of Islamic socialism, stating in a February 1951 speech, that 'Islamic Socialism did not allow any class struggle.'[7] The Raja of Mahmudabad argued cogently in favour of Islamic socialism at the Katrak Hall, Karachi, in 1967.[8]

With this consensus among the Muslim League stalwarts, it is not possible to exclude Islamic socialism from the ideological history of Pakistan. However two questions arise; how is it possible for leaders to differ on the need for an Islamic state, but to agree on Islamic socialism? Secondly, when there was a consensus among the founding generations, why was it never implemented? As to the first question, the latitude given by the Holy Quran in the political sphere, is more than that given in the economic sphere. The Holy Quran (68:7–14) specifies the types of persons who should not be obeyed:

> And obey thou not those who cry lies. They
> Wish that thou should compromise, then
> They would compromise
> And obey thou not every mean swearer,
> Backbiter, going about with slander,
> Hinderer of good, guilty aggressor,
> Coarse-grained, moreover ignoble,
> Because he has wealth and sons.[9]

This is a formidable list, but it does not proscribe any political system, presidential or parliamentary. Ideally, a republican caliphate encompassing the entire world would be preferred, but nation states cannot be termed un-Islamic, because even welfare societies formed to regulate the affairs of localities, or apartment blocks cannot be proscribed, because they help in fulfilling social requirements obligatory under Islam. To regulate water supply, sanitation and security are bare necessities and are not dependent on the larger ideological dispensation of the state.

On the other hand, strictures against economic crimes are not only more severe, but determine to a greater extent the nature of the state Muslims can adopt. These are: usury, hoarding, gambling, cheating in weights and measures. All the economic crimes listed here affect the ethical mores of society, but the proscription of usury, conjoined with the payment of *zakat*, or the tithe meant for charity, determine the nature of the state. This aspect became most conspicuous during the Cold War (1945–1990).

Islam grants the right of private ownership, but simultaneously dislikes the concentration of wealth in some hands. This is to avoid the exploitation of the masses. Islam preceded both the capitalist nation state as well as the communist state, so while Islamic socialism may be a new term, the concept of social justice is old. The west had also not allowed interest until John Calvin legalized it. As long as usury is practiced, only a capitalist system can exist. This is the reason why, in answer to our second question, Islamic socialism remained a pious hope and was never implemented.

During the era following Liaquat Ali Khan, Islamic socialism was rarely mentioned, however when the movement against Ayub Khan began, Maulana Abdul Hamid Khan Bhashani (president, National Awami Party), and Zulfikar Ali Bhutto (chairman, PPP) raised the slogan of Islamic socialism. Bhashani did not contest the 1970 elections, but Bhutto did, and eventually came to power. In reply to a question by Abul Hashim, Z.A. Bhutto explained in this author's presence that 'Islamic socialism means that part of socialism, which is not in conflict with Islam'. During the 1970 election campaign, 122 Ulema issued a decree that socialism was *haram* (religiously forbidden), and that Islamic socialism was a contradiction in terms. This decree was ignored by the electorate, but in the 1977 Pakistan National Alliance (PNA) Movement, it gained credence.

Partly due to the constraints of the 1971 defeat, partly because of a feudal background, and partly because of his temperament, Z.A. Bhutto was unable to implement his programmes. He nationalized industries, banks, and insurance companies, and even introduced land reforms, but veered sufficiently away from the left to alienate the socialist component of his party, but not sufficiently to mollify the religious parties forming the PNA, who, in 1977, launched a movement to enforce Nizam-i-Mustafa or an Islamic order.

ISLAMIZATION

General M. Ziaul Haq who staged a coup d'etat, in the wake of the PNA movement, made Islamization the ideological basis of his regime. The aim, and even the destiny of the people of Pakistan is Islamization, but it should be made clear what Islamization means. It cannot be coercion, because the Holy Quran forbids it. Moreover it cannot be applied selectively. Islamic laws were imposed for all crimes except murder, because under Islamic law, Zia would have had to release the prime minister he had overthrown. Again, Islamic provisions in the laws of evidence and adultery, created an anomaly not permissible in Islam. For example, in 1983, two victims of rape were convicted of adultery. Being women, their evidence was not considered sufficient to convict the perpetrators, but their complaint was construed as a confession to unlawful sex. Women's rights and the rights of minorities suffered due to discrimination.

It is not that the ulema—even those who had agitated for an Islamic order—did not realize the implications of this type of Islamization. Firstly, when Nawaz Sharif learnt that the Shariah court, set up under Zia, had outlawed usury, including interest, he appealed against this decision. Again, when Nawaz Sharif moved the Fifteenth Amendment to make Shariah the supreme law of the land, even the religious parties did not support him. They feared that this would be a device to subordinate the constitution, by which means he would gain unbridled power. It is manifest to all that Islamic laws can come into operation only when social anomalies are not created.

A side effect of the Islamization process was an increase in sectarian violence. If the extreme verdict of Abu Musab al Zarqawi of Al-Qaeda is accepted, Shaikh Hasan Nasrullah of Hezbullah cannot be considered a Muslim. It was after the capture of Afghanistan by the Taliban that Islamization had come in for condemnation by the West. After the events of

9/11, this hostility has increased immeasurably. Islam does not allow militancy—either in the preaching of Islam, or even in times of war. Islam enjoins Jihad, but has strict rules governing Muslim conduct. The old, infirm, women, infants and other non-combatants are not to be harmed. Even trees are not to be cut down, or fields devastated.

ENLIGHTENED MODERATION

The régime of General Pervez Musharraf has eschewed the militancy attached to the fair name of Islam, and has opted for what he calls 'Enlightened Moderation'. This is all to the good. The challenge from without is weak. The challenge from within is strong. When custom is allowed to supersede Sharia, then Islamization is indeed remote. Islam is a religion of mercy, the Holy Quran begins in the name of Allah, Who is Compassionate and Merciful. We repeat these verses in our prayers. Yet a mother had her daughter, Saima Sarwar, killed in her presence, because she had sought divorce—a right that is guaranteed to her in Islam. Honour killing should be punishable by death in accordance with the laws of Islam. We must reiterate that Islamic laws cannot be applied selectively. It is those village or tribe elders who sentence women to gang rape, who are impeding the imposition of Islamic laws. Those who kill and rape are rebels unto God, and it is their audacity which explains why Islamic punishments are harsh.

There is no denying that Muslims all over the world are subject to oppression, but they are not subject to the type of oppression our Holy Prophet (PBUH) had to face—the oppression he forgave when he conquered Mecca. The Holy Quran has honoured Muslims by designating them as *Ummatan Wastan: Thus we appointed you a midmost nation that you might be witness to the people, and that the Messenger might be a witness to you.* (Q.2:143)

Midmost, medium, middle—all these words can be used to translate *wasatan*. It means above all that the Muslim community should not be extremist, and must not be seen as extremist by the other people on whom it must bear witness. Militancy and extremism are un-Islamic. The laws of God cannot be subject to human passion. The repression of Muslims in Chechnya is horrible. This does not justify the gruesome murder of innocent school children in Beslan (2 September 2004). Unless such means are condemned, the ends shall be despised. Islam permits retaliation, but the retaliation must be strictly measured. The Holy Quran (81:8–9) warns of the time when the buried infant shall be asked for what sin she was slain. It is clear that the burying alive of the girl child was a pagan practice, not a Muslim practice. Here the Holy Quran is decrying the slaying of non-Muslim children. Yet the ulema did not condemn the Beslan massacre. Islamic norms cannot be trampled upon, even in the pursuit of what are seen as Islamic causes.

If ideology is the value commitment of a people, as Eqbal Ahmad once said, then values take precedence over rituals. The Holy Quran says:

> It is not piety that you turn your faces
> To the East and to the West
> True piety is this:
> To believe in God, and the last Day,
> The Angels, the Book and the Prophets
> To give of one's substance, however cherished
> To kinsmen, and orphans, the needy
> The traveller, beggars, and to ransom
> The slave, to perform the prayers, to pay the alms (2:176)

Allama Iqbal, writing in the context of the above verse, comments: 'The form of prayer ought not to become a matter of dispute. Which side you turn is certainly not essential to the spirit of prayer.'[10]

Islam is a religion in which human rights are not infringed upon by Divine Right. If a person commits a crime against a fellow being, God, in His divine mercy shall not forgive the culprit over the head of the victim. Just above, we have mentioned the law of retaliation. We are encouraged to forgive, but the right of retaliation is not taken from us.

NOTES

1. Charles Bressler, *Literary Criticism*, New Jersey: Prentice Hall, 1994, p. 172.
2. Raja of Mahmudabad, 'Some Memories' in *India's Partition*, ed. Mushirul Hassan, New Delhi: Oxford University Press, 1994, p. 425.
3. Isha'at Habibullah, *Autobiography*. Unpublished typescript, graciously given to me by the author's daughter, Muneeza Shamsie, pp. 108–109.
4. John Esposito, *Unholy War*, Oxford University Press, 2000, p. 57.
5. M.A. Jinnah, *Speeches and Statements as Governor-General*, Karachi, 2000, p. 182.
6. Richard Symonds, *The Making of Pakistan*, 2nd edition, Islamabad: National Book Foundation, 1976, p. 182.
7. Khan Salahuddin Khan, *The Speeches and Statements of Mohtarma Fatima Jinnah*, Lahore: Research Society of Pakistan, University of the Punjab, 1976, pp. 25–26.
8. Muhammad Ali Siddiqui, 'Foreword' to The *Life and Times of the Raja Sahib of Mahmudabad*, ed. Syed Ishtiaq Hussain, Karachi: Mehboob Academy, 1998, p. 18.
9. A.J. Arberry (trans.), *The Koran* (Oxford World's Classics), Oxford Paperbacks; new edition, 1998.
10. Muhammad Iqbal, *Reconstruction of Religious Thought in Islam*, Lahore, Sang-e-Meel, 2004, p. 85.

MOHAMMAD ALI JINNAH (b. 25 December 1876–d. 11 September 1948) was a campaigner for India's freedom. M.A. Jinnah was an instrument of India's partition. Both claims are valid. Whether this represents an advance, or a derailment, depends on the meaning of the word 'freedom'. The Hindus had not gained freedom after the defeat of the Muslims. Would the Muslims gain freedom on the withdrawal of the British?

The first step in the direction of partition was taken when the Congress leadership transited from Jinnah to Gandhi. Both had emerged together as champions of India's freedom, both were disciples of Gopal Krishna Gokhale; and both gained prominence by protesting against the plight of Indians in South Africa; Gandhi with his novel *satyagraha*, and Jinnah by confronting the viceroy face-to-face. Then, was their later divergence an outcome of their vision, or their circumstances? These were not insuperable, and may not have come about without the fateful intervention of Motilal Nehru who primed Jinnah to oppose Gandhi's non-cooperation resolution at Nagpur, in 1920, and then resiled from his stand.[1] Only ten days before, Jinnah had spoken of his belief in the ideal of non-cooperation; and even at Nagpur (where he resigned), Jinnah had not opposed the principles, but he had opposed the impractical portions of Gandhi's resolution.

His resignation from Congress brought about a personality change. Dewan Chaman Lal, who knew Jinnah as a young man, described his 'uninhibited laughter and general bonhomie'.[2] Jinnah's formality and reserve developed as a reaction to the social treatment he received from his Congress compatriots—which was strange considering his close friendship with Nehru's father, and Patel's brother. Again, had Gandhi not gone against Jinnah's pleas, by raising the religious sentiments of the (Muslim) masses during the Khilafat Movement, the role of the Muslim League would have been limited to being a moderating influence in Indian politics.

His reserve also developed when his marriage with a young girl—whom he had pursued tempestuously—broke down. Kanji Dwarkadas—a mutual friend—was called home by Jinnah, the day after the heart rending scene of his wife's burial: 'Never have I found a man so sad and so bitter. He screamed his heart out, speaking to me for over two hours, myself listening to him patiently and sympathetically, occasionally putting in a word here and there. Something, I saw, snapped in him.'[3]

A number of freedom fighters were widowers: Gandhi, Jawaharlal Nehru, Vallabhbhai Patel and Abul Kalam Azad, but only Jinnah's wife, Ruttie, had been politically active.

Jinnah had resigned from Congress politically, not psychologically. Jinnah caused a split in the Muslim League over the composition of the Simon Commission, rather than abandon Congress (which he had left) in its struggle. Viceroy Lord Willingdon found Jinnah more Congress than Congress, but Jinnah was alienated time and again by Congress; by the abjuration of the Lucknow Pact, by resiling from the Delhi Muslim Proposals, by disregarding the tacit UP 1937 electoral understanding, and finally by reneging on the grouping clause. Without these rebuffs Jinnah would not have faced a choice between territorial loyalty and communal survival.

Jinnah was not elitist in politics. He led a mass demonstration against Lord Willingdon. He dealt with tough hecklers and their political patrons in a Bombay meeting held to promote the candidature of R.P. Paranjype.[4] Ian Bryant Wells has quoted Jinnah's speech on the Elementary Education Bill: 'Are you going to keep millions and millions of people under your feet for the fear that they may demand more rights'? In spite of these sentiments Indian historians favour a Jinnah who would bow before Nehru—not a Jinnah who would stand up to Lord Mountbatten. Only one reviewer, T.W. Hutton, has identified Jinnah's fear of emotion as central to both his politics and personality. This trait eluded his Congress contemporaries. Speaking at the All-Parties Conference, in 1928, Jinnah said: 'Every country struggling for freedom and desirous of establishing a democratic system has had to face the problem of minorities..... minorities cannot give anything to the majority and the majority alone can give...'

Twenty years later, addressing the Constituent Assembly of Pakistan, the Quaid-i-Azam said: 'You may belong to any religion, cast or creed, that has nothing to do with the business of the state. We are starting with this fundamental principle that we are all citizens and equal citizens of one state.'

Jinnah was upholding a lifelong principle ignored equally by the citizens of India and Pakistan.

NOTES

1. Kanji Dwarkadas, *India's Fight for Freedom, 1913–1937: An Eyewitness Story*, Bombay: Popular Prakashan, 1966, pp. 286–87.
2. Dewan Chaman Lal, 'The Quaid-i-Azam as I knew him', in Jamiluddin Ahmad (ed.), *Quaid-i-Azam as seen by his Contemporaries*, Lahore: Ashraf, 1976, p. 171.
3. Kanji Dwarkadas, *Ruttie Jinnah: The Story of a Great Friendship*, Bombay: Kanji Dwarkadas, 1963, p. 58.
4. V.N. Naik, *Mr Jinnah: A Political Study*, Bombay: Sadbhakti Publications, 1947, pp. 38–41.

CHAPTER 25

THE ESTABLISHMENT OF PAKISTAN: EARLY PROBLEMS

On independence, Pakistan was without any infrastructure to set up a new state. It had neither of the two capital cities, Calcutta or New Delhi, developed by the British in India. It established its capital at Karachi, which had become a provincial capital only ten years previously. It had no office buildings, furniture or stationery whereby the administrative machinery for the seat of a government could be set up. People sat under trees, bringing furniture from wherever they resided, and the government started functioning. Even Lord Mountbatten, then the governor-general of India, described Karachi as a 'tent' compared to the splendour of New Delhi.[1]

Apart from the practical difficulty of setting up government machinery, there was the political difficulty that the provincial government of Sindh resented the separation of Karachi from the province. The Sindh Muslim League began to function as an opposition party. The cash-strapped government of Pakistan promised financial compensation, but the provincial government did not consider the amount adequate.

RIOTS AND REFUGEES

The partition of India was accompanied by widespread riots throughout the subcontinent. Since the boundary awards had been delayed, rioting was most rampant in the Punjab. The riots were started by the Sikhs and the Rashtriya Swayamsevak Sangh (RSS), the militant Hindu organization, and were followed by a Muslim reprisal which was also swift and brutal. There was widespread murder, rape and arson on both sides. Partition had resulted in the largest human migration in recorded history. According to Pakistani estimates, approximately, 6,500,000 Muslims reached Pakistan from India; 5,200,000 came from East Punjab, including the princely states where rioting was severe. 500,000 lost their lives or were abducted. From Pakistan there was an exodus of about 5,500,000 Hindus and Sikhs. According to Richard Symonds, writing in 1950, the population of Pakistan increased by about 100,000 people.[2]

In the face of unspeakable atrocities, writers from all three communities, Hindu, Muslim and Sikh, led by Krishan Chandar, Sa'adat Hasan Manto and

Rajinder Singh Bedi rose to the occasion and most impartially showed that the riots were crimes not against communities but against humanity. Books are a poor defence against bullets, but these writers provided a bridge to mental reconciliation and normalcy. At first, numbers proved deceptive. Inevitably as news of atrocities spread in Karachi, there was rioting against the Hindus. On 9 January 1948, the Quaid-i-Azam warned the Muslim refugees 'not to abuse the hospitality that has been extended to them'.[3]

DIVISION OF ASSETS

Field Marshal Sir Claude Auchinleck, the British commander-in-chief of India had taken the position that regardless of the partition of India, the armed forces should not be divided. However, when a political decision to divide the armed forces was taken, he testified that the Indian government wanted to prevent the establishment of Pakistan. He did not admit that he had delayed the decision of physically dividing the military assets before Partition.

As far as financial assets were concerned, India was prepared to pay Pakistan only 5 per cent of the total capital on the condition that Pakistan accept the liability of 20 per cent of the debt. In November 1947, H.M. Patel, finance secretary of India, and Chaudhry Mohammad Ali, secretary general, Government of Pakistan agreed that the disputed portion of Pakistan's share of the cash balances in sterling would be 17.5 per cent. In terms of cash, it worked out to Rs 750 million. But even this agreed amount was not transferred to Pakistan. Nehru wrote to Liaquat Ali Khan that India could not release the money because Pakistan planned to use it against India in the ongoing Kashmir war. When Junagadh, with a Muslim ruler and Hindu majority, had acceded to Pakistan, India had forcibly occupied it, saying that Junagadh's accession to Pakistan was against the principles of the religious divide. India had occupied Kashmir, which had a Hindu ruler and a Muslim majority, against the principle it had recently expounded. Nehru's linking of the division of assets with the Kashmir war was a hollow argument that deprived India of its moral ground. Gandhi started a fast unto death, forcing the government of India to transfer Pakistan's share. Lord Mountbatten and Nehru had sidelined Gandhi, therefore they resented his intervention but were forced to pay an instalment of Pakistan's share of assets to induce Gandhi to break his fast. Gandhi was assassinated on 30 January 1948 by an RSS member, Nathuram Godse. Gandhi had rendered ineffective the Cabinet Mission Plan but had now paid with his life for helping Pakistan.

The payment of this instalment did not end Pakistan's crisis. The Nizam of Hyderabad sent a cheque for a large amount, but since it was based on Indian securities, Nehru did not allow it to be encashed. At this, Sir Adamjee Haji Dawood arranged for a loan on his guarantee from Mohammad Ali Habib, the founder of Habib Bank, thereby preventing the financial collapse of Pakistan.

THE KASHMIR WAR

Nehru had made a public reversal of the principle of Partition by occupying first Junagadh and then Kashmir. This diplomatic gamble could have only been taken on the expectation that Pakistan would not survive the blow. Pakistan had been denied its share of military and financial assets. The reorganization of the Pakistan Army was still underway when the Kashmir war was thrust on it. Within Kashmir, the state forces had started a massacare of Muslims in Poonch. These Muslims had relatives in the tribal areas of Pakistan who invaded Kashmir hoping to rescue their relatives. The Pakistan Army did not have the resources to halt their advance. They were unable to control the tribals even when they looted Muslim property in Rawalpindi. Secondly, had Pakistan taken action against the tribesmen, it would have popularized the demand for *Pakhtunistan*—an independent Pathan state, a demand supported by the Congress leaders.

The government of India made the plea that it entered Kashmir because the maharaja had signed an Instrument of Accession to India. The Instrument of Accession has never surfaced and Alastair Lamb has proved that it was never signed. Nehru promised the people of Kashmir and the whole world that the fate of Kashmir would not be decided by the accession, but by a free and impartial plebiscite of the people of Jammu and Kashmir.[4] India has since reneged on this promise and this is one of two issues which still beset Pakistan–India relations.

THE INDUS WATER DISPUTE

The Indus Water dispute, like the Kashmir war, had its origin in the Radcliffe Awards. Just as the award of Gurdaspur to India was responsible for giving India access to Kashmir, the award of Ferozepur and Zira to India resulted in the Canal Waters dispute. All three were Muslim majority districts, and were given to India for a purpose.

The British had developed the upper Indus basin as an integrated unit having a vast irrigation network. The Radcliffe Award gave India the Ferozepur Headworks that controlled the Sutlej River as well as the Madhopur Head-works controlling the Ravi River. An arbitral tribunal was set up under Sir Patrick Spens, which recommended that the flow of water to Pakistan should not be stopped. Immediately after the tribunal was wound up in April 1948, the Indian government actually cut off the flow of water to Pakistan. Since this was in breach of international law which holds that an upper riparian country cannot interfere with the existing irrigation of the lower riparian country, the supply was partially restored. This long standing dispute was apparently resolved in 1960 when Nehru came to Karachi to sign an agreement with President Ayub and Eugene Black, vice-president of the World Bank. India is continuing with its Baglihar project despite Pakistan's protests and this threatens to upset the Indus Basin Treaty of 1960.

Recently the World Bank has been asked to arbitrate between India and Pakistan and has prepared a report which awaits consideration.

THE JINNAH ERA

One of the greatest setbacks to Pakistan in its early days was the death of the Quaid-i-Azam, barely thirteen months after Independence. The presence of the Quaid-i-Azam as governor-general had been vital to the survival of Pakistan. Lord Mountbatten had publicly admitted that had he become the common governor-general of India and Pakistan, partition would have been temporary. In this design, he had the support of his Prime Minister Clement Atlee who while speaking on the Independence Bill, had expressed his hope that Pakistan would not last. It was to prevent this outcome that the AIML nominated M.A. Jinnah to be the first governor-general of Pakistan.

In these peculiar circumstances, the Independence Act was amended to make the governor-general and not the prime minister the chief executive of Pakistan. From 30 December 1947 all vital policy decisions would be taken by the governor-general in cabinet. M.A. Jinnah also became the chief executive of the Balochistan province. There had been no political reforms in Balochistan up until Independence, i.e there was no governor, no assembly.

M.A. Jinnah envisaged Pakistan as a modern state, not as a theocracy. He chastised Muslim migrants from India on 9 January 1948 for the anti-Hindu riots in Karachi.[5] His 11 August 1947 speech giving equal rights to minorities was the result of years of deliberation. On 5 November 1941 he told H.V. Hodson that minorities would be represented in the cabinet. His only reservation then had been that the Hindus being a minority 'could not dictate policy'.[6]

In the domain of foreign policy he held out friendship to all upholding the Charter of the United Nations. He believed in leaning towards the West without going out of the way to annoy the USSR. He noted later that the USSR was the only country not to congratulate Pakistan on its creation. He undertook a personal initiative with regard to Afghanistan, the only country to oppose Pakistan's membership of the UN. On 3 December 1947, the Afghan ambassador presented his credentials to the governor-general of Pakistan as the result of negotiations conducted by the special representative, Nawab Saeedullah Khan. Jinnah also strongly supported the Palestinian cause and upheld the independence of Indonesia.

In terms of internal politics, although the Congress ministry in NWFP had lost its representative status in the referendum, the governor-general let Dr Khan Sahib head the provincial administration. However, when Dr Khan Sahib refused to salute the Pakistani flag and persisted in his refusal, the governor-general was obliged to dismiss his ministry on 22 August 1947.

The Quaid-i-Azam was able to visit East Bengal only once as governor-general. In his speech at Curzon Hall, Dhaka, he reiterated the decision of the AIML Delhi Legislators Convention in March 1946, that Urdu would be the official language of Pakistan. In his speech on 20 March 1948 at Dhaka, on 12 April 1948 at Peshawar, and on 15 June 1948 at Quetta, he warned the people against provincialism.

He advocated Islamic socialism and Islamic social justice, although Pakistan had to depend on its few plutocrats for its solvency. Jinnah prescribed industrialization as the key to development. On 1 April 1948, he hailed the issuance of Pakistan's own currency as an assertion of Pakistan's economic viability and independence. On 1 July 1948, while inaugurating the State Bank he called upon it to undertake research to make banking compatible with Islamic principles. He told the youth to choose a career in commerce over one in the civil or government service.

At the Chittagong meeting on 25 March 1948, he told gazetted officers that the country would no longer be ruled by the bureaucracy and that they should have nothing to do with party politics. Addressing the military staff college at Quetta on 14 June 1948, he reminded the military of the oath which they were required to take, the text of which he read out.

By 12 April 1948, Jinnah's illness had overtaken him. In June he had to reside at Quetta and Ziarat in Balochistan. He was brought to Karachi without protocol on 11 September 1948. His ambulance broke down, and though his physicians said that Jinnah had not suffered due to the breakdown, he died the same evening.

The death of Jinnah created a sense of uncertainty. Sensing this, India attacked Hyderabad the next day. By all standards, the achievement of Pakistan was momentous. Jinnah had rarely displayed emotion, but his followers shed uninhibited tears, feeling the weight of history while carrying his coffin.

THE LIAQUAT ERA, 1948–1951

Liaquat Ali Khan (1895–1951), the prime minister of Pakistan, had been honorary secretary of the AIML and leader of its bloc in the interim government. Due to his role in the Pakistan Movement, he had the magnetism to pull the country out of its despondency over Jinnah's death and the consequent Indian attack on Hyderabad, Deccan. The challenges of nation building were still immense, and Liaquat Ali Khan was able to meet only some of them. As far as framing of the constitution was concerned, Liaquat Ali Khan presented the Objectives Resolution on 12 March 1949. This is a valuable document that has been retained in all subsequent constitutions. The interim report of 28 September 1950 proved so unpopular that it had to be withdrawn in November. In the interim report, the prime minister had recommended the concentration of power in the future president. Other major impediments such as differences over the constitutional role of Islam and the quantum of East Bengal's representation were not removed.

Liaquat Ali Khan's policy of giving precedence to the Muslim League over parliament, increased the tension between the centre and provinces and resulted in the formation of twenty-one opposition parties. Since one party was given overwhelming importance, opposition elements began forming new parties. Liaquat Ali Khan was popular with the masses but the political forces were aligned against him. Jinnah himself complained of rising provincialism and Yusuf Haroon, as Sindh chief minister, also warned against this trend on 27 July 1947. Liaquat dismissed both the Punjab governor, Sir Francis Mudie and the Punjab Assembly, and the situation did not improve till the end of 1950 when the Muslim League won the elections to the NWFP and West Punjab. This success did not extend to East Bengal because of their outstanding demand to declare Bengali one of the national languages of Pakistan.

The constitution and the Kashmir problem remained unresolved, but Liaquat Ali Khan obtained favourable resolutions on 13 August 1948 and 25 July 1951 from the UN, calling for an impartial plebiscite. Till today these resolutions are the bedrock of Pakistan's stand on Kashmir.

Liaquat Ali Khan made rapid strides towards industrialization. He formed two Pakistan Industrial Development Corporations, one for large and one for small-scale industries. He did not wait for private entrepreneurs, but kept provision for their partnership. Pakistan was the largest jute producer in the world, but at the time of Independence it had no jute mill. It had a large cotton crop but only fourteen cotton mills. Liaquat's boldest decision was his refusal to devalue the rupee following the British and then Indian devaluation on 15 September 1949. India refused to buy jute and other commodities at the new rate. Liaquat was demonstrating Pakistan's financial viability with a vengeance. This caused the greatest stress to the jute growers of East Bengal. Liaquat travelled to Dhaka to assure them that if the Indians did not buy jute at the new rate, the government of Pakistan would buy the entire crop. Since Liaquat Ali Khan was a man of unassailable character, the peasants relied on him and refused to sell at the old price.

Liaquat Ali Khan accelerated Bengali recruitment in both the armed and civil services. The government gained financial respite because of the Korean war which gave a boost to Pakistani exports. This may have been a modest and ephemeral respite for Pakistan's economy, but it was a much needed one. Similarly Liaquat's efforts to achieve economic independence may have taken its toll on institution building. Liaquat could not decentralize power when immense efforts had gone into building a centre.

Liaquat Ali Khan constructed the 107 miles long BRB canal on the Punjab border and in July 1951, he de-escalated tension by a show of strength. He negotiated the Liaquat–Nehru Pact giving protection to minorities in both countries. Liaquat Ali Khan had put Pakistan on the road to progress when, in Rawalpindi on 16 October 1951, he was assassinated. His last words were: 'May God protect Pakistan'.

NOTES

1. Allen Campbell-Johnson, *Mission with Mountbatten,* London: Robert Hale, 1972, p. 87.
2. Richard Symonds, *The Making of Pakistan,* Islamabad: NBF, 1976, p. 87.
3. *Jinnah: Speeches and Statements 1947–1948,* Karachi: Oxford University Press, 2000, p. 92.
4. Jawaharlal Nehru, AIR broadcast, 2 November 1947.
5. Waheed Ahmad, (ed.), *The Nation's Voice,* Karachi: QAA, 2000, pp. 831–43.
6. Ibid.

NAWABZADA MUHAMMAD LIAQUAT ALI KHAN (b. Karnal, 1 October 1896–d. Rawalpindi, 16 October 1951) was the last honorary secretary of the AIML, the leader of the AIML block in the interim government, and the first prime minister of Pakistan. More worth recalling is that the Pakistan High Commission, in India, is housed in Liaquat Ali Khan's property. He did not file any claim for any property left behind in India, nor did he exchange any property. The chief minister of Sindh had cut off water supply to his official residence. When his mother asked for a car to bring her from the border to Karachi, Liaquat Ali Khan respectfully declined, saying that she would have to come in 1947, like any other refugee. When he was assassinated, he was discovered to be wearing a patched shirt. His bank balance was meagre. His sacrifices for the cause of Pakistan were second to none; yet he remains the most maligned Prime Minister of Pakistan.

Both in the 19–21 December 2006 centennial of the AIML, under the Quaid-i-Azam University, and in the 19–20 February 2007 Punjab University Conference on Peace and Security, Liaquat Ali Khan was blamed for derailing the destiny of Pakistan. His ambition, his flawed foreign policy, and his neglect of democratic norms are cited. As for his ambition, on 27 December 1947, he had sent in his resignation:

> You are the architect of Pakistan and, as such, I feel that it is but fair that you should have only such persons around you in building it up who can command your complete confidence and good will. I would never dream of doing anything which would, in any way injure Pakistan in the slightest degree, but as everyone knows, my health has not been well for the last two months; my slipping out quietly will not create any misunderstanding or difficulties.[1]

Liaquat's relations with Jinnah need comment. Jinnah often heeded Liaquat's suggestions: they worked out strategies and itineraries together, and entertained each other's objections. Yet, there seems to have been something elusive; Liaquat wrote to Jinnah, on 29 May 1940: 'In reality, it is the Congress alone which is responsible for this unsatisfactory state of affairs. You have hit the nail on the head by issuing your statement.'[2] Which is all perfectly true, yet the fact that he had to spell out explicitly the position of the Muslim League to Jinnah is an oddity. It is also enigmatic that their correspondence tells us more about the reserved and reticent Jinnah, than about the amiable and affable Liaquat Ali Khan.

How much Liaquat was his own master needs to be reconsidered now. Giving an interview to Nicholas Mansergh, in March 1947, Liaquat proposed that there be a capital in each wing: one administrative, one parliamentary ('I have made his suggestion.'[3]) Yet, when Shaista Ikramullah made the same proposal in the Constituent Assembly, Liaquat opposed it.[4] In the same interview, about the United States, Liaquat had said: 'We did not dislike them, we just feel that there is nothing in common. Therefore we are likely to think of Britain as an associate since we know her. The Soviet Union is an uncertain factor and her materialism is repugnant to Muslims.'[5]

That the materialism of the USSR was repugnant was a point reiterated by Jinnah on 7 September 1947. By the phrase 'uncertain factor,' Liaquat could not then have meant that the USSR would collapse, rather, that its policy with regard to a new Muslim country, near Central Asia, would be uncertain. The Pakistan Cabinet pre-empted Liaquat by retaining his reservations about the USSR, but discarding them with regard to the US. The stage was set for spreading a myth about the Moscow visit. Liaquat had thwarted two military coups—one in India (1947), and one in Pakistan (1951). His reputation was bound to suffer.

NOTES

1. Roger Long, 'Jinnah and his Right Hand' in M.R. Kazimi (ed.), *M.A. Jinnah: Views and Reviews*, Karachi: Oxford University Press, 2005, p. 138.
2. Muhammad Reza Kazimi (ed.), *Jinnah–Liaquat Correspondence*, Karachi: Pakistan Study Centre, University of Karachi, 2003, p. 88.
3. Nicholas Mansergh, *Independence Year*, New Delhi: Oxford University Press, 1999, p. 245.
4. Shaista Ikramullah, *From Purdah to Parliament*, Karachi: Oxford University Press, 1998, p. 229.
5. Nicholas Mansergh, op. cit., p. 246.

CHAPTER 26

EXPERIMENT IN DEMOCRACY, 1951–1958

The assassination of Liaquat Ali Khan was followed by a period of instability. No less than six prime ministers served during the next eight years.

Khwaja Nazimuddin stepped down as Pakistan's second governor-general to become the second prime minister. He was temperamentally unsuited to combat the intrigues of the new governor-general, Ghulam Mohammad, who had given himself overriding powers. Khwaja Nazimuddin became the target of criticism due to a shortage of food, and his ineffectual handling (initially) of the anti-Ahmadi riots in the Punjab. Being a Bengali, his opposition to the declaration of Bengali as a national language, brought the Language Movement to a head. By and large he retained the esteem of the masses and the confidence of the Constituent Assembly. This did not prevent Ghulam Mohammad from dismissing Khwaja Nazimuddin as prime minister on 17 April 1953. The success of this *coup* signalled the fragility of parliamentary democracy in Pakistan.

Mohammad Ali Bogra was inducted as prime minister. The induction of a nonrepresentative Bengali prime minister did not pacify the Bengalis, and in the ensuing 1954 provincial elections in East Bengal, the ruling Muslim League was defeated by the United Front. A.K. Fazlul Haq, the new chief minister of East Bengal stated on 3 May 1954, in the Indian city of Calcutta, that he did not believe in Pakistan. According to H.S. Suhrawardy this statement sparked off protests in his own province, one led by his erstwhile ally Maulana Abdul Hamid Khan Bhashani. Fazlul Haq promised to retire from politics and was eventually removed. Later he was appointed governor of the province.

The governor-general, emboldened by Nazimuddin's removal, dissolved the Constituent Assembly on 24 October 1954. The prime minister acquiesced in the decision, but the speaker, Tamizuddin Khan (1889–1963), challenged the action in the Sindh High Court. The court upheld the stand of the speaker, but the Federal Court, in a majority decision on 10 May 1955, decided against the speaker and in favour of Governor-General Ghulam Mohammad. This was the first verdict to uphold the dissolution of an assembly. Since Prime Minister Mohammad Ali Bogra had already tried, in 1954, to curtail the powers of the governor-general, and because he was without a popular base, he too was eased out of office on 10 August 1955.

The new Prime Minister, Chaudhry Mohammad Ali, was a bureaucrat having served as secretary general in 1947. He supported the move to merge the four provinces of Pakistan into One Unit which came into effect on 5 October 1955. Chaudhry Mohammad Ali became the first prime minister to give Pakistan a Constitution on 29 February 1956. Pakistan remained within the British Commonwealth but was designated an Islamic Republic. This achievement did not prove sufficient to prevent his fall. The newly created Republican Party forced Chaudhry Mohammad Ali's resignation on 8 September 1956.

The next Prime Minister, Huseyn Shaheed Suhrawardy was the only seasoned politician after Liaquat Ali Khan to hold this office; he had the credentials to bring about the now much needed stability to Pakistani politics. He was a leading barrister of his time, and the most successful since Jinnah. He was also chief minister of Bengal during the great Calcutta killing and had stayed with Gandhi to keep peace in Calcutta during Partition. He, along with Kiran Shankar Roy, the leader of the opposition in Bengal, and with Sarat Chandra Bose, had drafted a scheme for a united and independent Bengal, which M.A. Jinnah had immediately accepted.[1] Later, Gandhi and Liaquat Ali Khan also voiced acceptance but Nehru, the prime minister designate, turned down this scheme saying that the Hindus of Bengal could not live under perpetual Muslim majority.[2] He refused the offer of becoming the governor-general's personal roving ambassador or rehabilitation minister and insisted on becoming deputy prime minister.[3] This Jinnah interpreted as lack of confidence in Khwaja Nazimuddin, then chief minister of East Bengal. Later his membership of Pakistan's Constituent Assembly was cancelled because he had decided not to take up permanent residence in Pakistan. The result was that H.S. Suhrawardy ceased to be a member, while Kiran Shankar Roy remained a member of the Pakistan Constituent Assembly.

With the Language Movement, Suhrawardy's political role was enlarged, and he (quite rightly) called himself the last bridge between the eastern and western wings of Pakistan. Earlier his observation that East Bengali demands were largely met by parity representation in the National Assembly and the recognition of Bengali as a national language of Pakistan (under the 1956 Constitution) held out hope for national integration. Unfortunately, he became prime minister when he espoused a most unpopular cause. The Suez Crisis had resulted in the Anglo–French–Israeli invasion of Egypt in 1956 and while the people of Pakistan were outraged by the invasion, H.S. Suhrawardy justified his desertion of the Arab cause by describing Muslim countries as 'zeroes'. This phrase was earlier employed by President Iskander Mirza on 26 July 1956 but was noted largely when echoed by the prime minister. His foreign policy initiatives, and the impact left by this charismatic leader both on foreign affairs and interior politics was weak and temporary. He was the first prime minister to state that the Two-Nation theory had lost its validity after the creation of Pakistan and his main success was the induction of joint electorates in Pakistan. The defection of Maulana Bhashani from his party and thereafter, the desertion of the Republican Party enabled President Iskander Mirza to force his resignation.

The next Prime Minister, I.I. Chundrigar (15 September 1897–26 September 1960), had been a stalwart of the Bombay Muslim League. In the interim government he had been member for commerce. He was ambassador to Afghanistan and governor of NWFP. His was the shortest term as prime minister (18 October to 16 December 1957). He resigned over the question of separate or joint electorates.

The seventh Prime Minister, Sir Feroz Khan Noon (7 May 1893–9 December 1970), had even more impressive political credentials. He became the first native to become defence member of the Viceroy's Executive Council (1942–45) and was Indian high commissioner to Britain (1936–41). Sir Feroz Khan Noon remained prime minister for only 9 months (11 December 1957 to 7 October 1958) when he was removed in Pakistan's first military coup.

This democratic but unstable era saw progress in the industrial sector. The economy had survived the recession following the end of the Korean war (1952). The democratic dispensation was severely inhibited by Governor-General Ghulam Mohammad and President Iskander Mirza, who had the support of the bureaucracy and perhaps some elements in the armed forces. The franchise base was too narrow to provide succour to prime ministers and parliaments, but the politicians cannot be absolved of the charge of discrediting democratic rule.

On 20 September 1958, Abdul Hakim, the speaker of the East Pakistan assembly was physically expelled from the House amidst loud allegations that he was insane! On 23 September 1958, the deputy speaker, Shahed Ali, who had unfortunately to preside over the proceedings, died as the result of the violence in the sssembly.

Such incidents, coupled with allegations that Kalat was preparing to secede created alarm. President Iskander Mirza, abrogated the 1956 constitution, dismissed the prime minister and dissolved the assemblies.

On 7 October 1958 martial law was proclaimed. The Commander-in-Chief, General Mohammad Ayub Khan was appointed chief martial law administrator, and on 24 October, General Ayub was designated prime minister. On 27 October, he exiled President Iskander Mirza and occupied the office of the president. The despondent public widely and sincerely hailed the military coup, and President Ayub, regarded as a saviour, began his rule with expressions of approval from the public.

Notes

1. H.V. Hodson, *The Great Divide,* 2nd ed., Karachi: Oxford University Press, 1989, p. 246 (First edition London, Hutchinson 1969, published when Bengal separatism had gathered momentum).
2. S.M. Burke and S.A.D. Qureshi, *The British Raj in India,* Karachi: Oxford University Press, 1995, p. 513.
3. Ata Rabbani, *I was the Quaid's ADC,* Karachi: Oxford University Press, 1996, p. 171.

Huseyn Shaheed Suhrawardy (b. Midnapur, 8 September 1892–d. Beiru, 5 December 1963) was born to Sir Zahid Suhrawardy, a judge of the Calcutta High Court, and Khujesta Akhtar Bano—a pioneer of the Urdu novel. Suhrawardy was educated at Oxford, became a barrister, and as a practicing lawyer, led the profession in Pakistan. As a politician he rose to become chief minister of Bengal and prime minister of Pakistan (12 September 1956–13 October 1957), but in his personal life he suffered tragedies, and as a consequence, he took refuge in humour. His first wife died three years after marriage. His second marriage—to a Russian—was also brief. The greatest tragedy was that of his son, Shahab, who had graduated from Christ Church College, Oxford, and who died in 1940, at the age of 20. Suhrawardy adopted a fast lifestyle—even indulging in pranks. Khwaja Nazimuddin shuddered when he recalled how Suhrawardy brought a toy Panda—which squeaked—to a cabinet meeting.[1] Towards independence, he admitted to the viceroy that he had lied to Jinnah.[2]

His heart led his head. He minted money as a lawyer, but frittered it all away by doling it out to the deserving as well as the undeserving. In Calcutta, Sheikh Mujibur Rahman discovered that Suhrawardy made monthly payments of over Rs 3000 to the needy.[3] Such a man does not start riots, and although Suhrawardy suffered obloquy for the Great Calcutta killings of 1949, Chief Justice Sir Patrick Spens, exonerated him. In order to avoid a repetition of the holocaust at partition, Suhrawardy persuaded Mahatma Gandhi to join him in a mission to promote communal harmony. This mission induced him to refuse high office in Pakistan: 'Jinnah had been kind enough to offer me, successively, the refugee ministry, permanent representative to the UN, ambassador to the countries of the Middle East, and even the defense ministry.'[4]

Ever since Suhrawardy defended the leftist stalwarts in the Rawalpindi Conspiracy case, 1951, whom Liaquat prosecuted, his reputation had become coloured. Syed Jaffar Ahmad writes: 'Liaquat Ali Khan did not hide his dislike of Suhrawardy, who was humiliated when he was voted out of membership, while he was present on the floor of the house.'[5] What Liaquat had said was: 'My honourable friend is having a very mistaken sense of his importance if he thinks this amendment has been brought forward only for the purpose of eliminating Mr Suhrawardy from the constituent assembly of Pakistan. Mr Suhrawardy, if he so desires, can become a permanent resident of Pakistan tomorrow.'[6]

H.S. Suhrawardy was evasive in his address: 'I think that there is no anomaly in a member, in a citizen of the Indian Dominion being a member of the constituent assembly of Pakistan…and I feel, Sir, that the greatest loyalty is a loyalty to humanity, which transcends all parochial loyalties.'[7]

There is no doubt that Suhrawardy was the most able and popular prime minister after Liaquat Ali Khan, but he had compromised himself even before assuming office. He issued a statement in support of Urdu as the state language of Pakistan, also saying that Urdu be taught as a compulsory second language in east

Bengal.[8] On 17 April 1953, he publicly endorsed the dismissal of Khwaja Nazimuddin.[9] As prime minister, he had to uphold the most unpopular foreign policy by supporting the invasion of Suez, and added insult to injury by calling the Arabs a collection of zeroes. His exchange of visits with Zhou Enlai was a resounding success, but on his visit to the US, he dissipated its effect by lampooning China. Consider also his denunciation of Russia: 'The frequent purges, executions and massacres for political reasons the concentration camps, the farcical trials of alleged foreign spies...'[10]

Not even Liaquat (who has been accused time and again of alienating Russia) had used such strong language. It is no wonder, then, that his premiership occupies barely three pages in Suhrawardy's own memoirs.

NOTES

1. Shaista Ikramullah, *Huseyn Shaheed Suhrawardy*, Karachi: Oxford University Press, 1991, p. 12.
2. L.A. Sherwani, *The Partition of India and Mountbatten*, Karachi: Council of Pakistan Studies, 1986, p. 161.
3. S.A. Karim, *Sheikh Mujib: Triumph and Tragedy*, Dhaka: The University Press, 2005, p. 96.
4. M.H.R. Talukdar, ed., *The Memoirs of Huseyn Shaheed Suhrawardy*, Dhaka: The University Press, p. 106.
5. Syed Jaffar Ahmad, 'The Bengali Trio,' *Dawn*, 30 December 2006, p. 34.
6. M. Rafiq Afzal (ed.), *The Speeches and Statements of Quaid-i-Millat Liaquat Ali Khan*, Lahore Research Society, University of the Punjab, 1967, p. 157.
7. Shaista Ikramullah, op. cit., p. 153.
8. Badruddin Umar, *The Emergence of Bangladesh*, Karachi OUP, 2004, p. 217.
9. Ibid., p. 243.
10. M.H.R. Talukdar, op. cit., p. 115.

CHAPTER 27

THE FIRST MILITARY REGIME, 1958–1969

The Ayub Khan era began as a benevolent despotism, but ended as a discredited polity. In the beginning, the military regime succeeded in cracking down on corrupt civil servants, black marketeers and notorious smugglers. It also strictly imposed traffic regulations and civic rules, thereby earning the gratitude of the common man. This success was not replicated in East Pakistan, causing the General Officer Commanding, Major General Umrao Khan to admit that in his province, martial law had been a failure. In the exuberance following the reforms, people forgot that elections under the 1956 Constitution, scheduled for early 1959, had been relegated to oblivion.

Instead of general elections based on adult franchise, Field Marshal (since 1959) Mohammad Ayub Khan introduced a system of indirect elections called Basic Democracy (BD). Eighty thousand members (120,000 since 1967) would be directly elected to form the electoral college. Basic Democrats would then elect the president (which they did on 17 February 1960) and thereafter, the members of the national and provincial assemblies. These BDs would also run local government and union councils. Structurally, this system was designed to provide services to the people. Members would be available locally and be accessible throughout their term instead of only in the election season. Culturally it was a different story, since a limited electorate was open to coercion and corruption. Martial law punishments were harsh, some unwarranted, but as the presence of the military was not resented, reprisals were not vicious.

On 8 June 1962, President Ayub Khan lifted martial law and promulgated Pakistan's second constitution, which was presidential, not parliamentary. The four-year calm was broken by anti-constitution demonstrations led by a former Prime Minister H.S. Suhrawardy. The political and student protests could then be contained because of the great popularity enjoyed by the governor of East Pakistan, Lt.-Gen. Azam Khan. The first major rift between the ruler and ruled had been created and would only widen with time.

President Ayub Khan initiated a number of reforms in the law, education and population planning sectors. The president took a number of steps which he believed would accelerate economic progress in East Pakistan and the backward regions in West Pakistan. Contrary to the socialist tendencies then prevailing in Asia, the Pakistan Industrial Development Corporation set up units in the public sector and sold them to the private sector. Industrial development took long strides under Ayub, and even today, the development achieved in his era remains the mainstay of Pakistan's economy. Being conservative by nature, Ayub did not see the need for spreading wealth socially as much as regionally. Ultimately, because the distribution of wealth was not equitable socially, it proved to be unbalanced regionally. After he had resigned, Ayub told foreign journalists that there was a lack of managerial capacity in East Pakistan, which caused wastage of investment.[1] This may have been partially true then, but amidst the production of wealth, labour law was weighted heavily in favour of the capitalists. The chief economist of the Planning Commission, Dr Mahbub ul Haq, revealed that the wealth of the nation was held by only twenty-two families. Another aspect was that free import of capital goods gave an impetus to the consumer goods industry, while retarding development of heavy industries. In trade, a scheme of Bonus Vouchers (which could be purchased in the open market) was launched, which would subsidize imports. In spite of the boom of the sixties, the import of some articles, especially books, was severely curtailed.

In the agriculture sector, the labour force was not properly organized and Ayub's reforms were less effective than in industry. A Green Revolution was achieved by means of mechanized farming, chemical fertilizers and sinking of tube wells. The signing of the Indus Water Treaty with India in 1960, and the construction of the Warsak and Mangla dams increased the extent of irrigation. Water logging and salinity were tackled on a war footing. However, because of social constraints, most of the benefits were appropriated by the landlords and did not trickle down to the peasants.

On the diplomatic front, because of the arms imbalance, Ayub Khan told the American Congress that Pakistan was a country where US troops could land at any time. He withstood bravely the U2 crisis in 1960, when a US spy plane took off from Badaber base in Pakistan and was shot down over USSR territory. The US arming of India in the wake of the 1962 Sino–Indian War came as a rude awakening. Friendship with China grew and President Ayub became the first Pakistan head of government to visit the USSR in 1964. To offset western anger over Pakistan's wooing the Communist giants, a Regional Cooperation for Development (RCD)—was signed with Iran and Turkey, who were already pro-US CENTO allies. These were the conditions when the first presidential elections under the new 1962 constitution were announced.

Ayub Khan had a distinct advantage over the opposition: the only politician of consequence, H.S. Suhrawardy had died in 1963. Lt.-Gen. Azam Khan, a rival from within the military establishment, spoke out before the elections were scheduled and was countered tactically. The weakness of the disparate combination of the opposition was actually exposed when Miss Fatima Jinnah, Quaid-i-Azam's sister, was chosen as the Combined Opposition

Parties (COP's) presidential candidate. In spite of social disparities, stability had brought progress to Pakistan. The urge for democracy brought forth impressive rhetoric, but except in the politically charged cities of Karachi, Dhaka and Chittagong, Ayub won with a majority of 64 per cent. Had the 1965 war not intervened, political stability would have brought greater economic gains to Pakistan.

The 1965 war was preceded by the Rann of Kutch conflict, an area where the borders had not been demarcated at Independence. The Pakistan Army gave a good account of itself but yielded to British advice to submit the dispute to arbitration.

THE 1965 WAR

Causes: India abrogated Article 370 of its constitution which had given Jammu and Kashmir an autonomous status with a separate prime minister, and on 4 December 1964, enacted Articles 356/357 which in effect was an attempt to declare that Kashmir was an integral part of India. Unless Pakistan reacted now, its case on Kashmir would be lost by default. If it again appealed to the UN, it would again be frustrated by the Russian veto. If it simply sat back and let the ceasefire line become the international border (as some Pakistanis are now proposing) then constitutionally it would mean surrendering claims also to Azad Kashmir. If that came about, India could link up with Afghanistan from Kashmir and crush Pakistan. There was only one choice, to attract attention to the plight of the Kashmiris and cause international pressure on India not to treat Kashmir as a 'settled issue' and to allow self determination to Kashmiris in line with UNSC resolutions, and Nehru's repeated promises of an impartial plebiscite.

Under these circumstances Pakistan had to break the deadlock by sending infiltrators to Kashmir, which was not a novel step. President John F. Kennedy had recently sent infiltrators into Cuba. The leaders of Britain, Sri Lanka, Indonesia, even far off Brazil, and the majority of the world said that India was the agressor.

An example of Pakistan's folly is stated to be the assurance given by Zulfikar Ali Bhutto and Foreign Secretary Aziz Ahmad that India would confine its reaction to Kashmir and would not cross the international border; an assurance that Ayub accepted, and which turned out to be false. The suggestion that a military president relied on civilian assessment rather than military intelligence is too unrealistic to be taken at face value, specially when the Indian Prime Minister Lal Bahadur Shastri had publicly proclaimed that India would retaliate at a place of her own choosing.

The only rational explanation of the Pakistani initiative is that it was prompted by the Chinese leadership and was based on Chinese intervention.

In early 1965, the Chinese premier Zhou Enlai said to Ayub that a just settlement of the Kashmir dispute required sacrifices. On 4 September 1965 the Chinese Foreign Minister Chen Yi was told of the Pakistani sacrifices.[2] One Pakistani informant, Shamsuddin, told Keith James of the British high commission that the suggestion that regular troops be disguised as Kashmiri freedom fighters was a Chinese one.[3]

The Indian response to these moves was to take Kargil on 15 August 1965. This did not cause an international outrage as did Pakistani occupation of Kargil in 1999. Both the 1965 and 1999 actions were for the same reason, to cut Srinagar–Leh communications. Kargil was returned after the Tashkent Declaration and remained on the Pakistan side till the 1971 war. The fall of Kargil to India created a situation where surrender would lead inexorably to the ultimate liquidation of Pakistan or else Pakistan would have to disregard the arms imbalance, which could only grow worse with time, and defend itself.

Events: On 6 September 1965, the Indian forces crossed the international border and tried to capture the two cities of Lahore and Sialkot. The capture of these cities was calculated to break Pakistan's resistance. The assault on Lahore was halted with the help of the BRB canal. The defenders fought recklessly. A great battle was fought at Chawinda which Pakistan won. Pakistan had initially made headway in the Khem Karan sector, but beyond that line, the Indians flooded the area so that Pakistani tanks were bogged down. In Kashmir, the Pakistan advance was hampered by a midway change of command. Lt.-Gen. Akhtar Malik was replaced by Lt.-Gen. Yahya Khan. A spectacular aspect of the war was the superiority displayed by the Pakistan Air Force. The Pakistan Navy, though ill-equipped, took the Indian port of Dwarka. Pakistan performed well considering all the odds.

Results: The 1965 war is one of the most curious wars in history. Initially, both sides claimed victory, subsequently both sides admitted defeat. By 1990, Admiral Nandkarni of India and General Beg of Pakistan had stated that their respective countries had fared badly in the war. India was unable to take Lahore and Pakistan was unable to take Kashmir. After seventeen days of war, first India, and then Pakistan accepted a ceasefire.

The Role of Foreign Powers: All Third World countries with the solitary exception of Malaysia sided with Pakistan. Indonesia supplied a submarine and there were demonstrations favouring Pakistan in Iran and Turkey. Even Brazil showed solidarity with Pakistan. The British Prime Minister, Harold Wilson, stated that India's crossing of the international border was an act of aggression. Thereafter, all his efforts were centred on Pakistan accepting a ceasefire without securing a political settlement of Kashmir; above all, Britain was most anxious that Pakistan should eschew Chinese intervention. The British High Commissioner, Sir Morrice James, gave President Ayub the assurance that 'the world would not, repeat, not in the foreseeable future revert to the position that the future of Kashmir was a closed issue'.[4] In other words, James was cajoling Ayub into accepting a ceasefire without political progress in Kashmir. In his memoirs he justly claimed that he had played the vital role in persuading Ayub to accept the ceasefire[5] without accepting Chinese help.

US President Lyndon B. Johnson's initial reaction was to halt arms supply to both India and Pakistan, though fully conscious that India had an alternative source of supply from Russia, while Pakistan had none. The US had replied to Pakistan's invocation of the 1959 Mutual Defence Treaty with the charge that Pakistan had sent infiltrators on 5 August 1965. In the face of the Chinese factor, the US state office displayed a more measured response. US Secretary of State Dean Rusk told the Indian envoy on 18 September that in case of Chinese intervention, US would need Congressional sanction to commit its troops, an outcome Rusk said was unlikely.[6] US Under Secretary George Ball and Assistant Secretary William Bundy said, on 23 September, that Chinese movement would give US greater leverage over India.[7] In the midst of US recrimination was embedded Dean Rusk's statement upholding the principle of plebiscite.[8]

The Chinese role, as stated above, began before the hostilities broke out. The Chinese foreign minister was in Pakistan on 4 September. On 7 September, China declared that India's invasion of Pakistan was an act of naked aggression. On 8 September it sent warnings against Indian intrusions into Chinese territory. On 16 September, China issued an ultimatum that unless India dismantled its military posts in Chinese territory, stopped intrusions and undertook to refrain from hostile acts across the border, it would take appropriate action. On 19 September, the Chinese extended their ultimatum by three days and at the end of the period announced that India had complied with their demands.

It is obvious that the first Chinese ultimatum was to give Pakistan time to decide its course and the announcement of Indian compliance signalled that Pakistan had finally decided against taking advantage of this ultimatum. The Chinese condition for helping Pakistan was that Pakistan remain steadfast and not succumb to pressure,[9] but being conservative by temperament and training, Ayub was forced to give in to British blandishments, and threw away an opportunity. The American assessment was clear in analysing the chances of winning by the combatants. While they calculated that Pakistani ammunition (which the US had supplied) would run out before Indian ammunition did, the US also reckoned that if Pakistan won a major battle in the Punjab it could win the war. Another power to play a major role was the USSR. Its role could be best understood in the context of the Tashkent peace talks of 10 January 1966, which were called by the USSR.

THE TASHKENT DECLARATION

President Ayub led the Pakistani delegation, Prime Minister Lal Bahadur Shastri, the Indian delegation and Alexei N. Kosygin, Chairman, Council of Ministers, the USSR delegation. Tashkent is the capital of Uzbekistan, then in the USSR. The talks lasted from 4 to 10 January 1966. India had opposed the drawing up of an agenda.

The outcome of the 1965 war was that Pakistan spurned the offer of help from China which had consistently supported it, and accepted the good offices of the USSR which had consistently opposed it. The statements of US Secretary of State Dean Rusk and his deputies show that Chinese intervention would have given more time to Pakistan, thus demoralizing India before the US counter intervention took place. Even in the British estimation 'India had come off best on the ground, but had no great victory to announce'.[1] To create an air of neutrality, the USSR Prime Minister, Alexei Kosygin, remarked that Kashmir was a disputed area.[2]

This explains why the Indian prime minister was apprehensive, and sought Anglo–American clearance before accepting the USSR invitation to talks in Tashkent.[3] President Ayub was, on the other hand, aggressively defiant, terming the Russian offer a propaganda stunt. He openly said that if he and Shastri met face to face they would merely restate their cases and depart without reaching an agreement. Ayub favoured arbitration under UNSC as has been the case with the Rann of Kutch engagement.[4] Thus, Ayub went to Tashkent against his better judgement and had the US not put its weight behind the Soviet initiative, Ayub would not have attended the peace talks. As we now know, he would have been able to prevent his fall.

It was Pakistan that had imposed conditions for accepting a ceasefire on 11 September 1965. Foreign Minister Bhutto told Sir Morrice James that the UNSC resolution of 4 and 6 September favoured India by asking for a return to 5 August position without providing for a Kashmir settlement.[5] The British stated that the problem could be approached in four stages: (i) Both sides stop fighting (ii) both sides agree to return of status quo (iii) measures be taken to neutralize and quieten the situation within Kashmir and (iv) future settlement of the whole problem of Kashmir.

Britain approached the problem it had created, gingerly. The first two stages would be unacceptable to Pakistan unless followed by the last two.[6] This was the objective Pakistan pursued at Tashkent and this was the objective that eluded it.

The Indian objective was to secure a No-War Pact from Pakistan so that the Kashmir dispute was permanently put into cold storage. At one point in the negotiations, Shastri prevailed on Ayub to inscribe in his own hand on the typed draft, a renunciation of force. Z.A. Bhutto had the undertaking cancelled. Kuldip Nayar, an Indian journalist who retained Ayub's inscription, surmises that this was the secret clause in the Tashkent agreement to which Z.A. Bhutto later referred.[7]

The only pressure the USSR exercised over India was to return the Kargil area, and it is on this point that Ayub was forthright. Otherwise the pressure was on Pakistan, as Kosygin stated that if no accord was signed, the world would get the impression that disputes could be settled only by force. According to another version, Kosygin stated that he would not allow the meeting to be unproductive. Kosygin also dismissed a proposal for independent Kashmir, citing the ethnic diversity of the state.[8]

It was India that was dependent on the USSR for arms and money, not Pakistan. Therefore, it was held anomalous that Pakistan, and not India, yielded to Soviet pressure. Meanwhile, China had issued another ultimatum to India on 6 January while negotiations were in progress.

NOTES

1. Roedad Khan, (ed.), *The British Papers*, Karachi: Oxford University Press, 2002, p. 410.
2. Mahboob A. Popatia, *Pakistan's Relations with the Soviet Union*, Karachi: Pakistan Study Centre, University of Karachi, 1988, p. 95.
3. Roedad Khan, (ed.), *The British Papers*, p. 395.
4. Ibid., p. 408.
5. Ibid., p. 326.
6. Ibid., p. 321.
7. Kuldip Nayar, *India: The Critical Years*, New Delhi: Vikas, 1971, p. 245.
   In his later publication *Distant Neighbours*, New Delhi: Vikas, 1972, p. 136, Kuldip Nayar has reproduced Ayub's handwritten concession.
8. Iqbal Akhund, *Memoirs of a Bystander*, Karachi: Oxford University Press, 1997, p. 118.

PROVISIONS

The Tashkent Declaration was finally signed on 10 January 1966. It provided for: (a) the reaffirmation by both sides of their obligation under the United Nations Charter, to settle disputes by peaceful means; (b) the withdrawal of all armed personnel by 25 February 1966 to positions held prior to 5 August 1965; (c) discontinuance of hostile propaganda; (d) restoration of full diplomatic representation; (e) machinery to continue joint India/Pakistan discussions on other issues of direct concern.

The only mention of the cause of the conflict was as follows: 'It was against this background that Jammu and Kashmir was discussed, and each of the sides set forth its respective positions.'

This was a disappointing outcome, and though the Soviet Union had been protective of India's occupation, Kosygin realized that the solution he had imposed did not have portents for peace, and *after* the Tashkent Declaration was signed Kosygin asked Shastri to solve the Kashmir problem. Shastri offered minor adjustments along the ceasefire line, which Pakistan rejected.

REACTIONS

The Indian reaction to the Tashkent Declaration was naturally favourable. The death of Lal Bahadur Shastri in Tashkent had sanctified the Declaration. In Pakistan, anti-Tashkent demonstrations were set off by a war widow who appeared at the Punjab University campus with her fatherless infants. These demonstrations swelled to a widespread movement. On 10 June 1966 Foreign Minister Z.A. Bhutto advocated overstepping the Tashkent Declaration to obtain a solution to the Kashmir problem.[10] Eventually he came to lead the movement. The killing by police gunfire of a student, Abdul Hamid, on 7 November 1966 accelerated the movement. The arrest of Z.A. Bhutto on 13 November 1968 only served to inflame the masses, and the movement was sustained for three years, leading ultimately to Ayub's resignation on 25 March 1969.

Another factor which led to disenchantment with Ayub was the prominence given by the government-controlled press to his son, Captain Gohar Ayub. This bred the suspicion that he was being groomed for succession. Gohar Ayub's unpopularity was due to a January 1965 victory procession he had led in Karachi that had turned violent. There were wild rumours that Gohar Ayub was buying up every profitable enterprise. This rebounded on a president who had been elected to put an end to corruption. In 1967, Ayub published his political autobiography *Friends Not Masters*[11] which took away the mystique of his reforms, and caused the 'Decade of Development' which could have justly been celebrated, to become an occasion for derision.

In East Pakistan, the cause of disaffection was not Tashkent which most opposition leaders had hailed. During a Lahore meeting in 1966, of opposition leaders, the Awami League President Sheikh Mujibur Rahman (1920–1975), presented his six points programme: a confederal formula for East and West Pakistan. Agitation for this programme, further inflamed by the Agartala Conspiracy trial, led to violent demonstrations, entailing what was called 'Besiege and Burn' (*Gherao Jalao*) operations. If Ayub had resigned on 21 February 1969 instead of just saying that he would not again run for president, the momentum towards disintegration could have been contained. He resigned on 25 March 1969 when anti-government demonstrations became anti-state demonstrations. People calling for regime change began calling for secession. Thus while Ayub's removal was inevitable and of course popular, it was mistimed, because it created uncertainty.

NOTES

1. *Morning News*, Karachi, 2 April 1972, p. 4.
2. Anwar Husain Syed, *China and Pakistan*, London: OUP, 1974, p. 117.
3. Roedad Khan (ed.), *The British Papers*, Karachi: OUP, 2002, p. 422 (hereafter abbreviated as BPs).
4. Ibid., p. 388.
5. Sir Morrice James, *Pakistan Chronicle*, Karachi: OUP, 1993, p. 153.
6. BPs, p. 372.
7. Ibid., pp. 375, 410.
8. Ibid., p. 384.
9. M. Asghar Khan, *The First Round*, London: Islamic Information Services, 1979, p. 22.
10. BPs, p. 573.
11. Mohammad Ayub Khan, *Friends Not Masters*, Karachi: Oxford University Press, 1967.

FIELD MARSHAL MOHAMMAD AYUB KHAN (b. Rehana, 1907–d. Islamabad, 1974) had a dominating presence, but a vulnerable personality. He was educated at Aligarh and Sandhurst. As president, he brought stability, and in its wake unequalled economic prosperity. Ayub's prescription for prosperity however proved to be too conservative, giving rise to a backlash from which Pakistan has never recovered. Ayub was the first military ruler of Pakistan, and while the novelty lasted, he was more popular than the ephemeral prime ministers he replaced. His was the only military regime which brought about a respite from corruption to a degree that surprised even him.

Take the example of how readily people declared their untaxed hidden wealth—they declared Rs. 1,700 million. I asked a businessman 'Why did you do it?' He said, 'In one of your photographs, I saw you with your finger pointed like this, and your mouth screwed up like this.' I said to myself, 'This man will not leave us alone.'[1]

Even more revealing is his analysis of the prospects of a military coup d'etat in India:

The fools don't realize that even if he [General Kondar Maddapa Cariappa], 1899–1993 was inclined that way, he being a retired man, has no power or influence to do such a thing. I told him that even if circumstances warranted, take over of seventeen provincial governments and a central government was not a feasible proposition. However what is possible is that someone like Yashwant Balwant Rao Chavan may take over with the backing of the army.[2]

In other words, the necessary ingredients were either a military personality capable of overshadowing politicians, or conversely, a political personality capable of dominating the military, and a compact administrative apparatus, simple to take over. In connection with capitals, Ayub's critical faculty went on and off. He objected that Lahore as capital of the west wing was too close to the border.[3] This idea did not cross his mind while determining the location of Islamabad.

It is apparent that in his later years, his protégé Zulfikar Ali Bhutto became quite an obsession with him, and Altaf Gauhar explains why. In Tashkent, 'When Ayub was relating how Shastri kept saying that he was answerable to the people, Bhutto interrupted quite sharply, 'But you too are answerable to the people'. '[4]

Even in his diary, his reason for Bhutto's removal appears as an afterthought: 'His real trouble was that he started running a personal policy assisted by a few elements in the foreign office, instead of the national, also, he was distrusted and disliked in most capitals'.[5]

What Ayub considered 'national' policy was telling the Chinese Ambassador, just one year after the 1965 war, that the Chinese government's treatment of Muslims would have repercussions in Sinkiang, Central Asia, and Pakistan![6] The following April 1987, he criticized the past action of Bhutto and Aziz Ahmad for bending over backwards to establish close relations with Nepal, and even Sikkim and Bhutan.[7]

During the 1971 crisis, he received information—which he believed Bhutto shared—that many PPP men had sworn allegiance to Mujibur Rahman. He conceded that Bhutto's stand was logical in view of Mujibur Rahman's uncompromising attitude, but his object was difficult, as indeed it was.

Ayub was innately a gentleman—very patriotic—but his days at Sandhurst had rendered him incapable of taking the plunge at crucial times. In this trait he was not followed by his son, Gohar Ayub, who proved to be an intrepid Foreign Minister.

NOTES

1. Mohammad Ayub Khan, *Friends not Masters*, Karachi: Oxford University Press, 1971, p. 76.
2. Craig Baxter, (ed.) *The Diaries of Field Marshal Mohammed Ayub Khan*, Karachi: Oxford University Press, 2007, p. 165.
3. Ibid., p. 91.
4. Altaf Gauhar, *Ayub Khan, Pakistan's First Military Ruler*, Karachi, Oxford University Press, 1996, p. 262.
5. Craig Baxter, op. cit., p. 3
6. Ibid., p. 10.
7. Ibid., p. 84.
8. Ibid., p. 452.

CHAPTER 28

THE SECOND MILITARY REGIME, 1969–1971

On 25 March 1969, Field Marshal Mohammad Ayub Khan (1908–1974) imposed martial law, abrogated the 1962 Constitution and transferred the offices of chief martial law administrator and president to Gen. Yahya Khan (1917–1980). He temporarily banned all political activity, vowing to lead the country back to sanity, as the demonstrations against Ayub Khan had assumed violent proportions. The 1962 constitution had provided for transfer of power to the speaker of the National Assembly, Abdul Jabbar Khan, a Bengali leader who had not spared even his son Rashid Khan Menon for his revolutionary activities. Constitutionally and personally, Abdul Jabbar Khan had a better chance than anyone else to address the tide of Bengali nationalism, but he was never given the chance.

General Yahya Khan asserted that he had neither staged a *coup d'état*, nor was he the elected representative of the people. He was instead, a soldier on 'deputed duty'. Later, with the encouragement of political parties, he took two decisions in advance of the constitution-making process. On 28 November 1969, he announced the dissolution of One Unit; the restoration of the three West Pakistan provinces and the creation of Balochistan. He also announced that parity between the two wings was being revoked. This had meant an equal number of seats in the National Assembly for both wings. Yahya Khan affirmed the principle of one man, one vote which meant that East Pakistan would have a majority in the next assembly. The Legal Framework Order (LFO) had made a simple majority sufficient for framing the constitution.

The LFO was promulgated on 30 March 1970. This prescribed the limits in which elections would be held and within which the constitution was to be framed. The LFO provided that:

> Pakistan shall be a Federal Republic to be known as the Islamic Republic of Pakistan in which the Provinces and other territories which are now and may hereafter be included in Pakistan shall be so united in a Federation that the independence, the territorial integrity and the national solidarity of Pakistan are ensured and that the unity of the Federation is not in any way involved. (para 20).

In addition, the LFO provided that the constitution was to be framed within 120 days, failing which the National Assembly would be dissolved.

Shorn of constitutional terms, federating unit meant West Pakistan on one hand, and East Pakistan on the other. After the break up of One Unit, the term federating unit would apply equally to Sindh, Punjab, NWFP and Balochistan. All provinces, according to the Six Points would have separate currencies, separate foreign currency accounts and separate militias. The politicians immediately understood that the LFO and the Six Points were not compatible. Sheikh Mujibur Rahman, the Awami League president said, on 2 May 1970 at Hatiya, that the Constituent Assembly should be made sovereign. He pointed out that 'the coming elections were not for achieving power, but to frame the country's constitution...' He regretted that certain provisions in the LFO had negated the principles of democracy.[1] On 3 May Awami League leader Tajuddin said that the Six Points were a must.[2] On 8 May 1970 Sheikh Mujibur Rahman reiterated that there was no possibility of compromise on the Six Points.[3] Thus we see that the incompatibility between the LFO and Six Points was glaringly apparent even before the 7 December 1970 general elections. On 14 August 1970 Independence Day, students of Dhaka University, in a meeting presided over by the Vice-Chancellor Abu Saeed Choudhry displayed a new map and flag of Bangladesh.[4] Former professor and chair of Political Science at Dhaka University and a member of Yahya's cabinet G.W. Choudhry later commented that Mujib's scheme of a centre with only two responsibilities, defence and foreign affairs, was devoid of financial or administrative means to carry out its obligations.[5]

Mujibur Rahman had stressed that the elections were for framing a constitution and not for achieving power. There would be no provision under constitutional law to limit the Six Points to only one province. The Awami League insisted that the constitution be framed only by the simple majority it enjoyed and vehemently rejected the suggestion that the constitution be passed by a 61 per cent majority. This figure was proposed as a compromise since it is a universal convention to frame or amend a constitution by a two-thirds majority. The importance of the Six Points became clear after the Awami League won the 1970 elections.

THE SIX POINT PROGRAMME

1. The character of the government shall be federal and parliamentary in which the election shall be direct and on the basis of universal adult franchise; the representation in the federal legislature shall be on the basis of population.
2. The federal government shall be responsible only for defence and foreign affairs and, subject to conditions provided in (3), below, currency.
3. There shall be two separate currencies mutually freely convertible in each wing for each region, or in the alternative, a single currency with regional federal reserve banks to prevent the transfer of resources and flight of capital from one region to another.
4. Fiscal policy shall be the responsibility of the federating units (provinces). The federal government shall be provided with requisite revenue resources for meeting the requirements of defence and foreign affairs.
5. Constitutional provisions shall be made to enable separate accounts to be maintained of the foreign exchange of each of the federating units, under the control of the respective governments.
6. The government of the federating units shall be empowered to maintain a militia or para-military force in order to contribute effectively towards national security.

THE ELECTIONS OF 7 DECEMBER 1970

These were the first ever general elections to be held on the basis of direct and universal adult franchise throughout Pakistan. The framing of the constitution had been an elusive exercise, therefore the enthusiasm of the voters to secure a lasting constitution for Pakistan was unprecedented. It was generally recognized that the conduct of elections had been free and fair. For this Yahya Khan was rightly praised. In East Pakistan, the Awami League won 167 out of 169 seats. Out of the 144 seats allotted to the west wing, the PPP, led by Zulfikar Ali Bhutto won 81 seats initially. After independent members joined the PPP its representation grew to 88. The Awami League had not won a single seat outside East Pakistan, and since One Unit had been done away with, the PPP, on the same basis of regional representation, represented only the Punjab and Sindh; as in Balochistan and NWFP the National Awami Party, led by Khan Abdul Wali Khan (d.2006), had the majority representation. Thus three parties represented three regions: East Bengal, Sindh and Punjab, and Balochistan and NWFP. The party caught in the middle, the PPP set off the constitutional crisis.

The Awami League leader Sheikh Mujibur Rahman was also making disquieting observations but was neither loud nor categorical. He told Ardeshir Zahedi and Ihsan Sabri Cagliyangil, the foreign ministers of Iran and Turkey, that 'he would rather be the father of a new nation than the Prime

Minister of Pakistan.'⁶ On 14 January 1971, Yahya Khan declared that Sheikh Mujibur Rahman was the next prime minister of Pakistan. On 17 January, Yahya went to Larkana to confer with Z.A. Bhutto. This created a bad impression since Yahya had not visited Mujibur Rahman at his house, but called him to the Governor's House, Dhaka. According to Bhutto, he expressed to Yahya, his misgivings about the Six Points.⁷ Bhutto thereafter, went to Dhaka to confer with Mujibur Rahman about the Six Point formula from 27 to 30 February 1971. These talks proved inconclusive and on his return Bhutto asked Yahya to delay convening the Constituent Assembly.

THE CONSTITUTIONAL CRISIS

Yahya did not accede to Bhutto's request and fixed 3 March 1971 as the date when the Constituent Assembly would be convened at Dhaka. At this, Z.A. Bhutto set off the constitutional crisis by stating, on 15 February 1971 in Peshawar, that he would not attend the Constituent Assembly on 3 March. In Bhutto's own words, 'unless assured that our point of view would be heard, and if found reasonable, accepted by the Awami League',⁸ he would not attend. On 28 February in Lahore, Bhutto said he was willing to go to Dhaka if the pre-condition of framing the constitution within 120 days was lifted. Bhutto's position was equivocal; he had denied at Peshawar that he was boycotting the session, but this was only a play of words because his refusal to attend, and, moreover, his refusal to let his party members attend was, in effect, a boycott.

In East Pakistan, Mujibur Rahman told the *New York Times* on 4 March 1971, that each wing should have its own prime minister. As M. Rafique Afzal aptly says: 'No one took notice of this extreme statement, but ten days later, a similar statement by Bhutto evoked an uproar'.⁹ Whatever the objective situation, Bhutto's ambition is a factor which nobody is willing to discount. Whether Bhutto was justified in depicting the Six Points as secessionist can be judged by tracing the history of Bengali nationalism.

THE COURSE OF ETHNIC VIOLENCE

On 25 March 1971, General Tikka Khan (1917–2002) ordered military action which was indiscriminate and reprehensible but not unprovoked. The violence was initiated by Bengali militants and not by the Pakistan Army. In fact, there were two broad phases of violence, a limited phase dating from 1954 and a second phase beginning in 1966. The first ethnic riot took place on 23 March 1954 at Chandraghona Paper Mills (near Chittagong), the second took place in the Adamjee Jute Mills at Narayanganj (near Dhaka) on 15 May 1954. The majority of victims were non-Bengalis, lumped together under the name of *Biharis* as most of them had sought refuge from anti-Muslim riots in Bihar.

The next round of ethnic riots took place in Chittagong early in May 1966, when a Khoja family refused to allow their daughter to marry a Bengali boy, (for sectarian rather than ethnic reasons).[10] Following Yahya's martial law, on 7 August 1969, there were attacks on non-Bengali localities in Dhaka,[11] and another attack on 1 November 1969.

On 1 March 1971, when General Yahya Khan announced that the Constituent Assembly session scheduled for 3 March was being postponed, Mujib held a press conference and called for a strike and civil disobedience. This was the signal for widespread genocide against the non-Bengalis. This was a pogrom during which around 30,000 non-Bengalis, men, women and children, were killed.[12]

HISTORY OF BENGALI NATIONALISM

Following are excerpts from different books and journals that trace the various stages of Bengali nationalism:

1. Since the dawn of history, Bengal had been a problem, demanding political independence against imperial domination whether Hindu or Muslim, since the age of Harsha down to the age of Akbar.[1]

2. Ethnic animosity between Bengalis and Biharis, specially, Hindu Bengalis and Hindu Biharis surfaced before Partition. The Congress Working Committee formed a sub-committee to deal with this problem. It finally adopted Dr Rajendra Prasad's proposal of doing away with ethnic distinction, by abolishing the provision of Domicile Certificates.[2]

3. Netaji Subhash Chandra Bose was forced by Mahatma Gandhi to resign as Congress President in 1939. To show his solidarity with the great Bengali leader, the great Bengali poet Rabindranath Tagore hosted a reception in honour of Bose and delivered the welcome address.[3]

4. In 1947, Huseyn Shaheed Suhrawardy, then chief minister, and Kiran Shankar Roy, then leader of the opposition in the Bengal Legislative Assembly, presented a scheme of a United and Independent Bengal. M.A. Jinnah,[4] Liaquat Ali Khan, Sarat Chandra Bose and even Mahatma Gandhi agreed, but the Congress President, Jawaharlal Nehru refused, saying that 'there was no chance of Hindus there agreeing to put themselves under permanent Muslim domination.'[5]

This led to Nehru endorsing the Two-Nation Theory, he had otherwise detested and ridiculed. It was wrong for Hindus to be permanently subjugated in Muslim majority Bengal, but it was acceptable for Muslims to be permanently subjugated in Hindu majority India. Nehru had realised that if a single province, Bengal, was allowed independence, other provinces would make the same demand, and the Princely states would be encouraged to retain their freedom.[6]

In 1947, Nehru blocked the independence of Bengal to preserve the integrity of India. In 1971, Yahya blocked the independence of Bangladesh to preserve the integrity of Pakistan. Three out of five provinces, East Bengal, NWFP and Balochistan had voted for pro-USSR parties (Awami League in the post-Suhrawardy era and NAP). While M.A. Jinnah could agree to an independent Bengal, there was no constitutional device by which he could refuse the accession of East Bengal to Pakistan.

NOTES

1. Kalikaranjan Qanungo, *Sher Shah and his Times* Calcutta: Orient Longman, 1965, p. 303.
2. *Star of India*, Calcutta, 16 January 1939, p. 6.
3. Stanley Wolpert, *Gandhi's Passion*, New York: Oxford University Press, 2001, p. 188. Shakeel Ahmad Zia, *Sindh Ka Muqaddama* (Sindh's Case), Karachi, April 1987, p. 25.
4. H.V. Hodson, *The Great Divide*, Karachi: Oxford University Press, 1989, p. 246.
5. S.M. Burke and S.A.D. Qureshi, *The British Raj in India*, Karachi: Oxford University Press, 1995, p. 513.
6. Sailesh Kumar Bandopadhya, *Quaid-i-Azam Mohammad Ali Jinnah and the Creation of Pakistan*, New Delhi: Sterling, 1991, p. 323.

A British technician who crossed the border on 6 April 1971 reported the massacre in Dinajpur. 'After the soldiers had left, the mobs set upon the non-Bengali Muslims from Bihar. I don't know how many died, but I could hear the screams throughout the night'. The European manager of a Chittagong bank said, 'It was fortunate for every European living here that the Army arrived when it did; otherwise, I would not have lived to tell the tale'. Most of the non-Bengalis were killed before 25 March.[13]

All these atrocities are well-documented. The effect of the violence was to shape the outcome of the three-sided negotiations being carried out between Yahya Khan, Mujibur Rahman and Zulfikar Ali Bhutto.

The negotiations began on 22 March 1971. Tajuddin conveyed the Awami League decision that it would not allow any central or national cabinet, and demanded that power be transferred to the two wings directly.[14] This meant that the Awami League, which had already called for martial law to be lifted, wanted not a transfer but an abdication of power. The next day—Republic Day—Kamal Husain submitted the final proposal of the Awami League to Yahya Khan.[15] According to G.W. Choudhry, who personally saw the draft, the Awami League set forth the procedure for framing two constitutions by two sovereign constitutional conventions. 'In fact, the Mujib plan was nothing but an unqualified scheme for splitting the country into two separate entities, Bangladesh and Pakistan.'[16] Although G.W. Choudhry is critical of Z.A. Bhutto throughout, his analysis of the Six Points is the same as Bhutto's.

Thus the crisis had nothing to do with transferring power to the majority party. It was a constitutional crisis. As Bhutto had explained, the Six Point programme was a confederal not federal scheme. In a confederal set up, the majority party of one unit cannot become the majority party of another federating unit,[17] for example, both Britain and Australia are members of the Commonwealth and both have Queen Elizabeth II as their head of state, but the majority party of Britain cannot form a government in Australia. If the Awami League wished for power at the centre it would have had to compromise on the Six Points. Mujibur Rahman could not become the prime minister and yet retain a Six Point mandate.

Bhutto became the main adversary for pointing this out. The slogan chanted by the Awami League protesters was '*Bhuttor Mukkhe Lati Maro*' (Kick Bhutto's face). It is clear from the conclusion reached by all political analysts that the Six Point programme was a scheme of secession. Why did Mujibur Rahman not make a direct declaration of independence? G.W. Choudhry's explanation is that Mujibur Rahman wished to employ a weak confederal link to extract financial benefits. He writes: 'While the Central Government was denied any financial powers or resources as far as Bangladesh was concerned, it might be liable to pay dues to the Bangladesh Government on the basis of the 1970–71 budget'.[18] This marked the end of the talks and was the signal for action by the Pakistan Army on 25 March 1971.

PAKISTAN ARMY ATROCITIES

G.W. Choudhry, a professor of Political Science, was present during the crisis and was able to depict unerringly the events that unfolded. He concedes that armed rebellion had to be encountered, but condemns the action taken by the army and then asks: 'But could there be any justification or rationale for the killing of thousands of innocent villagers who had not the slightest idea of the issues involved?'[19] The atrocities cited in the Hamoodur Rahman Commission Report are sufficient to convey a sense of the trauma: 'There was a massacre in Comilla Cantonment on 27 March 1971, ordered by Lt.-Gen. Yaqub Malik. Seventeen officers, nine hundred and fifteen soldiers were killed. In Salda Nadi another five hundred persons were killed'. Brigadier Arbab also asked Lt.-Col. Aziz Ahmad Khan to destroy all houses in Joydebpur, who carried out the order to a great extent. In May, Brigadier Abdullah Malik gave a written order to kill Hindus. Lt.-Gen. Gul Hassan used to ask the soldiers 'how many Bengalis have you killed?'[20]

The Hamoodur Rahman Commission stated that there was indiscriminate killings of Bengalis.[21] While it is to the credit of West Pakistanis that no Bengalis were killed in the west wing, it is a matter of grave discredit that the terrorists were allowed to escape and innocent people were killed.[22] When asked, about the army action, General Tikka Khan said, 'it was a complete distortion of history to believe as everyone in the world does, that we started everything. Mujib wanted a showdown'.[23]

As far as this statement goes, it is true. He complained about exaggeration by the Awami League. His own estimate of the number of Bengalis killed was 30,000! The Hamoodur Rahman Commission estimated 26,000 Bengalis killed. The verdict of the Hamoodur Rahman Commission Report is that: 'No amount of provocation by the militants of the Awami League or other miscreants could justify retaliation by a disciplined army against its own people'.[24] It is in the background of this verdict, perhaps, that President Pervez Musharraf apologized on 29 July 2002, in Dhaka for the army action.

WEST PAKISTAN ARROGANCE

Just as important as recounting the history of Bengali nationalism, is the need to analyse the mindset of West Pakistanis. The history of Bengali nationalism and the language issue encompass policy, but not conduct, as all the portents of nationalism could have remained latent, possibly even contained, even after having emerged from the Calcutta and Noakhali communal riots. The arrogance of the ruling elite towards the Bengali population had a cumulative effect in creating alienation.

The language factor had led the Bihari refugees to side with the Urdu speaking West Pakistan, but this was a purely sentimental attitude of a largely lower middle class community. In practice, the Biharis were fluent in Bengali and only needed to learn the script. This involved effort, since the scripts were so different and there were few facilities for on-the-job training.

The Bengali population was overwhelmingly responsive to rulers who showed sensitivity to their feelings. The popularity of Lt.-Gen. Azam Khan as governor of East Pakistan is irrefutable evidence that the population of East Pakistan was actively constructing Pakistan nationalism. It is in the governorship of Azam Khan that we find the factor that kept East Pakistan loyal to Pakistan. His term and style as governor should be studied in any analysis of the crisis. In spite of being a military governor and a Pathan, and ethnically poles apart from the Bengalis, he identified with the masses.

On the occasion of the state visit of Queen Elizabeth II, while the road connecting Dhaka airport to the city was under repair, Azam Khan shared food and drink from the earthernware vessels of the labourers, squatting with them during visits which were round the clock. Apart from labourers, he identified with fishermen and farmers. Even after braving the shock of his removal and a presidential election which was bitterly contested in 1965, the population of East Pakistan had solidly supported the 1965 war. It was apparent, but not expressed then, that there was not a single anti-aircraft gun in the whole of East Pakistan.

It was this spirit of patriotism that had to be broken before a secessionist plan could succeed. The fourteen points of 1954 had similarities to the Six Points of 1966. When, in 1954, the popular and newly-elected Chief Minister, A.K. Fazlul Haq, made a statement in Calcutta decrying the creation of Pakistan, there were widespread protests in the province and the largest protest was led by Maulana Abdul Hamid Khan Bhashani (1885–1976). The same man called for outright secession in 1970. It was only after the 1965 war that politicians waiting in the wings could bring secessionist feelings into the mainstream of Bengali politics.

It is now admitted that the east wing was treated as a colony. This is true only of the urban areas; the rural areas were treated worse than colonies. It is also ridiculous to blame, as some authors do, Hindu teachers for spreading disaffection. By 1965 Hindu teachers were in a minority and did not feel as secure as their Muslim colleagues, who were the ones preaching secession. It is also true that the literary and cultural bias of the east wing was different from that of the west wing but this was not an insuperable problem. The killing of Dr Govind Chandra Dev, and Prof. Jyotirmoy Guhathakurta were tragedies.

CROSS-BORDER TERRORISM

By 1970, the Bengali militant cadre had been organized. The Indian government took advantage of the ethnic unrest to train saboteurs. The Indian Prime Minister, Mrs Indira Gandhi, admitted in an interview with Oriana Fallaci that Indian help to the Mukti Bahini (Liberation Army) marked the beginning of the 1971 war; she openly admitted that India started the war.[25] The Indian general who trained and led the Mukti Bahini was Shahbeg Singh, who shaved his beard for the purpose.[26] In order to give an ideological cover to cross-border terrorism, Indira Gandhi began to negate the sovereign status of Pakistan. She stated in London on 1 November 1971, that India and Pakistan were not equal, and that India would not accept such treatment.

In a further development, the USSR and India concurred that 'if Pakistan attacked India in retaliation against Indian assistance to the Mukti Bahini, it would be considered aggression. USSR regarded the Mukti Bahini as a liberation movement, and its support was just and defensible'.[27]

THE ROLE OF FOREIGN POWERS

The concord between the USSR and India reflects on the role of foreign powers in the 1971 war. Paradoxically, Pakistan's relations with the USSR had improved considerably. On 15 June 1970, the USSR and Pakistan had signed a pact for cultural and scientific cooperation.[28] Relations thereafter were deliberately worsened, to take advantage of the 25 March 1971 military crackdown. Only three days later, the USSR Prime Minister Alexei Kosygin expressed his concern about the situation in Pakistan and on 2 April, the USSR President Nicolai Podgorny threatened Yahya Khan with dire consequences. Yahya called it a blatant interference in Pakistan's internal matters. The same day, the US State Department issued a statement that the Awami League insurgency was an internal matter. This would be the first and last time the US State Department would issue a statement openly supporting Pakistan. Both President Richard M. Nixon (1913–1994) and the National Security Advisor, Henry Kissinger, mention in their memoirs that the Secretary of State, William Rogers, was pro-India and obstructed the efforts of President Nixon.

In April, the Chinese prime minister told a Pakistani delegation that China would side with Pakistan, but would not be able to support military measures.[29] When Henry Kissinger made his clandestine trip to China on 11 July 1971, he said that the US would support Pakistan in the crisis but could not take military action.[30] Thus, though Pakistan won the diplomatic support of the US and China, it was unable to secure military guarantees for its integrity. At different times each country would encourage the other to intervene militarily on Pakistan's side, but this never materialized.

Henry Kissinger's secret trip to China and the announcement that President Nixon had accepted an invitation to visit China created quite a stir. Pakistan had suffered badly in the 1965 war and the Tashkent negotiations because of US and USSR collusion with the aim of containing China. With this change in world alliances there was hope for Pakistan. This hope was not fulfilled. As a counterpoise to the thaw in US–China relations, India and the USSR signed a Treaty of Friendship and Cooperation on 9 August 1971, which included military collaboration.

Instead of showing solidarity with Pakistan or China, the US State Department chose to contradict the contention of Benjamin Oehlert Jr., a long-serving US Ambassador to Pakistan, that the US had obligations towards Pakistan.[31] By issuing this statement, the US State Department undermined the joint efforts of the US and China to support Pakistan. The US had not still formally recognized China, and the secret assurances of Henry Kissinger were not considered reliable enough by China to take a military initiative. Later, on 11 December, Z.A. Bhutto carried the intelligence that the Chinese were confused by the split in the US establishment.[32]

Thereafter, the pace of events increased. On 2 December 1971, President Yahya Khan invoked the 1959 Mutual Defence Treaty. On 3 December war began on the western front. On the same day, the Washington Special Action Group (WSAP) held a meeting in which President Nixon's wish to tilt towards

Pakistan was raised. William Rogers continued to be obstructive but George Bush Sr. then US envoy to the UN, condemned India as the aggressor. The UNSC considered a resolution for a ceasefire and withdrawal of forces to their own countries, but the USSR vetoed it. On the following day, 6 December, India formally recognized Bangladesh. On 7 December, the UN General Assembly called for a ceasefire and withdrawal from each others' territory. The 104 against 11 votes for the motion reflected international support for Pakistan. There is no veto in the UN General Assembly but its resolutions are not binding.

The US State Department deplored Indian intervention the same day, but Henry Kissinger confides that when Maj.-Gen. Rao Farman Ali's offer of ceasefire was received at the UN, the State Department personnel were jubilant.[33] On 9 December, Nixon said he reprimanded the State Department. However, Nixon accepted the State Department assessment that the independence of East Pakistan was both inevitable and desirable.[34] Nixon and Kissinger violently disagreed with another assessment of the US State Department. The State Department held that India had no designs on West Pakistan. India gave the US an undertaking that it would not invade West Pakistan but, much to the chagrin of India, Nixon insisted that this undertaking would have to include Azad Kashmir.

Henry Kissinger explained, first to Huang Hua and then to Bhutto, that the military conditions on the ground were deteriorating so fast that if efforts were directed at saving East Pakistan, Azad Kashmir and West Pakistan would meanwhile fall.[35] India could mount a single air attack with a hundred planes. Kissinger took the precaution of telling General A.N. Raza, the Pakistani ambassador, that Pakistan should insist that any ceasefire proposal should include ceasefire in West Pakistan as well. On 9 December, *after* East Pakistan was a lost cause, President Nixon ordered the Seventh Fleet's USS *Enterprise* to move towards Bengal.[36] At about the same time the USSR moved its troops to the Chinese border. The USSR ambassador assured India that they would divert Chinese troops and would not allow the Seventh Fleet to intervene.[37] Another explanation of how the USSR prevailed over the US and China is provided by a Yale professor. In 1971 the USSR deployed nuclear submarines off the east coast of the USA, from where they could attack US targets in eight minutes.[38] In view of the lengths to which the USSR had gone to dismember Pakistan, it was no consolation to be told by its deputy foreign minister that: 'The game is being played for high international stakes. It has nothing to do with you. You are the victims of an objective situation.'[39]

THE OUTBREAK OF WAR

On 22 November 1971, without a formal declaration of war, India started an all out offensive in East Pakistan. On 3 December 1971, to relieve some pressure on the eastern front, Yahya Khan ordered a counter offensive in the west. The total result was the loss of Kargil to India. The defeat of Pakistan was expected. With the simultaneous US arms embargo on Pakistan and the Russian supply of arms to India, no other result, short of foreign intervention, could be expected. President Yahya Khan was to complain that his orders on the western front were not being carried out, while the soldiers complained of not receiving orders. President Yahya Khan attempted to retain power even after the surrender in Dhaka on 16 December but, by 20 December, he was forced to resign. His comment on the outcome of the war was:

> There was always the possibility that events in East Pakistan might take the course they have taken, but I had no alternative. People would not have excused me if I had allowed East Pakistan to secede.[40]

THE POLAND RESOLUTION

On 15 December 1971, when surrender had already been agreed upon, Poland, then a Russian satellite, moved a resolution, which called for: (a) Power to be transferred to Sheikh Mujibur Rahman as the elected representative of East Pakistan (b) After the Awami League had been installed, there would be an initial ceasefire of seventy-two hours (c) Thereafter, steps would be taken to evacuate Pakistani troops to preset positions (d) West Pakistan civilians would be allowed to go home, through the auspices of the UN (e) Indian armed forces shall start their withdrawal after the Pakistan troops, at a time fixed in consultation with the Awami League government.

The Pakistani permanent representative to the UN rejected the resolution on the ground that it provided for Pakistan to first withdraw from its own territory. Only then the occupying Indian forces would begin to withdraw.[1] Other analysts have pointed out that (1) the resolution mentioned no ceasefire in the west[2] (2) it was the most stringent and specific of all the drafts so far moved.[3]

NOTES
1. Sultan M. Khan *Memories and Reflections*, London: Centre for Pakistan Studies, 1997, p. 384.
2. Iqbal Akhund, *Memoirs of a Bystander*, Karachi: Oxford University Press, 1997, p. 203.
3. Hasan Zaheer, *The Separation of East Pakistan*, Karachi: Oxford University Press, 1994, p. 414.

1971 IN RETROSPECT

Of late, some new material about the 1971 crisis has surfaced. More papers from the US archives have been declassified, but they do not add substantially to what has been revealed in the *American Papers* (1999) and *The White House and Pakistan* (2002) or in the memoirs of Richard M. Nixon and Henry Kissinger (see bibliography).

Bangladeshi writers like Badruddin Umar[1] and S.A. Karim[2] have written that Sheikh Mujibur Rahman was indeed involved in the Agartala Conspiracy but as Karim relates Mujib would not call it a conspiracy but 'a striving for independence'. While Pakistani writers like Syed Shahid Husain have argued that the Six Points were not secessionist[3] Bangladeshi writers do not bother to argue. But here also the honours go to Bangladeshi writers. While B. Umar and S.A. Karim mention some killings of non-Bengalis; Pakistan HRCP director, I.A. Rehman, says killings of non-Bengalis is 'not relevant'.[4] More than documents, retrospection has been valuable. Sarmila Bose, an Indian Bengali belonging to an illustrious political family, gave a verdict that all the combatants of 1971 should consider. After stating that allegations of Pakistani atrocities were grossly exaggerated, she added:

> 'The Civil War of 1971 was fought between those who believed they were fighting for a united Pakistan and those who believed their chance for justice and progress lay in an independent Bangladesh. Both were legitimate political positions. All parties in this conflict embraced violence as a means to the end, all committed acts of brutality outside accepted norms of warfare, and all had their share of humanity. Their attributes make the 1971 conflict particularly suitable for efforts towards reconciliation, rather than recrimination.'[5]

NOTES

1. Badruddin Umar, *The Emergence of Bangladesh*, Karachi: Oxford University Press, 2006, Vol. II, p. 137.
2. S.A. Karim, *Sheikh Mujib: Triumph and Tragedy*, Dhaka: The University Press, 2005, p. 111.
3. Syed Shahid Husain, 'Of Lessons Not Learnt', *Dawn*, 11 December 2005.
4. *Newsline*, Karachi, February 2001, p. 49.
5. Sarmila Bose at a New York seminar, *Dawn*, 7 July 2005.

NOTES

1. *Dawn*, Karachi, 2 May 1970, p. 1.
2. Ibid., 4 May 1970, p. 3.
3. Ibid., 9 May 1970, p. 1.
4. G.W. Choudhry, *The Last Days of United Pakistan*, Karachi: Oxford University Press, 1998, p. 99.
5. Ibid., p. 135.
6. Sultan M. Khan, *Memories And Reflections*, London: Centre for Pakistan Studies, 1997, p. 288.
7. Zulfikar Ali Bhutto, *The Great Tragedy*, Karachi: PPP, 1971, p. 28.

8. Ibid.
9. M. Rafique Afzal, *Pakistan: History and Politics 1947–1971*, Karachi: Oxford University Press, 2001, pp. 416–417.
10. Roedad Khan (ed.) *The British Papers*, Karachi: Oxford University Press, 2002, p. 535.
11. *Pakistan Times,* Lahore, 18 August 1969, p. 1.
12. *Times,* London, 6 April 1970.
13. Lawrence Ziring, *Bangladesh From Mujib To Ershad*, Karachi: Oxford University Press, 1992, p. 64. A.O. Mitha, *Unlikely Beginnings,* Karachi: Oxford University Press, 2003, pp. 402–410. Tajul Islam Hashmi, 'The Bihari Minorities in Bangladesh' in Mushirul Hasan (ed.) *Islam, Communities and the Nation,* New Delhi: Manohar, 1998, pp. 392–398. Raunaq Jahan, Pakistan: *Failure of National Integration,* New York: Columbia University Press, 1972, p. 202.
14. *New York Times*, 11 May 1971.
15. Ibid., 28 April 1971.
16. G.W. Choudhry, op. cit., p. 176.
17. Zulfikar Ali Bhutto, op. cit., p. 19.
18. G.W. Choudhry, op. cit., p. 173.
19. Ibid., p. 182.
20. Hamoodur Rahman Commission Report (HRCP), *Dawn*, Karachi, 14 August 2000 and 6 February 2001.
21. Ibid., p. v.
22. Ibid.
23. Safdar Mahmood, *Pakistan Divided*, Lahore: Jang, 1984, p. 143.
24. HRCP, op. cit., p. vi.
25. Oriana Fallaci, *Interview with History*, Boston: Houghton and Muffin, 1976, p. 160.
26. Khushwant Singh, *Truth, Love and a Little Malice,* New Delhi: Viking, 2002, p. 315.
27. Pran Chopra, *India's Second Liberation,* 2nd ed. Cambridge Massachusetts: MIT Press, 1976, p. 100.
28. *Dawn*, Karachi, 16 June 1970, p. 1.
29. Sultan M. Khan, op. cit., p. 308.
30. Henry Kissinger, *The White House Years*, London: Weidenfeld and Nicolson, 1979, p. 862.
31. Ibid., p. 893.
32. Ibid., p. 905 and p. 908.
33. Richard M. Nixon, *The Memoirs of Richard Nixon*, New York: Grosset and Dunlop, 1978, p. 526.
34. Henry Kissinger, op. cit., p. 907.
35. Richard Nixon, loc cit.
36. S.M. Burke and Lawrence Ziring, *Pakistan's Foreign Policy,* 2nd ed. Karachi: Oxford University Press, 1996, p. 404.
37. *The New York Times,* 11 January 1972.
38. Paul Bracken, *Fire in the East,* New York: Perennial, 2002, p. 102.
39. Sultan M. Khan, op. cit., p. 380.
40. Hasan Zaheer, *The Separation of East Pakistan*, Karachi: Oxford University Press, 1994, p. 409.

 SHEIKH MUJIBUR RAHMAN (b. Tungipara, 1920–d. Dhaka, 15 August 1975) was the leader who founded Bangladesh, and in the process dismembered Pakistan. What was his precise role during the last round of negotiations remains unclear, even after the release of US State Department papers. One report says that Mujib reneged on an agreement with Yahya Khan which called for (a) immediate establishment of provincial governments, (b) temporary continuation of the central government under Yahya, and (c) a constitutional scheme in which the central government would deal only with defence, foreign affairs and currency.[1]

A subsequent report stated that Mujibur Rahman wanted confederation, not separation.[2]

Sheikh Mujibur Rahman began his political life in Mission High School, Gopalpur, when he told A.K. Fazlul Haq and H.S. Suhrawardy, who were jointly on inspection, that the roof leaked. The principal thought he had spoken out of turn, but in the years ahead, Mujib's encounter with the two leaders would continue. He went on to Islamia College, Calcutta and the University of Dhaka. He became an ardent Muslim Leaguer, and in the 1946 Bihar riots, played a leading role in rehabilitating the refugees in East Bengal.

It was in the wake of the 1948 Bengali Language Movement that Mujibur Rahman gained prominence. He was able to persuade H.S. Suhrawardy to retract his statement favouring Urdu as the sole national language, but was unable to associate Fazlul Haq with the Language Movement. This defined his attitude towards them. On 5 January 1956, he criticized Fazlul Haq for challenging the leadership of HS Suhrawardy.[3]

The number of times Sheikh Mujibur Rahman was sent to jail needs to be noted: (i) he was arrested while picketing the Dhaka Secretariat on 11 March 1948; (ii) he was again arrested while agitating for better working conditions in the Dhaka University; from 10 April to 29 July 1949; (iii) he was jailed on 1 January 1950 for two years; (iv) he was already in jail when he was indicted under the Agartala Conspiracy Case. This writer saw him being tried by a magistrate in 1965. He was released in 1968 to participate in the Round Table Conference. (v) The last time he was arrested was after the Army Action on 25 March 1976. He looked at the (burning) skyline and asked the commanding officer: 'Was it necessary to do all this?' Sheikh Mujibur Rahman had courted arrest to avoid a crackdown: other than him, each and every Awami League legislator had escaped.

Sheikh Mujibur Rahman remains a living factor in the politics of Pakistan. This is because most Pakistanis blame only Yahya and Bhutto for the 1971 debacle.

He has more ardent supporters in the country he divided, than in the country he emancipated. While his Bangladeshi biographer has accepted that Mujib had indeed gone to Agartala,[5] and that the militants who killed the Dhaka intellectuals on 14 December 1971 were Bengalis and not Biharis,[6] his Pakistani reviewer complained: 'Mr Karim's considerable capacity to respect the truth is likely to deepen a Pakistani majority's miscomprehension of the events of 1971.'[7]

In those fateful days, Z.A. Bhutto recalled Mujib saying: 'If they (the army) destroyed him first, they would also destroy me.'[8] What Bhutto said to the army commander was far more poignant: 'In spite of what Sheikh Mujibur Rahman stood for, he was a leader of the people and merited respect.'[9]

NOTES

1. *Daily Times*, Karachi, 11 May 2005.
2. *Dawn*, Karachi, 7 July 2005.
3. S.A. Karim, *Sheikh Mujib: Triumph and Tragedy*, Dhaka: The University Press, 2005, p. 63.
4. Ibid., p. 200.
5. Ibid., p. 110.
6. Ibid., p. 284.
7. I.A. Rehman, 'Anatomy of a Tragic Hero', *Newsline*, October 2006, p. 111.
8. Zulfikar Ali Bhutto, *The Great Tragedy*, Karachi: Pakistan Peoples Party, 1971, p. 43.
9. Ibid., p. 50.

CHAPTER 29

THE FIRST PPP GOVERNMENT, 1971–1977

On 20 December 1971, the office of the chief martial law administrator and president was transferred to Zulfikar Ali Bhutto (1928–1979) as the elected representative of what remained of Pakistan. Under the cover of martial law which was then the basic law of the country, Bhutto nationalized all heavy industrial units except textiles. This created an environment in which educational institutions were nationalized. The nationalization of education was not in the original Pakistan Peoples Party manifesto, but took place under pressure from teachers' unions guided by recommendations made by the Nur Khan Commission. Labour reforms could be effected as capital and labour were drawn from different ethnic groups.

Stringent agricultural reforms were announced but not strictly implemented as Zulfikar Ali Bhutto had previously cabled Yahya Khan against the imposition of agricultural tax.[1] After keeping commerce and business in suspense, the government nationalized banks and insurance companies on 1 January 1974.

Bhutto was the first populist leader of Pakistan since the generation of the founders. He adopted the creed of Islamic socialism which was considered anathema by over a hundred ulema representing fundamentalist Islamic parties, although Islamic socialism as a concept was favoured by Allama Iqbal and Maulana Hasrat Mohani (1881–1951). The term itself was used by Jinnah,[2] and projected as the state ideology by Liaquat Ali Khan,[3] the Raja of Mahmudabad (1913–1973)[4] and Fatima Jinnah[5] as we have seen in the Ideological History of Pakistan.

After the trouncing of conservative parties by the Awami League, PPP and National Awami Party (NAP), Chaudhry Mohammad Ali, the former prime minister, and Gen. Sher Ali Khan, Yahya's information minister, had urged Yahya to cancel the results of the 7 December 1970 elections. Some officers solemnly contemplated transferring power to Air Marshal (retd.) M. Asghar Khan who had lost his own seat in the elections.[6] The electoral victory of the PPP had broken the traditional patterns of results and many feudals and other entrenched politicians had lost.

In the urban constituencies, especially in Karachi, Bhutto faced opposition even from the liberal sector, when he recognized Sindhi as the official language of Sindh. This decision resulted in rioting between Urdu and Sindhi speaking groups. It had great destabilising potential but Z.A. Bhutto overcame it by making a direct sentimental appeal to all contenders. The industrial and commercial interests having already been alienated, Bhutto next eliminated radical elements from his own party.

Bhutto eschewed revolution and veered round to reaction, but the war of attrition between the political and economic forces of the country, begun by his reforms, did not end. The nationalization of industries was accompanied by handcuffing and briefly detaining the top industrialists Ahmad Dawood and Fakhruddin Valika. The psychological impact was greater than the economic, as the units taken over had marginal production.

The nationalized sectors gradually showed a dismal performance. The nationalized banks performed professionally during Bhutto's term and only later faced bankruptcy when huge loans were advanced without collateral and even written off under political pressure. On the whole, however, security of service combined with lack of incentive, had a detrimental effect on services for which the major and moral responsibility is vested in the employees.

Bhutto had an uneasy relationship with the NAP–JUI coalitions in the NWFP and Balochistan provinces. On assuming power he had lifted the ban on the NAP imposed by the Yahya regime, and even gave them governors appointed by their party. An arms cache was discovered in the Iraqi embassy; becoming suspicious of their intentions, Bhutto dismissed the government of Balochistan, in consequence of which the NWFP government also resigned. There was army action in Balochistan, and the nationalist trend in that province and NWFP was heightened, but Bhutto pre-empted them diplomatically by engaging with Afghanistan which had supported the NAP–JUI irredentist claim, which means that parts of Pakistan should have been part of Afghanistan. At the height of the 1971 war, King Zahir Shah had been in Moscow and had refused to endorse the USSR policy of dismembering Pakistan. Even when Zahir Shah was ousted by Daud Khan, Bhutto visited him while he incarcerated the NAP leaders.

In the domain of foreign policy there was a see-saw pattern. In the beginning Bhutto had to contend with the USSR and towards the end of his term he had to contend with the US which was infuriated at Bhutto's attempt to counteract India's nuclear explosion of 1974. Bhutto leaned to the left, pulling out of CENTO and SEATO and extending recognition to North Korea, North Vietnam and East Germany. Bhutto had a signal success with the Muslim world; following the Arab–Israeli war, Bhutto allegedly advised the policy of an oil embargo and in 1974 he hosted the second Islamic Summit at Lahore, taking time out to recognize Bangladesh.

Bhutto's most enduring legacy is the near-unanimous Constitution promulgated on 12 August 1973, under which Bhutto became prime minister (see Chapter 33). He also laid the foundation of the nuclear programme which enabled Pakistan to test in 1998. Bhutto was to complain that this initiative caused his overthrow. However, in 1976 Bhutto felt confident enough to schedule general elections for March 1977. Almost overnight, large urban centres became bastions of opposition; a nine party opposition alliance called the Pakistan National Alliance was formed. There was a hard-hitting campaign in which the opposition promised to establish an Islamic order. Claiming that inflation was due solely to the extravagance of the ruling clique, the PNA vowed to bring prices back to 1970 levels. They also termed their campaign a movement for democracy.

There were reasons behind the bitterness of the campaign, apart from ideological, class and ethnic conflict. Zulfikar Ali Bhutto was imperious by nature, and there were many who became victims of his fits of rage, the most prominent among them being J.A. Rahim, the secretary general of the PPP and a federal minister, who was dismissed, beaten and humiliated. Bhutto veered more to state power than people's power, and while welcoming feudals into the PPP fold, he alienated the committed socialist radicals of his party. Yet he retained sufficient oratical skill to strike a direct rapport with the masses.

There matters stood when the 1977 general elections were held. The PPP won more seats than Bhutto expected. The Pakistan National Alliance refused to accept the results claiming that the polls had been rigged. That there were glaring and striking polling irregularities is quite evident; yet it is doubtful that they extended to an actual controversion of the public mandate. That is why Bhutto's military successor, General Ziaul Haq kept on postponing elections. Two surviving members of the three-man PNA team, Professor A. Ghafur and Nawabzada Nasrullah Khan, stated on national television on 5 July 1989 that the PPP and PNA had reached an agreement and that General Ziaul Haq's coup of 5 July 1977 had been unwarranted.

Zulfikar Ali Bhutto regained popularity immediately after his removal. To neutralize his popularity the military regime tried Bhutto for aiding and abetting in the murder of a political opponent. Despite discrepant ballistics evidence and a divided bench, Zulfikar Ali Bhutto was executed on 4 April 1979. With his all too human failings Bhutto possessed a political mystique. On 18 September and 5 October 2004, Z.A. Bhutto's lifetime opponents joined in paying him tribute.

THE SIMLA AGREEMENT

The Simla Accord signed between India and Pakistan on 2 July 1972 had as its main provisions:

(i) That the principles and purposes of the Charter of the United Nations shall govern the relations between the two countries (ii) That the two countries are resolved to settle their differences by peaceful means through bilateral negotiations or by any other peaceful means mutually agreed upon between them. Pending the final settlement of any problems between the two countries, neither side shall unilaterally alter the situation (iv: ii) In Jammu and Kashmir, the line of control resulting from the ceasefire of 17 December 1971 shall be respected by both sides without prejudice to the recognized position of either side.
(*The numbering is from the original document*)

This agreement was the greatest challenge to be faced by Zulfikar Ali Bhutto, since his popularity had been based on his denunciation of the Tashkent Declaration. Had he failed in Simla, despite the military defeat, his tenure would have immediately ended. Predictably, both sides gave different interpretations of the text. On 4 April 1995, P.N. Dhar, who had been secretary to Indira Gandhi, claimed that there had been a secret clause in Simla. This is a tacit admission that the official Indian interpretation was unsupported by the text. Opposition leaders in both countries, including Mahmud Azam Faruqi of Pakistan's Jama'at-i-Islami, upheld the Indian interpretation that the Simla Agreement precluded a reference to the UN, while Atal Bihari Vajpayee the future Indian Prime Minister said that Z.A. Bhutto had achieved regaining the territory under Indian occupation, securing the release of the prisoners of war and reopening the Kashmir issue.[1] Vajpayee's interpretation was supported by party man Bhai Mahavir.[2] Abdus Sattar from the Pakistan side pointed out that P.N. Dhar was not present at the one to one talks between Mrs Gandhi and Mr Bhutto; he recalls that Mrs Gandhi had denied any secret clause in the Simla Agreement. He also quotes Zulfikar Ali Bhutto's speech in the National Assembly that by bifurcating and delinking the international boundary from the ceasefire line in Kashmir, Kashmir had been acknowledged as a disputed area...[3]

NOTES

1. G.S. Bhargava, *Success or Surrender*, New Delhi, Sterling 1972, p. 68.
2. Ibid., p. 70.
3. Abdus Sattar, 'Simla Agreement-IV', *Dawn*, 5 July 1995, p. 12.

NOTES

1. Roedad Khan (ed.), *American Papers*, Karachi: Oxford University Press, 1999, p. 632.
2. *Jinnah Speeches as Governor-General*, Karachi: OUP, 2000, p. 166.
3. On 26 March 1948, M. Rafique Afzal, *Speeches and Statements of Quaid-i-Millat Liaquat Ali Khan*, Lahore: Research Society, 1976, p. 267.
4. Ishtiaq Husain, *The Life and Times of the Raja Saheb of Mahmudabad* II, Karachi Mahboob Academy, 1998, p. 18.
5. 25 December 1961, in Khan Salahuddin Khan ed. *Speeches, Messages and Statements of Mohtarma Fatima Jinnah*, Lahore Research Society, 1976, passim.
6. A.R. Siddiqi, *East Pakistan: The Endgame*, Karachi: OUP, 2004, p. 211.

... The noble Brutus
Hath told you, Caesar was ambitious
If it were so, it was a grievous fault
And grievously hath Caesar answered it

ZULFIKAR ALI BHUTTO (b. Larkana, 5 January 1928–d. Rawalpindi, 4 April 1979). No other lines apply more aptly to the dramatic course of Z.A. Bhutto's political career. Shock and grief over his death touched new depths, while exultation over his execution opened a new, sordid dimension in the politics of Pakistan. Even, thirty years after his deposal, Z.A. Bhutto remains Pakistan's most controversial figure. Already, with the exception of Jinnah, he is the subject of more studies than any other leader of Pakistan.

A federal minister at the young age of 30, Bhutto held diverse portfolios before becoming foreign minister, in 1963, which proved to be his real metier. On his removal from this office, he produced a treatise on foreign affairs, called *The Myth of Independence*. This contains his concept of bilateralism, and his dicta on the survival of small states against great powers. It is hazardous to deduce from theoretical principles, the guiding elements of a practicing statesman, but in this case they not only apply, they guide. Bhutto's postulate was that barring glaring exceptions, the great powers sought to unite former colonial states in order to better exploit them.[1] As regards India-Pakistan relations, Bhutto's main plank of resistance was elaborated in the following words, which eerily recall the present situation:

It has been suggested that Pakistan should become realistic and seek *rapprochement* with India without the settlement of outstanding disputes...It would mean capitulation by instalment and eventual liquidation[2]...In exploring the possibilities available in capitulation by instalment, it must be remembered that it is a function of diplomacy to look for various approaches and to avoid abrupt decisions which sound like an ultimatum.[3]

Even with finesse, a search may not yield a solution. This point is reiterated in Bhutto's aphorism: 'Pressure is a worm if you stamp on it, but it becomes a monster if you recoil.'[4] Bhutto was indeed under pressure on the nuclear issue, as declassified documents from the national security archives of the George Washington University testify. Safeguards are not enough, he was told, because one side could break an agreement,[5] an argument not followed in the 2006 India–US nuclear agreement, Bhutto's prescription on pressure is a reminder that character is destiny. He was successful in foreign policy because in that domain, one cannot be a feudal lord. The pages of this book attest that during the East Pakistan crisis, which brought him into power, his choices were constricted, and during the Pakistan National Alliance agitation, which ushered him out, he had none. Were both events portents of a greater design? The transfer of power to Bhutto, as the elected representative, held an element of defiance resembling post-Great War Hungary, where Prime Minister Michael Károlyi had brought out from prison Bela Kun, and transferred his office to him. Bela Kun promulgated a Soviet constitution, nationalized land, paid unemployment wages, and accepted health and education as state responsibilities. When these measures resulted in national awakening and revitalization of the proletariat, Bela Kun was exiled, and the Romanian army was unleashed on Hungary.[6] Bhutto's fate was deferred, but in the end more tragic. It is curious that in the long gallery of role models suggested for Bhutto, extending as it does from Napoleon to Nehru, Bela Kun has found no place.

There is an esoteric element which links his tyranny to his charisma. As Stanley Wolpert discovered, none of his behaviour, even when well documented, seemed to diminish his political appeal for most Pakistanis.[7]

He regained his popularity when he was deposed, and his passion—much more than his discourse—made him a legend.

NOTES

1. Zulfikar Ali Bhutto, *The Myth of Independence*, Dacca: Oxford University Press, 1969, p. 10.
2. Ibid., p. 177.
3. Ibid., p. 106.
4. Ibid., p. 13.
5. *Dawn*, Karachi, 28 May 2006.
6. J. Hampden Jackson, *The Post War World*, London: Victor Gollancz, 1935, pp. 36, 37.
7. Stanley Wolpert, *Zulfi Bhutto of Pakistan*, New York: Oxford University Press, 1993, p. 314.

Chapter 30

The Third Military Regime, 1977–1988

The clash between the PPP and PNA had polarized the nation, destabilized the state and ruined the economy. A beleaguered Z.A. Bhutto had banned night clubs and liquor, horse-racing and gambling and declared Friday as the weekly holiday instead of Sunday, but these concessions to Islamic sentiments proved of no avail. Only while the PPP and PNA teams negotiated, was the violence suspended.

General Muhammad Ziaul Haq (1924–1988) said he was staging his coup so that the army could act as a neutral force between the PPP and PNA, hold elections within ninety days and retire to the barracks immediately afterwards. In his inaugural address to the nation Ziaul Haq said that he supported the movement for Islamization. It was this pronouncement that dispelled the notion that the coup had been staged at Bhutto's behest. Ziaul Haq imposed the *Zakat* and *Ushr* ordinance which allowed the government to deduct the Islamic tithes on savings and land revenue. Ziaul Haq introduced Islamic punishments for all crimes except murder, since Islamic laws would ensure Z.A. Bhutto's release. Ziaul Haq's alteration of the law of evidence resulted in legal perversities. A victim of rape would be convicted of adultery while the perpetrator would be let off for lack of evidence.

Ziaul Haq, in need of political anchor, gave a boost to religious parties which hitherto had been badly mauled in every election. This led to heightened sectarian militancy. Soon the banning of political activity resulted in the emergence of ethnic parties. The influx of Afghan refugees fleeing their country in the wake of the Soviet invasion added to the chaos. The cumulative effect of all this was an unprecedented brutalization of society, and the introduction of Kalashnikov and drug cultures. Drugs, till then almost unknown, registered a widespread consumption.

Yet, despite these crippling social defects, Ziaul Haq's policy of containing and combating the Soviet presence in Afghanistan was basically sound. For Pakistan to refuse aid against the Soviet presence on Pakistan's borders would have tempted the Soviet army to extend its presence to Pakistan and add a warm water port to its possessions. The social consequences of the Soviet invasion alone could have hardly been worse than was the result of the Afghan influx.

Under cover of the Afghan crisis, Ziaul Haq was able to replenish both the coffers and the arsenals of Pakistan and, more vitally, he was able to continue Pakistan's nuclear programme, notwithstanding the 28 April 1977 statement of his predecessor Z.A. Bhutto that he was being punished for pursuing nuclear detterence. In the domain of defence, the loss of Siachen to India can be weighed against him. The Soviet invasion of Afghanistan was an ad hoc situation and as such led to ad hoc results in terms of western support. The liberal parties in the US and Europe had muted, but not dropped, their demand, for democracy in Pakistan. In 1983, Ziaul Haq was able to militarily crush the Movement for the Restoration of Democracy (MRD) but realized that at least a cosmetic exercise in democracy had become unavoidable. As a first step he held a referendum on his Islamization policy, so worded that it meant a validation of Zia's term for a further five years. There was a low turn-out in the referendum, but in February 1985 the electoral response was greater.

A parliament based on non-party polls was ushered in. Mohammad Khan Junejo (1932–1993) was appointed prime minister on 23 March 1985. General Ziaul Haq made the restoration of parliament conditional on the passage of the Eighth Amendment. The amendment had a clause 58(2)(B) which empowered the president to dismiss the prime minister and dissolve the parliament (See Chapter 33). After initial resistance from a group headed by Senator Saifullah, the legislature capitulated and enacted the Eighth Amendment giving constitutional cover to martial law regulations. On 31 December 1985 martial law was lifted but Ziaul Haq remained president as well as chief of army staff.

Mohammad Khan Junejo, contrary to General Ziaul Haq's expectations, wished to pursue an agenda of his own.[1] He signed an accord in Geneva which paved the way for Soviet withdrawal from Afghanistan. Although this conformed to Pakistan's official policy, in reality Ziaul Haq had hoped to prolong the withdrawal process, thereby retaining a front line state status for Pakistan, for a longer period. Mohammad Khan Junejo practised and imposed austerity in government expenditure. He put both military and civil officers in small cars. His character was impeccable, but since he was perceived as a product of the military regime, his sterling qualities were recognized only retrospectively. The National Assembly was showing restlessness and Syed Fakhr Imam was elected speaker against Zia's favoured candidate.

Ojhri Camp, a munitions depot in Rawalpindi, blew up with considerable loss of life on 10 April 1988. The prime minister launched an inquiry resented by the military top brass. Public bickering between young military officers and ruling party legislators added to the tension. On 29 May 1988, President Ziaul Haq dismissed his own hand-picked prime minister and dissolved the National Assembly which was elected on a non-party basis under clause

58(2)B of the Eighth Amendment. This proved to be a more complicated course of action than an outright coup, since the president was forced to order fresh elections within ninety days. Before the world could discover whether this second promise would be kept, President Ziaul Haq was killed in an aircrash on 17 August 1988. In accordance with the 1973 Constitution, the Chairman of the Senate, Ghulam Ishaq Khan (1915–2006) assumed the office of president.

NOTE

1. K.M. Arif, *Working With Zia*, Karachi: Oxford University Press, 1995, p. 395.

CHAPTER 31

THE DEMOCRATIC INTERREGNUM, 1988–1999

From 3 December 1988 to 12 October 1999 Pakistan witnessed a partial respite from autocratic rule. This period also saw an increase in ethnic and sectarian strife. With the role of political parties having previously been constricted, ethnic and sectarian forces acquired greater public space. Since sectarian strife raised the spectre of greater violence, the heightening of ethnic feelings was grasped as an alternative involving lesser violence. Due to discriminatory legislation regarding employment and education quotas Muhajir ethnic feeling cut through sectarian fanaticism which led to the emergence of the Muhajir Qaumi Movement (MQM).

In the November 1988 elections, the PPP emerged as the party with the largest number of seats, but President Ghulam Ishaq Khan was visibly reluctant to name its leader, Benazir Bhutto, as prime minister. He only did so when all efforts to set up a counter coalition against her failed. On 3 December 1988 Benazir Bhutto became the first woman prime minister in the entire Muslim world. She had become a world celebrity as well because of the courageous struggle she had waged against despotism. Power was transferred to her under stringent conditions including signing a pre-negotiated IMF agreement.

In her first press conference Benazir Bhutto made it clear that she was not a free agent and that she had to work under a system. The largest province, Punjab, in an almost overnight turn around between the national and provincial elections, voted her political rival Nawaz Sharif into power. The establishment headed by President G.I. Khan, and the Punjab government headed by Nawaz Sharif, kept her in a crucible. Her parliamentary coalition with the MQM fell apart revealing the precarious nature of her government.

The MQM clandestinely broke its alliance with the PPP on 6 October 1989 and made its hostility public only when a no confidence motion was tabled against the prime minister. Her response was more impolitic than the MQM's and the shooting down of women protestors in the Pucca Qila in Hyderabad tarnished her image as a champion of democracy and human rights. No other domestic strife has had a more disastrous fall-out. On her own admission she handed over a list of Sikh dissidents to Indian Prime Minister Rajiv Gandhi which enabled him to crush the Sikh separatist movement in India.[1] With the conflict raging in East Punjab, the Kashmiri struggle would have had greater chance of success, but this chance was wasted and the MQM started a series of strikes which internationally obfuscated the news and impact of the Kashmir uprising which had then newly begun. This disaffection against Benazir Bhutto in the main cities of Karachi, Lahore and Quetta set the stage for her dismissal on 6 August 1990, on charges of misrule and corruption attributed to her husband. A sympathetic biographer admits that Benazir Bhutto had been distracted by her opponents and had not fulfilled her promises.[2]

The damage to the nascent democracy could have been contained if an impartial interim prime minister had been appointed ahead of the new elections, but President G.I. Khan took the novel step of transferring power to the Leader of the Opposition, Ghulam Mustafa Jatoi who had lost his seat in the elections and had to be inducted to the National Assembly through a by-election in a different constituency. The dismal showing of the PPP coalition (only forty-five seats) was immediately seen by PPP supporters as the result of rigging.

Later, when the then-ruling clique was out of office, it did not contradict allegations of rigging. Nevertheless, Nawaz Sharif had an electoral base in the Punjab and it was expected that his government would be stable. For no rational or vital reason, this expectation was belied. The term of Mian Mohammad Nawaz Sharif saw the first Gulf War which clearly showed up the contradictions of Pakistan's polity. President Ghulam Ishaq Khan, Mirza Aslam Beg (COAS), and Begum Nusrat Bhutto (Chairperson of the main opposition party, the PPP) issued statements favouring Iraq. Nawaz Sharif and Benazir Bhutto (leader of the parliamentary opposition) were firmly on the side of Kuwait, fully realizing that Muslim solidarity took second place to national sovereignty, and understanding all the implications of supporting an invasion of a sovereign state.

With Nawaz Sharif inclining towards reconciliation with the PPP and stating openly his intention of scrapping the Eighth Amendment, the president moved to prevent curtailment of his powers, dismissed Nawaz Sharif, and dissolved the National Assembly on 18 April 1993. On 26 May 1993 the Supreme Court restored the parliament and premier; the only instance when the Supreme Court has ruled against the plea of 'state necessity'. President G.I. Khan stuck to office despite this judicial rebuff, but a situation in which the relations between the president and prime minister were openly strained was proving detrimental to the state, and on 18 July 1993 each had to resign his office.

This term of Nawaz Sharif's Pakistan Muslim League (PML-N) also saw heightened tension in Sindh province. The president had imposed a ruthless minority government under Jam Sadiq Ali to keep the PPP (which had an enhanced presence in the Sindh Assembly) out. In this the chief minister had the enthusiastic support of the MQM. When it was perceived that the MQM was irrevocably cut from its Sindh moorings, it was subjected by its allies to military action. Although its fortunes went on fluctuating, the MQM never fully recovered from this blow, and for a long time Karachi remained a city of insecurity and economic stagnation.

Benazir Bhutto won the 6 October 1993 elections by securing eighty-six seats. This time, the Punjab Assembly as well as the office of the president went to her party members, making her second term as prime minister seemingly more secure. Benazir Bhutto was able to improve the economy by increasing inward investment and trade. This was only to the extent permitted by the ethnic strife which continued to plague her administration. Military action against the MQM continued, with the MQM retaliating with strikes, damaging the economy. On 1 September 1996, an opposition leader, the prime minister's only surviving brother, Murtaza Bhutto, was killed in a police shoot out. After offering formal condolences, President Farooq Leghari had the Supreme Court opened on a holiday[3] to file a case against the bereaved prime minister, and she was finally dismissed on 5 November 1996 on grounds of extra judicial killings and corruption. Benazir Bhutto's petition for the restoration of her government was dismissed by the Supreme Court.

During his second term, Mian Nawaz Sharif took pre-emptive legislative measures to secure his government. On 4 April 1997, the anniversary of Z.A. Bhutto's execution, the National Assembly unanimously, and in a matter of minutes, passed the Thirteenth Amendment partially repealing the Eighth Amendment, i.e. the power of the president to dismiss the prime minister and dissolve the assemblies. On 1 July 1997, the Fourteenth Amendment was passed preventing floor-crossing or flouting of party discipline by legislators. The Chief Justice of Pakistan, Sajjad Ali Shah, had his court stormed by the PML-N (ruling party) members while he was hearing an appeal to strike down the Thirteenth Amendment. This would have enabled the president to dismiss the prime minister. Frustrated at being unable to dismiss Nawaz Sharif as he had dismissed Benazir Bhutto, Farooq Leghari resigned as president on 2 December 1997.

Some destabilizing factors intruded from external sources. On 25 May 1997, Pakistan, along with US allies including Saudi Arabia and the United Arab Emirates, recognized the militant Taliban regime in Afghanistan. This was later to be the cause of friction with the US. On 11 May 1998, India conducted a series of nuclear tests and threatened to occupy Azad Kashmir. Since India had already demonstrated its nuclear capacity in 1974, the new threats were taken very seriously. Pakistan responded on 28 May, after international guarantees of security were not forthcoming.

Unfortunately, simultaneous with the announcement of nuclear success, the prime minister, also announced the freezing of foreign currency accounts and the construction of the Kalabagh Dam which was opposed by three out of four provinces of Pakistan. This dissipated the political advantage gained by the prime minister.

After the nuclearization of both countries, the Indian Prime Minister, Atal Bihari Vajpayee, visited Lahore on a bus on 20 February 1999 and held talks with his Pakistani counterpart in an atmosphere of cordiality. It was noted that the joint statement of the two prime ministers ignored the Kashmir issue. Frustrated by this omission and the stalled talks on the Siachen issue, Pakistani irregulars, supported by regulars, crossed the Line of Control (LoC) and took up positions in the Kargil sector. Kargil, as mentioned above, had been part of Pakistan till 1971, and after the 1971 war, it was India which had pressurised the UN to withdraw its observer group from that sector.

Tactically, the Kargil episode was the consequence of, in the words of a high ranking Pakistani diplomat, 'unstructured, personalised decision making'. The propaganda war was lost by Pakistan, because the nuclearization of the adversaries had focused world attention away from the causes to the consequences. Attention, in other words, shifted from the evasion of UNSC resolutions by India to the issue of cross-border terrorism by Pakistan. Nawaz Sharif travelled to the US to announce Pakistan's withdrawal from Kargil; this was in exchange for the vaguest of promises made by President Bill Clinton to use his influence to solve the Kashmir dispute. It was transparently clear that the promise was not to be taken seriously.

On the domestic side, the prime minister tabled the Fifteenth Amendment designed to make the Quran and Sunnah the supreme law of the land.[4] Even the religious parties would not support this bill, although on the surface it met their longstanding demand. They understood it to be a measure to completely undermine the constitution, and give a free hand to Nawaz Sharif. The constitution was inadvertently undermined when Nawaz Sharif attempted to dismiss the army chief, General Pervez Musharraf, while he was on a flight from Sri Lanka. The attempt rebounded on him and on 12 October 1999, Nawaz Sharif was ousted in a coup led by General Musharraf in retaliation for the prime minister's attempt to dismiss him and endanger the lives of all the passengers.

THE NUCLEAR CHOICE

'Your money or your life', said the marauder to the traveller. 'Take my life' said the traveller, 'I am saving my money for my old age.' Here was a man who knew his priorities, a man who would have opted for economic aid and international goodwill. Don't go nuclear and we will reward you. We shall deliver to you the F-16s you have already paid for. No, the F-16s are no deterrent against nuclear attack, but have faith in us. After you have been destroyed in a nuclear attack, we shall reschedule your debts and offer you new loans on soft terms.

This nice old lady told her son's class teacher: 'My child is very sensitive, when he is naughty, slap the boy next to him.' The teacher agreed. Ever since India exploded a nuclear device in 1974, Pakistan has had country specific sanctions slapped on her. This comes out of experience. If the US had been as mature at the outbreak of the Second World War, they would have imposed sanctions on Britain immediately after Hitler invaded Poland. Already the Kashmiris feel that the description of a terrorist has begun to fit Marquis La Fayette.

When Pakistan lost her moral advantage by carrying out her own tests, Prem Shankar Jha expounded the theory that Pakistan's nuclear explosions carried out later were a justification for India's nuclear explosions carried out earlier. In the immortal words of the sensitive child: 'It all started when he hit me back.'

NOTES

1. Mehtab Ali Shah, *The Foreign Policy of Pakistan*, London: I.B. Tauris 1997 vide *Dawn*, 17 February 1994.
2. Diane Sansevere-Dreher, *Benazir Bhutto*, New York: Bantam Skylark, 1991, p. 74.
3. Ajmal Mian, *A Judge Speaks Out*, Karachi: Oxford University Press, 2004, p. 203.
4. On 9 October 1998, this bill was passed by the National Assembly, but not the Senate.

CHAPTER 32

THE FOURTH MILITARY REGIME, 1999

Pakistan's second democratic interregnum ended when General Pervez Musharraf (b.1943) reacted to his midflight dismissal as COAS by Prime Minister Nawaz Sharif, by staging a *coup d'état*. His was the first military regime which did not declare martial law. General Musharraf chose initially the designation of chief executive. The United States accepted the legitimacy of the military regime on 6 December 1999. The Supreme Court gave its final judgement on the legitimacy of the military regime on 12 March 2000. General Musharraf's *coup* was justified but the Supreme Court ruled that he was bound to hold elections within three years.

Gradually, General Musharraf was able to sidestep his constitutional obligations. On 20 June 2001, he assumed the office of president after obtaining the resignation of President M. Rafiq Tarar. On 30 April 2002, Pervez Musharraf held a referendum to confirm himself as president. He later admitted that there were flaws due to 'over enthusiastic officials'. However, the crisis ran deeper. Had the Supreme Court struck down the referendum programme as unconstitutional, the people of Pakistan would have been absolved of responsibility, but since the legality of the referendum was upheld, the people had no choice but to participate in it, as an unrepresentative government at such a sensitive security juncture was a high risk.

Again the blame for enabling President Musharraf to transform constitutional provisions by stages is shared by the gullibility of the religious alliance MMA, whose concessions to the military over the constitution in effect weakened the position of the centrist ARD opposition. Elections were held as per the Supreme Court verdict on 10 October 2002, but General Musharraf only shared power with the parliament, and did not effectively transfer power to it. The first prime minister under Pervez Musharraf was Mir Zafrullah Khan Jamali (b.1944) who held office from 23 November 2002 to 26 June 2004. Chaudhry Shujaat Hussain (b.1946) served as prime minister for forty-five days. There is no provision for an interim prime minister in the constitution but Chaudhry Shujaat served as interim prime minister to pave the way politically for his successor. Prime Minister Shaukat Aziz (b.1949) took office on 23 August 2004 as the twenty-third incumbent.

A National Security Council (NSC) was inducted which alone would be empowered to dismiss prime ministers or dissolve parliaments. The NSC would include the leader of the opposition. Superficially this is fraught with risk as he or she would have the incentive to replace the prime minister, but in normal conditions it could be a forum where continuity and briefing could be imparted to the leader of the opposition. At present it is a supra-cabinet. Its membership consists of: the president, prime minister, leader of the opposition, all service chiefs and the chairman of the joint chiefs of staff committee, governors and chief ministers of all four provinces, and of course the defence and foreign ministers and secretaries.

The real challenge to the regime has been the Afghanistan problem. General Ziaul Haq had sown the wind of terrorism and General Pervez Musharraf has reaped the whirlwind. As the Zia policy was basically sound for halting the Soviet advance, despite the disastrous social fall out, the policy of Pervez Musharraf of joining the US war against terror is basically sound. During the democratic interregnum the military establishment attempted to bring Afghanistan into an alliance to obtain defence in depth. This military establishment was slow to realize that although defence in depth had value in conventional warfare, in nuclear warfare it can prove a liability.

During the Zia era the Mujahideen had been trained, armed and financed by the US. After the Soviet withdrawal from Afghanistan, these religious warriors were left to their own devices, and took fanaticism and militancy to its extreme limits. The Taliban regime of Afghanistan, which personified these tactics, was initially given tacit western support because it provided a sectarian counterpoise to the 1979 Irani revolution. It was like the support given in the 1980s to Iraqi leader Saddam Hussain on the other flank of Iran.

Following the terrorist attacks on US targets on 11 September 2001, the Pakistani support for the fanatical Taliban regime was withdrawn. Pakistan had been one of only three countries to recognize the Taliban regime in Afghanistan, the other two being Saudi Arabia and the United Arab Emirates. Since these were traditionally pro-US countries, there was widespread speculation that Pakistan had recognized the Taliban regime with US approval. Thus Pakistan's turnaround on the Taliban regime was not an isolated step. Neither was it harmful. Pakistan's pro-Taliban policy had strained the country's relations with its most benign neighbours, China and Iran. Most usefully, its alliance with the west on this issue secured for it US support during the 13 December 2001 to 16 October 2002 military standoff with India, which started with a terrorist attack on the Indian parliament.

As with the Zia regime, the present regime has faced a domestic backlash over a foreign policy option. This has centered in the South Waziristan vicinity of Wana. Wana had been the recurring scene of battle against the British in 1894, 1919 and 1937. In 1947 Wana was the scene of revolt against newly-established Pakistan by the Faqir of Ipi. Since April 2003 roughly, Wana has again become the centre of armed resistance to the pro-US policy of the government. There were air attacks on 11 June and 9 September 2004. Militants laid down their arms on 20 April and 5 August 2004, but this did not stem the violence. The economic blockade imposed on Wana was lifted by Prime Minister Shaukat Aziz on 25 September 2004 but to no avail. On 9 October 2004 two Chinese engineers were kidnapped by the tribals one of whom was killed. Wana still continues to bleed and a major initiative is required to restore peace there.

Pervez Musharraf's alliance with the West allowed him to ride out the storm over the A.Q. Khan affair. A.Q. Khan, the father of the Pakistani bomb, came under pressure for nuclear proliferation when Libya admitted to US authorities that it had received help from him. At the time of the first Gulf War of 1990, Iraqi scientists had also named A.Q. Khan as the architect of their nuclear programme. In 1995, the Pakistan government had actually put him on an exit control list, but he was soon exonerated because of his national standing. Pakistani commentators were quick to point out that the US had the occasion to pardon J. Robert Oppenheimer, architect of the US bomb. The cases were dissimilar, and even if there had been similarity, proliferation was too alarming a prospect to induce judicial review, and without US support President Musharraf would not have been able to stand between A.Q. Khan and international agencies, especially after his televised confession on 1 February 2004.

According to the eminent historian Stanley Wolpert:

> The positive achievements of General Pervez Musharraf's regime have included stabilization of the economy and overall improvement in Pakistan's relations with other countries—notably with the USA, with whom Pakistan is allied in the 'War against Terror', and with India.[1]

President Musharraf has also been able to withstand pressure to commit Pakistani troops to Iraq. The American war in Iraq and Afghanistan is unpopular in Pakistan, but all diplomacy requires give and take, and an appreciation of the differences between the West's Middle East policy and South Asia policy; the USSR consistently supported the Arabs against Israel but that did not prevent it from dismembering Pakistan.

On the economic front the investment climate does not seem to have improved; in fact there was friction when retailers observed a three day strike beginning on 19 May 2000. Nevertheless stability and the control of ethnic conflict had a salutary effect. It was reported that Pakistan's economy had grown by 4.9 per cent in the 1999–2000 financial year. Principally because of the War on Terror, Pakistan has not been able to cope with sectarian violence so effectively. The regime has had to contend with an almost new dimension to religious strife. Christians and their churches have been attacked; most notably the church in the Islamabad Diplomatic Enclave (17 March 2002), a boarding school at Murree (4 August 2002), a Christian charity office in Karachi (25 September 2002).

There are signs of national reconciliation too. Asif Zardari, the husband of Benazir Bhutto, originally incarcerated by Nawaz Sharif, was finally released after eight years, on 22 December 2004. Benazir Bhutto made guarded references praising Musharraf for increasing women's representation in legislatures and for the 26 October 2004 bill for enhancing punishment for so called honour killings.

It was Sam Goldwyn who wanted 'a story that starts with an earthquake and works its way up to a climax.'[2] This is essentially the story which has unfolded since 8 October 2005, when an earthquake hit the northern part of Pakistan leaving 100,000 dead, 70,000 injured, and 3.5 million homeless. Initially the nation was united by grief, but when the relief measures proved hopelessly inadequate: fissures began to appear. The homeless have already endured two winters in the high mountainous areas that are naturally exposed to frost.

In a terrain of another type, the simmering discontent in Balochistan erupted. In the first crisis, under Ayub, Balochistan was bombed and Nawab Akbar Bugti was sentenced to death. The death sentence was commuted at the behest of Z.A. Bhutto, and when the National Awami Party led an insurgency in Bhutto's own time, Akbar Bugti (and after him the Khan of Qalat) were made governors to deal with rival tribes. During the present regime, Nawab Akbar Bugti and a number of associates who had taken refuge in a cave were blasted to death on 26 August 2006.

It needs reflection that this round of protest and defiance, had started with the rape of a lady doctor, Shazia Khalid. Balochistan is the province with the lowest population, but it has the largest area, the largest energy reserves, and the largest mineral resources. A rationalization of returns from its own resources may even now, pave the way for national reconciliation. This is vital if the strategic value of Balochistan is to be appreciated, both as the littoral of the Gwadar seaport being built with Chinese cooperation, and the transit area of the lucrative Iran-Pakistan-India pipeline.

The events moved from a calamity to a catastrophe, when on 9 March 2007, the president, on the advice of the prime minister, moved a reference against the Chief Justice of Pakistan, Iftikhar Mohammad Chaudhry. The merits of the case cannot be commented upon as the matter is *sub judice*, but the fall out has been totally unexpected in its extent. The manhandling and hair pulling of the chief justice was shown live on the private television channels of Pakistan. This outraged the people and what was generally perceived as an ingenious move, the SHO of Kohsar Police Station, stated before an inquiry tribunal, that the pictures were genuine but the man committing the outrage was a stranger in police uniform.[3] The bar associations demonstrated against the suspension of the chief justice and were joined by multitudes of demonstrators, who braved the weather and kept nightlong vigils to receive the chief justice when he arrived to address bar associations of various districts.

The motorcade of the chief justice took twenty-five hours to reach Lahore High Court from Islamabad.[4] This is a measure of the crowds lining the road: normally only one-fifth of the time is required. The military government has not been able to prevent such demonstrations, and this is what political parties in Pakistan have not been able to organize. Previously, it was generally assumed that political parties had not been able to rally the people against the regime because of a pervasive apathy. Indeed, unprecedented numbers of suicides caused by poverty and hunger underlined this.[5] Apathy is quite contrary to the fires igniting revolution. The lawyers' struggle is stark evidence that people are willing to come out on the streets, brave police brutality and court arrests. The political parties have only jumped on the lawyer's bandwagon of protest.

On the other hand, the regime's move was not whimsical: it was driven by desperation. The chief justice overturned the privatization of the Pakistan Steel Mills, and was pursuing, with unprecedented assiduity, the cases of people who had gone missing, and whose dependents had accused the intelligence agencies of causing their disappearance. It is true that the Pakistan Steel Mills had been grossly undervalued, but any setback to privatization could be viewed as a setback to IBRD/IMF conditionality. Similarly, the US/NATO's ever rising refrain to do more to contain acts of terrorism caused the concerned agencies to use high-handed methods, putting suspects into the Pakistani equivalent of Guantanamo Bay. The government's methods lacked finesse, thus making its position difficult to defend on 27 March 2007.

The government blamed Jihadi groups for the disappearances.[6] It could hardly be imagined that the situation could get worse, yet when the chief justice accepted an invitation to address the Karachi Bar Association on 12 May 2007 and the MQM scheduled a rally on the same day, trouble was clearly anticipated. In the National Assembly, the former Prime Minister, Zafarullah Jamali, made a humble request to the MQM to postpone their rally. The response of the MQM leader, Nawab Mirza, was chilling: 'No one will be allowed to do anything in Karachi. The country belongs to every one, but Karachi belongs to us.'[7]

This position was not only extra constitutional, but ensured the MQM's political isolation.

The violence on the following day set the course for the events that were to follow. On 10 July after a prolonged stand off, and a fruitless rounds of negotiations, the Lal Masjid (the Islamabad stronghold of the militants) was finally stormed. The leading *alim* Abdur Rashid Ghazi with a number of die-hard supporters perished in the assault. The other *alim* Abdul Aziz (brother of Abdur Rashid), had earlier been caught trying to escape. Not only Pervez Musharraf but George W. Bush were reaping the whirlwind, while Jimmy Carter, who had sown the wind unjustly arraigned the incumbent president. Muslim militants were given a boost above their electoral standing to destabilize the first PPP regime in 1977. Later Jimmy Carter rewarded India for its 1974 nuclear explosion and imposed sanctions on Pakistan two days after Bhutto's execution. This impelled even Bhutto's adversaries to seek the nuclear option. Hopefully the Lal Masjid operation will not trigger a series of suicide bombing retaliation.

On 20 July 2007, the Supreme Court bench reinstated the chief justice, putting the seal of futility on a concerted campaign by government supporters. These supporters mainly consisting of the members of the Pakistan Muslim League (Q) received a jolt when it surfaced that President Musharraf had held direct talks with Benazir Bhutto, on 26 July. It further transpired that this had been the second such meeting. Another former prime minister, Nawaz Sharif received an apparent reprieve on 23 August when the Supreme Court ruled he could return to Pakistan. The political import of this verdict was that Nawaz Sharif could participate in the forthcoming elections.

To offset this contingency, the Saudi Intelligence Chief, Muqrin bin Abdul Aziz and Sa'ad Hariri son of the slain Lebanese Premier Rafiq Hariri produced on 8 September 2007 the original of the signed undertaking of Nawaz Sharif to stay away from Pakistan for ten years. Earlier Sharif had denied the existence of this document, and when confronted with it, said that the ten-year exile had verbally been reduced to five years. Whether this admission dampened the ardor of his supporters, who were unable to prevent his re-deportation when Nawaz Sharif arrived on 10 September, is not known. The only notable development in this connection is that the former Prime Minister Chaudhry Shujaat Husain, and the ruling PML (Q) resolved by a majority that Nawaz Sharif be allowed by return to Pakistan.[8]

Simultaneously, it decried a possible deal between the president and the PPP. The party leadership present in Pakistan bravely kept on reiterating its principled stand against dictatorship, but their dissonance with Benazir Bhutto's attempts to find a negotiated transition to democracy was audible. On 1 September 2007, Benazir Bhutto said that she had not reached an agreement with Musharraf and on the fifth, when emissaries resumed talks, she called for a direct meeting with the president. However, their differences seem unbridgeable, and negotiations have petered out.

We must end our narrative at a point when the election schedule of the president has been announced while a Supreme Court bench is adjudicating the issue. Neither the Supreme Court nor the presidency has had the last word. Let the verdict be recorded by a better chronicler.

On 3 November 2007, General Pervez Musharraf proclaimed a state of emergency sending back the superior judiciary for the second time. Almost immediately seven judges of the Supreme Court led by the Chief Justice Iftikhar Mohammad Chaudhry overturned the Provisional Constitutional Order under which the emergency was proclaimed. If the amendments are *ultra vires* (beyond the power) of the basic provision of the constitution, even a two-third majority provides no remedy.

President Pervez Musharraf doffed his uniform on 28 November 2007 and the National Assembly completed its five-year tenure, amidst congratulations that it had not been dissolved. The lifting of emergency should have instilled confidence, but the caretaker government did not appear neutral. The assassination of Benazir Bhutto on 27 December 2007 caused a violent backlash which destabilized the government. On 21 January 2008, President Musharraf reacted to foreign press criticism by asking western nations to stop their 'obsession with democracy'.[9] What this means in practical terms remains to be seen.

Notes

1. Stanley Wolpert 'Pervez Musharraf' in Hafeez Malik and Yuri Gankovsky (eds.), *Encyclopedia of Pakistan,* Karachi: Oxford University Press, 2005, p. 183.
2. Sam Goldwyn, *Dictionary of Modern Quotations*, Harmondsworth: Penguin, 1980, p. 134.
3. *Dawn*, 29 March 2007.
4. Ibid., 7 May 2007.
5. abbas@sdpi.org
6. *Dawn*, 28 March 2007.
7. *Newsline*, Karachi, June 2007.
8. *Dawn*, 27 January 2007.
9. *Dawn*, 22 January 2008.

 ENAZIR BHUTTO (b. Karachi, 23 June 1953–d. Rawalpindi, 27 December 2007). She was the only politician to suffer the trauma of her father's execution. She held no State office at the time of her death; yet the United Nations Security Council was convened to condemn her assassination. She had represented hope. In her autobiography *The Daughter of the East* she had noted that: 'Pakistan is no ordinary country. And mine has been no ordinary life'.[1] To this, to our regret, we have add that she had no ordinary death. She openly spoke that her life was at risk, but she had to undertake the risk to rid Pakistan of the militants. In another context, she said: 'we had heard rumours that the [Zia] regime was going to get the Afghan *mujahideen* to kill me.[2]

Off lasting impact are the reactions of people who had been subordinate to her Kamran Shafi wrote: 'She came out as someone from one's own family: relaxed, easy, and eager to put her guest at immediate ease...Benazir was a very decent person at heart.'[3] Another journalist M. Ziauddin wrote of his experience: 'I had gone to the meeting after hearing many stories about her arrogance, hot temper, and short fuse. But the Benazir I met was a person one could communicate, enter into heated debate and argue with'.[4]

She did not excise from the second edition, Faisal Hayat's account of his resistance to torture and his refusal to abandon her cause, even though, in between, he had joined the cabinet of General Musharraf. This is symptomatic of people having resisted Ziaul Haq and having joined Pervez Musharraf. But the shrinkage of dictatorial space has been greater. After Benazir Bhutto's assassination, an array of generals, admirals, and air marshals gathered together asking President Pervez Musharraf to step down.[5]

She spent most of her life in jail or exile. Her years in power were not her years of triumph. She fought an uphill battle to become Prime Minister twice. She fought a losing battle both times, unable to complete her terms. Her husband suffered terms of imprisonment. His mettle showed when he could handle the crisis of her assassination with more responsibility than the regime.

Instead of stressing that Pervez Musharraf had met Benazir Bhutto twice in Dubai, and that he and she shared common enemies, her death was put down not to the assassin, not to the suicide bomber, but to a lever on her vehicle. The manufacturers of the vehicle threatened to sue.

In contrast Asif Zardari, her widower, responded by saying 'we have decided to turn our grief into our strength'.[6] This is the strand of hope that her legacy holds out.

Notes

1. Benazir Bhutto, *Daughter of the East*, 2nd ed. London, Simon and Schuster 2007, p. xi.
2. Ibid., p. 328.
3. *Dawn*, Karachi, 28 December 2007.
4. Ibid., 30 December 2007.
5. Ibid., 23 January 2008.
6. *Newsline*, Karachi, January 2008, p. 24.

PART VI

CONSTITUTIONAL HISTORY

CHAPTER 33

CONSTITUTIONAL DEVELOPMENTS: 1947, 1956, 1962 AND 1973

THE CONSTITUTIONAL HISTORY OF BRITISH INDIA

1. *Regulating Act 1773*: The East India Company was required to submit all material correspondence to the King's ministers.
2. *Pitt's India Act 1784*: Company affairs subordinated to a Board of Governors appointed by the Crown (6 members). This system of dual government, with more amendments in 1813, 1833 and 1853 continued till the Company's rule ended.
3. *An Act for the Better Government of India 1858*: It abolished the Company's rule and appointed a Secretary of State for India with a council of 15 members. The Governor-General was given additional designation of Viceroy.
4. *Indian Councils Act of 1861*: A 5th member was added to the Viceroy's Council. Between 6 to 12 members were added to act as legislature. The portfolio system was introduced, and a measure of decentralization adopted. Indians were included in the Council and provinces were given legislative councils.
5. *Indian Councils Act of 1892*: Enlarged the Imperial and Provincial Councils memberships. Although direct elections were not the norm, the councils became more representative, as the chambers of commerce, university bodies, municipal bodies and district boards sent their nominees, though official majority was retained. The powers of criticism of the councils increased.
6. *Indian Councils Act 1909*: Morley–Minto Reforms. Central and provincial legislatures were enlarged, their functions extended and the principle of election was legally recognized. An official majority was maintained in the centre but not in provinces. Separate electorates was ceded.
7. *The Government of India Act 1919*: (Montagu–Chelmsford Reforms) Central and provincial subjects were divided. Central subjects were foreign affairs, defense, communications, taxation. Provincial subjects being education, health, agriculture, law & order and justice. Bi-cameral legislature in the Centre. In the provinces there were two categories. Reserved subjects were under nominated members with no responsibility to the House whereas transferred subjects were under directly elected members. This was known as Dyarchy. Separate electorates was extended to Sikh and Christian groups.

8. *Government of India Act 1935*: The Federal Act was never carried out as the Congress, and Muslim League, and Princes opposed it. It sought to impose Dyarchy in the centre. However, it gave greater power to the provinces. Dyarchy was removed from the provinces, Assemblies replaced councils in the provinces. Burma was separated from India. Sindh was separated from Bombay and NWFP was given full provincial status with an Assembly.

Framing a constitution for Pakistan has been an uphill task, while preserving the constitution has proved to be a daunting task. Simply put, Pakistan enacted three constitutions, in 1956, in 1962 and in 1973; there are also some documents preceding the 1956 constitution and a series of amendments succeeding the 1973 constitution, which have to be taken into account in tracing the constitutional development of Pakistan. It is unusual for a country to have had more than one constitution. That we have had so many, with so many amendments, speaks volumes for political instability in Pakistan. While describing the constitutional history of British India, it was explained that a constitution embodies the set of rules according to which a people agree to live with each other. The Oxford English Dictionary's definition is that 'a constitution embodies' the fundamental principles by which a state is governed'. It is thus the basic law from which other laws proceed. Constitution-making has proved elusive and contentious because of the inability to arrive at a consensus on two issues: the role of religion in the state and the degree of autonomy to be granted to the provinces. Both issues are covered under separate headings below. But first we need to trace the early history of constitutions in Pakistan.

EARLY CONSTITUTIONAL HISTORY

Pakistan gained independence as a Dominion of the British Commonwealth of Nations. Two documents governed the dominion: the Indian Independence Act 1947 and the Government of India Act 1935 (GOI Act 1935), which was to function as an interim constitution. There was a departure from the norm when the Jinnah chose to be governor-general, instead of prime minister, who is usually the chief executive in a parliamentary democracy.

The reason why Jinnah assumed the office of governor-general was to pre-empt the appointment of Lord Mountbatten, who wished to undo partition as governor-general. The GOI Act 1935 gave discretionary powers to the viceroy/governor-general; the British withdrew this provision when they handed over power. It has been pointed out[1] that Provision C to Section 8(2) of the Indian Independence Act precluded the governor-general from exercising personal discretion and individual judgement and made it mandatory for him to follow the advice of the prime minister.

On the other hand, Pakistan was being governed by the Provisional Constitution Order 1947. The centre had full power to alter the interim constitution under Section 9(1) of the Indian Independence Act. Until 1949, the governor-general was personally entitled to alter the interim constitution and after 1949, the Constituent Assembly was so empowered. Jinnah died before 1949 and thus he was able to alter the interim constitution. His first act was to change the form of the oath to be taken by the governor-general. It originally read: 'to bear true faith and allegiance to His Majesty (the King of England). Jinnah had it changed to 'bear true allegiance to the Constitution'.

It was under this amended form of the interim constitution that Jinnah took his oath of office as governor-general of Pakistan. Until 1949, the governor-general rather than the prime minister had been the chief executive of Pakistan. To enforce this further, on 30 December 1947, the cabinet decided that no matter of policy or principle could be decided unless its meeting was presided over by the governor-general. This provision was personal to Jinnah, since much depended on the prestige of the office holder. Had Jinnah been bound by decisions taken by Liaquat Ali Khan, it would have been a reversal of their pre-independence equation. This factor was also illustrated by the fact that Liaquat Ali Khan did not have to wait till 1949 to become chief executive. He became prime minister and chief executive following Jinnah's death in 1948, because in the freedom movement he had been far more prominent than the new Governor-General, Khwaja Nazimuddin. The division of power at the centre did not become a constitutional issue at that time, but later it was held responsible for weakening the tradition of parliamentary governance.

The first contentious issue was the role that religion was to play in the polity of Pakistan. Since protagonists of both a secular or a religious state quote Jinnah, his statements are detailed below:

1. 'Let us lay down the foundations of our democracy on the study of truly Islamic ideals and principles.'[2]
2. 'You are free to go to your temples, you are free to go to your mosques or to any other place of worship in this State of Pakistan. You may belong to any religion, caste or creed—that has nothing to do with the business of the State... we are starting with this fundamental principle that we are all citizens and equal citizens of one State.'[3]
3. 'The constitution of Pakistan has yet to be framed by the Pakistan Constituent Assembly. I do not know what the ultimate shape of this constitution is going to be but I am sure that it will be a democratic type, embodying the essential principles of Islam...In any case, Pakistan is not going to be a theocratic state—to be ruled by priests with a divine vision. We have many non-Muslims they will enjoy the same rights and privileges as any other citizens.'[4]

The first quotation is cited by protagonists of an Islamic state, the second by the secularists. It is the third quotation that needs to be considered most. It is within one speech that we have reference to Islamic values as well as a denunciation of theocracy. By considering both parts together, it emerges that Jinnah considered *liberty, equality* and *fraternity* to be Islamic values that had to be followed. Democracy and Islam, according to him, were identical. Theocracy means rule of the priests and this certainly is a concept opposed to democracy. He also knew that there is no provision for an ordained priesthood in Islam. Jinnah spoke simultaneously against theocracy and in favour of Islamic norms, because the majority was Muslim. No constitutional guarantee could neglect this aspect of Pakistan's polity. The form was secular, but the content was religious, and both these realities had to be reconciled. Then there is another vital aspect of Jinnah's third speech: The Constituent Assembly as a body, and not its president as an individual, would determine the nature of the constitution. Much of these statements reflected Jinnah's experience as the champion of minorities.

THE ROLE OF MINORITIES

Jinnah knew from experience that if a minority community of whatever following was discriminated against, it led to disintegration. He observed that it was Hindu–Muslim discord which had been responsible for India's enslavement. He also noted that there were caste and sectarian differences among Muslims and Hindus. These internal dissensions had to be contained. Then again, the role of the minorities was of more than symbolic value. Jogendra Nath Mandal presided over the inaugural session of the Pakistan Constituent Assembly. The casting vote of S.P. Singha, the Christian Speaker of the Punjab Assembly enabled it to join Pakistan. H.S. Suhrawardy and Kiran Shankar Roy were co-authors of the united and independent Bengal scheme. H.S. Suhrawardy was denied his seat in the Constituent Assembly because he did not take up permanent residence in Pakistan. Kiran Shankar Roy took up residence and made one of the most moving speeches in support of Pakistan. Therefore, in any constitutional dispensation, the minority communities representation could not be denied an honourable place.

The contribution of the Parsi community to the development of Pakistan is immense. They too have contributed to civic life and education, and their expertise in commerce has stood Pakistan in good stead.

THE ROLE OF THE ULEMA/OBJECTIVES RESOLUTION

The demand that Pakistan be declared an Islamic State was put forward by Maulana Abul Ala Maududi (1902–1979), the founder of the Jama'at-i-Islami, who had earlier opposed the creation of Pakistan. He addressed meetings all over Pakistan and asserted that the future constitution should embody the following principles:

(1) The sovereignty of Pakistan belongs to Allah alone and the Government of Pakistan has no right other than to enforce the will of Allah. (2) The basic law of Pakistan is the *Shariah* of Islam. (3) All those laws which are repugnant to Islam are to be revoked and in future, no such law should be passed. (4) The Government of Pakistan will exercise its authority within the limits prescribed by Islamic *Shariah*.

Apart from the fact that Jinnah was opposed to theocracy, some practical problems come in the way of applying the *Shariah* smoothly. The *Shariah* has four legal systems, *Hanafi, Maliki, Shafii* and *Hanbali*. Since there is no accord on what constitutes the *Shariah*, the law prescribed by one school of thought could be proscribed by another. As an example, the *Hanafi fiqh* does not make the consent of a guardian binding on a bride; other *fiqhs* do. The social fall outs are the 'honour killings' which clearly transcend the *Shariah*. This movement of the Jama'at-i-Islami gathered wide support and momentum, and the Objectives Resolution tabled by Liaquat Ali Khan represented an attempt by the prime minister to defuse this tension. The Objectives Resolution was passed by the Constituent Assembly on 12 March 1949. It served as a preamble to the constitutions of 1956, 1962 and 1973 and has proved to be the most resilient document in the constitutional history of Pakistan.

OBJECTIVES RESOLUTION

1. Whereas sovereignity over the entire Universe belongs to Allah Almighty alone, and the authority which He has delegated to the State of Pakistan through its people for being exercised within the limits prescribed by Him is a sacred trust.
2. This Constituent Assembly representing the people of Pakistan resolves to frame a constitution of the sovereign independent state of Pakistan; wherein the state shall exercise its power and authority through the chosen representatives of the people.
3. Wherein the principles of democracy, freedom, equality, tolerance and social justice as enunicated by Islam shall be fully observed.
4. Wherein the Muslims shall be enabled to order their lives in the individual and collective spheres in accordance with the teaching and requirements of Islam as set out in the Holy Quran and the *Sunnah*.
5. Wherein adequate provisions shall be made for the minorities to freely profess and practice their religions and develop their cultures.
6. Whereby the territories now included in or accession with Pakistan and such territories as may hereafter be included in or accede to Pakistan shall form a federation wherein the units will be autonomous with such boundaries and limitation on their powers and authority as may be prescribed.

7. Wherein shall be guaranteed fundamental rights including equality of status, of opportunity before law, social economic and political justice and freedom of thought, expression, belief, faith, worship and association subject to law and public morality.
8. Wherein adequate provision shall be made to safeguard the legitimate interests of minorities and backward and depressed classes.
9. Wherein the independence of judiciary shall be fully secured.
10. Wherein the integrity of the territories of the federation, its independence and all its rights including its sovereign rights on land, sea and air shall be safeguarded.
11. So that the people of Pakistan may prosper and attain their rightful and honoured place amongst the nations of the world and make their full contribution towards international peace and progress and happiness of humanity.

The points on which the Objectives Resolution departed from the Jama'at-i-Islami formula are:

Point 1: meant that sovereignty was to be exercised by the people, reintroducing the democratic principles. The rights other than to enforce the will of the sovereign was removed. Point 2: specifically mentioned tolerance. Point 3: says that Muslims shall be 'enabled', not compelled to order their lives in accordance with the *Shariah*. The Objective Resolution is in accord with the 256th Verse of the Quran (*Surah Baqra*) where 'there is no compulsion in religion'. Point 4: mentions minority rights and Point 6: mentions fundamental human rights, both of which were not part of the Jama'at-i-Islami demand. Point 8: reiterates the rights of minorities and backward classes.

The Jama'at-i-Islami found Jinnah's declaration at the Sibi Durbar, that the foundation of democracy would be on the basis of truly Islamic ideals and principles, inadequate. Since it did not support Jinnah's view of equal rights for the minorities, as soon as it entered government, it imposed separate electorates on the minorities against their will. Maulana Abul Ala Maududi was arrested under the Safety Act on 4 October 1948. Some ulema such as Allama Shabbir Ahmad Usmani and Umar Hayat Khan, who had supported the Pakistan Movement, joined hands with them and the Jama'at-i-Islami, far from being deterred by the arrest of its leaders, widened its base and mounted intense pressure on the government. Point 6 and points 9 to 11 are not directly concerned with religion but with the distribution of power between the centre and provinces, but even these were related to the demands made by the ulema.

PROVINCIAL AUTONOMY

East Pakistan was larger than all the provinces of West Pakistan put together in terms of its population. In any democratic dispensation, the representatives of East Bengal would command a majority. This the politicians from West Pakistan wished to avoid. The point was raised that East Bengal was greater in population by virtue of its Hindu community, otherwise the *Muslim* population of both wings was equal. By cutting down minority rights it was possible to reduce the franchise of the East Wing.

BASIC PRINCIPLES COMMITTEE REPORT

The next document to be produced after the Objectives Resolution was the Basic Principles Committee Report. The committee, consisting of twenty-five members, was headed by Maulvi Tamizuddin Khan, president of the Constituent Assembly. Its interim report was submitted on 7 September 1950, but it pleased no one. The religious faction was angry because of the provision that the head of state could be a non-Muslim and the Bengalis were angry because their language was not given national status. The interim report indemnified the governor-general, prime minister and legislators from appearing in court. On this score the indignation of the ulema was justified, as the pious caliphs had readily appeared before courts when summoned. Since the interim report drew on the GOI Act 1935 it gave sweeping powers to the head of state, who could assume control of the provinces and, in case of emergency, could suspend the constitution in part or fully. This provision was circulated in advance of any constitution being framed! The interim report provided, moreover, for the head of state to be indirectly elected by the legislature. The form of government would be federal, as provided by GOI Act 1935. A federal form has more than one level of government, one at the level of the federation—in the centre—and the other governing the federating units or the provinces. The legislature was to be bicameral, having two houses, the lower being directly elected and the upper being indirectly elected. The upper house was to give equal representation to all the provinces. Thus if East Bengal had a majority in the lower house, it became a minority in the upper house. Since the powers of both houses were equal, the majority of East Pakistan would be neutralized in this manner.

The final report of the Basic Principles Committee was presented during the term of Khwaja Nazimuddin's prime ministership in July 1952. Both east and west wings were to have equal representation. Unlike the interim report, which mentioned Urdu as the only national language, the final report made no mention of any national language. One provision was made to conciliate the ulema. An ulema board was formed, at both the federal and provincial levels to prevent legislation which was un-Islamic. This fell short of conciliating the ulema as the government would have the power of nomination. The Prime Minister, Khwaja Nazimuddin withdrew the final report on 21 January 1953 without informing Maulvi Tamizuddin Khan, president of the Constituent Assembly. On 17 April 1953 the Prime Minister, Khwaja Nazimuddin was dismissed by the Governor-General, Ghulam Mohammad. Constitution framing, which had hitherto been contentious, had now assumed the proportion of a crisis.

1954 DRAFT CONSTITUTION

In 1954, Mohammad Ali Bogra, (d.1963) who was appointed prime minister in place of Khwaja Nazimuddin, formulated his constitutional proposals. He represented nobody but hailed from East Bengal. When he came across West Pakistani opposition to allow his province a majority, he proposed a solution to overcome it. His solution was given the name of the Mohammad Ali Formula. The federation was to have a bicameral legislature (two houses of Parliament). In the upper house, each of the five provinces would have ten seats, in the lower house the total membership would be three hundred of which one hundred and sixty-five would be from to East Bengal. Thus in both houses taken together, each wing would have one hundred and seventy-five seats. This parity between the two wings offered a workable compromise and had there been the political will to enforce this formula, there would have been no insurmountable crisis in the future. After a hectic and prolonged session, the Constituent Assembly took a recess on 14 November 1953. During the recess the Muslim League lost the provincial elections in East Bengal, causing some to observe, with justice, that the Constituent Assembly had become unrepresentative.

When the Constituent Assembly reconvened on 14 March 1954, it carried on business as usual. On 7 May, Mohammad Ali successfully moved a resolution making Bengali a national language along with Urdu. The Constituent Assembly stood poised to give the country a constitution, but trouble was brewing in another quarter. The Governor-General, Ghulam Mohammad, was not satisfied with the Mohammad Ali Formula. He felt that some smaller provinces like NWFP or Balochistan could join hands with East Bengal and pass measures not to the liking of his Punjab constituency. He therefore planned a merger of all four West Pakistan provinces, Sindh, Punjab, NWFP and Balochistan to be called One Unit. Another piece of legislation which the Constituent Assembly was enacting surreptitiously, but of which Ghulam Mohammad learnt, was to curtail the powers of the governor-general.

On 21 September it was enacted that the governor-general would have no powers to dismiss the prime minister or dissolve assemblies. The prime minister would hold office as long as he enjoyed the confidence of the house, and not at the pleasure of the governor-general. One day earlier the Constituent Assembly had repealed the Public and Representative Officer (Disqualification) Act (PRODA), which was the main weapon the governor-general could use to coerce individual politicians. Therefore, when the Constituent Assembly had almost passed the constitution, the governor-general intervened and dissolved the Constituent Assembly on 24 October 1954.

THE 1956 CONSTITUTION

A constitution for Pakistan was finally enacted in 1956 when Ghulam Mohammad had retired. Prior to his retirement, in 1955, the One Unit Scheme had been put into effect in 1955. Therefore, the first difference between the 1954 draft and the 1956 Constitution was that it had a unicameral legislature, that is, having only one chamber, but 150 or an equal number of seats was allotted to the two wings which meant parity (total 300). Bengali was declared a national language alongside Urdu.

The constitution had an involved system in relation to the head of state and government. According to the constitution, the country was to be known as the Islamic Republic of Pakistan. The president would be a Muslim male adult of at least forty years of age. He would be indirectly elected by the federal and provincial assemblies for a period of five years and be eligible for re-election only once. The president could be impeached by two-thirds of the National Assembly. He was required to act on the advice of the cabinet. On the other hand, the president could veto any legislation, subject to the provision that two-thirds of the members could override the veto.

The president could issue ordinances when the National Assembly was not in session. No money bill could be introduced without the consent of the president. The president possessed the power to proclaim an emergency and suspend human rights. The list of human rights was long, but as one commentator has remarked, compromised by the proviso[5] 'subject to any reasonable restrictions imposed by law'. Not only was 'reasonable' very imprecise, but what 'law' would apply was also ambiguous. The only guarantee of human rights in the constitution was an independent judiciary. Although proclaimed a republic, Pakistan would remain a member of the British Commonwealth.

In spite of the provision that the president would act on the advice of the cabinet, the position of the president was far more secure than that of the prime minister. The last Governor-General Iskander Mirza, had become the first president, but he outstayed a number of prime ministers: Chaudhry Mohammad Ali (who gave the constitution), Huseyn Shaheed Suhrawardy,

I.I. Chundrigar and Feroz Khan Noon. President Mirza complained about the polity but abrogated the constitution. Only when the 1956 Constitution was abrogated, Mirza's new prime minister and chief martial law administrator, General Mohammad Ayub Khan was able to oust him and take his place. (Islamic provisions of the three constitutions are listed separately in Chapter 34).

THE 1962 CONSTITUTION

Two years after staging his *coup*; on 17 February 1960, President Ayub Khan appointed a constitution commission. It was entrusted with examining the causes of the failure of the parliamentary system, implying that, as if the constitution had abrogated itself. It was charged to suggest a form of democracy suited to 'changed circumstances'. A cabinet committee was appointed to study the recommendations of the constitution commission. On the submission of this committee's report a two-member team was appointed to study the administrative problems which the introduction of the new constitution would bring. Finally, on 1 March 1962, President Ayub Khan broadcast features of his one-man constitution. He had disregarded the recommendations of his own constitution commission, which had recommended a strong presidency, but an equally strong parliament. Ayub retained the first and rejected the second.

The 1962 Constitution replaced the parliamentary system with the presidential system. Rather than go through the tedium of frequently changing prime ministers, the post was abolished altogether. Direct Adult Franchise was done away with for an electoral college of Basic Democrats, themselves directly elected, in February 1960. They totalled eighty thousand—forty thousand in each wing. They constituted four tiers of local government and formed the electoral college for the president and the members of the national and provincial assemblies. The legislature was unicameral and there was no vice-president. The president appointed judges, armed forces' chiefs and ministers. Two-thirds of the National Assembly could impeach the president. One redeeming feature was that the president could not dissolve the National Assembly without losing his own office as well. As we have seen in the political section, Ayub Khan effectively abrogated his own constitution on 25 March 1969 by transferring power to the army chief instead of to the speaker of the National Assembly.

THE CONSTITUTIONAL CRISIS 1969—71

There was a conflict between the Legal Framework Order (LFO) of General Yahya Khan and the Six Points of Sheikh Mujibur Rahman. There were some decisions taken in advance of electing the Constituent Assembly which were at the behest of the political forces, such as, restoration of direct adult franchise, and the parliamentary system, and abolition of One-Unit.[6] No constitution commission was appointed to probe the causes of the failure of the presidential system. Only one (and the most) contentious issue remained: the degree of provincial autonomy. On 11 January 1970 Sheikh Mujibur Rahman asked Yahya Khan not to grant autonomy in advance of the election.[7] On 7 March Mujib said that he would launch a movement *after* elections to achieve autonomy.

The constitutional crisis over the degree of autonomy could not be resolved until Indian armed intervention caused the secession of the East Wing. The power of the chief martial law administrator and president was transferred to Zulfikar Ali Bhutto on 20 December 1971. Although Z.A. Bhutto emerged as the elected representative of residual Pakistan, the transition could only be made by transferring the office of the chief martial law administrator under the only basic law in the country.

Martial Law was lifted and an interim constitution, enacted on 17 April 1972, came into force on 21 April. The presidential form was retained. It was strongly rumoured that Bhutto preferred a presidential system for the permanent constitution as well, and it was this discord which ultimately led to the resignation of the Law Minister, Mian Mahmud Ali Qasuri.

The National Assembly doubled, as before, as the Constituent Assembly. On 17 April 1972 a committee to draft the permanent constitution was appointed. On 20 October 1972, a draft bill was signed by all parties represented in the Assembly. On 2 February 1973 a constitution bill was moved, and the bill was passed almost unanimously on 10 April 1973 and promulgated on Independence Day 1973. Zulfikar Ali Bhutto stepped down to become prime minister, and the speaker, Fazal Ilahi Chaudhry became the fourth president of Pakistan.

WHAT IS A FEDERATION?

This question is relevant to deciding whether the Six Points were federal, or confederal, which is a loose arrangement. This also forms the basis whereby Z.A. Bhutto sought consensus on the 1973 constitution. Federation is a term of American origin when thirteen States who found themselves individually weak against Britain or France, came together in a federation for mutual security. Alexander Hamilton, formulated on 18 December 1787 the purpose and functions of a federation:

'The principle purposes to be answered by Union are these—the common defence of the members—the preservation of the public peace as well against internal convulsions as external attacks—the regulation of commerce with other nations and between the States—the superintendence of our intercourse, political and commercial, with foreign countries.'

The Federalist Papers No. 27.

EFFORTS FOR CONSENSUS

Zulfikar Ali Bhutto was conscious of the fact that firstly, constitution framing in Pakistan had been delayed, and secondly, it could be abrogated because it had no firm foundation. Pakistan had recently been dismembered ostensibly because no consensus could be built between the Awami League and the PPP. Now the PPP–NAP/JUI equation in residual Pakistan was the same as that between the Awami League and the PPP. The National Awami Party (NAP) chief, Khan Abdul Wali Khan, said as much. Consequently, opposition parties were brought together and on 20 October 1972, a constitutional accord was signed effecting a compromise. Z.A. Bhutto thanked the opposition for its cooperation.[8]

The dismissal of the NAP–JUI government in Balochistan and its resignation in NWFP intervened between the accord and the passage of the constitution. Without giving in on the political issue, Z.A. Bhutto was still able to gather their support for his draft 1973 Constitution.

The constitution was to be a federal and parliamentary system of government. For the first time a bicameral legislature was brought into being; the upper house was called the Senate and the lower house would be called the National Assembly. Members of the National Assembly would number two hundred, elected directly by the people. The senate would consist of sixty-three members to be indirectly elected. Each provincial assembly would elect fourteen members, five would be elected by the Federally Administered Tribal Areas (FATA) and two by the federal capital area. The senate would not be subject to dissolution. The term of their office would be four years, half the members retiring after two years. The National Assembly members would have a tenure of five years.

The president would act on the advice of the prime minister. He could exercise the power to pardon prisoners condemned to death. Only a male Muslim of more than forty-five years of age would be eligible to stand for office. The president would be elected by the members of the National and Provincial assemblies.

The prime minister would be elected by a majority of the National Assembly.

Since the first era of parliamentary government had seen a succession of prime ministers, it was provided that any motion of no-confidence against the prime minister would have to name his successor. Since it is easier to secure agreement on the removal of a serving prime minister, than to agree upon a common candidate to succeed him, this provision was designed to give stability to the prime minister's office.

In the provinces, the governor would be the nominee of the federal government, while the chief minister would be elected by a majority of the provincial assembly, to which he was responsible. The structure of the federal system was replicated in the provinces.

There was a list of human and provincial rights but those were used to secure a consensus and sadly, compromised later, by the majority enjoyed by the ruling party.

AMENDMENTS TO THE 1973 CONSTITUTION

The constitution can be amended by a two-thirds majority of both houses of parliament. Seven amendments were moved by Z.A. Bhutto, the architect of the 1973 Constitution.

1. The first amendment allowed the government to ban political parties from operating in a manner prejudicial to the sovereignty or integrity of Pakistan. This decision had to be confirmed by the Supreme Court. This was the amendment Bhutto used in banning the NAP.
2. The second amendment declared the Ahmadis as non-Muslims.
3. The third amendment softened safeguards against arrest and detention and facilitated continuation of a Proclamation of Emergency under which basic human rights could be curtailed.
4. The fourth amendment curtailed the writ powers against arrest and detention. The high courts were largely precluded from granting freedom or bail to people who were detained.
5. The fifth amendment further curtailed the power of the higher judiciary. Their terms of office were to be determined not solely by age, but by a fixed term. Judges could be transferred from one High Court to another for one year without their consent.
6. The sixth amendment clarified the retirement age of judges.
7. The seventh amendment provided for a referendum. This was to avoid re-election after the 1977 allegations of poll-rigging. Politically, Bhutto was unable to use this amendment, but two military rulers, General Ziaul Haq and General Pervez Musharraf, used it.

Except for the first amendment, which was subject to the decision of the Supreme Court, and the second, which was thrust upon him, there was no real necessity for Bhutto to subject his own constitution to so many amendments. They were aimed mainly at human rights and the judiciary which would uphold them. The amendments followed a constitutional procedure and were passed by a two-thirds majority, but weakened the moral force behind the near consensus that the 1973 Constitution had achieved, and compromised the sanctity of this document when it was challenged by extra-parliamentary forces.

LATER AMENDMENTS

8. President Ziaul Haq made the passage of the eighth amendment a condition for lifting martial law. By this amendment, the electoral college for the president came to include the senate in addition to the national and provincial assemblies. It contained clause 58(2)B according to which the president could dismiss the prime minister and dissolve the assemblies. President Ziaul Haq exercised this power once, President Ghulam Ishaq Khan twice and President Farooq Leghari once. When President Leghari was unable to dismiss his second prime minister and the eighth amendment had been repealed, he had to resign. This amendment increased the strength of the senate from sixty-three to eighty-seven; five seats from each province were reserved for ulema, technocrats or professionals. The number of seats reserved for women was increased from ten to twenty. The Federal Shariat Court was set up. Its task was to rule whether any existing law was in accord with Islamic laws and pass verdicts on government measures in any domain of life.

9. The intent of the ninth amendment was to make the Quran and Sunnah the supreme law. It was passed by the senate, but because of the dismissal of Prime Minister Junejo in 1988, the amendment did not become effective.

10. The tenth amendment provided that the interval between two National Assembly or senate sessions should not exceed 130 days.

11. The intent of the eleventh amendment was to revise the number of seats reserved for women in the National Assembly. This was enacted in the seventeenth amendment with the number of reserved seats increased.

12. The twelfth amendment provided for the setting up of speedy trial courts.

13. The thirteenth amendment was enacted by the PML (N) government to repeal the eighth amendment especially 58(2)B. It simultaneously struck down the provision by which governors could dismiss chief ministers and dissolve provincial assemblies. The president's powers to appoint judges and the three armed forces' chiefs were curtailed. He would have to make these appointments on the advice of the prime minister.

14. The fourteenth amendment prevented floor-crossing or horse-trading by elected members.

15. The fifteenth amendment was again meant to make the Quran and Sunnah the basic law of the land. Since this would have resulted in drastic curtailment of the constitution, even the religious parties did not oblige Nawaz Sharif. This amendment was passed by the National Assembly on 9 October 1999, but not by the Senate.

16. The sixteenth amendment related to extending the quota system in the services for another forty years from August 1993. This was to amend

Article 27 of the constitution which provides for safeguards against any form of discrimination including domicile or place of birth.

17. General Pervez Musharraf took over the government on 12 October 1999. The Supreme Court justified his takeover on 12 May 2002 in the Zafar Ali Shah case on 30 April 2002. General Pervez Musharraf held a referendum to justify his assumption of power on 20 June 2001. On 21 August 2002, he promulgated the Legal Framework Order (LFO). Again, by this LFO, the president and not the prime minister would have the power to appoint the armed forces' chiefs and judges of the supreme and high courts. The office of the prime minister would be restored, but the constitution would, in its orientation, become presidential rather than parliamentary.

THE SEVENTEENTH AMENDMENT

The LFO originally provided for the establishment of a National Security Council.[9] General Musharraf extended his term as president by five years, secured indemnity for all his orders since his take-over and reinstated the rule that the president and not the prime minister would have the power to appoint armed forces' chiefs and members of the higher judiciary.

Some features of the LFO were positive and political leaders have not stinted from characterizing them as such. These are the reduction of the voting age from 21 years to 18, increasing the number of National Assembly seats from 217 to 342, and of Senate seats from 87 to 100. Women's representation was increased. Candidates for assemblies had to be at least graduates and finally, separate electorates for minorities was abolished. This was to fulfil a long-standing demand of the minorities.

After the 10 October 2002 elections, some modifications to the LFO were deemed advisable. The treasury benches contended that the LFO was a part of the constitution whereas the opposition benches disagreed. One opposition alliance, Muttahida Majlis-i-Amal (MMA), to the exclusion of another component the Alliance for the Restoration of Democracy (ARD), negotiated with the government and the resultant compromise was enacted as the seventeenth amendment on 29 December 2003. The seventeenth amendment had originally required the president to resign as chief of army staff on 31 December 2004, but the parliament passed a dual offices bill before that date enabling the president to retain his uniform.

As a compromise, the pre-LFO retirement age of the higher judiciary was restored; this resulted in the retirement of the chief justice and a number of other judges. Under this amendment, the local government system would function for a further six years. The local government system had been inducted under a Devolution of Power Plan on 23 March 2000 which was put into operation through the National Reconstruction Bureau. The regime criticized the earlier local government systems on the ground that the provincial administration had controlled it through bureaucrats at every stage. As a result, the post of divisional commissioner was abolished, and the deputy commissioners were re-designated as district coordination officers.

Two innocuous amendments to the LFO were made. The president would retain the power to appoint the military chief, but in doing so would consult the prime minister. The invocation of 58(2)(B) would be referred to the Supreme Court, a recourse which, with a solitary exception in 1993, was found ineffective. A former judge of the Supreme Court, and a former Attorney General, Fakhruddin G. Ebrahim, has observed that the Supreme Court gave three years to General Musharraf when he had not even asked for it, and the power to amend the constitution even though the constitution was in abeyance for three years. This judgement, dated 12 May 2000, gives judicial cover to the seventeenth amendment.[10]

NOTES

1. *Dawn*, Karachi, 5 October 2002.
2. Sibi Durbar speech, 14 February 1947.
3. *Jinnah: Speeches and Statements 1947–1948*, Karachi: Oxford University Press, 2000, p. 28, (11 August 1947).
4. Ibid., p. 125, Broadcast to USA, February 1948.
5. Louis D. Hayes, *The Struggle for Legitimacy in Pakistan*, Lahore: Vanguard, 1986, p. 92.
6. Abdur Rahman Siddiqi, *East Pakistan: The Endgame*, Karachi: Oxford University Press, 2004, p. 225.
7. Ibid.
8. Rafi Raza, *Zulfikar Ali Bhutto and Pakistan 1971–1977*, Karachi: Oxford University Press, 1997, p. 176.
9. Charles H. Kennedy and Cynthia A. Botteron (eds.) *Pakistan 2005*, Karachi: Oxford University Press, 2006, p. 2.
10. *Dawn*, 14 January 2005.

CHAPTER 34

THE ISLAMIC PROVISIONS OF SUCCESSIVE CONSTITUTIONS

The definition of religious jurisdiction is not unique to Pakistan. In Britain, the mother of parliaments, the constitution of Clarendon (1641), set the limits of civil and ecclesiastical (church) jurisdictions. The king or queen is designated *Defender of the Faith*. Originally, *Defender* meant the Defender of the Roman Catholic Church and, after King Henry VIII, the British sovereign became the Defender of the Church of England.

This example has been given to show that the original intent of the founder is capable of being altered. Taking the dicta of Jinnah together, we can reach the conclusion that he expected secular principles to devolve from Islamic values. Such a concept needs adjustment. However, as much as we deplore the induction of religion as a coercive force, we must acknowledge that the demographic composition kept the door ajar for Islamization.

THE 1956 CONSTITUTION

1. The country was named the Islamic Republic of Pakistan.
2. The Objectives Resolution 1949 was adopted as a preamble indicating State policy.
3. The moral teachings of Islam would be encouraged and vices such as gambling, drinking and prostitution would be curbed.
4. *Zakat* and *Auqaf.* The government was instructed to collect and administer alms and trusts.
5. Article 24 of the constitution obliged Pakistan to maintain friendly relations with Muslim countries.
6. No law repugnant to Islam was to be passed. Existing laws (inherited from the British) would also be examined with a view to make them conform to Islamic laws.
7. The government was required, under Article 197 to set up an Islamic Research Institute to examine laws. During the period the 1956 Constitution remained in force, such an institute was not set up.
8. The president was required to be a Muslim male adult. However, the speaker of the National Assembly who was to officiate in the president's absence, or infirmity could be a non-Muslim. No non-Muslim speaker has

ever been appointed save Joginder Nath Mandal who inaugurated the Constituent Assembly of Pakistan.

1962 CONSTITUTION

1. Initially the country was called the Republic of Pakistan, but by its first amendment on 25 December 1963, the words Islamic has been added.
2. The Objectives Resolution was again retained as the preamble, only the word Islam was substituted for 'Quran and Sunnah'.
3. The government would provide for the compulsory education of the Quran and Islamiat to Muslim students.
4. Under an amendment the 1956 provision of bringing existing laws in conformity with Islam was restored.
5. An Islamic Advisory Council was to be set up consisting of no less than five and no more than twelve members. It was meant to answer the queries of the president and legislators. Its advice was not binding.
6. For the framing of Islamic laws, an Islamic Research Institute was set up with the head office in Islamabad and provincial offices in Lahore and Dhaka.

THE 1973 CONSTITUTION

1. This was the first constitution in which Islam was declared to be the state religion.
2. The Objectives Resolution was adopted.
3. All legislation was to be in conformity with the Quran and Sunnah. All existing laws were to be brought in conformity within nine years. Personal law for non-Muslims was according to their respective creeds.
4. Both the president and prime minister were required to be adult Muslims. The president would be male.
5. The government of Pakistan would take the responsibility of printing the Holy Quran. Article 31 required copies to be free of all types of printing errors.
6. The government would provide maximum facilities for the promotion of the Arabic language.
7. A Council of Islamic Ideology (CII) would be formed having eight to fifteen members. Two had to be either serving or retired judges of the supreme or high courts. The chairman would also have to be a serving or former judge of the Supreme Court. At least one member had to be a woman, and all sects were to be represented. The CII had to complete Islamization within seven years.
8. The second amendment declared all Ahmadis and Qadianis as non-Muslim.

The framing of the existing constitutions were reflective of a desire to Islamize the government and society. Islamization is called the destiny of Pakistan, and indeed it is a natural and noble goal. However, we must be vigilant against those versions which are not in accordance with the beneficial spirit of Islam.

RESULTS AND CONSEQUENCES OF THE ISLAMIC PROVISIONS

One of the initial impediments to the framing of the constitution was the controversy over the degree and role of Islam in the collective lives of its citizens. The 1973 Constitution, had more Islamic provisions than the previous constitutions; it was the first constitution to declare that Islam was the state religion, but this did not mollify the ulema. Instead, a movement for complete Islamization of the legal system was started. During the 1977 Pakistan National Alliance (PNA) campaign, Z.A. Bhutto banned gambling and drinking, closed down night clubs and from 1 July, Friday was declared the weekly holiday instead of Sunday. These measures did not halt the PNA Movement and as a result of this movement, General Ziaul Haq declared Martial Law and took further steps towards Islamization.

i) The first measure was to introduce separate electorates for minorities. In British India, Muslims obtained separate electorates because of their demand. In Pakistan, minorities had consistently opposed separate electorates. Since Ziaul Haq sensed that minorities would vote for the PPP whom he had overthrown, he imposed separate electorates on the minorities. A non-Muslim voter could only vote for non-Muslim candidates. It was finally rescinded by General Pervez Musharraf in the seventeenth amendment which was enacted on 29 December 2003.

ii) On 21 June 1980, *Zakat* and *Ushr* were introduced in the domain of Public Law. *Zakat* is paid at the rate of 2.5 per cent of annual savings. This is compulsory in Islam, but now it was not left to personal conscience but collected and administered by the state, with the donor having no say over it's utilization. *Ushr* is land tax; it literally means one tenth of the produce of the land. This, like *Zakat*, is levied on Muslims only.

iii) On 1 January 1981, interest-free banking and risk-free insurance was introduced. Islamic banking became the model, but in reality, a profit and loss system was launched, in which interest was introduced under another name. When the Shariat Court ruled that Interest was Usury and un-Islamic, the Nawaz Sharif government appealed against the judgement. However, some public good resulted from this measure: widows and orphans were exempted from paying interest against the loans they had taken from the House Building Finance Corporation, which is a public sector institution.

iv) Islamic punishments (*Hudood* in Arabic) were introduced. Bhutto's June 1977 measures were deemed insufficient, and Islamic punishments and Islamic laws of evidence were prescribed for every major crime except murder, specifically for theft, adultery and false accusation of adultery. The prohibition on drinking was strictly applied and severely punished. Non-Muslims were allowed drink on ceremonial occasions, as were foreigners, behind closed doors.

v) The Council of Islamic Ideology (CII) was enlarged to 19 members and terms of its reference were extended to oversee all laws of the land and to rule which existing law was Islamic or not. This applied mostly to the laws inherited from the British. Parliament could seek the opinion of the CII on any legislation being considered or reviewed.

vi) In December 1977, a Federal Advisory Council was also established to accelerate the pace of Islamization.

vii) A federal and four provincial ombudsmen (*Mohtasib*) were appointed. Apart from probing charges of corruption, the ombudsmen could issue directives to government functionaries, if they felt that a decision was unwarranted. Usually retired members of the higher judiciary were appointed to this post.

viii) A Shariah Appeal Bench was set up, composed of both *ulema* and lawyers. Any decision of the Shariah Appeal Bench could not be challenged in the Supreme Court or High Courts.

ix) The Islamic Research Institute was rejuvenated and its task of conducting research was enhanced.

x) A faculty of Shariah was introduced in Quaid-i-Azam University, Islamabad, and Peshawar University. The International Islamic University, Islamabad also has a large faculty of Shariah.

xi) Under Educational Reforms of 1979, the teaching of Islamic and Pakistan Studies was made compulsory for all faculties of Science, Arts, Commerce, Engineering and Medicine.

Some constitutional aspects of Islamization are covered in the chapter on Human Rights. It must be acknowledged that Islamization is a noble purpose. If it is carried out with honest intent, it would result in the moral uplift of society.

A BUL ALA MAUDUDI (b. Aurangabad, 25 September 1903–d. Buffalo, 25 September 1979). It is true that Maulana Maududi opposed the Pakistan Movement. That he anathemized the founder of Pakistan is also true. That he refused to characterize the 1947–48 Kashmir war as Jihad is even truer. What is equally true is that while he opposed the Muslim League, he also denounced the Congress, and by doing so, he endorsed the Two-Nation Theory. This sets him apart from the other *ulema* who opposed Pakistan. It needs to be conceded that he is not the only party leader in Pakistan to make a volte-face. This apart, Maulana Maududi has been one of the most influential citizens of Pakistan; his works being absorbed by such Islamic ideologues as Syed Qutb of Egypt, and Ayatullah Khomeini of Iran. During the drafting of the Objectives Resolution (1949), his party—Jama'at-i-Islami—represented street power in Pakistan, forming the nucleus of the Lal Masjid—the Islamabad-based fanatical agitation, which now, in May 2007, threatens the state foundations of Pakistan.

Maududi was the maternal grandson of Qurban Beg Salik, who is familiar to all Ghalib scholars. Maududi composed poetry, and during the course of his literary and journalistic endeavours, come into contact with Josh Malihabadi and Niaz Fatehpuri—the poet and the critic who were most vociferously denounced as free thinkers. Maududi started his career in journalism as editor of *Medina*, Bijnaur, and *Taj*, Jabalpur. He went back to the Deccan, in 1928, from where he launched the *Tarjuman-ul-Quran*, which is still under publication. Maududi founded the Jama'at-i-Islami (JI), at Lahore, in 1941, with seventy-five members. The membership of the JI was to be graded according to piety and belief. At a later stage, this had an adverse effect when the JI's street power did not translate into electoral victory. Maududi was sentenced to death for his part in the 1953 anti-Qadiani agitation, but the sentence was commuted to three years imprisonment. He was arrested once more, in 1964.

Since Maududi came to the forefront at the time when the Objectives Resolution was being drafted, he faced a dilemma in trying to resolve the readiness of the Islamic state (which was the ideal) and the readiness of an Islamic constitution (which was to be the instrument). For Maududi, the Islamic State was not an evolving model, but an already perfect one, requiring no change.[1] On the other hand, about the Islamic constitution for which the immediate battle was raging, he said:

> When we say that this country should have an Islamic Constitution, we do not mean that we possess a constitution of the Islamic state in a written form and the only thing that is required to be done is to enforce it. The core of the problem is that we want an unwritten constitution to be transformed into a written one. What we term as Islamic constitution is in reality an unwritten constitution. It is contained in certain specific sources, and it is from that we have to evolve a written constitution in keeping with the present day requirements of our country.[2]

This was actually a post colonial exercise. Previous to this, law and jurisprudence had existed. The theoretical formulations of an Islamic state, as set down by such writers as Abul Hasan al Mawardi, were ex post facto. No wonder a category such as Imarat bil Istila—Emirate by seizure, existed. The JI had adopted a hierarchical form of membership, and when it called for the sovereignty of Allah, it ipso facto marginalized the electorate—the only method of constituting a government known to classical Islam. An analysis of all ideological arguments put forward by Maududi points to a religious oligarchy, as recently witnessed in Iran, where a council of guardians reduced an elected president (Muhammad Khatami) to the state of the leader of the opposition. Some mechanism is visibly necessary to prevent the enjoining of virtue and forbidding of evil being reduced to compelling virtue and expirtating evil, the challenge being issued from Lal Masjid, Islamabad, on 2 April 2007, which proclaims that only six Taliban enforced Islamic law in Afghanistan, and we are ten thousand.[3]

NOTES

1. Seyyed Vali Reza Nasr, *Maududi and the Making of Islamic Revival*, New York: Oxford University Press, 1996, p. 89.
2. Ibid., p. 96 vide Abul A'la Maududi, *First Principles of the Islamic State*, Lahore: Islamic publications, 1983, p. 1.
3. *Dawn*, 3 April 2007, p. 1.

PART VII

HISTORY OF THE INSTITUTIONS

Bureaucrat is a term which originated in France. Bureau means desk (it also means office) in French, and people who worked at desks were called bureaucrats. In time this term became associated with certain characteristics: it denoted a body of public servants who devised and followed certain set rules which slowed the process of implementation, who sought to make policy subservient to their rules and had passed a lifetime in their careers, knew all the rules and could implement, reject, delay or hasten a decision or verdict. This power could make a section of the bureaucracy open to corruption.

These were the characteristics of those who came to be known as clerks, or the lower bureaucracy. It is often said that Pakistan inherited its bureaucracy from the colonial model, which had a different set of characteristics. The colonial model was the Indian Civil Service (ICS) cadre. To this cadre, at first, no natives could be admitted and the examination for recruitment was for a long time, held only in England, and in India only after great agitation. After Indians appeared in centres in India, they became a class of their own. This exclusiveness stemmed from the fact that western education, and by implication, western culture, was considered superior.

The superiority of western culture, in time, overtook the notion of the superiority of western education. What India needed most to learn from England were the sciences and commerce. For centuries these had been taken away from the formal syllabi of Muslim India. Yet the class to whom the highest echelons of service were entrusted were those with a classical or general education. Even when the system of patronage was extended, scions of well-connected native families needed to acquire a Bachelor of Arts (BA) degree, to be appointed honorary magistrates. In those days, no Indian rose higher than a deputy commissioner. The ICS officers were exceptionally brilliant and, by inclination or by training, learnt to distance themselves from the people they ruled.

This distance was distinct from ignorance. A candidate passing the ICS examination was sent as a probationer to one of four institutions: the universities of Oxford, Cambridge, and London or Trinity College, Dublin. Once in India, the first appointment would be as an assistant district officer serving under a district officer with a seniority between seven to twenty years and who served under a commissioner who headed a division comprising a number of districts. Normally an ICS officer would retire from this post.

Those ICS officers who staffed the central or provincial secretariats had to start their careers in the provinces and were seconded from their district offices. In the words of one officer:

> This constant interchange was in my opinion one reason for the general excellence of the Indian administration, since a great many personal relationships were formed and desk bound bureaucrats were never too far away from the way things were worked in the provinces.[1]

Service in the provinces involved a great deal of touring, mostly on horseback, but this same officer mentions that a superior advised him against mixing with Indians even if they were also ICS officers.[2] The Pakistani successor to the ICS were members of the Central Superior Services (CSS), having a number of cadres, the first being an addition. The Pakistan Foreign Service trainees were sent to the Fletcher School of Diplomacy at Duke University, USA. The nearest cadre to the ICS was the Civil Service of Pakistan (CSP). The CSP followed the ICS formula for postings in the central secretariat, 'For the first six years the trainees were rotated in the districts and only then were they posted in the secretariat as under-secretary. Nine years as under-secretary qualified a civil servant to be posted as deputy secretary.' The deputy secretary is the lynch pin of the administration; this is quite understandable as the deputy secretary was half way between the junior and the senior officers. The deputy secretary would be promoted joint secretary, and only the few at the top would be posted to the highest post of Secretary to the Ministry.

At the time of Independence, the Civil Service was headed by Chaudhry Mohammad Ali, as secretary general. This experience stood Chaudhry Mohammad Ali in good stead when he became the prime minister of Pakistan.

A deputy secretary in the secretariat was equivalent to the deputy commissioner in the district. It has been remarked that he was the lynch-pin of the operation although the British had no corresponding post in Britain.

The CSS included cadres such as the Information Service, Military Accounts Service, Income Tax Service, Office of the Controller of Imports and Exports, (which has been abolished) Police Service (where the recruitment was central and posting was provincial) in addition to the Foreign and Civil Service. Medicine, Education, Archaeology or Geological Survey perhaps did not merit admission to these superior services.

A change was brought about in the Ayub era, when the post of additional secretary was added between the posts of secretary and joint secretary. During the first PPP government, Z.A. Bhutto abolished the service cadre. The CSP became the District Management Group, the Secretarial Group, and so on. There was a unified pay scale and the grades were from 1–23. Grade 23 was for the secretary. What had previously been Class One Service began from Grade 17. There was no great shake-up except that the nomenclature had changed and inter-cadre posting was somewhat easier. Bhutto also made a provision for lateral entry into the superior services by examination.

This came about because Z.A. Bhutto had ordered a 'screening', that is a major purge of civil servants who numbered 1330.[3] Bhutto was the third president to screen officers. This process had begun with President Ayub and continued with Yahya Khan. The reasons for the purges were said to be corruption and inefficiency. On the whole, both inefficiency and corruption had crept in, but there was some dispute about particular bureaucrats. For example, Abbas Khalili was dismissed by Ayub but re-instated by Bhutto, and made secretary of defence production. On the other hand, others who had died or had already retired from the service found their names on Bhutto's lists. This affected the morale of the officers and made them more subordinate to the rulers than the rules.

The administrative structure at the centre was replicated in the provinces— except for purely central departments such as Defence and Foreign Affairs. The chief secretary of a province headed its administration with secretaries of various ministries under him. The purges affected even the provincial cadres, and the overall effect of insecurity was, increased corruption.

Corruption, not inefficiency, has been the main bane of Pakistan's bureaucracy despite the quota system. No inefficient officer can be corrupt, but in analysing the causes of corruption one cannot repeat the Actonian cliché. When the bureaucracy was invaded by corruption, provides the answer to why. At the time of independence there was a shortage of bureaucracy at all levels, gazetted and non-gazetted. Officers were given the option to serve in Pakistan, and in those early years no one cared to know the ethnic composition or even the sectarian composition of any cadre. Everyone served not only selflessly, but paid from his own pocket for the stationery and furniture. Without the honesty, dedication and efficiency of the first batch of officers, Pakistan would not have survived. It was political instability in the first instance, and long periods of non-political regimes, which created the corrupt practices. Mahbub ul Haq estimated that millions of rupees were syphoned off from government funds by bureaucrats.

Reforms under President Musharraf, in the form of the local government system have affected the District Management Group. A Devolution of Power Plan was announced on 23 March 2000 and was put into operation through the National Reconstruction Bureau, newly set up by the military government. The regime took the position that the previous local government systems were governed by the provincial administration. Also criticized were the separate provisions for local governments in the city and town areas as opposed to local government in the rural areas.

As a first step, divisions and the connected posts of commissioner were abolished. The district or deputy commissioner's post was retained along with that of assistant commissioner, but they were redesignated as district coordination officer etc., and their direct jurisdiction was curtailed. The administrative structure of local government was formed at three levels (i) District or *Zila*, (ii) Subdistrict or *Tehsil* and (iii) Union (a subdivision of subdistrict). Each level is headed by a *nazim* or administrator and *naib nazim* or deputy administrator. These officials are responsible to a legislative council and have to work in conjunction with an administrative unit headed by a bureaucrat (e.g. the district coordinator).

This system of bypassing divisions has led to political criticism that by devolving power to the districts directly, provincial autonomy is being circumvented. It is undeniable that local bodies are revived and empowered under dictatorships, and either made to lapse, or to weaken under democratic regimes.

The police officer has also been redesignated the town police officer, but the extent of his jurisdiction is at present being debated. The local governments at present deal with a very long list of departments, Agriculture, Works and Services, Heath, Education, Literacy and Community development. Provincial governments have appointed a director general, Implementation, Monitoring and Evaluation cell. This may serve as a link between local and provincial governments. How much the people are empowered, and how much the local government, remains to be seen. At present this experiment seems more far-reaching than the restructuring of cadres under Z.A. Bhutto.

NOTES

1. Denis Judd, (ed.), *A British Tale of Indian and Foreign Service: The Memoirs of Sir Ian Scott*, London: The Radcliffe Press, 1999, pp. 39, 40.
2. Ibid., p. 36.
3. S. Irtiza Husain, *Compromise with Conciliation*, Karachi: Pak-Amercian Commercial, 1997, p. 197.

CHAPTER 36

THE ARMED FORCES

The cause of Muslim decline was the fact that what the Mughal army lacked was not courage but organization. Naval superiority ensured the triumph of Britain over India, and no ruler, with the solitary exception of Sher Shah Suri, had devoted attention to the strengthening of naval forces of India. The lack of organization had also impeded modernization, and the real military worth of the youth became apparent when they provided manpower to the British forces. We have discussed how the East India Company was able to recruit the cream of military talent and turn it into such an efficient fighting machine as to make the numerical superiority of natives a liability rather than a source of strength.

Even to die-hard imperialists it was apparent that India needed to consolidate her defences before British control loosened.[1] It suited the British to create regiments by purposely mixing Hindus and Muslims of different castes. When Britain needed Muslim troops from India to station in Egypt in 1882, the India GHQ informed London that such a dispatch would not be possible because the Indian army was deliberately not organized on religious lines. However, the exigencies of the vast British Empire were many and from 1892 onwards recruitment was on the basis of caste and creed.[2]

With the advent of the twentieth century, this phase was over. The recruitment was no longer on religious lines. Up until the First World War native soldiers were refused commissions and it was this point which led to the first clash between M.K. Gandhi and M.A. Jinnah. Gandhi was in favour of unconditional cooperation with the British, even going to the extent of making the offices of the Home Rule League a recruiting agency, while Jinnah and B.G. Tilak took the position that unless Indian troops were given Royal Commissions (as they were then called), the Home Rule League would not cooperate with the British. Jinnah was then championing the cause of an Indian and not a Muslim army, but by the time of the Second World War, the Muslim presence in the British Indian army brought great political benefits to the Muslims of India. The Muslim soldiers hailing mainly from the Punjab and NWFP were so important to the British War effort that their aspirations could not be disregarded during the course of the War, and even after, they were such a major factor that even the Labour Government could not override these aspirations. British Intelligence had intercepted the letters of Muslim soldiers to M.A. Jinnah.

This debt, we tend to overlook when we complain of the political or administrative role of the armed forces. Indeed, the image of the privileged few obscures the hardship and privation officers have to endure for the defence of the country. The armed forces were of the essence and both M.A. Jinnah and Liaquat Ali Khan had refused to accept power in Pakistan unless they were given an army immediately. Since the British were of the view that Pakistan would be temporary, they delayed the division of the armed forces when they decided to divide India. As it was, although there were pure Hindu and Sikh units there were no all-Muslim units, which according to Stephen Cohen was a result of British distrust dating back to 1857.[3]

At Independence, the officer corps of the Pakistan army consisted of one major general, two brigadiers and fifty-three colonels. The rest of the required officers were British, and it was from this small corps of officers that the Pakistan army has developed. The present strength of the Pakistan army is 520,000. It was earlier headed by a commander-in-chief, but since 1971 it is headed by the chief of army staff. Below him are lieutenant generals each of whom heads a corps made up of two or more divisions. The divisions are headed by major generals and consist of three or more brigades. A brigade is headed by a brigadier. Also below the chief of staff are four central command officers (i) chief of general staff (ii) adjutant general (iii) quartermaster general and (iv) master general of ordnance.[4]

THE NAVY

The present strength of the navy is 22,000. It is headed by the chief of naval staff. The next senior officer is the vice-chief of the naval staff who is responsible for maritime operations and planning. The deputy chief of naval staff is responsible for recruitment, administration and planning. There are three principal staff officers responsible respectively for operations, personnel, and material.[5] At present there are ten surface ships and nine submarines. A most vital adjunct is the navy's aviation wing.

THE AIR FORCE

The Pakistan Air Force has a strength of 45,000 men. The chief of air staff is assisted by five principal staff officers, each responsible respectively for (i) operations, (ii) engineering (iii) administration (iv) training and (v) personnel.[6]

CIVIL ACTIVITIES OF THE ARMED FORCES

The armed forces are often called upon to perform civilian functions, such as managing airlines and other institutions, building roads in difficult places such as the Karakoram Highway, and conducting rescue operations at times of natural calamities such as the earthquake of October 2005. They have also taken over the running of the whole country several times in the history of Pakistan. The armed forces take on all these responsibilities because it is felt that civilians are too corrupt, undisciplined and untrained to perform these functions well.

While it is quite true that the armed forces are far better trained and disciplined than most civilian workforce, the answer to the problem of civilian incompetence lies not in marginalizing civilian workers but in training them better. This can only be achieved if the people of Pakistan are educated and trained. The armed forces are after all recruited from the civilian population of Pakistan and are the same people. They are trained for the defence of Pakistan and should not be distracted from it.

NOTES

1. Arthur Vincent, *The Defence of India*, Bombay, 1922, p. 91.
2. M.E. Chamberlain, *Britain and India*, Devon, 1974, p. 160.
3. Stephen P. Cohen, *The Pakistan Army*, Los Angeles: University of California Press, 1984, p. 6.
4. Pervaiz Iqbal Cheema, *The Armed Forces of Pakistan*: Karachi, Oxford University Press, 2003, p. 46.
5. Ibid., p. 86.
6. Ibid., p. 104.

PART VIII

DIPLOMATIC HISTORY

CHAPTER 37

INTRODUCTION: AIMS AND OBJECTIVES

The terms on which a state wishes to conduct its international relations is called its foreign policy. The purpose of foreign policy is to gain for the state such a place in the comity of nations that is has no difficulty in sustaining its sovereignty and integrity, to give it a voice in the formulation of international principles conducive to its interests, and to extend its influence beyond its frontiers and within international fora.

FORMULATION OF FOREIGN POLICY

A. The formulation of foreign policy has three structures. The first of them is within the executive:

(i) The president or prime minister of a country. For example the US President Harry Truman said, the 'President makes foreign policy'. In 1956, the British Prime Minister, Sir Anthony Eden did not consult his full cabinet before the invasion of Egypt.

(ii) The foreign minister. If the head of government lacks any special interest in foreign policy, or if the foreign minister is the head of a coalition party, he may play a more decisive role. The classic example is the British Foreign Minister, Ernest Bevin under Prime Minister Clement Atlee.

(iii) The Foreign Office. This is the government department responsible for the formulation and execution of foreign policy. It has many sections known as 'desks' which deal with specific countries or groups of countries. Because of close focus and specialization, they provide inputs of detailed, even secret, information and give expert opinions on this basis. The bureaucracy along with career diplomats provides continuity to foreign policy when the elected government changes.

Sometimes foreign policies can cause tension. In 1971, for example, the pro-Pakistan policy of the US president was nullified by the state department headed by the secretary of state.

Apart from the foreign office, the military establishment and scientists also formulate foreign policy in some measure. The military brings security considerations to the foreign ministry's notice. Scientists have a better insight into the scientific capacity of contending countries, and their expertise can increase the options a government can exercise. Nuclear capability is the most obvious example. Between the Executive and the Foreign Office, an intermediary body like the National Security Council (NSC) can intervene. The Defence Committee of the Cabinet also has a strong bearing, but a NSC can have information on a wider spectrum of both political and technical interests.

B. There is the intermediary structure consisting mainly of parliaments. These are usually multiparty bodies, therefore they are usually unable to initiate foreign policy, but they monitor it closely. 'Their main power lies in the ratification of treaties.'[1] The US Congress is the most prominent example of exercise of this power. In 1919, it refused to ratify the Treaty of Versailles by which the League of Nations would be formed. The US President, Woodrow Wilson had taken the initiative in its foundation, but Congress would not allow the US to join. The Comprehensive Test Ban Treaty (CTBT) is a treaty that the US urged other countries, including Pakistan, to sign. In 1999, the US Congress itself refused to ratify it, thereby relieving Pakistan of pressure. The Symington, Pressler, and Brown Amendments of the US Congress played a leading role in the maintenance of US relations with Pakistan.

C. The outer structure reflects Public Opinion and/or Ideology. If there had not been a strong public opinion in favour of carrying out retaliatory nuclear tests in May 1998, the government would have succumbed to world pressure. Similarly, the Tashkent Declaration (1966) went against public opinion and a movement was unleashed which toppled the Ayub regime. During the Simla Summit (1972) public opinion was sober because Pakistan had lost the 1971 war.

This brings us to instances where public opinion is strong, but since all other elements formulating foreign policy are united, the government goes against public opinion. For example, Pakistan took an anti-Arab stance in the 1956 Arab–Israel War. Public opinion was in favour of Iraq in the 1990 Gulf-War; but since the underlying principle, that the invasion of a neighbouring state was obviously dangerous, Prime Minister Nawaz Sharif, against much of the establishment and with the solitary support of the former Prime Minister Benazir Bhutto, was able to pursue an anti-Iraq policy. Ideology is often bound up with public opinion but not necessarily. Pakistan does not recognize Israel out of ideological differences, practical incentives notwithstanding. This is not because of anti-Zionism but because Israel is perceived to be established on Arab lands. Pakistan has ideological sympathy with the people of Chechnya, but nevertheless recognizes it as a part of Russia.

In addition to the above three structures there are politicians and academics who have theories on foreign policy but have no means to impose them. Mehtab Ali Shah states that the provincial bodies should have an input.

He further states that Pakistan's policy on Kashmir is only for the benefit of Punjab and not the remaining three provinces of Pakistan. He advocates a compromise over Kashmir and says that Pakistan can live without it if it can live without East Pakistan.[2] M.B. Naqvi advocates accepting Indian hegemony.[3] This policy would be very sound, if the disappearance of Pakistan could guarantee also the disappearance of India. Previously East Pakistani intellectuals expressed the opinion that the Farakka Barrage issue was raised by West Pakistani politicians to embitter the relations between Bengal and India. Now, thirty-four years after the liberation of Bangladesh, the Farraka Barrage is again a very contentious issue between Bangladesh and India. Therefore, goodwill alone does not lead to solutions of international disputes.

HISTORICAL PERSPECTIVE

Pakistan came into being when its name was unfamiliar, when the notion of a state founded on religion was unpopular, and when, almost simultaneously with its creation, it was forced into a war over Kashmir with India—the same country which had withheld its military and financial assets. Moreover, Pakistan came into existence when the Cold War had already begun.

Pakistan had barely formulated the principles of its foreign policy when it was forced to define its objectives which were security and sheer survival. The principles of Pakistan were broadcast by its Founder as honesty and fair play, the extension of moral and material support to oppressed and supressed nations (e.g. Indonesia), and the upholding of the United Nations Charter.

There was some dissonance in the beginning; while the Governor-General, Mohammad Ali Jinnah, although stressing neutrality as a principle, gave preference to the USA over the USSR on ideological grounds. The Prime Minister, Liaquat Ali Khan also stressed neutrality but voiced his preference for Britain over the United States. While the regimes of Jinnah and Liaquat lasted, Pakistan remained officially neutral, but under Governor-General Ghulam Mohammad, Pakistan entered into military alliances with the West, CENTO and SEATO.

Pakistan's alliances with the West gave the Indian Prime Minister, Pandit Jawaharlal Nehru the excuse to renege on his repeated promises to hold a plebiscite in Kashmir ('Pakistan has brought the Cold War to India's door') and since Russia gave India all out support against Pakistan, our intelligentsia has bitterly regretted this decision. In reality, Pakistan stayed neutral for a longer time than its resources warranted. As Franceso Guicciardini stated early in the sixteenth century, while neutrality was good for a powerful state, it was dangerous for a weak state. Pakistan was weak, it badly needed arms to secure itself against India, and its strategic location was also suited to American strategic interests, most notably for bases suited to the surveillance of the USSR (such as one established later at Badaber), bases for which the United Stated had approached the British before Independence.

During the 1965 war, Zulfikar Ali Bhutto characterized India's non-alliance as double alliance, as it indeed was, but Pakistan could not match the resources and market potential of India and it was sheer naivete to suppose that the standards which were being applied by the US and the UK to India would be applied to Pakistan. From the 1960s to the 1980s, Pakistan's, relationship with the Peoples Republic of China was the cornerstone of Pakistan's foreign policy. Relations with the Muslim world, which were initially uneasy, plumetted during the 1956 Suez War. Some improvement was achieved during the 1967 Six Day War, but the solidarity Pakistan sought remained elusive. Relations with the newly-independent Central Asian States provided a real opportunity for Pakistan to extend its influence, but Pakistan's policy over Afghanistan, apart from causing tension with its most friendly neighbours China and Iran, actually led to a resurgence of Russian influence in central Asia.

Pakistan regained its non-aligned status after the 1971 war when India and the USSR jointly acted against Pakistan, making its eastern wing (East Bengal) the only state since the Second World War to have successfully seceded. Having lost a war and a province, in 1971, Pakistan also lost strategic posts like Kargil in the conflict. When, eighteen years later, and subsequent to the loss of Siachen, Pakistan reoccupied Kargil, it led to a crisis in which world opinion went against Pakistan. The re-focusing of world opinion away from UN resolutions on Kashmir to cross-border terrorism was the greatest ever foreign policy failure of Pakistan. In the previous year, Pakistan had finally tested and proved its nuclear capability but the diplomatic advantage of going nuclear was dissipated by integrating the announcement with two very contentious domestic issues, the Kalabagh Dam and the freezing of Foreign Currency Accounts. The 12 October 1999 coup initially compounded Pakistan's difficulties, but when Pakistan joined the US led alliance against terror following the 9/11 terrorist attack it was able to emerge from isolation. Pakistan was therefore successful in containing the fall-out of the revelation that Pakistani scientists had been engaged in clandestine nuclear proliferation, but this has been a fragile success, and to emerge victorious from this crisis will require the highest order of vigilance and confidence building.

NOTES

1. Joseph Frankel, *International Relations*, London: Oxford University Press, 1964, p. 37.
2. Mehtab Ali Shah, 'Soul Searching On Kashmir' *Dawn*, Karachi, 4 September 1999.
3. M.B. Naqvi, 'Portents of the 1996 Indian Polls' *Dawn*, Karachi, 3 October 1995.

CHAPTER 38

PAKISTAN AND THE WORLD POWERS

Countries which can influence decisions and events in most parts of the globe are called world powers. These powers are the United States of America, Russia, China and Britain. We shall trace the relations of Pakistan with these powers in turn. In the background we must consider the relations these powers maintained mutually.

During the entire course of the Cold War from 1946 to 1999, there was an ideological war between the countries led by the United States who stood for democracy and market economy on the one side, and the Union of Soviet Socialist Republics (USSR), which subscribed to dictatorship of the proletariat and a planned economy, on the other. These were described as the two worlds, capitalist and communist, and those countries which kept themselves away, and were, incidently, developing countries were said to belong to the Third World. This was called the Bipolar Age.

From the beginning of the Cold War which encompassed the Korean and the Vietnam Wars, relations between the United States and the Peoples Republic of China were hostile right until 1970, when ideological differences were subserved to strategic considerations as both confronted the USSR. At present there is no mutual hostility, but there is also no warmth between the two powers.

The Cold War lasted as long as USSR remained a communist power and held sway over the Central Asian States. Since 1991, the USSR as such has ceased to exist and no longer remains an ideological adversary for the United States. It is still a large country with immense resources and still retains, like the US and China, a huge nuclear arsenal. Russia may not have lost its importance, but since it is no longer opposed to the United States, what has emerged is called a Unipolar world, as opposed to the Bipolar phase when the two world powers were dominant.

Britain too has seen its status reduced, but had anticipated this reduction and planned accordingly. It has retained sufficient heirlooms of the Empire, and from the time of the partition of India in 1947, to at least the 1956 War, when its invasion of Egypt was disliked by both the US and the USSR, it remained, for practical purposes, a world power. It also has a nuclear arsenal, but this alone does not account for its world power stature. France, which also has a nuclear arsenal and, like the world powers mentioned above, is a permanent member of the United Nations Security Council, has not been able to exercise the same measure of influence as Britain. With this brief introduction, we come to world power relations with Pakistan.

PAKISTAN AND THE UNITED STATES OF AMERICA

The year 2003 is a good point from which to view the nature of US–Pakistan relations. On 15 March 2003 the United States waived democracy-related sanctions against Pakistan. On 24 March the US imposed sanctions on the KRL nuclear facility of Pakistan. On 3 April the US waived one billion dollars debt payable by Pakistan. On 4 April the majority view at a Johns Hopkins University seminar was that Pakistan was a greater challenge than Iraq. On 10 April, Secretary of State, Colin Powell rebutted the assertion of the Indian Foreign Minister Yashwant Sinha that there was a stronger case for military action against Pakistan than against Iraq. However, Powell also stressed that the situation across the Line of Control in Kashmir was difficult and painful, in other words accusing Pakistan of cross border terrorism in Kashmir. During 2004, Pakistan was granted the most favoured non-NATO ally status, and was enmeshed in the A.Q. Khan nuclear proliferation scandal.

These developments show that there are no other two countries in the world whose relations are so chequered as those of the US and Pakistan. There is no sustained cordiality and there is no sustained hostility. From Colin Powell's 10 April 2003 statement it can be concluded that bilateral concerns are not adverse, but they follow an erratic course because of third party considerations. An example of this is the divergence, indeed deflection of views regarding the Arab–Israeli conflict. During the Cold War, Pakistan detested the role of the USSR in South Asia but applauded its role in the Middle East. Since the Cold War has ended, Pakistan must give precedence to US support in South Asia and not make US policy in the Middle East an over-riding concern.

When the US and Pakistan established relations in 1947, they had different reasons for doing so. Pakistan needed help against India which had withheld its military assets, while the war had broken out in Kashmir; the US wanted Pakistan's assistance in encircling the communist states of the USSR and China. The lead taken in establishing relations on a discordant basis was taken by Pakistan, not the US.[1] In October 1947, a Pakistani delegation led by Mir Laiq Ali, offered the country's services to halt the progress of communism for the sum of two billion dollars.

That amount of money was not forthcoming but the United States viewed Pakistan sympathetically and supported its position on Kashmir in the UN. Liaquat Ali Khan, as the first prime minister of Pakistan made a successful visit to the United States but still held back from committing troops to Korea.

On his return from the US, Liaquat announced that Pakistan was completely neutral because it was not beholden to any country. After Liaquat's assassination during Ghulam Mohammad's tenure as governor-general, Pakistan signed SEATO and CENTO (originally Baghdad Pact) accords in 1954, and a Mutual Defence treaty in 1959. The implications of these have already been covered. Briefly, India went back on its promise to hold a plebiscite in Kashmir, and the USSR vetoed every UNSC resolution which urged action on the plebiscite.

These pacts with the US enabled Pakistan to assemble a large arsenal, especially in the Air Force. During the 1950s Pakistan was called the 'most allied ally'. President Dwight D. Eisenhower visited Pakistan on 8 December 1959. President Ayub Khan told the US Congress on 12 July 1960 that the US could land its troops in Pakistan whenever it wished. In the same year a U2 American spy plane, which had taken off from Badaber in Pakistan, was shot down over the USSR territory and the pilot, Gary Powers, was captured alive. Ayub remained placid in the face of a direct threat from Nikita Khrushchev, the Soviet Premier.

Even at the outset of the 1959 Sino–Indian tension, President Ayub left his country aghast when he proposed a joint Indo–Pakistan Defence Pact against China. Luckily for Pakistan, the Indian prime minister turned this offer down. Two successive foreign ministers, Mohammad Ali Bogra and Zulfikar Ali Bhutto, were able to secure the support of China. Pakistan's growing relations with China crossed what the US termed 'acceptable limits', and the American action of arming India became a source of contention during which Pakistan's Foreign Secretary, Sami Khan Dehlavi, was removed from his post. Relations remained cold when the 1965 Indo–Pakistan war broke out. The US imposed an arms and aid embargo on both India and Pakistan, but harmed only the latter, as India had an alternate source of supply in the USSR.

Relations remained sour until 1970 when the US revised its anti-China policy and sought Pakistan's help in establishing contact with it. This Sino–US detente raised Pakistan's hopes but these hopes were countermanded by the Indo–Soviet Treaty of Friendship of 1971. Although the Sino–US partnership was active in the UNSC, India and the USSR moved swiftly to pre-empt it and dismembered Pakistan. Only one side of the atrocities had been reported in the United States, consequently members of Congress as well as the State Department thwarted the attempts of President R.M. Nixon to prevent the secession of East Pakistan. The new President, Z.A. Bhutto publicly acknowledged that President Nixon had saved West Pakistan and Azad Kashmir.

The United States' so called 'tilt' towards Pakistan lasted until the beginning of the Jimmy Carter era, when Pakistan, in response to the 1974 Indian nuclear explosion, started its own defensive programme. Pakistan's pursuit of a defensive nuclear armoury seemed unreasonable to the Carter administration. This phase continued until 1979 when the USSR invaded Afghanistan.

Pakistan became a front-line state and under both Jimmy Carter and Ronald Reagan received massive military and financial aid. The Pakistani government under General Ziaul Haq took complete advantage of the lifting of American pressure and went ahead with the nuclearization programme. One other consequence of the Afghan war for both the US and Pakistan was the induction and arming of Islamic military groups from Afghanistan itself and the Middle East, against the Soviet Union. After the Soviet withdrawal from Afghanistan, this policy was to have catastrophic consequences for both countries.

Once Pakistan lost its front line status, events moved at a fast pace. Within two years the USSR was fragmented and with the end of the Cold War the United States resumed its nuclear non-proliferation pressure on Pakistan with a spate of legislation. First came the Symington Amendment of 1975, passed to stop aid to non-nuclear countries who were importing uranium enrichment technology. It was followed by the Glenn Amendment of 1977 which sought to bar assistance to countries importing nuclear reprocessing technology. (A French Nuclear Reprocessing Plant had been negotiated by Z.A. Bhutto). These amendments were first invoked by President Jimmy Carter on 6 April 1979 (two days after Z.A. Bhutto's execution) but soon had to be suspended in view of the Soviet invasion of Afghanistan. It should be noted that this situation was more critical for Pakistan than for the US, since Pakistan could hardly have been able to survive had Russian troops advanced into Pakistan.

It was to seek suspension of the earlier amendments and to help Pakistan that the Pressler Amendment was passed in 1985. Only later did it work against Pakistan. This provided for the reaffirmation of the 1959 Mutual Assistance Treaty relating to aggression from a communist country. It also had a provision that the US president had to certify annually that Pakistan did not possess a nuclear explosive devise. When, after the end of the Cold War, President George Bush refused to issue such a certificate, the Symington and Glenn Amendments came into operation against Pakistan.

The restoration of democracy brought about a thaw in mutual relations. President Bill Clinton said, on the occasion of Benazir Bhutto's official visit, that it was wrong on the part of the US to retain both the F16 aircraft and the money paid for it. In November 1995, Senator Hank Brown moved his amendment which restored US economic and non-military aid. The Brown Amendment did not repeal or modify the Pressler Amendment but this was done by the Harkin–Warner Amendment on 17 July 1997.

When Pakistan responded to the Indian nuclear tests in 1998, the US did not question the rationale of Pakistan's nuclear tests, but was nevertheless unhappy. Relations plunged again during the 1999 Kargil crisis. US officials issued no statements when India siezed Kargil from Pakistan in 1965, nor when India violated the LoC by taking Siachen in 1985, but the nuclearization of both combatants had an alarming effect when Pakistani irregulars occupied Kargil in 1999. Pakistan was forced to withdraw under international military pressure led by the US.

When Pakistan once again came under military rule in 1999, President Clinton showed his displeasure by condescending to spend only a few hours in Pakistan on 26 March 2000, when he delivered a homily on television. The succeeding George W. Bush administration indicated that it would objectively review bilateral relations. By an ironic twist Pakistan was being held responsible for the puritanical deeds of the Taliban regime in Pakistan. The Taliban were the residue of the Islamic militant groups jointly fostered by the US and Pakistan to combat Soviet occupation. After the Soviet withdrawal, these groups turned against the US. Pakistan's support for the Taliban alienated all and conciliated none. This was a serious aberration. According to an American chronicler, Dennis Kux, the initial US response to the Taliban regime had been positive, and saw 'nothing objectionable' in the steps the Taliban had taken to impose Islamic law.[2]

It is not simply that the US were taking ad hoc measures. They planned to raise whole generations of Jihadis. In her book, *I is for Infidel: from Holy War to Holy Terror*, Kathy Gannon shows how small children were given books to indoctrinate them. Francis Robinson pertinently commented: 'It is well known that the rise of the Taliban was in part the outcome of western measures in Pakistan and Afghanistan to resist the Russian invader.'[3]

The 11 September 2001 terrorist attacks gave Pakistan an opportunity to cut its Taliban connection. The US ultimatum and Pakistan's opportunity to withdraw from a most unpopular alliance were the flip sides of a coin. Pakistan again became a front line state and an ally in the war against terror. President Pervez Musharraf was received warmly in the US on 12 February 2002, and a number of times thereafter.

OUTSTANDING ISSUES

The United States dominates the unipolar world, therefore the issues between it and Pakistan and the attitudes taken by citizens of both countries are not only the most urgent foreign policy concerns of Pakistan, but central to Pakistan Studies itself.

CROSS BORDER TERRORISM

The United States shows concern over cross-border terrorism by Pakistan in Kashmir. It believes that the uprising in Kashmir is not indigenous but the result of infiltration from the Pakistan side.[4] One way of verifying this claim is to have the UN monitor the border. Pakistan proposed this not only in the 1990s but in 1971 as well.

> Referring to allegations that East Pakistan guerrillas were operating from Indian soil, Mrs Gandhi said: 'How can we check it? Our border with East Bengal is so long that even if India deployed her entire army it would not be able to stop them'. Mrs Gandhi hinted that she was opposed to a plan proposed by Pakistan for posting UN (forces) in East Pakistan. She could see no purpose in it.[5]

The Soviet stance was more belligerent: If Pakistan attacked India for Indian assistance to the Mukti Bahini, the Soviet Union would consider it an act of agression.[6] If Pakistan's plea for UN monitoring had been accepted, there would be no invasion of East Pakistan in 1971 and no Kargil crisis in 1999. The following words of Bill Clinton are worth pondering over:

> Essentially I believe a policy that causes so many civilian casualties without a political solution ultimately cannot succeed.[7]

This he said with reference to Chechnya; it would apply more aptly to Kashmir. The testimony of an American reporter Martin Sugarman who constantly reports on the human rights violations in Indian held Kashmir, could be heeded.[8]

DEMOCRACY

Since both the US and India are huge democracies, they are allies, much to the discomfiture of Pakistan. India's definition of a democracy should be taken into account. According to the *Dawn* of 12 November 1971, Mrs Indira Gandhi said, on 11 December 1971,

> India was hurt to discover that certain countries which called themselves democracies had preferred to ignore the repression in East Pakistan during the last eight months.

Accordingly countries which take recourse to repression cannot be called democracies. Indian repression in Kashmir exceeds eight months, it also exceeds eight years, and seven hundred thousand Indian troops are stationed in Kashmir.

NUCLEAR PROLIFERATION

The Abdul Qadeer Khan scandal highlights the proliferation fears of the US. This episode has a history. During the 1991 Gulf War, Americans discovered that A.Q. Khan had been helping Iraq with its nuclearization programme. In a little-publicized move the government of Pakistan had placed A.Q. Khan on its exit control list on 21 January 1995. This points to the proliferation role of the Pakitani scientist. But the press and public opinion play a very potent role here. The day after the Pakistani president issued a pardon to A.Q. Khan, two leading columnists rushed to print the case of J. Robert Oppenheimer, father of the US bomb, who was deprived of security clearance.[9] The words used for Oppenheimer were found to fit A.Q. Khan: Although the US owed a 'great debt of gratitude for his magnificent service, his continuing conduct and associations reflected a serious disregard for the requirements of the security system'.[10]

The A.Q. Khan affair acquired an intriguing aspect when Ruud Lubbers, former Netherlands prime minister, revealed on 9 August 2005, that his government could not arrest A.Q. Khan in 1975 because of CIA intervention. Again in 1979, the CIA prevented the Netherlands from further investigation. The next day, an American State Department spokesman refused to comment on the report on the grounds that it dealt with long past events and with intelligence matters. Thus, there is more to the A.Q. Khan affair than meets the eye.[11]

While hardly anyone ever refers to the fact now, and the US is known as the only power to use the bomb, the Manhattan Project was actually a race with Nishina's Laboratory in Japan, where efforts to build an atomic bomb were underway. Oppenheimer and his team pre-empted an atomic attack on the USA. The principle is that a difference must be made against a bomb for hegemony and a bomb for survival. If the US had not turned a blind eye to Indian efforts to go nuclear, Pakistan would not be in possession of a bomb. The only way to stop proliferation is to stop discrimination. No country other than India has needled and goaded another country into nuclear retaliation. It was Pakistan that proposed a Nuclear-free South Asia, and it was India that opposed it.

In contrast to fears of proliferation by Pakistan, the news that a container carrying uranium was stolen in India was almost ignored. The chief minister of Jharkand Madhu Khoda revealed three weeks after the theft: 'It was not highly enriched but neither was it just yellow cake' (*Dawn*, 24 December 2006). A year earlier, police had arrested two uranium thieves in Assam. Thus, there are non-State actors in India as well; where religious fundamentalists organize pogroms.

THE CHINA FACTOR

Pakistan's friendship with China became the first cause of friction between the US and Pakistan. Yet when world power configurations changed, a

Sino–US rapprochement was favoured. Relations between the US and China still remain intact, yet there is a lobby which projects China as the long-term adversary of the US. This is calculated on the basis of China's size, population and nuclear capacity. Ideological differences between China and the US had not impeded a strategic alliance during the Cold War. With ideology now scaled down, no cause of conflict is apparent. As far as purely strategic factors are concerned, the same potential for conflict which exists between the US and China also exists between the US and India. From China there emanates no intent of hostility; from India it has been frankly conveyed:

> Soon, predict some BJP seers, India must come into conflict with the US and China for possession of Mideast oil. India must be militarily prepared.[12]

THE PAKISTANI PERCEPTION

While it is necessary to clear up some American perceptions about Pakistan, it is equally imperative to clear the Pakistani perception about the US. It is usually thought that the US is only a fair weather friend and we would have fared better by being neutral or with an alliance with Russia. The accusation of being a fair weather friend was made by Foreign Minister Gohar Ayub to Strobe Talbott.[13] On other occasions, US emisarries like Bill Gates[14] and Anthony Zinni[15] have been blunt; this means that when the US feels it is on weak ground, it listens. Most of Pakistan's complaints relate to the 1965 and 1971 wars. The complaints are valid but nevertheless warrant closer inspection. The US did not abide by the 1959 treaty during the 1965 war. Secretary of State Dean Rusk cited as the reason that Pakistan had sent infiltrators into Kashmir.[16] Since this charge has been repeated by Air Marshal Nur Khan, then PAF chief and subsequently by a former Foreign Secretary, Humayun Khan,[17] there remains no ground to censure the US on this point. However, this statement is not representative of the US efforts during the 1965 war. How the China factor influenced reactions needs to be set out. Dean Rusk told the Indian ambassador that in the unlikely event of sizeable Chinese intervention, the US would first ask India to stop the fighting, moreover there was little chance of the US committing troops to the conflict.[18] The American Ambassador, Walter MacConaughy said that destruction of Pakistan's military capacity would not be in US interests. Under Secretary, George Ball and the Assistant Secretary, William Bundy, advanced the view that were the Chinese to indulge in some mild harrasing action, it would give US leverage over India. The consequences of the US stopping arms supplies were immense and were appreciated later by Henry Kissinger but on balance, the US was supportive, even though behind the scenes, and publicly, Dean Rusk endorsed the plebiscite principle.[19]

As for the 1971 war, we have already seen that the Russians had stationed two nuclear submarines off the US coast in 1971.[20] Despite a hostile Congress and insubordinate State Department, the US saved both West Pakistan and Azad Kashmir. Again when we see *Pakistani* journalists blaming Henry Kissinger for condoning the genocide of Bengalis in 1971, and say that Kissinger's advice to Nixon to tilt towards Pakistan was 'infamous', we can well imagine the extent of US feeling against him.[21]

Finally we must note that no matter how low our relations have plunged, there have been strong votaries of Pakistan in the United States. Senators Dan Burton, Tom Harkin, John Warner, Hank Brown and Sam Brownback have vigorously supported Pakistan. Congressman Dana Rohabracher criticized his government for inaction on Kashmir and savaged the Indian representative and called for a plebiscite.[22] In no other country do we have such eloquent spokesmen.

THE USSR AND PAKISTAN

On 25 May 2002, Russia invited the leaders of India and Pakistan to attend a peace conference.[23] Pakistan agreed, India refused. Russia blamed Pakistan.[24] This exchange defines the relations between Pakistan and the USSR. These relations began in the Cold War when not only strategic but ideological rifts existed. Pakistan's founder, while he found no ideological affinity with the USSR, made the proviso that Pakistan should not go out of its way to annoy Moscow. In a meeting on 11 September 1947, he noted that the USSR was the only country not to congratulate Pakistan on its creation. Moscow was informed that the British embassy would represent Pakistan's interest in the USSR. There seems to be a behind-the-scenes move in this decision; prior to independence, Muslim League leader, Yusuf Haroon had contacted the Soviet Foreign Minister W.M. Molotov to secure the emergence of Pakistan, but the central leadership of the Muslim League disowned his representative status, most probably under British pressure.

When the Indian Prime Minister Pandit Nehru was invited to the US, the USSR looked for an opening in South Asia. On 2 June 1949, Josef Stalin invited Liaquat Ali Khan to the USSR and on 7 June Liaquat announced acceptance and proposed 20 August as the date of the visit. It was against the background of these moves that Liaquat stated, on 10 June, that, 'Pakistan cannot afford to wait. She must take her friends where she finds them'. But from then on the USSR back-pedalled. On 19 July Liaquat was informed that the date of his visit had been advanced and he must arrive on 15 August. Since this would have meant his absence from Pakistan during its first Independence Day since the death of Jinnah, Liaquat proposed 18 August, but from then on until Liaquat's assassination on 16 October 1951, no date was set.

A section of the intelligensia have blamed Liaquat Ali Khan for strained relations with the USSR, maintaining that he obtained an invitation from Moscow only to use it for soliciting an invitation from the US. There is no factual foundation, no archival basis, for this story. Hasan Zaheer who has seen the Pakistani records, and Mansoor Alam who has seen the Soviet records, are among those writers who have sought to destroy this myth. In 1956, Anastas Mikoyan, then deputy foreign minister, came to Karachi and issued another invitation, but this invitation was not accepted. This was after Pakistan had become a military ally of the West, and Soviet leaders had publicly sided with India over Kashmir.

It was during this phase that, on 7 May 1960, a U2 American spy plane that had taken off from Badaber near Peshawar, was shot down over USSR territory. The Soviet Prime Minister, Nikita Khrushchev, directly threatened Pakistan with reprisals. The following year, however, Z.A. Bhutto, then fuel and power minister, successfully negotiated with the Soviet Union an oil and gas exploration agreement (4 March 1961). The Sino–Indian war of 1962 and the western arming of India created dissatisfaction with a pro-west policy. President Ayub Khan made a state visit to the USSR in April 1965. In the same year the India–Pakistan war broke out. Now the new Soviet Prime Minister Alexei Kosygin inched closer to Pakistan, acknowledging that Kashmir was a disputed issue. After the ceasefire the USSR hosted the Tashkent conference. Ayub visited Moscow again in 1967. Kosygin visited Pakistan in April 1968 and May 1969 and concluded a token arms deal.

Even as late as 1970, relations were on the upswing and the USSR had signed a cultural pact with Pakistan. But as soon as military action began in East Pakistan, President Nicolai Podgorny threatened President Yahya Khan. In his reply Yahya referred to Soviet military suppression of Hungary and Poland. A meeting between the two presidents in Tehran was not cordial. An Indo–Soviet treaty of friendship was signed under which any action against cross-border terrorism by Mukti Bahini from Pakistan would be treated as an act of war.

During the December 1971 debates in the UNSC, the USSR vetoed every proposal for ceasefire, and made Pakistan's withdrawal from its own territory a condition for peace. After the war, the new President, Z.A. Bhutto, made an official visit to Moscow from 16–18 March 1972, but was told plainly by his hosts that the USSR would again act in a similar manner in a similar situation as had prevailed in East Pakistan. This was interpreted as a Soviet invitation for the secession of NWFP and Balochistan provinces. Z.A. Bhutto's second visit from 24–26 October 1974 was far more cordial. Nevertheless, Leonid Brezhnev's Plan to include Pakistan in a security arrangement with what he called the 'States of Hindustan' showed that Indian hegemony over South Asia was the lynch-pin of Soviet policy.

Meanwhile some progress was witnessed in trade and economic cooperation including an agreement to build a Steel Mill which eventually became operational in 1980.

Relations deteriorated sharply again when the USSR invaded Afghanistan in 1979. In this crisis the US again helped Pakistan against the USSR. President Zia tried to maintain relations regardless of the Afghan crisis, but his visits to Moscow for State funerals proved fruitless. Finally, the Soviet withdrawal began after the 14 April 1988 Geneva Accord and they vacated Afghanistan on 15 February 1989.

This was actually a prelude to the break up of the Soviet Union which provided an opportunity to review relations. On 24 December 1995, the Russian Ambassador, A.U. Alexeyev stated that state and national interests and not ideology would guide Russo–Pakistan relations. No change was perceptible in practical terms. There were two irritants: Pakistan's support to the Taliban regime in Afghanistan, and Russia's conviction that the Taliban were behind the resistance in Chechnya, in spite of Pakistan's stated position that it considers Chechnya to be a part of Russia. There was a meeting between President Vladimir Putin and President Pervez Musharraf at the UN in 2000, but no concrete result was obtained.

In October 2000, President Putin visited India and signed a new Defence Pact which was described by the Indians as more comprehensive than the 1971 Treaty of Friendship. The only perceptible thaw in relations between Russia and Pakistan was when Russia helped Pakistan launch a satellite in 2003. There are irritants between Russia and India, but never to the advantage of Pakistan. On 2 December 2004, Indian sources reported that Russia had imposed conditions on India for the continued supply of arms. However, during President Putin's visit to India all such conditionalities were withdrawn. Indeed, Russian support for India has never been conditional. On 3 January 2005, the Pakistani ambassador to Russia said that economic relations between the two countries would improve.[25] The Russian ambassador to Pakistan made no corresponding statement.

A ripple was created in the uneventful relations between Russia and Pakistan, when Prime Minister Mikhail E. Fradkov arrived on 11 April 2007 at Islamabad at the head of a large delegation. Apart from delivering a formal message from his President Vladimir Putin to President Musharraf, he held a joint press conference with Prime Minister Shaukat Aziz on 12 April, advocating economic diplomacy and expanded cooperation in the war against extremism and terrorism. Shaukat Aziz said that both sides had agreed to promote trade ties, using Iran as a corridor for this purpose (*The News*, 13 April 2007). Delegation members accompanying the Russian premier offered Pakistan high speed locomotives and train coaches (*Dawn*, 13 April 2007).

PAKISTAN AND CHINA

The People's Republic of China was established in 1949, two years after Pakistan's creation. No ideological restraint marked Pakistan's relations with Communist China, as it had with Communist Russia. Pakistan was one of the first countries to recognize China, diplomatic relations had been established by 1951. The Pakistani leadership had had an unhappy exchange with Chiang Kai-shek and was more receptive to the regime headed by Mao Zedong. The relations were initially formal and China was not pleased at Pakistan joining SEATO and CENTO, yet there was no bitterness. The Pakistani Prime Minister, Mohammad Ali Bogra, was able to strike a rapport with the Chinese Premier Zhou Enlai during the Bandung Conference of 1955,[26] which Pakistan had co-sponsored. Bogra's successor, H.S. Suhrawardy, visited China on Zhou Enlai's invitation in October 1956 and Zhou Enlai paid a return visit to Pakistan in March 1957. Unfortunately Suhrawardy, on his visit to the United States, not only played down relations with China but also voiced criticism of the Chinese regime.

This damage was contained due to China's diplomatic maturity, but an episode occurred which had greater potential for misgivings. At the start of the Sino–Indian conflict in 1959, President Ayub most injudiciously offered India joint defence against China which the Indian Premier, Jawaharlal Nehru, inexplicably refused. At this stage the Foreign Minister, Mohammad Ali Bogra, who, as prime minister, had established first contacts with China, was able to nullify Ayub's indiscretion and cement ties with China.

On 2 March 1963, the Sino–Pakistan border was demarcated, and later agreements on trade, and much more significantly, direct air communications were signed. China was culturally insular and diplomatically isolated, therefore, air links were a boon to both countries. During the 1965 War, China offered Pakistan military support, reportedly on the condition that Pakistan sustain the conflict and not accept a ceasefire precipitously. On 16 September, when the war was at its height, China issued an ultimatum to India to return some border outposts, yaks and other chattels. Alarmed by Chinese support for Pakistan, the British High Commissioner, Sir Morrice James, played on Ayub's conservatism and dissuaded him from accepting Chinese help. China issued another ultimatum to India on 6 January 1966, while the Tashkent Conference was in progress, but Ayub again succumbed to Soviet pressure.

In the 1965 war, when Pakistan had a sizeable arsenal, it did not seize the offer of Chinese help; in 1971, when Pakistan had a depleted arsenal, China fell short of promising armed intervention. We have seen earlier in the chapter how in US eyes Chinese intervention had room for manoeuvre despite their postures. In 1971, active Sino–American partnership could not result in gains for Pakistan. In 1970, President Yahya helped the US establish links with China, but China was too cautious and unable to decide between the mixed signals it was receiving from the White House and the State Department to commit troops to Pakistan, especially in the face of Russian deployment. In 1965, since China was not in contact with the US, Russia did not raise the stakes as it did in 1971.

Even before the 1971 war, Pakistan actively supported China's bid to regain its seat in the UN and opposed the American Two Chinas formula. It voted for the draft resolution which seated China in the UNSC and expelled Taiwan from the UN.

Z.A. Bhutto regarded Sino–American relations as an important factor in consolidating Pakistan's position in Asia and visited China in January 1972, May 1974 and May 1976. China became one of the main suppliers of arms to Pakistan. This continued despite the death of Zhou Enlai, and Mao Zedong in 1976 and the execution of Zulfikar Ali Bhutto in 1979.

During the 1980–90s, relations between China and Pakistan remained stable and friendly. In November 1989, Li Ping, head of the Chinese government, visited Pakistan when China promised to help Pakistan in the development of nuclear energy including providing technical equipment for a nuclear plant. In 1990, Pakistan launched a satellite from Chinese territory.

At the end of the Cold War, Sino–American relations were strained but had not broken down. Russo–Chinese relations also improved when ideology was no longer a key factor. Thus no power required Pakistan to encircle China. The year 2003 marked a number of developments showing that even in changed circumstances China was helpful to Pakistan. On 19 June 2003, when India blocked Pakistan's membership of the Association of South East Asian Nations (ASEAN), China strongly supported Pakistan. President Pervez Musharraf visited China on 4 November 2003, when Prime Minister Hu Jintao agreed to enhance defence cooperation.

Pakistan's pro-Taliban policy cast its shadow over its relations with China. The nuclearization of North Korea caused adjustments on a global scale. The incursion of Islamic militants into the Xinjiang province with an Uighur Muslim majority became a source of Chinese concern. Sino–Indian relations, even amidst heavy rhetoric, improved. On 20 January 1995, China, though loudly declared by India to be the main reason for Indian nuclearization, gave India thirty tonnes of uranium. On 22 October 2003, China and Pakistan conducted joint naval exercises, the first China had conducted with any country. On 15 November 2003, China conducted similar naval exercises with India. By the beginning of 2005, Indian Foreign Minister Natwar Singh said that China was no longer regarded as an adversary.[27]

On a more serious note, China expelled seven hundred Pakistani traders from Xinjiang, albeit under a 1985 agreement. Both China and Pakistan have decried US sanctions[28] on them for alleged transfer of nuclear technology. In mid-January 2005, American sources revealed that the US had constantly urged China not to help Pakistan in its quest for nuclearization citing documents dated from 1977 to 1997.[29] While China has reaffirmed its commitment to non-proliferation, its discretion in the face of such pressure has shown that China still values Pakistan's friendship.

The following Pakistani projects have been undertaken with Chinese help and are still continuing: the Karakorum Highway, the Heavy Mechanical Complex at Taxila, the Heavy Electrical Complex at Kot Najibullah, the Thermal Power Station at Guddu, SPARK, an agricultural cooperation programme, the Saindak Metallurgy Project and the on going development of Gawadar Port, and a jointly developed fighter aircraft, the JF-17.

The relations between China and Pakistan have continued to grow despite changes in the imperatives. During his visit to Pakistan, President Hu Jintao, declared Pakistan to be 'an indispensable partner'.[30] Omitting reference to extremism or terrorism which have been the main cause for Chinese concern, President Hu Jintao advocated a greater role for Pakistan in world affairs, saying that 'Pakistan's standing was rising steadily in Asia and beyond.' The same day, an accord on the construction of the Karakoram Highway from Rai Kot to Sazeen, an additional 200 kilometers was signed.

It was a joyous day when two JF-17s were welcomed at Karma on 12 March 2007. On 19 April 2007, Prime Minister Shaukat Aziz said in Chengdu that Pakistan would recover investment by selling the aircraft.[31] It was stated on 13 May 2007 that China would supply F-22P frigates. These frigates would have six helicopters each.[32] Nevertheless Sino–Indian relations had also grown. There was speculation that China would also sign with India a nuclear cooperation treaty.[33] Despite all confidence building measures, it has surfaced that China has not given up its claim to the territory that India calls 'Arunachal Pradesh'.[34] A major crisis was averted on 24 June 2007 when the government secured the release of nine Chinese nationals abducted by the Lal Masjid brigade. One of the greatest pressure tactics of terrorists is to abduct or kill Chinese nationals in Pakistan, to lay bare the country's most secure base of integrity. China gave a $327 million loan for the next phase of the Karakoram Highway.[35]

ANGLO–PAKISTAN RELATIONS

Pakistan was created when it gained independence from Britain. The last Viceroy, Lord Mountbatten, was given a brief to partition India only if unavoidable. Even before Lord Mountbatten, arrived, it was decided to concede a Pakistan in which Punjab and Bengal, Muslim majority provinces, were to be divided. It was decided more than a year before independence that Pakistan, in the event of its creation, would not be given the Muslim majority district of Gurdaspur.[36] H.C. Beaumont later confessed that a further gift of Firozpur and Zira was made to India by Sir Cyril Radcliffe. Thus all the disadvantages with which Pakistan was born were due to British manipulations. In a way, this was to be expected as India was a larger market and was strategically more important to the east of Suez interests of the British Empire.

The Labour Party's commitment to the Indian National Congress was so firm that it was a wonder that partition was at all conceded. Sardar Patel complained to Richard Symonds that Winston Churchill was responsible for the creation of Pakistan.[37] This was a manifest exaggeration, but the basic fact remained that there was a powerful and influential Conservative element better represented in the House of Lords, which was mindful of British promises to the minorities. Churchill's speech in the House of Commons, following the announcement of the Cabinet Mission Plan, is an example of this.

Pakistan came into existence as a Dominion of the British Commonwealth and even when it became a republic in 1956, it retained its membership of the Commonwealth. In the 1956 invasion of Egypt, Pakistan angered its population by siding with Britain and France against Egypt. At the initial stage there was also tension between Britain and the US over exercise of influence over Pakistan. British influence remained strong till the 1965 war. The statement of Prime Minister Harold Wilson in 1965, that India was the aggressor was the highest point in mutual relations. Subsequent to his announcement, he received inadequate support from the Foreign Office, and scaled down his rhetoric. The British High Commissioner, Sir Morrice James, was able to persuade President Ayub against accepting Chinese aid, promising never to let the Kashmir issue be sidelined, but when Ayub took him at his word, he betrayed that trust.

When the 1971 war broke out, Harold Wilson was still prime minister and he led the charade against Pakistan. When a deputation of British parliamentarians under Mrs Jill Knight gave a favourable report on Pakistan, he despatched another delegation under Arthur Bottomley to obtain a second, adverse report. In January 1972, Pakistan left the Commonwealth in protest against Britain's recognition of Bangladesh as an independent state. In July 1973, Zulfikar Ali Bhutto visited Britain and in January 1978 Prime Minister James Callaghan visited Pakistan. The Afghan crisis caused by the Russian invasion saw Prime Minister Margaret Thatcher visit Pakistan, but cooperation was confined to the Afghanistan crisis.

In October 1989, Prime Minister Benazir Bhutto restored Pakistan's membership of the Commonwealth. Anglo–Pakistan relations came under mild strain as a result of Pakistan's nuclear tests, and severe strain during the 1999 Kargil crisis. When the military government of General Pervez

Musharraf took over, the Commonwealth suspended Pakistan's membership. Since Pakistan joined the anti-terror coalition, relations have thawed to a degree that can be called cool but correct. A sizeable Pakistani population has made Britain its home and this, in addition to some commercial interests, keeps Anglo–Pakistani relations on an even keel.

The British Prime Minister, Tony Blair visited Pakistan, and on 19 November 2007, signed an accord with President Musharraf and Prime Minister Shaukat Aziz to strengthen cooperation to fight terrorism, drug trafficking, illegal immigration and trans-national organized crime (*Dawn*, 20 November 2006).

Tony Blair announced that Britain had doubled development assistance, as well as pledged £20 million to reduce poverty. There was a plea for greater British market access for Pakistani goods on which the British prime minister was non-committal.

In the Honours list issued on Her Majesty's Birthday, a knighthood was awarded to Salman Rushdie, author of the blasphemous *Satanic Verses* (London, 1988). Previously a knighthood had been awarded to V.C. Naipaul, author of *Among the Believers: An Islamic Journey* (1982), a book which is unsympathetic to Muslims. The foreign secretary said that the reason of the award was self-evident. It was hardly that, since an internationally celebrated author Colin Wilson was consistently passed over. When the Beatles were awarded the OBE in 1962, a number of recipients returned their awards. So soon after the cartoon fiasco, why the sentiments of Muslims had to be injured is not self-evident. So while hopes for better relations had been raised in November 2006, in June 2007 they have been dashed.

NOTES

1. K. Arif (ed.), *American–Pakistan Relations*, Lahore: Vanguard, 1984, p. 5.
2. Dennis Kux, *Disenchanted Allies*, Karachi: Oxford University Press, 2001. Excerpts: *Dawn*, 25 September 2001.
3. Francis Robinson, *Islam, South Asia and the West*, New Delhi: Oxford University Press, 2007, p. 275.
4. Michael Krepon, *New Friday Times*, Lahore, 8 August 2003, p. 6.
5. The *Times*, London, 3 December 1971.
6. Pran Chopra, *India's Second Liberation*, Cambridge: Massachusetts MIT Press, 1974, p. 100.
7. *Dawn*, 5 June 2000.
8. Suroosh Irfani, (ed.), *Fifty Years of the Kashmir Dispute*, Muzaffarabad: University of Azad Jammu and Kashmir, 1997, pp. 83–88.
9. The *News*, Karachi, 10 February 2004.
10. Ibid., 11 February 2004.
11. *Dawn*, 10 and 11 August 2005.

12. Eric Margolis, *War at the Top of the World*, New Delhi: Roli Books, 2001, p. 96. See also Gen. S. Padmanabhan. *The Writing on the Wall India Checkmates America 2017*, New Delhi: Manar Publication, 2004. In which a former chief of the Indian army staff projects his vision of defeating the United States.
13. *Dawn*, 23 January 2005.
14. Ibid., 2 June 1999.
15. Ibid., 4 June 2004.
16. Roedad Khan (ed.) *British Papers*, Karachi: Oxford University Press, 2002, p. 276.
17. Ibid., p. xix.
18. Ibid., p. 372. *The American Papers* also edited by Roedad Khan, Karachi: Oxford University Press, 1999 (does not have as many details about the US reaction as the *British Papers*).
19. *British Papers*, p. 384.
20. Paul Bracken, *Fire in the East*, New York: Perennial 2000, p. 102.
21. Mahir Ali, *Dawn*, 11 December 2002.
22. Ibid., 31 October 2003.
23. Ibid., 26 May 2002.
24. Ibid., 7 June 2002.
25. Ibid., 4 June 2005.
26. Qutbuddin Aziz, *Exciting Stories to Remember*, Karachi: Islamic Media, 1995, p. 54.
27. *Dawn*, 28 January 2005.
28. *The News*, Karachi, 22 November 2000.
29. *Dawn*, 15 January 2005, p. 3.
30. *Dawn*, 25 November 2006.
31. Ibid., 20 April 2007.
32. Ibid., 14 May 2007.
33. Ibid.
34. Ibid., 15 November 2007.
35. Ibid., 22 January 2008.
36. Penderel Moon, *Wavell: The Viceroy's Journal*, Karachi: Oxford University Press, 1974, p. 245.
37. Richard Symonds, *In the Margins of Independence*, Karachi, Oxford University Press, 2001, p. 92.

CHAPTER 39

PAKISTAN'S RELATIONS WITH THE SAARC STATES

South Asian Association for Regional Cooperation (SAARC) comprises Bangladesh, Bhutan, India, Maldives, Nepal, Pakistan and Sri Lanka. It was founded in Dhaka in December 1985. The total population of South Asia was then more than a thousand million. It was established to enhance economic relations among the member countries in what has been termed as no-conflict areas, which exclude bilateral issues. South Asian relations with the outside world are beyond the scope of SAARC. The association has held twelve annual sessions so far. The 13th session scheduled for February 2005 was postponed. The King of Nepal dismissed his cabinet, and India took this as an affront and had refused to attend. At the Dhaka Summit, when it was belatedly held there two important developments took place. Afghanistan was made a member, and China was given observer status. These developments promise to bring stability to SAARC and make it more effective.

RELATIONS WITH INDIA

Relations between India and Pakistan remain contentious on both sides. After Partition, the state to state relations did not turn a new leaf, but rather remained a continuation of the relations between the Indian National Congress and the All India Muslim League. Some of the rancour comes from the frustration caused by missed opportunities. Even after securing an electoral endorsement for Partition in 1946, the Muslim League compromised by accepting the Cabinet Mission Plan which provided for a central power between the Hindustan and Pakistan areas, controlling Defence, Foreign Affairs and Communications.

Some writers have defended Nehru's rejection of the Cabinet Mission Plan by asserting that it would have resulted in the creation of Pakistan. This argument would have been forceful, had its rejection prevented the emergence of Pakistan. Even if the Muslim League had had the desire to create Pakistan from the Cabinet Mission Plan, it did not have the means.

After the creation of Pakistan, the next issue to sour Indo–Pakistan relations was Kashmir. In the matter of integrating the Princely States, India did not display the patience required to tackle the issue. If India had not forcibly resisted the accession of Junagadh to Pakistan, it would have had a more convincing case over Kashmir. India not only resisted the accession of Junagadh, a stragically negligible state with a Hindu majority ruled by a Muslim prince, but characterized the accession of Junagadh to Pakistan as being 'against the principle of partition'. Then finally, Prime Minister Nehru rejected President Ayub's offer of joint Indo–Pakistan defence against China. Thus three decisions by Nehru eventually resulted in the emergence of a nuclear Pakistan.

After Kashmir, the next issue was the sharing of the Indus waters between India and Pakistan. This problem was considered permanently solved, but since 2004, the spectre of the Baglihar Dam built on the Indian side has reopened the issue and again brought the World Bank into the scene. Kashmir, however, has not been the only problem. The 1971 war was caused by the crisis in East Pakistan', an integral part of Pakistan under International Law. Kashmir came to be discussed only during the 1972 Simla Conference.

Another problem between India and Pakistan was the valuation of the Pakistani rupee in the face of Indian devaluation. The communal riots which broke out between Hindus and Muslims were addressed in the Liaquat–Nehru Pact of 1950. These agreements, together with the arbitration over the Rann of Kutch in 1965, show that when there has been a political will, there has been a way, and that the outstanding disputes are not dictated by nature.

In the political development chapters we have already discussed the three wars and the Kargil crisis. The nuclear stand off of 1998 cut through the posturing and resulted in the visit of the Indian Prime Minister, Atal Bihari Vajpayee, to Lahore. This was overtaken by the 1999 Kargil crisis. Relations worsened because of a terrorist attack on the Indian parliament on 13 December 2001 which resulted in military confrontation at the border for two years before it was called off on 12 October 2002. This crisis caused a break in diplomatic relations since India recalled its envoy and threatened to send back the Pakistan envoy. Simultaneously, over-flights were banned. This has been remedied: diplomatic relations have been re-established, over-flights have been restored, and both armies have withdrawn from offensive positions. However, confidence-building measures and meetings between India's and Pakistan's leaders have not yet led to the resolution of any outstanding dispute, least of all Kashmir.

REASONS FOR INDIA'S DIPLOMATIC SUCCESS IN THE KASHMIR DISPUTE

While the arguments are in favour of Pakistan, Kashmir is in the possession of India. It is necessary to explain why.

1. India has done well by following the golden rules of unity, faith and discipline. It has worked at building its country's image. Nehru was a chain smoker, but it would be difficult to find a photograph showing him smoking, because the patriotic Indian press did not publicise even what was a fashionable practice in those days. They revere Nehru for his role in securing India's freedom and disregard his errors of judgement that resulted in Partition.

   On our part we ridicule Prime Minister Liaquat Ali Khan and persistently perpetuate a completely baseless myth, that he solicited an invitation from Russia, and used it instead to maneouvre an invitation from the USA. Instead of showing appreciation we revel in criticizing him.

2. Every Indian is united on the claim that Kashmir is an integral part of India, while our own intellectuals and politicians create confusion. Some advocate a compromise on the LoC, even giving up Kashmir altogether, some press for a neutral or independent Kashmir. It is because of the unity of the Indian people that the Kashmir problem is viewed internationally not as an unfulfilled UN resolution, but as a case of cross-border terrorism. This is India's greatest diplomatic success, and Pakistan's greatest diplomatic failure. It was this failure that led to Pakistan's withdrawal from Kargil in 1999, although the comparable Indian occupation of Siachen in 1985 occasioned no international outrage.

3. Hardly any Indian ever blames his government for invading an integral part of Pakistan in 1971, and violating the principle of non-interference in the internal matters of Pakistan. On the other hand our own newspapers are replete with biased stories of genocide in 1971. Our intellectuals constantly complain that power was not transferred to the Awami League, the majority party in 1971, but no one advocates giving Six Points to NWFP (Wana) or Balochistan (Sibi) which would give these provinces separate currencies and provincial militias, as well as placing the responsibility for international aid and trade directly in the hands of provinces, completely bypassing the central government. Whether these writers are aware of it or not, whether they are doing this with honest intent or not, it amounts to propaganda.

   What is the purpose of this propaganda? Its purpose is to take away the will to fight. Reference will be made to some writers and their suggestions but before we come to that stage we need to examine all aspects of the Kashmir dispute.

THE ORIGINS OF THE KASHMIR DISPUTE

Kashmir was one of more than 500 princely states in India. It was ruled by a Hindu Maharaja, Hari Singh, but the population was overwhelmingly Muslim. It had a very strategic location. Most other states were completely surrounded by either India or Pakistan but because of the division of the Punjab, Kashmir had equal access to India and Pakistan. The ruler was inclined towards India, the people towards Pakistan.

The importance of Kashmir was clear to all, and even before the division of India was agreed upon in principle, efforts were afoot to block the accession of Kashmir to Pakistan.

PRE-PARTITION MOVES

On 23 January 1946, the Reforms Commissioner, V.P. Menon wrote to George Abell that Gurdaspur be excluded from Pakistan.[1] On 15 April 1946, the brief prepared by the Cabinet Mission for talks with Jinnah proposed a Pakistan without Gurdaspur.[2] The importance of Gurdaspur was that it provided India with all-weather access to Kashmir. It was a Muslim majority district. On 14 June 1947, Krishna Menon wrote to Lord Mountbatten that: 'there might be dire consequences for the future of Anglo–Indian relations if Kashmir were permitted to go to Pakistan.'[3] Menon had asked Mountbatten not to keep this letter, but he preserved it.[4] On 17 June 1947, V.P. Menon again favoured Gurdaspur becoming part of India.[5]

The above quoted correspondence shows that preparations for preventing the accession of Kashmir to Pakistan began even before Lord Mountbatten arrived as governer general.

THE BOUNDARY AWARD

We have seen in the section on the national struggle that Arthur Henderson, H.C. Beaumont, Sir Ian Scott and others gave evidence that Radcliffe altered the awards at the behest of Lord Mountbatten. In the first instalment, Gurdaspur was given to India and in the second instalment Ferozpur and Zira were also given to India. All three were Muslim majority districts. When Liaquat Ali Khan sent Chaudhry Mohammad Ali to Lord Ismay to protest, he blandly denied any such changes.

THE OUTBREAK OF FIGHTING

The conflict began when the Dogra state forces started terrorizing Muslims in the Poonch district of Kashmir. Tribal Pathans who had relatives in Poonch, mounted an attack to rescue the Muslims. This is what is described as Pakistan's invasion of Kashmir. The genocide at Poonch is suppressed from all accounts published in India. It is alleged that the people of NWFP had not wanted accession to Pakistan, but here we see them trying to rescue Muslims in Kashmir. The Pakistan army had yet to complete its reorganization, and it could not risk interfering with the Tribal Pathans. It is true that their progress was ultimately barred by the Indian army. We must reflect that whatever areas of Kashmir we have, are the result of these tribal incursions.

THE INSTRUMENT OF ACCESSION

It is alleged that frightened by the tribal reprisal, Maharaja Hari Singh signed an Instrument of Accession to India. After it was signed, the Indian army entered Kashmir to combat the tribals. Alastair Lamb has established that the Maharaja never signed an Instrument of Accession and that such a document does not exist. Nevertheless, as we have seen above, when the Muslim ruler of Hindu majority Junagadh acceded to Pakistan, India militarily blocked the accession, saying that such an accession was against the principle underlying Partition. Having made such an assertion, India could not have accepted the accession of Kashmir.

PROMISES OF A PLEBISCITE

At the time India accepted the supposed accession of Kashmir, it also stated that the final disposition of Kashmir would depend on a free and impartial plebiscite of the people of Jammu and Kashmir. India made this promise not only to the people of Kashmir but to the international community as well.[6] The dates on which Nehru repeated his promise of a plebiscite were 26 October 1947, 27 October 1947, 30 October 1947, 2 November 1947, 12 February 1951, 27 June 1952 and 7 August 1952. Despite these repeated promises it is now claimed by India that Kashmir is its integral part. On 3 November 1947 Nehru had assured Liaquat that: 'we have agreed to an impartial international agency like the UN supervising any referendum'. Thus any internal election held by India is not valid.

Nehru went back on his solemn pledges on 24 February 1955 on the excuse that Pakistan had become a military ally of the USA.

UNSC RESOLUTIONS

The United Nations Security Council Resolution which says that the accession of Kashmir will be decided by a free and impartial plebiscite was passed on 21 April 1948 and reiterated on 5 January 1949. Any election held by Indian authorities in Kashmir cannot replace the provision of a free and impartial plebiscite. Hence it cannot be asserted by India that Kashmir is its integral part. Such an assertion is not upheld by International Law. In 1957 the UN resolved that this step was in conflict with a plebiscite.

The cause of the 1965 war was Kashmir. The Indian parliament had taken steps to integrate Kashmir into India constitutionally. Before 1965 India had kept up the pretence of the autonomy of Kashmir. The head of the Kashmir administration had been designated prime minister, now he was designated chief minister, like the head of any province in India. Pakistan sent infiltrators inside Kashmir, just as President John Kennedy sent infiltrators inside Cuba, with equally disastrous results. Most of the infiltrators were arrested. Pakistan took this desperate step because if it had remained silent it would have acquiesced to the integration of Kashmir into India. As Ayub had replied, India had no legal title to Kashmir, hence intrusion was not agression.

When friction along the ceasefire line increased, Kargil fell to India. As stated earlier, Kargil was part of Pakistan until 1971. The course of the war and the Tashkent Declaration have been discussed in the chapter on Ayub Khan. The only point to stress is that Pakistan's reoccupation of Kargil in 1999 set off a crisis whereas the 1965 fall of Kargil to India did not.

The 1971 war did not take place because of Kashmir, but at the Simla Summit, India tried to take advantage of Pakistan's military defeat to impose a unilateral solution for Kashmir. The Simla Agreement could also be concluded because in a skirmish after the ceasefire in 1971, Pakistan was able to take the Lipa Valley in Kashmir. On 5 February 1973, Zulfikar Ali Bhutto called for a strike which was observed on both sides of the Line of Control. This was a signal that Pakistan had not surrendered in Kashmir.

Barring the allegations of ceasefire violations on both sides, there were no momentous development until 1985 when Indian troops occupied the Siachen Heights. In a similar action, Pakistan occupied Kargil in 1999, but because of hostile world opinion had to pull out.

Since the conflict has remained unresolved for more than fifty years, certain commentators have offered different solutions. One solution has been to establish an independent Kashmir. It is forgotten that Alexei Kosygin had turned down this option in Tashkent. An independent Kashmir, he told Ayub, would fall under the influence of third parties.[7] An American representative identified the third party as China.[8] It is again fortunate that Kosygin did not let Ayub proceed with this proposal. Once Pakistan itself floats independent Kashmir as a solution, the only tangible result would be the renunciation of Pakistan's claim to its side of Kashmir. India's initial promise to hold a plebiscite had also appeared as a reassuring and reasonable solution, but when sufficient time had elapsed after the ceasefire, that solution proved elusive.

How long a united and independent Kashmir can remain free depends on factors much beyond Pakistan's control. When the dismissal of his prime minister by the king of Nepal can cause India to feel affronted, when it claims that Bangladesh is harbouring terrorists, a much more innocuous development in an independent Kashmir may cause India to intervene. This could spell the end of Kashmir's neutrality and this time round there may be no UN resolutions in Pakistan's favour.

Then there are politicians who favour accepting the Line of Control as the permanent international border. Again, such acceptance by Pakistan cannot result in India's renunciation of her claim over Pakistan's Northern Areas. Hunza and Chitral would provide India with a spring board to enter Afghanistan; a foothold in Afghanistan would enable India to drive a strategic wedge between China and Pakistan.

President Pervez Musharraf also tried to propose a satisfice solution to Kashmir. On 18 December 2003, he said that Pakistan could move half way from demanding a plebiscite under UN resolutions; he thought both countries could move from their stated positions. Reacting, the peace activist Pervez Hoodbhoy proposed accepting the LoC as the border.[9] Perhaps Pervez Musharraf was fazed by the US describing his willingness to set aside the UN resolutions as a 'constructive development'. Since then the president has clarified that flexibility has to be mutual. At present such prospects are bleak. Nevertheless there is no reason for Pakistan to blink first. If India compromises, it compromises an outpost, if Pakistan compromises on Kashmir, it compromises its sovereignty.

There was scarcely any evidence when President Pervez Musharraf gave an exclusive interview to Prannoy Roy, on 5 December 2005. The president reiterated his four point solution to Kashmir. He had put it forward in an October 2005 interview also but he interrupted watching the unfolding of his plan. The four point formula is clearly carried in the 5 December 2005 interview:

1. Kashmir will have the same borders but people will be allowed to move freely back and forth in the region.
2. The region will have self-governance or autonomy, but not independence.
3. Troops will be withdrawn from the region in a staggered manner.
4. A joint supervision mechanism will be set up, with India, Pakistan and Kashmir represented.

The president was still asked just as he unfolded these four points, whether he was giving up plebiscite and giving up the UN resolution, although that is inherent in the four points. Explaining the first point he had stated: 'Therefore the solution lies in making the line of control irrelevant and this is a term I am borrowing from your leadership, this is the word they used and I keep saying it now.'

It needs to be realized that from making the LoC irrelevant, to making the international border irrelevant is but a short step. When the Indian leadership asserts that 'redrawing of boundaries is out of the question',[10] it clearly means that it makes no such distinctions. This too, is a position which has solidified gradually. Previously Swaran Singh had complained that Pakistan had not reciprocated on this point: 'India had proposed ceding to Pakistan 110,000 square kilometres of a total of 275,000, whereas Pakistan had not even ceded Jammu—a state where there was a majority of Hindus.'[11]

So not only was a redrawing of borders proposed, it was proposed to be redrawn on religious lines. The second position, autonomy, has been tried at least constitutionally, on both sides, but it had led nowhere near a solution. The third point, demilitarization, was the point on which the earliest Kashmir negotiations had failed. The fourth point is impractical as it was also ruled out, even though the British Commonwealth prime ministers had offered the troops and money necessary to inaugurate this idyllic arrangement.

INDIAN LEADERS ON KASHMIR

Although now every leader in India insists that Kashmir is an integral part of India, this was not the position early in the conflict. Below are some statements of Indian leaders. One sample statement of Pandit Jawaharlal Nehru, the first Prime Minister of India was:

1. 'We have declared that the fate of Kashmir is ultimately to be decided by the people. That pledge we have given, not only to the people of Kashmir, but to the whole world. We want it to be a fair, just referendum and we shall accept the verdict.'
   – Nehru AIR Broadcast, 2 November 1947

2. 'Those who accepted the partition of India—the Congress—on the basis of communal majority should have agreed to the inclusion of Kashmir in Pakistan, as undeniably Kashmir has a Muslim majority.'
   – Dr N.B. Khare, President, Hindu Mahasabha, APP, 3 May 1951

3. 'If the Muslims of Kashmir do not want to remain with us, let them go away, but Kashmir must and will be ours.'
   – Shyama Prasad Mukherjee's Speech, Patiala, 20 April 1953

4. 'The Mahasabha is convinced that an over all plebiscite will mean loss of both Jammu and Kashmir to India.'
   – V.G. Deshpande, General Secretary, Mahasabha, Bombay, 14 September 1953

5. 'Knowing that Kashmir is predominantly Mussalman, it is one day bound to become a Mussalman State.'
   – Mahatma Gandhi on 5 May 1934

Source: Prem Nath Bazaz, *The History of the Struggle for Freedom in Kashmir*, New Delhi: Kashmir Publishing Co. 1954, p. 343.

RELATIONS WITH BANGLADESH

The tragic and bloody circumstances in which Bangladesh seceded from Pakistan have already been recounted. We can start from 22 February 1974 when Pakistan recognized Bangladesh and Sheikh Mujibur Rahman, president of Bangladesh attended the Lahore Islamic Summit of 1974. On 9 April 1974, representatives from Pakistan, Bangladesh and India met in Delhi to agree to normalise relations. The repatriation of Bangladeshis from Pakistan, and the repatriation of some non-Bengalis to Pakistan (mainly divided families) took place under this declaration. On 27 June 1974, Prime Minister Zulfikar Ali Bhutto was given a popular and tumultuous reception in Dhaka, 'Let us forget the enmity and bitterness of the past and inaugurate a new chapter of hope and prosperity' said President Mujibur Rahman, the founder of Bangladesh.

In 1978 President Ziaur Rahman of Bangladesh was heartily welcomed by President Ziaul Haq of Pakistan. Quite astoundingly, there were demonstrations in Dhaka on 5 April 1979 to protest against the execution of Zulfikar Ali Bhutto. In 1983, Foreign Minister Sahibzada Yaqub Khan, who as GOC in East Pakistan had resigned rather than take Military Action in 1971, visited Dacca (now Dhaka) and addressed two outstanding issues between the two countries, the division of assets and the repatriation of non-Bengalis to Pakistan. Neither of these issues has been resolved to the satisfaction of Bangladesh, but nor have they become impediments to improved relations.

In June 1986 and in July 1987 President H.M. Ershad visited Pakistan. Prime Minister Benazir Bhutto visited Dhaka in 1989. Tributes were paid to Sheikh Mujibur Rahman at an Islamabad meeting on 17 March 1998. On 27 November 2000, the deputy high commissioner to Bangladesh said at a Dhaka seminar that Pakistan would not apologize to Bangladesh because the violence had been initiated by Awami League 'miscreants'. Although Pakistan had announced his withdrawal, the Bangladesh government expelled the deputy high commissioner. Two years later on 29 July 2002, President Pervez Musharraf apologized in Dhaka for the army action. Since the induction of Khalida Zia's government in October 2001, relations have improved.

The government of Bangladesh is locked now in disputes with India over the Farakka Barrage, which dates back to when this was an East Pakistan problem, and the Gozaldoba Barrage, and the interlinking of rivers in India. On 21 September 2003, large areas of Bangladesh were flooded. Bangladesh and India accuse each other of harbouring terrorists. Against this background the relations between Bangladesh and Pakistan have further improved.

RELATIONS WITH AFGHANISTAN

The Muslims of India used to look to the Afghans for help against the Hindu majority. Ahmad Shah Abdali's defeat of the Marathas in 1761 is symbolic of that sentiment. During the Khilafat Movement there was also a migration movement. Muslims migrated to Afghanistan, but soon found its gates barred. At Independence, Pakistan's membership of the UN was challenged only by Afghanistan. However, due to Jinnah's personal diplomacy, the Afghan envoy presented his credentials to him. Yet Afghanistan did not recognize the Durand Line which had been established in 1893 by an Anglo–Afghan treaty; it claimed Pakistan territory up to Attock.

From 1961 to 1963 diplomatic relations between Pakistan and Afghanistan remained broken, and were revived only due to the mediation of the Shah of Iran. However, during the 1965 and 1971 wars, in spite of its hostile posturing, Afghanistan did not embarrass Pakistan. On 13 December 1971, King Zahir Shah was in Moscow but, as foreign diplomats noted, did not endorse President Podgorny's condition of transfer of power to the Awami League as a requirement of ceasefire.

Shortly after, King Zahir Shah was ousted in a coup, a number of pro-Russian regimes ruled, finally culminating in the 1979 Russian invasion of Afghanistan. At first Pakistan joined the US in its efforts to counter the Russian invasion. After an interlude, Pakistan joined the war against terror in Afghanistan. Until there is peace in Afghanistan and US troops withdraw as the Russian troops did, the real nature of Pakistan–Afghanistan relations cannot be defined.

The situation across the Afghan border has worsened after President Hamid Karzai's assumed power in Kabul. Unable to stem the resurgence of the Taliban, Karzai's government has constantly blamed 'cross-border terrorism' from Pakistan for their anarchy. Their dilemma is that they want Pakistan to secure a border (Durand Line) that they do not wish to recognize. Those crossing over from Pakistan are not Pakistan but Afghan nationals. On 20 November 2006 Foreign Office spokesperson Tasnim Aslam said that: 'The only solution to Afghanistan's complaints of cross-border terrorism is that it should take back the three million Afghan refugees who live in Pakistan.'[12] She added that Afghanistan would not allow fencing or selecting of the border which had as many as 97 posts.

Afghanistan is not willing to take back its citizens who are mostly armed and have the potential to destabilize the host country. On 31 March 2007 the United Nations High Commissioner for Refugees had to suspend repatriation following the killing of an Afghan national near its verification centre 15 April had been set as the deadline for the registration of Afghans.[13]

Previously when US/NATO forces bombed sites within Pakistan, killing civilians, only Pakistan had protested. Hot pursuit into its territory was where Pakistan drew the line. On 23 June 2007, a barrage of artillery killed sixty civilians whom the NATO command described as 'insurgents'.[14] However, many children were killed, and one person seeing nine members of his family dread, committed suicide. Since the 'insurgents' included Afghan's, Karzai also criticized 'indiscriminate and imprecise' operations by US/NATO forces. The Karzai regime has been receiving open ended support, which might end now.

OTHER SAARC COUNTRIES

With other SAARC countries, Sri Lanka, Nepal, the Maldives and Bhutan, Pakistan enjoys normal relations. They have no disputes with Pakistan and the SAARC meetings, especially the Summit meetings, have brought these countries closer than otherwise would have been the case.

NOTES

1. S.M. Burke and S.A.D. Qureshi, *The British Raj in India,* Karachi: OUP, 1995, p. 562ff.
2. Penderel Moon (ed.), *Wavell: The Viceroy's Journal,* Karachi: OUP, 1974, p. 245.
3. Alastair Lamb, *Incomplete Partition,* Karachi: OUP, 1992, p. 108. vide *Transfer of Power Papers,* London: HMSO, Vol. xi, No. 201.
4. Ibid., p. 118.
5. S.M. Burke and S.A.D. Qureshi, op. cit., p. 587.
6. Alastair Lamb, *Kashmir: A Disputed Legacy,* Karachi: OUP, 1992, p. 182.
7. Iqbal Akhund, *Memoirs of a Bystander,* Karachi: OUP, 1997, p. 118.
8. Roedad Khan, op. cit., p. 411.
9. *Dawn,* Karachi, 23 December 2003.
10. Ibid., 15 January 2007.
11. Jean Alphonse Bernard, *From Raj to the Republic: A Political History of India, 1935-2000,* New Delhi: Har Anand Publications, 2001, p. 241. Also for a confirmation that India was willing to redraw boundaries in Kashmir see Kuldip Nayar, *India: The Critical Years,* New Delhi: Vikas, 1971, p. 195.
12. *Daily Times,* Karachi, 21 November 2006.
13. *Dawn,* Karachi, 1 April 2007.
14. *Dawn,* Karachi, 24 June 2007.

CHAPTER 40

PAKISTAN, THE NON-ALIGNED MOVEMENT AND THE MUSLIM WORLD

NAM MOVEMENT

Pakistan was a non-aligned country from 1947 to 1954, and allied with the West from 1954 to 1979. From 1979 onwards it became once again non-aligned. In the first phase, the Cold War was raging and both America and the USSR were actively inducting allies. The American Secretary of State, John Foster Dulles, (1888–1959) under President Dwight D. Eisenhower (1890–1969), had a dictum that 'those who are not with us are against us'. It was against this background that Pakistan joined SEATO and CENTO. In the second phase, pacts had less to do with the conduct of foreign policy; NATO is still maintained though the Soviet counter part, the Warsaw Pact, has disappeared. NATO now serves as a US superimposition upon the European Union (EU) states.

Pakistan had co-sponsored the Bandung Conference in 1955 even after joining CENTO and SEATO, but its non-aligned status was challenged and it could not continue. CENTO and SEATO petered out when both sponsors and client states considered them redundant; Pakistan after its breakup and Iran after its Revolution in 1979. Pakistan joined the Non-Aligned Movement (NAM) during its 1979 Havana Conference. Now there are so many economic configurations such as ASEAN, G8, etc., that the NAM no longer has the cohesiveness to be very active. At present the North/South division between developed and developing countries has become a more prominent issue.

THE MUSLIM WORLD

After the demise of CENTO it could be observed that all Muslim countries were non-aligned. After 1969, Muslim countries started becoming members of the Organization of Islamic Conference (OIC). In the last quarter of the twentieth century NAM and OIC had come to overlap. The unity and the glory of the Muslim world is one of the most sentimental concerns of Pakistani citizens, yet Pakistan's entry into the Muslim world was resisted and delayed.

1947–1967

At the time of its creation, Pakistan was the largest Muslim nation in terms of population. During the Freedom Movement, Indian Muslims had been blamed by their Hindu compatriots for looking outside India for inspiration. This referred not only to the religious duty of Muslims to look toward Makkah, but also to their greater interest in the fortunes of the Middle East.

Although the Khilafat Movement had ended in failure, it showed the extent to which pan-Islamic sentiments could politically galvanize the Muslims of India. Quite naturally, on creation, Pakistan approached the Muslim world with its long nurtured feelings of brotherhood, and voiced sentiments echoing Muslim solidarity. Its leadership had, from time to time, called Pakistan a 'fortress of Islam' and a laboratory for Islamic state craft. These Pakistani sentiments did not strike a responsive cord in the Muslim world.

The outcome was that the stress on Islam did not obtain for Pakistan a foothold in the Muslim world (especially the Middle East) but had a contrary effect. Sultan M. Khan, who was posted to Cairo, said that Pakistan had put forward proposals for an Islamic banking system, an Islamic Steamship Company, an Islamic news agency and an Islamic Conference to discuss important issues. This was considered trespassing on the preserves of the Arabs who felt that non-Arab Muslim countries would form a bloc with Pakistan.[1]

These were not merely racial feelings, it accorded with the historical enmities in the Middle East. Arab countries led by Egypt had lost their independence to Britain and other western countries. Therefore, on attaining freedom, Arab countries were averse to the west and looked to the USSR, the new enemy of the west. Non-Arab countries, particularly Turkey and Iran had a centuries-old conflict with Russia. They also shared frontiers with the USSR, and for their preservation they looked to the US, its post-war enemy. With the Cold War dividing the Muslim world, Pakistan could not cater to a unified Muslim world. Its welcome in the non-Arab camp led to its being mistrusted in the Arab camp.

India had succeeded in portraying the creation of Pakistan as a British conspiracy, which is the opposite of the truth. However, after the assassination of Liaquat Ali Khan, Pakistan signed military pacts with Britain and America. This in itself was not too harmful. What happened was that in the first test of solidarity, Pakistan failed the Arabs. In July 1956, Britain, France and Israel invaded Egypt because President Gamal Abdel Nasser had nationalized the Suez Canal. Pakistan sided with Britain against the Arabs, reinforcing the Indian propaganda that Pakistan was a British creation. First President Iskandar Mirza (on 26 July 1956), and then Prime Minister H.S. Suhrawardy explained to an indignant Pakistani public that, since the Arab world was of no consequence, Pakistan was siding with the invaders. 'Zero plus zero plus zero is equal to zero.'

This was adding insult to injury. Relations with Arab countries became bitter, a far cry from October 1951 when Pakistan had tried to form a block with Iran and Egypt, both countries then having anti-British administrations. One year later King Saud of Saudi Arabia visited Pakistan and India.

In 1956, despite its anger with Egypt, the USA forced Israel to vacate most of its Arab territory as did the USSR. After the war there were changes in the region. There was a revolution in Iraq. Although Pakistan was allied to the West, due to its experience in the 1962 Sino–Indian war and 1965 Indo–Pakistan war, Pakistan firmly sided with the Arabs in the 1967 Arab–Israeli war. The Six Day War in 1967 was disastrous for the Arabs, but it was only in this war that Pakistan was able to rehabilitate itself in the Middle East.

1968 ONWARDS

After the 1967 war, neither was the USA inclined, nor the USSR able, to have the Arab lands vacated. 1968 saw the Arab world trying to return to normalcy after its trauma. In 1968 there were widespread student demonstrations in France as well as in Pakistan; both President Charles de Gaulle and President Ayub resigned. In 1969 a fanatic Jew set fire to the Al-Aqsa Mosque in Jerusalem. This outrage brought Muslim countries onto a single platform after centuries of division. The first Islamic Conference was held in Morocco. An Indian delegation was initially invited on the plea that India had a large Muslim minority, but when President Yahya Khan threatened a boycott, the Indian delegation was forced to withdraw. It was during the Ayub era that Pakistan began to woo the Arabs and it was in 1969 that this effort produced results. Had the first Islamic conference been held in the 1950s, India would have ousted Pakistan.

The second Islamic Conference was held in the aftermath of the 1973 Arab–Israeli war, in Lahore. It was a grand success but on another level the heightened relations with Arab nations resulted in a sliding of relations with non-Arab nations. Because Anwar Saadat of Egypt and Muammar Qaddafi of Libya came, neither the Shah of Iran nor his prime minister attended. It is rumoured that Pakistani Prime Minister Zulfikar Ali Bhutto had advised Middle Eastern countries to use the oil weapon to withhold oil from supporters of Israel and sell it for a high price generally. The Organization of Petroleum Exporting Countries (OPEC) was not made up exclusively of Muslim countries, but was dominated by them. The assassination in 1975 of King Faisal of Saudi Arabia, the co-host of the 1974 Lahore Conference, and the overthrow of Zulfikar Ali Bhutto in 1977 removed two of the most dynamic leaders of the Muslim world.

RCD/ECO

Iran's cold response to the Lahore OIC was a new development. Turkey and Iran were Pakistan's partners in CENTO as well as in the Regional Cooperation for Development (RCD). Later, it was revealed that the RCD comprising Pakistan, Iran and Turkey was set up in 1964 to counter the influence of China over Pakistan. Neither CENTO nor RCD survived the 1979 Iranian Revolution, but the RCD was later transformed into a larger-based but low key organization called the Economic Cooperation Organization (ECO). ECO signified Pakistan's approach to the newly independent Muslim Central Asian States. Turkey, Iran and Pakistan, the original RCD members, joined the Central Asian States Azerbaijan, Kyrghystan, Tajikistan, Turkmenistan, and Uzbekistan in February 1992 to form the ECO. A number of joint projects have been undertaken and trade barriers have been removed. The leaders of the Central Asian States (CAS) all accepted the invitation of Pakistan's Prime Minister, Nawaz Sharif, in 1991 to visit the country with a view to fostering closer relations between the states. The next important step was the visit, from 24 November to 18 December 1991, of a delegation led by Sardar Assef Ahmad Ali (Minister of State for Economic Affairs to the Central Asian States).

A number of trade agreements were signed and an opportunity for a new vista in foreign relations was being opened up. Pakistan was willing to extend credit and provide facilities for privatizing Central Asian economies. This was a sound basis, but then relations cooled after 25 May 1997 when Pakistan recognized the Taliban regime in Afghanistan. Since Afghanistan lies between Pakistan and the ECO countries, this step had a cataclysmic effect. To Central Asian countries, the Taliban projected a militant and fanatical image of Islam. Even Iran and China, the closest neighbours of Pakistan, did not appreciate Pakistan's step and felt that friendship with Pakistan would bring Taliban-like regimes to their countries.

Even before the Taliban insurgency, the Central Asian States signed a mutual pact in 1996 to reduce armed forces along the former USSR and Chinese borders. In the Shanghai Cooperation Organization (SCO) set up in the same year, the CAS joined hands with Russia and China. This removed the thrust of their development from the South. Russia, from which CAS had gained freedom, gained a partial come back because of unresolved disputes. Previously the Amu Darya and Syr Darya flows were controlled by the USSR; after independence the northern states began hampering the flow of water to the southern states. Russia was called upon for the purpose of co-ordination, resulting in further loss of influence by Pakistan.

Big power rivalry surfaced briefly in 2001 when the US set up military bases at Manas in Kyrghystan, and Khanabad in Uzbekistan. Russia later on (25 October 2003) opened an airbase in Kant, thirty-five miles from the US base. It publicly demanded that the US pull out from its Central Asian bases. This, in conjunction with Pakistan's post 9/11 anti-Taliban, volte-face afforded an opportunity of improving relations with the Central Asian States and revitalizing the ECO.

The resurgent Taliban Movement, which has distinct sectarian overtones, moved into neighbouring Iran. A sound bomb exploded in Zahedan on 15 June 2005. In an almost unprecedented move, the foreign office summoned the Pakistani Ambassador, Shafqat Saeed 'to give explanations'.[2] It is quite apparent that Iran is adding its voice to the voice of the US/NATO forces to 'do more'. Suspicions were raised by the Iraq war, an Arab, non-Arab polarization raised concerns when Islamabad hosted a mini OIC Foreign Ministers summit on 25 February 2007. On 9 March, President Pervez Musharraf telephoned President Mahmud Ahmedinejad assuring him 'that Pakistan would always guard Iran's interests' reassuring Iran that the mini-summit was not directed against it.[3] In the meanwhile, the President of Iran visited Saudi Arabia on 4 March 2007 and agreed with King Abdullah that the sectarian violence stalking Iraq and Lebanon be jointly countered.[4]

PAKISTAN AND ISRAEL

Should, or should not Pakistan recognize Israel, is the most debated question about Pakistan's relations with the Muslim World. There are two sides of the question; Ideological and Practical.

Ideologically Pakistan should refrain from recognizing Israel, as it is a country which is set up on usurped and occupied land. It has a bad human rights record and is the cause of the displacement of millions of Palestines who have been stateless since 1948. Pragmatically Pakistan should recognize Israel because it would neutralize US and Western objection to Pakistan's nuclearization and end the discrimination which Pakistan's nuclear programme faces. This is all the more urgent in view of the A.Q. Khan scandal. Libya has suffered no obloqy for exposing A.Q. Khan. It is not probable that the Arab world would criticize Pakistan for such a measure. India has suffered no dent in Arab relations because of its ties with Israel. The case of Palestine and Kashmir also, are not parallel, as Egypt and Jordan already recognize Israel.

A third factor is opportunity. Z.A. Bhutto recognized Bangladesh under the cover of the Islamic Summit. Pakistan has had only one such opportunity. The recognition of Israel should have been announced alongside the attainment of nuclear status. The Israeli ambassador to the US was desperately trying to contact his Pakistan counterpart in May 1998, to assure him that Israel had no intention of attacking Pakistan's nuclear facilities. Perhaps lack of contact between two nuclear states is not good for world security.

The demilitarization of the Gaza strip provided an opportunity, and on 1 September 2005 the Israeli Foreign Minister Shalom Silvan met his Pakistani counterpart, Khurshid Mahmud Kasuri, in Istanbul. The latest development is the congratulation of the Israeli President on the re-election of President Pervez Musharraf.

NOTES

1. Sultan M. Khan, *Recollections and Reflections*, London: Centre of Pakistan Studies, 1997, p. 65.
2. *Dawn*, 19 February 2005.
3. Ibid., 9 March 2007.
4. Ibid., 18 March 2007.

PART IX

ECONOMIC HISTORY

CHAPTER 41

ECONOMIC DEVELOPMENT

The first objection to be made to the creation of Pakistan was that the state would not be economically viable, that is, it would not have the finances to survive. After Pakistan was created, the government of India refused to give its share of financial assets. The excuse that Nehru gave for this was that since there was a war over Kashmir, by handing over the financial resources India would be helping Pakistan to defeat it. Mahatma Gandhi, however, saw the injustice of this stance. He went on hunger strike against the government of India, so that it was forced to hand over 17.5 per cent of Pakistan's share. Gandhi was killed by a member of an extremist political group in India, one of the reasons for his anger with Gandhi was the fact that he had helped Pakistan.

Yet, despite the amount that was received, which was just one installment of the amount due, Pakistan was seriously short of finances. As has been mentioned before, the Nizam of Hyderabad sent a cheque for a large sum of money, but Nehru did not allow it to be encashed. Pakistan overcame this financial crisis, the worst in its history, with the help of its businessmen.

Pakistan's economy was indeed very weak at the time. It was too dependent on agriculture, which contributed 60 per cent of its income. The savings rate was as low as 5 per cent of the gross domestic product (GDP), which is very low. GDP means the total value of the goods and services produced by the country in one year. To take an example, suppose a country produces 100 tons of bananas which sell for Rs 50,000 a ton, the income from the domestic product, bananas, is Rs 50 million in a year. The country now also offers tourism, which fetches Rs 20 million a year. Tourism is a service and like bananas it is also a 'product' since it is marketed by the people of the country. The GDP of this country is then, Rs 70 million.

The financial system was very basic and at Independence, Pakistan had no central bank. A central bank is required to control a country's money supply, which helps in determining the buying power of money. A central bank fixes monetary policy which includes the rate of interest. This further helps people in calculating the risks and gains of their ventures. A central bank is also required to regulate other, mostly private banks. A central bank is subject to political control. Therefore, under those hostile circumstances it was even more necessary for Pakistan to set up its own central bank which could issue its own currency notes if its economic independence was to be upheld. This was the reason why Jinnah, despite his severe illness, travelled from Ziarat to Karachi to open the State Bank of Pakistan on 1 July 1948.

In the agriculture sector, the land tenure system and the low level of agricultural technology were responsible for low productivity. The only redeeming feature was that Pakistan had inherited part of a well-developed irrigation system. Industries were inadequate, rather informal, and at that time could not be optimally utilized because of riots and mass-migration. There was a small nucleus of industrial units around Lahore; diesel engines were being manufactured, electric fans were produced and the machine tool factories had actually started exports in 1942. The Darra Khel Arms factory, although efficient, was considered to be outside the formal sector of the economy. The witholding of military assets by India had raised disappointment to a level that even these available resources were not visible, even during the Kashmir war.

Pakistan survived, as Richard Symonds has observed, because the harvest in 1947 was good, and there were sufficient peasants to harvest it. The two initial years involved the management of the economy on a daily basis and there was no real development except for the establishment of the State Bank during Jinnah's lifetime.

In those early years, industrialization was seen as the only road to progress, therefore, Liaquat Ali Khan set up two corporations in the public sector, one for heavy and one for light industries. Under these corporations, the government would provide financing to an extent not forthcoming from the private sector. As a priority it planned to set up three jute mills in East Bengal. This need can be understood when we recall that it had a large crop of jute fibre but no mill at all to process it. There were a few cotton mills in the western wing, but hardly in proportion to the size of the cotton crop in Sindh and Punjab.

However, once the economy stabilized there was progress. All governments gave priority to development. Gross national product (GNP) increased on an average by 5 per cent a year. Undeniably there have been setbacks, there have been lapses, but Pakistan survived not only the partition of the Punjab in 1947 but also the loss of East Pakistan in 1971.

Economic History

The economic history of Pakistan can generally be divided into five phases:

    (i) The initial era of crisis management: this corresponds to the first democratic era of 1947 to 1958.

    (ii) The era of determined planning: this characterizes the Ayub era.

(iii) The re-orientation of growth strategy: This covers the first PPP regime 1971–77.

(iv) Distancing the economy from state capitalism: the Zia era reaction to Bhutto's policy, and finally

(v) Attempting structural reforms; the current phase.

The establishment of the State Bank of Pakistan in 1948 proved to be the first symbol of Pakistan's economic independence, and in the following year Pakistan asserted itself by refusing to fall in line with Britain and India when they devalued their currencies by 37 per cent This was not rancour on the part of Pakistan as imagined. Devaluation, a political decision to decrease the value of one's currency in relation to other currencies, may have enhanced exports but would also have increased the domestic price of imported goods on which Pakistan relied much more than India did. In retaliation, instead of paying higher prices to Pakistan for the same goods, India suspended all trade links. Among those who exported raw material to India, the most important were the jute growers of East Bengal. If India did not buy jute, they would have no other means of subsistence. Liaquat Ali Khan approached the jute growers and undertook to buy the whole crop to prevent it from being sold at devalued rates.

As an indication of how Pakistan weathered the crisis, the per capita income increased by 1.4 per cent. Per capita income means the income of a country divided by the number of its inhabitants. Agriculture increased by 2.6 per cent and the manufacturing sector by as much as 23.5 per cent. External factors were responsible for constricting Pakistan's economy, but the Korean war (1950–53) proved to be a factor highly conducive to growth. The Korean war created a demand for raw materials at enhanced rates. Pakistan's decision not to devalue in 1949 paid off, since it was able to sell at a higher exchange rate. It was also able to sell to different countries, which meant, in other words, diversifying the market.

Along with the Korean war boom, planning was needed to deal with the recession that would follow, when the war ended and the demand ceased. Pakistan had two choices. The first involved devaluation coupled with the rationing of imports. Rationing meant fixing the amount of a particular item that could be imported. The second was to re-impose trade and foreign exchange controls. The government of Pakistan exercised the second option, with the expectation that the manufacture of goods that were previously imported, would grow. The government imposed tariffs, a tax on imports and exports, which meant that consumer goods would become more costly. Since rising costs could reduce profits it was thought that investing in such industries that produced goods already in demand, would increase.

The government decided to make the process of imports a category of reward for the companies which had imported during the crisis period. In other words, to those firms who placed reliance on the government and had imported goods when the prospects were not bright, the government issued licences to import. Ultimately, this step led to a sale of licences. Uneven management skills or confidence in firms induced them to sell their licences to other parties who were more confident of making a larger profit on those licences. This system had the effect of engendering rent seeking, a practice which became entrenched and still persists. Rent seeking means that instead of trying to improve the quality of the goods and services they provide, businessmen approach the government to enact legislation to make their businesses more profitable.

When countries set priorities it means that some sectors of the economy perform better than others. But those segments of the economy which were earlier neglected, also need to be developed. If a country has the resources, it can allow all segments of the economy to develop together, but when the resources are limited, some segments are neglected. Thus initially, while industry progressed, agriculture lagged behind. It was also felt, at that time, that investment in education and social development had been too low, and this neglect would have an impact on other sectors of the economy. For example, if there were not enough educated people who could perform their functions in a commercial firm, or if health-care facilities were not provided, it would reduce the commitment and efficiency of the workforce.

One reason for the concentration on industry was that western countries had been extremely reluctant to sell Pakistan, components for those industries which already existed in India. In their scheme of business, western countries wanted Pakistan's industry to be subordinate to Indian industry. In practical terms it meant that Pakistan must depend on Indian industries to purchase its raw material at prices of their choice. Pakistan needed to avoid this. In these circumstances, only some East European countries, strapped for hard cash, were ready to sell industrial units or components to Pakistan. Since these countries were also Soviet satellites, political exigencies prevented this market from expanding.

The decision to promote import substitution industrialization, was based on the premise that the terms of trade would, in the long run, prove unattractive to producers of primary commodities, and also on the premise that the capitalist sector had a greater propensity to save. It was hoped that the aggregate savings ratio could be enhanced by incentives for capital formation.

This brings us to planning, which is covered separately in the next chapter, but here we need to outline the initial efforts and the delay in beginning to plan. The Pakistan Planning Board was set up in 1951, but did not prove to be very active. Before 1955, no serious planning was undertaken. Even when the First Five Year Plan (1955–60) was made, the objectives were too ambitious, therefore only a modicum of them could be achieved. The Plan had sought to reduce regional disparities, increase both agricultural and industrial production, to increase exports, and to increase the rate of savings.

Naturally not all of these objectives could be achieved, at least, not at a uniform rate. Nevertheless the exercise in planning was essential since it was long overdue. The exercise had begun a full eight years after the creation of Pakistan. This exercise accelerated the process of consolidation and experimentation. The plan did provide incentive, to industry, but not to agriculture or education. This was not surprising as agriculture had been allocated only 11 per cent of the total investment. This stagnation of agriculture naturally constrained other sectors of the economy.

THE AYUB ERA

After the first democratic phase of Pakistan's history there came the first military regime of Ayub Khan. A Green Revolution was set in force, during the Second Five Year Plan (1960–65), by increasing irrigation and introducing mechanized farming and fertilizers. The growth rate of agriculture increased from 1.43 to 5.1 per cent. To boost exports the Ayub regime introduced, in 1959, a Bonus Voucher Scheme which was intended to provide price incentives to the exporters of selected manufactured goods. Within three years, the net export of commodities covered by the Bonus Voucher Scheme saw a 40 per cent increase.

The Second Five Year Plan was viewed as successful and Pakistan was held up as a model for other countries, for, contrary to the socialist trend in Asia, Pakistan was setting up units in the public sector and then selling them to the private sector. Of course, as noted, when priorities are set, they are achieved at a cost. In this case the cost was social and ideological. When Dr Mahbub ul Haq, a bureaucrat during the Ayub era, stated that the wealth of Pakistan was concentrated in the hands of twenty-two families, people turned their focus away from the production of wealth to its distribution. The flow of production had to be slowed down due to the 1965 war. Thereafter, production was decreased, and wealth continued to be distributed unevenly.

The 1965 war proved to be a serious economic setback, not only because foreign aid was curtailed but also because the crops failed that year. This forced Pakistan to change its development strategy, especially as far as sectoral allocations were concerned. Agriculture was given greater importance. Greater attention was given to installed industries and consumer goods because they required less foreign exchange and had better export prospects.

The 1971 war proved far more calamitous. It is often asserted that the 1971 war had its origin in the economic deprivation of the east wing. The eastern wing had greater resources such as jute, but these were exploited mainly by non-Bengali investment and enterprise. This not only caused resentment but led to attacks on non-Bengali jute workers.

Z.A. BHUTTO'S RE-ORIENTATION OF GROWTH STRATEGY

Zulfikar Ali Bhutto's nationalization programmes are widely regretted today, but they were an inevitable outcome of Mahbub ul Haq's pronouncement that twenty-two families controlled the country's economy, and, of a sense of ethnic deprivation. Bhutto's nationalization received great condemnation, but Mujibur Rahman's simultaneous nationalization did not receive any condemnation although it was more disastrous. Bhutto at least had the excuse of the massive dislocation caused by the war. Two essential items, match boxes and paper were exclusively supplied by the eastern wing. West Pakistan was also the largest market for tea from East Pakistan. The residual Pakistan had to arrange its emergency imports at high costs.

By 1972, the PPP government had nationalized thirty-two large manufacturing units in eight major industries. On 1 January 1974, Bhutto nationalized local banks and all life insurance companies as well. During Bhutto's term, there was a 50 per cent reduction of private investment; the capital that could not be transferred abroad was used to finance small-scale industry. S. Akbar Zaidi has shown that these small units, unafraid on the account of nationalization, came forward and were proved to be expanding the economy.[1]

When PPP nationalized, it was forgotten by its opponents that the unmitigated dependence on the private sector, the pro-industry bias, the increasing dependence on foreign aid and the neglect of human development had led to some distortions and regional imbalances which had come to the political forefront. The reliance on the private sector was based on the expectation that the capitalists had a better propensity to save, but Pakistani capitalists were not as frugal as had been expected.

On the other hand, since a substantial part of the saving was done by the twenty-two families, they were able to pre-empt credit facilities from commercial banks and specialized financial institutions. It was this factor which led to the clamour for better income distribution that Bhutto had to deal with.

Zulfikar Ali Bhutto re-oriented growth strategy in the face of East Pakistan's secession, to take the edge off the more abrasive aspects of development planning, and, in doing so, he had to redefine the concept of a mixed economy. Unfortunately, Bhutto began this process in a most unseemly manner by arresting the two leading industrialists of Pakistan. This set off a war of attrition between the political and economic forces of the country, and worse, Bhutto referred to his tenure as commerce minister in a manner which indicated industry-agriculture rivalry. Thus his economic policies encountered more resistance than was warranted by his reforms.

Bhutto was justified in giving the government a greater share in economic planning. He scaled down economic planning and nationalized according to political strategy. For example, after leaving the business community in suspense, he nationalized banks and insurance companies on 1 January 1974. Meanwhile, he had consolidated the nationalization of industrial units.

Since Bhutto had been blamed for being softer on the agricultural sector than on the industrial sector, he overreached himself by nationalizing small agro-based industries. This was an important reason why the small town businessman participated in the 1977 upheaval against Bhutto. It is also forgotten that Bhutto's reforms had an unlucky start; his announcement of reforms was greeted by massive floods and exceptionally high oil prices, which were keenly felt because Bhutto had devalued the Pakistan rupee by 57 per cent.

However, since Bhutto was adept at both granting and witholding concessions, he removed all official bottlenecks for a wave of temporary migration to Arab countries. This improved the employment opportunities in the urban centres which had been polarized because of the language controversy, and increased the income of the lower and middle classes. Another feature was that, at a time when slow growth in output had increased inflation, the home remittances gave a fillip to price pressure since they increased the demand for consumer goods.

In a similar development, we see that because of the nationalization, the sustainability of large-scale industry allowed small-scale industries to emerge as a major economic factor. S. Akbar Zaidi observes that since small-scale industry did not fear nationalization, it went ahead under its own steam without government finances. It was the small-scale industries which benefited by the devaluation which offset the excessive fiscal advantage that accrued to large-scale industries. On the political level, it was increased trade union activity which led businessmen to move towards smaller units. The government had simplified import procedures and this also contributed to the greater advantages of the smaller units.

Between 1969–70 and 1976–77, the Yahya and Zia years, the commodity-producing sector grew by 2.2 per cent per anum as against the 6.4 per cent output growth in the service sector. This increased price levels. In the 1970s the consumer price index rose, on average, by 12.5 per cent per annum, up from 3.2 per cent in the 1960s. Although the PPP's economic performance was marred by a slow output rate and high inflation, objectively viewed, it was not dismal. It was cruel and ridiculous for Bhutto's opponents to claim that they would be able to reduce prices to pre-1970 levels when Bhutto was removed. Although this may not sound like an achievement, Bhutto not only laid the foundations of the capital goods industry, he also protected the incomes of the industrial labour force and low wage-earners in the public sector. The performance of the nationalized industries was not a as bad as alleged, and the banks showed a profit, until lending large sums of money without collateral became a means of patronage in the Zia era.

THE ZIA ERA—DISTANCING ECONOMY FROM STATE CAPITALISM

The two defining trends of the Ziaul Haq era (1977–88) were the Soviet invasion of Afghanistan, and the sharply rising fiscal deficits. Fiscal deficits mean that the government was granting more in subsidies than it was collecting in taxes, leading to a deficit. The Afghan war led to a large increase in aid inflow, since Ziaul Haq had wisely refused to accept 'peanuts' from the USA. On an ideological basis, the government made some attempts at denationalization and privatization, but despite a sense of triumph over Bhutto's removal, capital remained shy, and even now it has not regained confidence. The rate of savings at 9 per cent average was quite low, therefore foreign exchange was far more welcome than Ziaul Haq had claimed.

Pakistan's economy grew in this period by 6.5 per cent and the rate of inflation averaged at 7.3 per cent. The growth of public debt remained under control under the PPP in the 1980s, though the domestic debt grew far too high. On the other hand, Pakistan, during the 1980s, became self sufficient in all types of foods except edible oils.

STRUCTURAL REFORMS 1988

By the time democratic regimes were reinstalled, debt-servicing comprised 80 per cent of the GDP. This growth of public debt was caused by neglect of financial discipline, poor use of fiscal resources and the high cost of borrowing. External debt also rose sharply but this was not due to internal slackness, but because international capital was available on extremely onerous terms. Between 1972 to 1999, the percentage of concessional aid had fallen from 73 to 53 per cent. The official rate of interest increased, bringing it close to the market rate.

The 11 September 2002 terrorist attack on the US brought Pakistan on the right side of the war on terror. Pakistan again (as from 1979 to 1986) became a front-line state. It received short-term debt relief, debt forgiveness and debt restructuring. Trade concessions and an increase in formal home remittances provided further respite. Fortunately, this time round, Pakistan had effective policies to reduce external debt and liabilities. These were structural adjustments which will be explained. During the present Pervez Musharraf regime, and for the last three consecutive years, Pakistan has had a current account surplus. (Current accounts are where transaction means income for the recipient. This is in contrast with capital account where no actual rise in income takes place, but the form in which assets are held, changes).

Apart from home remittances, exports also increased, and after a long time, foreign exchange reserves are high. External debt and liability considered as a percentage of GDP fell from 51.7 per cent in the financial year 1990 to 2000 to 37.8 per cent in 2003–04. Considered as a percentage of foreign exchange earnings they have decreased from 297.33 to 168.7 per cent during the same period. It is because of a hostile security environment that these figures have not been heartening.

STRUCTURAL ADJUSTMENT PROGRAMME 1988

Realizing that a mere reversal of the PPP's nationalization programme was not enough, a structural adjustment programme was put into effect which basically means the encouragement of the private sector's participation in the expansion of the rural/agricultural sector. The government not only abolished regulatory restrictions such as making business dependent on government licence, but also provided the infrastructure like roads and ports so that the private sector could benefit from government measures. Power generation was opened to private enterprise with government subsidies on power and grains being withdrawn. Tax exemptions, previously extended to urban areas, have been extended to the rural areas since 1995.

The Structural Adjustment Programme has come in for some criticism. Firstly for its belief that marketization is the only route to economic progress. This, in other words, means that markets are allowed to govern economic decisions. This system disregards the external forces which loom large in Pakistan. Monopolies can distort the market because of a collective decision like any taken by any government department, and income distribution is affected, as was witnessed at the end of the Ayub era.

Pakistan has gone for budget cutting, that is, removing items from the budget due to financial constraint, exchange rate depreciation, interest rate liberalization, realistic prices without subsidies and trade liberalization. These are positive features but were considered ill timed. Trade liberalization was premature because it resulted in de-industrialization. An estimated 4000 industrial units have closed down. Budget cutting at a time when Pakistan was faced with a recession made economic revival more remote. The exchange depreciation increased the rupee value of external debts without enhancing exports. An interest rate liberalization meant that the government had to borrow at a higher rate of interest.

What is important is that this fallout was managed soundly because of the support of the international institutions, local political support, consistency and transparency of policies. In 2003–04 the GDP grew by 6.4 per cent, per capita income by 4 per cent and the manufacturing sector registered a growth rate of 17 per cent. During 2005, the fiscal deficit was contained at 4 per cent of the GDP and the government was able to repay more than 1.6 billion dollars to its foreign lenders.

Since Pakistan has achieved macroeconomic stability over the last five years, many economists expect the government to enlarge the Public Sector Development Plan, while others argue that the base is not broad enough.

There is an argument that the private sector should be encouraged to increase expenditure. Here the focus is on the textile industry. Apart from its large size, the textile industry is notable for two features: firstly, it was not touched by nationalization, and secondly it has had to cope with the industry-agriculture tension: while cotton growers wanted to export directly at a higher price, cotton mill owners claimed primacy over crops.

Since 2000, more than four billion dollars have been invested in the textile sector, but over all private investment has been languid, at a rate of about 11 per cent of the GDP during this time. The principal reason cited for this is that there is considerable excess capacity in some industries. This fact underscores the need for a modicum of planned economy. As the Multi Fibre Agreement (MFA), which ensured a share in exports, has expired, the only way to survive is to be competitive.

THE CHALLENGE OF GLOBALIZATION

Globalization of the economy means free international trade and free movement of capital across the globe. This is based on common information which enables multi-national firms to calculate the widest parameters for their products and to select the cheapest locations for any product in terms of labour, availability of raw materials or transport.

We can survive globalization by being competitive which means that we make technological progress, develop our human resources by imbuing the working force with better knowledge and skills, encourage flexibility and adaptability in organizations and ensure that the role of capital and finance is positive. In Pakistan, firms are generally small, and technologically they are underdeveloped, they have unskilled workers and, of course, an undeveloped financial sector.

Firms by themselves are unable to remedy these defects. The government will have to help, chiefly by investment in public infrastructure, providing low cost transportation and by facilitating exports. Experience has shown that sound economic policies without sound economic institutions are not very effective. The government could help by removing infrastructural bottlenecks, for example by repairing the irrigation system. Water supply dominates the discourse of the present (ninth) Five Year Plan and future agricultural development will have to rely on greater efficiency in water management. With the ideological debate now behind us, we can pursue pro-poor policies. This could be done by building a network of institutions at village level. The devolution of power scheme can be instrumental in achieving this. There is need to focus on infrastructure projects that can provide greater employment. The growth of small industries must be accelerated and greater education opportunities and expanding health care can help to achieve this goal.

THE RISE AND FALL OF THE BCCI

One of the most spectacular successes of private enterprise in Pakistan was the establishment of the Bank of Credit and Commerce International (BCCI). Its fall therefore, proved most confounding. At its height, the BCCI had 398 branches in 72 countries. The moving spirit behind the bank was Agha Hasan Abedi (1922–95) Obtaining an MA in English Literature and a Law degree, Abedi joined the Habib Bank in 1946. In 1959, he received financial backing from the House of Saigols to set up the United Bank Ltd. in 1959. The United Bank became synonymous with push and drive, or to put it in less staid terms, ambition. The United Bank in time set up 912 branches in Pakistan, and 24 branches in foreign lands. The opening of a new bank branch was perceived as a repository of more deposits and more capital. The Habib Bank remained conservative; insisting for example, that its staff acquire academic expertise in banking, the United Bank, allegedly waived this requirement if the employee under reference was able to attract sizeable deposits. Symptomatically, Habib Zurich the second largest international bank did not have a sensational success nor did it suffer a dramatic decline and still carries on.

Although the incoming PPP regime was to nationalize banks on 1 January 1974, Abedi, as head of the United Bank anticipated the move, and as early as 1972, he had founded the BCCI in cooperation with the Bank of America. This institution ran anti-clockwise to the socialist direction of the economy. Just as employment in the Gulf and Middle Eastern countries, offset the constricting elements of nationalization; obtaining employment in the BCCI was considered striking bonanza because the pay scale and perquisites were much higher than those prevailing then in Pakistan. The cream of the Pakistani banking talent, was recruited, but the recruitment went on till after the Bank was incurring losses.

Abedi was not neglectful of the demands of philanthropy. On the one-side he inducted former US President Jimmy Carter to Global 2000, one of its benevolent institutions. He set up the Orangi Pilot Project in 1980, a project to take up city planning to sanitation, in the largest urban area in Karachi. The BCCI foundation set up two prestigious educational institutes in Pakistan, FAST, now a university specializing in Information Technology and the Ghulam Ishaq Khan Institute at Topi. These are flourishing despite the closure of the BCCI.

What could cause such a massive enterprise to fail? Only a massive lack of collateral. *The Wall Street Journal* reported that huge loans were given to Gokals, the shipping magnates: $30 million in 1978, $70 million in 1979 and $71 million in 1981. Although no direct connection can be proved, this was around the time that Mustafa Gokal was a member of Ziaul Haq's cabinet. Testifying before the US Senate, Masihur Rahman, an employee, pinpointed the Gokals as the biggest reason for the bank's downfall.[1] The salaries and emoluments of the employees was also a major reason. BCCI showed an operational loss of $40 million in 1988, but instead of retrenchments, new appointments continued.[2]

The year 1988 proved to be the inauspicious year. Agha Hasan Abedi suffered a heart attack and had to withdraw from the bank's affairs. In the October of the some year, drug money laundering charges were brought against the BCCI. There was some discrepancy between the roles of the employers and the employees who were indicted at Tampa. The prosecutors conceded in December 1988 that the defendants 'did not receive any personal monetary gain from this alleged money laundering, neither did they accept the bribes offered by the undercover agents.'[3]

Was it a bubble that had burst on the pin of laundering charges, or was it an exercise to liquidate an institution which could stand in the way of imposing World Bank/IMF conditionalities? It was, it seems, a little of both. The BCCI pleaded guilty to the charges. Other banks charged simultaneously with the BCCI were treated more leniently. The American Bank of Dade County which confessed to laundering $90 million, more than six times the amount the BCCI was accused of laundering. Banco de Occident, Panama had to pay a fine of $5 million for laundering $411 million, which is a slap on the wrist compared to the liquidation of the BCCI.

A crucial factor was the US endeavour to charge Manuel Noriega for drug money laundering, and even today the President of Panama languishes in a US jail. The New World Order had begun. Meanwhile, in February 1991 Agha Hasan Abedi was set to launch his third venture. It was to be called the Progressive Bank.

NOTES

1. *Newsline*, Karachi, September 1991, p. 56.
2. Ibid., June 1990, p. 100.
3. *Herald*, Karachi, March 1991, p. 125.

NOTE

1. S. Akbar Zaidi, *Issues in Pakistan's Economy*, Karachi: Oxford University Press, 2005, p. 131.

CHAPTER 42

ECONOMIC PLANNING

Why do countries need to plan ahead? To ensure that the available resources of a country are utilized to their maximum advantage. Planning means deciding how to best organize the factors of production. The factors of production are land, which includes all natural resources employed in production; labour, which includes all mental and physical human resources; and capital which includes money and other goods and services utilized in the production of goods.

Planning means taking decisions about what and how much to produce, and how to distribute what is produced. To take these decisions, economists must have a comprehensive knowledge of what a country possesses and what a country requires. Planning has to be long-term and this is what differentiates it from annual budgets. Economic development, as Pervez Hasan states, 'must be sustainable'. Manufacturing should not be at the cost of depleting natural resources.

Planning is a governmental not private activity. Classically, its main objectives are a positive growth in GDP, that is, an increase in a country's total level of output, secondly, to control levels of unemployment, thirdly, to set a target rate of inflation, fourth to ensure that the current account balance is surplus, and finally to ensure that the exchange rate is stable, that is the value of the local currency does not fluctuate sharply in relation to other currencies.

Planned economy meant the socialist economy of communist states, most of which had collapsed by 1990. Price economy means that market forces determine the price of commodities; this corresponds to capitalist economy. We must be clear that planning in the context of Pakistan, is not planning as an ideological entity but a practical entity.

Economic planning began late in Pakistan, a full eight years after independence. It is possible that the government did not believe that it had a sufficient resource base to undertake economic planning.

THE FIRST FIVE YEAR PLAN (1955—60)

The First Plan set out the following targets:

1. A 15 per cent increase in GDP and 7 per cent increase in per capita income.
2. To create employment opportunities for 20,000,000 people.
3. A 13 per cent increase in food production, and ultimately autarchy and self sufficiency in food.
4. To improve 6,000 villages by providing power, water, sanitation and communications.
5. To irrigate 3,000,000 acres of land.
6. To produce 580,000 kilowatts of electricity.
7. To establish 1,500 new post offices.
8. To add Rs 250,000 hospital beds.
9. To earn Rs 50 crores worth of foreign exchange.

None of these targets was achieved. One reason is that the plan was actually sanctioned in 1957 and three years was too short a time for implementation, even if all the resources had been available. Thus, instead of 15 per cent, only 11 per cent increase in GDP was achieved. The per capita income was increased by 3 per cent instead of 7 per cent because the population increased faster than the rate of development. The plan failed, partly because the effort seems to have been half-hearted, and partly due to inexperience. On the other hand, a great increase in economic activity featured in the second plan.

The Second Five Year Plan (1960—65)

This Plan had as its goal a 24 per cent increase in the GDP, and a 12 per cent increase in per capita income, 6 per cent increase in heavy industry and 30 per cent increase in light industry. It aimed at food autarchy, and the removal of regional imbalances. This plan held out encouragement to private entrepreneurs to participate in profit-making activities, while the public sector moved into those activities which had little attraction for the private sector. This impetus to industry, alongside the Green Revolution which undertook to increase irrigation, enlarge mechanized farming and supply fertilizers, had an overall effect on development, and during the Ayub era all the economic indicators were positive. Towards the end of the plan period, the 1965 war broke out and resources from other sectors had to be diverted to defence. On the whole the Plan was considered very successful.

The Third Five Year Plan (1965—70)

The Third Plan had been designed on the lines of the Second Plan but proved unsuccessful because of the two wars. The Third Plan also showed, that foreign aid was an important factor in development, and if withheld or curtailed, it had an adverse effect on development. As against a 37 per cent target in GNP, 36 per cent was achieved. In agriculture the target was 5 per cent whereas 4 per cent was achieved. The export target of 9.5 per cent was actually achieved to the extent of 6.5 per cent.

The greatest shortfall was a poor performance in savings and capital development, and as Faruq Aziz has pointed out, this was the main reason for the economy not progressing at the desired rate. He also says that private enterprise in East Pakistan remained dormant, and the target of removing inter-wing disparity was not achieved. During the Ayub era, private enterprise was the key to development, but because it was in the hands of non-Bengalis, private enterprise was locally resented. The economists of the Dhaka University came up with a two economy theory, saying that the economies of the two wings were organically different. This made capital shy in East Pakistan, and it is possible that the steel mill planned for Chittagong was withheld on political grounds.

THE FOURTH FIVE YEAR PLAN (1970–75)

This Plan had to be abandoned because of the 1971 war and the secession of East Pakistan. When Zulfikar Ali Bhutto took over, he abandoned Five Year Plans and opted for annual plans. These too were not acted upon, consequently the Bhutto years came to be known as the non-plan years. However, this was the period when nationalization took place, and this agenda lasted throughout the Bhutto years, affecting future planning in Pakistan.

THE FIFTH FIVE YEAR PLAN (1978–83)

This Plan laid the foundation of long-term economic planning. The small agro-based units Bhutto had nationalized towards the end of his term, were denationalized. Ziaul Haq did not undertake large-scale denationalization, therefore those capitalists who were hit by nationalization remained wary. This provided an opportunity for a new class of entrepreneurs who wished to move from trade to industry. The Zia regime gave impetus to cement and fertilizer factories, a development this new class found conducive.

One notable feature was that half the amount of public sector funding was allocated to the lately established steel mill in Bin Qasim. This was a major step in basic industry development in Pakistan. The same period saw an increase in defence expenditure. The influx of Afghan refugees had both a financial and social cost with drug mafias acquiring a presence in Pakistan. Although the foreign aid in view of the Afghan influx was large, still the balance went against Pakistan since a section of entrepreneurs, mostly centred around Karachi, though otherwise willing to invest, was inhibited by the law and order situation. It must be noted that during this planning period Pakistan became self-sufficient in all basic food items except edible oils.

THE SIXTH FIVE YEAR PLAN (1983–88)

The Sixth Five Year Plan was essentially a continuation of the previous plan. It was aimed at maintaining the rate of economic development, harnessing modern technology and also avoiding the neglect of the social sector. Private investment in petro-chemicals and fertilizers fell short of the expected levels. On the other hand, investment in agro-based industries, textiles and pharmaceutical industries was between 2 to 8 per cent higher than the expected level. A growth of 6.5 per cent was registered. Severe droughts in 1986 and 1987 impeded a better growth rate.

THE SEVENTH FIVE YEAR PLAN (1988–93)

The Seventh Five Year Plan corresponded roughly with the induction of the first Benazir Bhutto and Nawaz Sharif democratic regimes. Benazir Bhutto tried to signal clearly that her regime did not intend to return to the nationalization of her father's regime, and encouraged private enterprise. Free enterprise, open markets, privatization and deregulation were to form the basis of a new economic framework. There was great emphasis on growth, though during the plan period there was no success in generating additional resources and even less success in curbing day to day expenditure.

The delay in the stabilization of the Afghan situation after the Soviet withdrawal, the break up of the USSR, and the Gulf war of 1991 were external factors which slowed progress. At home, ethnic strife and strikes took their toll. Between 1989 and 1993 there were two floods that affected progress.

THE EIGHTH FIVE YEAR PLAN (1993–98)

The Eighth Five Year Plan was actually approved on 31 May 1994 by the National Economic Council. In 1991, the government had inducted representatives from the private sector to seek guidelines for a programme. A balance was sought at between the public and private sector, between existing capital and new enterprise. The plan had a three-prong strategy which meant privatization, promotion of a free market and the development of small-scale industries. No great interest was shown during the period under review and the Five Year Plan somehow went out of fashion.

One problem facing the economy during the Pervez Musharraf regime was that successive governments had been experimenting with privatization but this had not proved a panacea for the economy. The economic crisis is paralleled by a moral crisis. To concede that only incentive and insecurity can make the wheels of the economy move means that the economic process can proceed on the basis of the baser instincts of mankind. Viewed ideologically private property needs protection. The only solution is to make the industries originally founded in the public sector more competitive.

The Pakistan Steel Mill is a major example. By 30 June 2000, the Pakistan Steel Mill had registered a colossal loss. The government formed a Restructuring Committee and its recommendations were carried out by cutting all unessential expenditure. A corporation forming a separate legal entity has been made responsible for all auxiliary duties including education. The steel mill has made a turn around and, according to Khurshid Anwar, the Finance Director, is operating successfully against imported steel products, despite the fact that its existing capacity of 1.1 million is an uneconomic size which makes the production costs higher. This, being an administrative problem, is capable of resolution.

Water has become the most serious resource problem and the issue of building a dam at Kalabagh has divided the nation politically. The people of Sindh are wary, saying that since insufficient water is being allowed to flow into the sea, the sea is claiming more and more upstream areas. On the other hand, if storage facilities are neglected, the whole area could suffer. This is the old struggle between the production and distribution of wealth.

VISION 2030

This is a plan which has a long term perspective. Approved by Prime Minister Shaukat Aziz on 3 March 2005, its key feature, predictably a key feature was a Rs293 million allocation for increasing water availability from 135.68 million acre feet to 150.35 million acre feet. The strategic direction was stated by Akram Sheikh, deputy chairman Planning Commission to be: A developed, industrialized, just and prosperous Pakistan through rapid and sustainable development in a resource constrained economy by employing knowledge inputs.

This focus on knowledge inputs needs not only a reordering of the administrative structure, but the social structure itself. The experience is that allocation is not enough, the teaching force needs both monetary and authority incentive coupled with empowered parents bodies. Human resource development, discussed further on, will have a more prominent role to play.

THE MEDIUM TERM DEVELOPMENT FRAMEWORK 2005–10

This is a component of Vision 2030, for both a short term and long term plan are needed to set priorities five, five year plans are envisaged as a whole all, naturally dependent on previous successes. A promising feature is that excepting for institutions and finance; the main objectives are more social than economic. They are Education, Justice and Health. The imperative of Education planning we have already discussed. Under Justice, reengineering of police has been proposed. This was attempted under local government, but the police is not willing to have its powers made subservient. The political ends of justice having erupted in crisis, a new approach needs to be applied. Health needs the greatest attention, not only by extending facilities to rural areas but by combating, on war footing, the unsanitary challenge in hospital management.

Under institutions, allocations of resources to achieve social justice are mentioned emphasis is placed on ending corruption and increasing accountability. Food, shelter, clothing have been conceded as requirements. How this can be achieved along with the structural adjustment plan is not clear. Under finances the necessity of promoting a just and non-regressive regime of taxation is mentioned. The tightening of the tax net is proposed, and a legal system to stop tax evasion by the corporate sector is emphasized. The spreading of the tax net should be given equal emphasis. It is proposed to improve the infrastructure of the corporate sector. Infrastructure needs in the agriculture sector are also important.

THE KALABAGH DAM PROPOSAL

The most burning controversy in the domain of economic planning is whether, a dam should be built at Kalabagh or not. Representatives of the most populous province, the Punjab, are vehement that it should be built. The representatives of all other provinces are equally vehement that it should not. For the Punjab it means greater irrigation, greater yield and greater prosperity. The other provinces argue that it would cause inundation of large areas, lead to dislocation of thousands of persons and cause large areas to go barren. This topic has not remained confined to discussions among engineers or economists, but has become a political issue, the topic of many slogans.

The World Bank has tried to bring about consensus between contending parties, and undeniably, it has a right to intervene, since it was the World Bank which brokered the 1960 Indus Badin Water Treaty. Lately it arbitrated over Pakistan's objections to the design of the Indian built Baglihar Dam. Pakistan's objections to the Baglihar, the objections of Bangladesh to the Farraka Barrage in India, and the conjoining of Indian rivers around Bangladesh show how far the era of the Mangla and Tarbela dams have been left behind when their construction was held up as a sign of progress.

The World Bank Report was prepared by John Briscoe and his associates, and contains interesting new material (i) There is only one industrial common effluent treatment plan for the whole country. (ii) There is no modern Asset Management Plan for any major infrastructure. (iii) The silt now causes the Indus River to shift vertically, not horizontally. (iv) Twenty to thirty per cent of water in the Indus Badin is consumed by weeds. (v) There are 20 million tons of salt accumulating in the system every year.

There are grave developments and unless remedied, the prospects of our economy are bleak. What is contended is whether storage will reduce silt and salinity, or will it increase them.

The World Bank experts recommend storage and dams. They also prophesy that investment in water infrastructure will reduce poverty. These recommendations are based on ecological studies. The melting of glaciers, which has already started in Pakistan, will cause a water glut, inevitably to be followed by water scarcity. They hold that midstream there is 20 per cent less flow of water, and downstream 20 per cent less than midstream. This brings us to the Sindhi objection to the Kalabagh.

There is a minimum amount of river water which needs to flow to the sea. The alternative is that the sea climbs up, filling the gap. Sea water being saline would render the present fertile area barren. Sindhi experts say that 10 million MAF is the minimum amount required for preventing sea intrusion. This estimate was contested *but no alternative estimate was forwarded*. As far as Balochistan and NWFP are concerned, the government of Pakistan can, as per World Bank's recommendation, give priority to developing storage infrastructure, but unless this complaint of Sindh is redressed, opposition to the Kalabagh Dam will not die down. Perhaps, the World Bank should have advanced the quantum of water required to flow downstream, and not have left the issue to political recrimination.

NOTE

1. *Dawn*, 4 May 2005.

M AHBUB UL HAQ (b. Jammu, 22 February 1934–d. New York, 16 July 1998) was one of the most influential economists that Pakistan has produced. He had the benefit of being educated in the universities of the Punjab, Cambridge, Yale, and Harvard. His brilliant academic accomplishments in Economics led to Mahbub ul Haq's induction in the Planning Commission of Pakistan, and in the 1960s, he rose to be its chief economist. It was in this latter position that Mahbub ul Haq delivered an address that changed the face of politics and development in Pakistan: 'The wealth of Pakistan was held by twenty-two families only.'[1]

This was at the height of the Ayub Khan era when all economic indicators were positive. This speech was highlighted by the socialist parties of Pakistan to offset the effects of the Ayub era boom. The East Pakistan fallout was wider. The economists of the University of Dacca, led by Dr Abu Nasr Mahmud, had formulated a Two Economies theory whereby the economy of the two wings had two separate bases. Since the overwhelming number of the twenty-two families belonged to non-Bengali entrepreneurs who had invested in East Pakistan, 'Twenty-two Families' became a slogan with Maulana Abdul Hamid Khan Bhashani (1880–1976), president of the National Awami Party, and in the western wing with Zulfikar Ali Bhutto, chairman of the PPP. Mahbub ul Haq provided these parties with support by another speech, made two years later: 'A mere reform of the capitalist system is no longer viable. The reforms cannot be built in Pakistan through an evolutionary process.'[2]

Mahbub ul Haq was taken at his word, and while the two socialist parties were rampant in both wings, in East Pakistan, the ingredients of '*Gherao, jalao*', (surround, burn) were added to the heady mixture of revolution. The ouster of Ayub led to nationalization in Pakistan under Zulfikar Ali Bhutto, and in Bangladesh under Sheikh Mujibur Rahman, but it was only in Pakistan that capital has shied away from investment.

Meanwhile in 1970, Mahbub ul Haq left Pakistan and until 1982, he was the director of the Policy Planning Department at the World Bank. To his credit, here also, he advocated the restructuring of the World Bank itself. In 1982, during the Zia era, Mahbub ul Haq returned to Pakistan and joined the Federal cabinet, serving in turn as minister of Finance, Planning and Development, Commerce, and Economic Affairs. He stood for tax reforms, poverty alleviation, and deregulation of the economy. In none of these could he claim a success.

From 1989–95, that is, during the democratic interregnum, Mahbub ul Haq left Pakistan to serve as special adviser to the UNDP administrator. He was the creator, chief architect, and principal author of the Human Development Reports of the UNDP. It was shortly after leaving this assignment that Mahbub ul Haq made his second celebrated observation: 'The magnitude of corruption in Pakistan, exceeds Rs.100 billion a year.'[3]

The corrupt have been more resilient than the capitalists in Pakistan, and Mahbub ul Haq had to concede that the incidence and volume of corruption had gone up. Dr Mahbub ul Haq can be held up as an example of the brilliant economists produced by Pakistan, who, despite having power and responsibility, were unable to influence the economy of their country in the direction and to the extent they desired.

Notes

1. Speech to Pakistan Management Association, vide *Pakistan Observer*, Dacca, 3 May 1968.
2. 'Pakistan's Choice For The 1970s'. Paper presented at the University of Rochester, 29–31 July 1970.
3. 'Ethics and Government'. Statement at the State of the World Forum, 21–23 November 1996, Guanajuato, Mexico.

CULTURAL

CHAPTER 43

CULTURE AND SOCIETY

What is culture? The search for a satisfactory answer to this question has given rise to a great deal of discussion and debate. What is Pakistani culture is another difficult question for which no completely acceptable answer has yet been evolved, but towards which we can draw closer by discussing and debating the question.

T.S. Eliot (1888–1965) the celebrated poet and critic called his treatise, *Notes Towards the Definition of Culture*.[1] In other words, Eliot does not claim to have arrived at a definition of culture, but can only to point to a definition. Then again, the reader must be warned that not only does the term culture have different meanings for different writers, but that it is used interchangeably with another term, civilization. The word civilization is of French origin (1734). It meant according to Michel Boivin,[2] to improve the social state of a community. Later, it denoted the higher state of humanity. In its origin, it is quite compatible with culture. We can see this in the writings of two theorists of history. For Oswald Spengler (1880–1936) Culture meant: 'Nobility, church privileges, dynasties, convention in art, and limits of knowledge in science.'[3] In other words, Spengler has used the word 'culture' as an extranational unit of society in which common features transcendig national boundaries are highlighted. His contemporary, Arnold Joseph Toynbee (1889–1975) employed the term civilization in almost the same sense. Toynbee found that a national state was not an intelligible field of study in isolation; and that 'a civilization is an intelligible field by comparision with its component communities—nations, city-states, millets, castes etc.'[4] In Eliot we find no attempt to determine the frontier between culture and society.[5]

A more recent author, Shireen Hunter, is more forthcoming: 'Culture, which subsumes civilization as its outward manifestation of itself'.[6] Oswald Spengler, the most influential exponent of culture as a unit of historial study states that: 'The Civilization is the inevitable destiny of the Culture'.[7] We ourselves speak of a Pakistani culture and an Islamic civilization. As an illustration, we can take the example of Faiz Ahmed Faiz (1911–84): the most internationally acclaimed poet of Urdu, complained that Urdu was an imposition, since only 8 per cent of Pakistani babies listen to lullabies in the national language.[8] We can deduce that for Faiz, culture is defined by mother tongue, which in 92 per cent cases means regional languages. It follows that

defined by Urdu, since Faiz not only composed the bulk of his
... urdu, he even, on occasion strayed into *Purbi*, a Hindi dialect
having no territorial representation in Pakistan.

The Oxford English Dictionary defines culture 'as the customs, institutions
and achievements of a particular nation, people or group'. Sir Edward Taylor
defines culture as 'that complex whole which includes knowledge, belief, art,
morals, law, custom, and any other habits acquired by human beings as
members of society'. The United Nations Economic, Social and Cultural
Organization UNESCO (2002) has defined culture as:

> culture should be regarded as the set of distinctive spiritual, material, intellectual
> and emotional features of society or a social group, and that it encompasses, in
> addition to art and literature, lifestyles, ways of living together, value systems,
> traditions and beliefs. In short, it requires unity in diversity.

THE MAIN COMPONENTS OF CULTURE

The following four elements can be considered to be the main components
of culture:
1. Values
2. Norms
3. Institutions
4. Artefacts

1. Values can be described as ideas of what seems important in life to a
group of people or a society. They are ideals that guide or qualify conduct and
interaction among people. They help to distinguish what is right from what
is wrong, and serve as a guide on how to conduct life in a meaningful way.
Culture is greatly influenced by values; and most often the ideas they generate
are brought together in religion from which society derives its values. For
example, honesty is a value shared by all religions, while honouring one's
ancestors is a value present in some religions but not in all. According to A.L.
Kroeber, 'culture embodies values'.[9]

2. Norms consist of what society considers as normal behaviour. Eating
with one's fingers is considered normal behaviour in South Asia but not in
Europe. Each culture has methods or sanctions, of making sure that people
live and respect its norms. If you eat with your fingers in a European city,
people may look at you with disapproval, so that you may stop eating that
way.

Sanctions may be strict or not, depending upon the importance of the
norm. Norms that a society enforces in a formal manner because it considers
them important, become the laws of that society. For example, drinking
alcohol is legally prohibited in Pakistan.

3. Institutions are the structures of a society within which values and norms are practiced and transmitted. Some institutions are exclusive to South Asian society, such as *mushairas*. However, marriage is an institution of our society which prevails in many other societies as well. In all these societies having a family and providing stability for them is considered an important norm. The rituals which are legal are religious, those which are cultural are social.

4. Artefacts are shaped by a culture's values and norms. A society's arts and crafts come under this heading. Geometrical design for example, has grown out of Islamic culture as a substitute for the artistic depiction of human bodies which is not acceptable in culture. This is an example of how a culture's values influence its artefacts. Some are developed by convention. The earliest mosque, at Medina, had no dome or minaret, but now a dome and minaret are the most recognizable feature of the mosque.

Culture has also been described as the result of 'the best that has been thought and said in the world'. In a progressive, developing and evolving culture, all achievements and accomplishments improve with time. In such a culture, improvement is given a great deal of importance, and since improvement becomes a value, people are open to listening to and acting upon the views of others.

Thought, and respect for ideas are forces inherent in the development of a culture's artefacts, just as thought and research are reflected in scientific advancement. Those who are courteous, tolerant and calm are considered cultured, as are those who are interested in the artefacts and institutions of their own and other cultures.

CULTURE AND CLASSES

It is often said that culture is the collective behaviour of the educated segment of society. Education is conceived to be a vital ingredient of culture. When we call a man 'cultured' we presuppose a certain level of education; when we speak of 'cultured pearls' we mean pearls having all the natural ingredients and produced in a shell, but whose production has been artificially induced. Therefore, we can confidently state that education is an important element in the diffusion of culture. We can relate our observation to the class structures of Pakistan.

We can say that the appreciation of art and the patronage of art belong to the Pakistani upper class, although the creation of art itself may be outside the purview of the upper class. Apart from the arts, as far as customs, manners and behavioural norms go, they belong more to the middle and lower classes. Dress and food varies from class to class in style, but in propriety, there is unity. Education is an important element in relation to the arts as well. There which cannot be appreciated naturally. They develop from an ....ste. For example, in Pakistan, classical music and modern art can be appreciated only by those who know the intricacies of these arts. Folk music and pop music have separate but overlapping audiences. People who can appreciate representational art far outnumber people who can appreciate abstract art.

Snobbishness in art is at an ebb. There is an effort by established artists to embrace the crude and garish artwork on trucks and buses. Literature is the only art which is available to all classes, but even here there is a distinction between serious and popular literature. However, taste distinction and class distinction are not congruent. Popular literature is devoured more by the middle class. Cinema has not yet found its bearings, in spite of three or four high class films. Television drama which played a formative role in fostering cultural awakening has seen technical advance and artistic decline at the same time.

CULTURE AND POLITICS

Culture acquires a political dimension when the culture of the conqueror is perceived to be higher than the culture of the conquered. Sir Percival Spear observes that a situation like this can bring about a real revolution and gives rise to rethinking. Since Pakistani culture cannot be divested of its British content, the clothes we wear, the language employed both by this writer and his readers and other technological improvements (or intrusions) into our life, mention must be made of three Englishmen who had a pronounced influence over us, Edmund Burke, Sir William Jones and Lord Macaulay. Edmund Burke's *Impeachment of Warren Hastings* transmitted British ideals to India, Sir William Jones made Indians aware of the grandeur of their early civilization, and on the opposite side Lord Macaulay made them aware of their shortcomings. Education in English overcame the separatist tendency of vernacular languages and provided an outer shell to culture. In other words, acting as a common language among speakers of various regional languages, English brought them closer, giving their cultures a better chance to merge.

In Pakistan, cultural varieties have been given a political meaning. It is reiterated that by neglecting regional cultures we are threatening the federation. One of the reasons why East Pakistan broke away was the issue of not giving Bengali its rightful place. On the break up of Pakistan two Russian historians, Gordon Polonska and Yuri V. Gankovsky, popularized the notion that Pakistan was composed of four nationalities, relating to the four provinces. Z.A. Bhutto, who took over after the secession of East Pakistan and was then engaged in military operations in Balochistan, banned this notion. It rarely serves to ban a concept. As an example, in order to show the failure of federation in Pakistan Syed Jaffar Ahmed highlighted the differences among the people of Pakistan: 'A people who have not coalesced into a nation, and are a disjointed lot'.[10] Writing in a very different context, at least three authors, Intizar Hussain, Bapsi Sidhwa and Attiya Dawood, coincidentally in the same issue, noted the similarities between India and Pakistan.[11] There is much to be said on the issue of federal myopia having fostered regionalism, but against this we note that Yusuf Haroon had warned against provincialism before the creation of Pakistan.[12]

Since regional tensions deal with language hegemony we shall resume this discussion in Chapter 44: Language and Literature.

CULTURAL HERITAGE AND MODERN CULTURE

Although culture is the term most used to interpret history, the historical component of culture is not unanimously acknowledged. While Clifford Geertz, defines culture as 'a historically transmitted pattern of meaning embodied in symbols'.[13] On the other hand, Philip Bagby defines culture as: 'Regularities in the behaviour, internal and external, of the members of a society, except those regularities which are clearly hereditary in origin'.[14] People wishing to reform, are mostly hampered by hereditary or historical norms; like the Mughal and British attempts to abolish *Sati*. The cultural scene in Pakistan attests to the compartmentalization of the historical and current.

In the domain of art, Abdur Rahman Chughtai represents cultural heritage, Sadequain represents modern culture; in music Roshan Ara represents cultural heritage, Fuzon represents modern culture; in literature Hafeez represents cultural heritage, N.M. Rashid represents modern culture. Apart from personalities, the Badshahi Mosque, Lahore is our cultural heritage, the Tooba Mosque in Karachi is a product of modern culture.

In historical terms it should be clarified that the possession of a great cultural heritage, to belong to a religion which has had a great cultural impact is not the same as possessing a great culture. A great culture is one that can overcome military superiority. The Hindus were able to assimilate conquerors like the Huns and the Scythians, and Muslims were able to convert Mongols and Tartars who were their conquerors, to their own religion.

When the British invaded India, European culture was in a dynamic state; scientific discoveries, political theorizing and literature were receiving an impetus, and at the same time the Muslims were reflecting on their decline. We mentioned earlier Edmund Burke, Sir William Jones and Lord Macaulay. Sir William Jones translated Kalidasa's *Shakuntala* and founded the Asiatic Society of Bengal. It was his mission to discover and propagate the glory of Hindu civilization. Lord Macaulay, on the other hand remarked that one shelf of western books contained more wisdom than whole libraries in oriental languages. Both Jones and Macaulay were right. Jones was concerned with cultural heritage, the past which was indeed glorious. Macaulay was concerned with the present, with what was, in his time, modern culture.

Gradually the mould of South Asian culture will become obsolete. The mould of modern Pakistan will come into play. Perhaps the present is not equal to the past, but nevertheless it will point to the future, to a Pakistan which is perforce nuclear, a Pakistan which is threatened, a Pakistan which, in addition, is beset with environmental hazards, which has serious gender inequalities, and which is sitting on a population time bomb. These are to be the future parameters of Pakistani culture regardless of whether we overcome these challenges, or whether they overwhelm us. If these trends are a danger, they are equally so to all Pakistanis and in that sense they have a unifying effect, for they call for all of us to put our heads together in order to evolve values and a mode of life acceptable to all.

NOTES

1. T.S. Eliot, *Notes Towards the Definition of Culture*, London: Faber and Faber, 1961.
2. Michel Boivin, *Jihad*, Chambery: Universite de Savoie, 1999.
3. Oswald Spengler, *Decline of the West*, New York: Vintage Books, 2006, p. 25.
4. A.J. Toynbee, *A Study of History*, Vol. XII, Oxford University Press, 1961, pp. 284 and 286.
5. T.S. Eliot, op. cit., p. 15.
6. Shireen Hunter, *The Future of Islam and the West*, Westport, Praegar, 1998, p. 8.
7. Oswald Spengler, op. cit., p. 24.
8. Faiz Ahmed Faiz, *Meezan*, Lahore, Minhas, 1962.
9. A.L. Kroeber, *The Nature of Culture*, Chicago: University of Chicago Press, 1952, p. 104.
10. Syed Jaffar Ahmed, *Dawn*, Sunday Magazine, 10 August 2003, p. 1.
11. Ibid., Books and Authors, pp. 1 to 4.
12. Ibid., 28 July 1947.
13. Clifford Geertz, *Interpretations of Culture*, New York: Basic Books, 1973, p. 89.
14. Philip Bagby, *Culture and History*, London: Longman, 1958, pp. 84 and 195.

CHAPTER 44

LANGUAGE AND LITERATURE

We have already noted how languages evolved. The evolution of speech is due to mimesis in a child, but the evolution of language has another dimension. Sanskrit was the language of the Aryans, and since Hinduism was common to South Asia, there could have been no ideological or political forces to promote regional languages. Regional languages like Pushto and Bengali, correspond to the climates in which they were nurtured. However, the spread of language does not follow the same process as the evolution of language. If a language contains knowledge required by other people, or if a language is championed by a politically dominant people, that language spreads far beyond the confines of its birth place. In both instances, English is the prime example. The language of a small island on the fringes of Europe has become not only the educational but literary language of people round the globe.

Then there are languages which are religiously sanctified. Sanskrit was the language of prayers and rituals for Hindus and spread all over the subcontinent. Yet, because regional languages evolved and Sanskrit became too difficult for common use, it became a dead language and was replaced by Prakrit and eventually by modern Hindi. There is also the case of Latin. It was the educational and religious language of the whole of Europe, but even in the country of its origin it was replaced by Italian which became an important literary language, and produced great poets like Dante and Petrach who are as revered as are Latin writers, such as Luctretius and Virgil. Arabic remains the living language of the Middle East, much beyond its original home in the Arabian peninsula; but in other Muslim lands where the Holy Quran and daily prayers are recited in Arabic, Persian, Turkish and Urdu evolved as distinct languages which not only produced great literature, but expounded the themes of Islam. It is in this light that we must view the relations between Urdu, the national language, and the regional languages of Pakistan. Since they have all been developed over time and reflect the disposition, the circumstances and the fortunes of the people who use them, we must acknowledge them as our treasures, just as we value the natural resources of our provinces.

URDU

When we view the language scene of Pakistan, we see a scene both stormy and complex. Urdu is the national language of Pakistan, but its position has never remained unchallenged. In 1867 there was a conflict between Hindi and Urdu, in 1952 there was a conflict between Bengali and Urdu and in 1972 there was a conflict between Sindhi and Urdu, and in every conflict Urdu proved to be the language of the minority. How then did Urdu become the national language of Pakistan? One reason is that all conflicts took place within three different borders. The Urdu–Hindi conflict took place within British India, the Bengali-Urdu conflict took place within divided India and the Sindhi–Urdu conflict took place within divided Pakistan.

In South Asia there was no true national language which was universally spoken, read and understood. Both Hindi and Urdu were actually inter-provincial languages, spoken in the same provinces: United Provinces (UP), Central Provinces (CP), and Bihar. However, there was one difference, Hindi was spoken all over, whereas Urdu was concentrated in the cities. Because Urdu was an urban language, it was used more in the urban centres than in rural areas. Urdu became associated with the Muslims and Hindi with the Hindus. Muslims, who had for a long time made Persian their official language, were confident that Urdu, the result of Hindu–Muslim interaction, would be equally acceptable to both communities, therefore, it came as a shock, when Babu Shiva Prasad, a poet of Urdu, led a movement in Benares in 1867 to replace Urdu with Hindi. It was this movement which led Sir Syed Ahmad Khan to articulate the Two-Nation Theory. Sir Syed said that the dissension between Hindus and Muslims originated with the language issue.

Why should there have been any resistance to Hindi at all, since it was the language of the majority? This question must be answered if we are to trace the history of Muslim nationalism in India. The answer is provided by Farman Fatehpuri: 'It was because the birth of Modern Hindi was not the result of natural or linguistic evolution.... It was brought forth at the instigation of the Fort William College authorities'[1] who commissioned Laloo Lalji to write *Prem Sagar*, and in the process remove Arabic and Persian words and replace them with Sanskrit. This was carried to such extremes that even Shiva Prasad was shocked. Tara Chand's comment on *Prem Sagar* was that: 'Modern Hindi was till then unknown, for no literature existed in it'.[2] As late as 1937, Piarey Lal, UP Minister of Education had refused to promulgate Hindi, which he considered 'rustic'.

In 1949, N.V. Gadgil, speaking in the Indian parliament on 13 September, admitted that 'Hindi today is admittedly a provincial language, and there are other provincial languages far richer in literature'.[3] R.R. Divakar, Information and Broadcasting Minister said in 1950 that he was receiving numerous complaints from people that the Hindi of All-India Radio was not intelligible to them and they had to listen to the Urdu of Radio Pakistan to follow the news.[4] Urdu became a political cause with Muslims because, more than Hindus, the British seemed bent on championing Hindi. In 1873, the Lt. Governor of Bihar, G. Campbell banned Urdu from educational institutions and the courts. The Lt. Governor of UP, Sir Anthony McDonnell passed a resolution replacing Urdu with Hindi.

The Muslims of India, alarmed at this turn of events formed, an Urdu Defence Committee under Sir Syed Ahmad Khan on 9 December 1873 at Allahabad. In 1900, first Nawab Mohsinul Mulk and then Nawab Viqarul Mulk led another Urdu Defence Association. In 1903, the Society for the Progress of Urdu was formed, and in 1910 when Aziz Mirza was honorary secretary, the society came under the aegis of the All-India Muslim League and the promotion of Urdu became one of the Muslim League's responsibilities. From then on Urdu became one of the symbols of Muslim League aspirations. In 1937, the possibility of compromise on Urdu, nurtured by the Nehru family, was finally ended when Mahatma Gandhi ruled: 'Urdu was the religious language of the Muslims; it was written in the Quranic script; Muslim rulers had devised and spread it. Muslims, if they wish can keep it and spread it'. It was at this juncture that Allama Iqbal offered his support to Baba-i-Urdu, Maulvi Abdul Haq.

This culminated in the AIML legislator's convention in Delhi in 1946, when M.A. Jinnah proclaimed that 'only Urdu would be the national language of Pakistan because it is the repository of Muslim culture, civilization and intellectual cohesion'. Jinnah's reiteration of this stand at Dhaka in 1948, could not have come as a surprise. However, for that independence year, the Federal Public Service Commission had allowed different languages in its examination including even Hindi, but Bengali was not included and this was the real reason that the language issue was raised.

This brings us to Urdu's relations with Bengali. At the time the rivalry between Hindi and Urdu began, it was clear that both languages were being backed by religious sentiments; regional considerations took second place. It was also a fact then, that no language confined to a province, no matter how rich, could challenge the hegemony of either Urdu or Hindi. Deena Nath Ganguly and Naveen Chandra Roy were the first of a complete cadre of Bengali writers who espoused the cause of Hindi. Presiding over the All-India Urdu Conference at Calcutta on 9 January 1936, A.K. Fazlul Haq reassured the delegates that the Muslims of Bengal were not against Urdu. A Calcutta meeting addressed by both Fazlul Haq and Suhrawardy, president and secretary of the Bengal Muslim League, on 8 April 1939, had stressed the 'need for protecting and promoting the Urdu language and script in Bengal'. Even now the Bengali speaking Muslims of Purnea district in India insist that their mother tongue is Urdu. Attitudes changed only when borders changed. Urdu was challenged only when Hindi was removed from the scene.

There is another factor which led to Urdu becoming the national language of Pakistan. In history, people have worked for the consolidation and advancement of other languages. Persians have served the cause of Arabic, Indians have served the cause of Persian, and Punjabis have served the cause of Urdu. This has not been confined to writers, but has extended to publishers. Not only Muslim publishers who are many, but Hindu publishers like Atar Chand Kapur and Narayan Das Saigol have played a pivotal role in the promotion of Urdu. Then Urdu acquired a national status because of its role in the Freedom Movement. Ninety per cent of the poems confiscated by the British were in Urdu.

When Pakistan came into being, the echoes of classical poetry were still strong and three classical poets—Seemab Akbarabadi (1880–1950), Arzu Lakhnawi (1872–1951), and Natiq Lakhnawi (1878–1950)—migrated to Pakistan when they were on the verge of death. The immigration of Josh Malihabadi (1895–1982) the poet of revolution was felt deeply because he had believed in Indian nationalism. Josh wrote most of his masterpieces in Pakistan and justified his stay in cultural terms.

Initially, the Progressive Writers Association was favoured because the Communist Party had supported partition, but because of its lukewarm response to the Indian occupation of Kashmir, eminent writers like Muhammad Din Taseer (1902–1950)—one of its founders—parted company with it. Extreme ideological exclusiveness and factional strife had already weakened the association when it was banned in the wake of the Rawalpindi Conspiracy, when Faiz Ahmed Faiz and Syed Sajjad Zaheer (1905–1973) were incarcerated. The two literary figures standing outside the Progressive Writers Association were Sa'adat Hasan Manto (1910–1955) and N.M. Rashid (1910–1975).

Sa'adat Hasan Manto illuminates his scenes, defines his theme sharply, and as far as the etching of his characters, the depiction of the shadowy world of harlotry, and his cynical exposé of bestiality, during communal riots is concerned, Manto is beyond the pale of comparison. He displays a dramatic flair, giving artistic credence to his surprise endings. Following closely is Ghulam Abbas (1909–1982) whose stories are known not only for artless and unobtrusive depicture, but also for delicacy and finesse.

Writers of the right wing also felt the pressure of religious groups; as a result Qurratulain Hyder (1927–2007) resentful of the tirade against her masterpiece, *Aag ka Darya* (1959), re-migrated to India. Soon after, Shaukat Siddiqui (1923–2006) published *Khuda ki Basti* which became an overnight success because of its strong social realism. By 1960, the experimental short story became dominant under Intizar Hussain (b.1923), Enver Sajjad (b.1934),

Masud Ash'ar, and Arsh Siddiqui (d.1997). Khalida Hussain (b.1938) received recognition rather late, but her mysterious and inscrutable treatment and choice of themes have left a lasting impression on Urdu fiction. The next generation, headed by Muhammad Mansha Yaad (b.1937) has original writers, Asif Farrukhi and Ali Haider Malik (b.1944). While Mansha Yaad has drawn his symbols from the rural myths and folk tales, another prominent contemporary, Rasheed Amjad (b.1940), has sought to break both the plot and linguistic structure.

Turning to poetry we encounter Nazar Muhammad Rashid (1910–1975): a sceptic with deep metaphysical insight, he transformed blank verse into abstract illuminations and formations, projecting the enigmatic, bizarre, and weird aspects of life, absorbing into poetry the themes that had been the preserve of prose. His contemporary, Miraji (1909–1949) became a cult figure and far more influential.

Side by side with a generation of neoclassical poets, a generation of post-modern poets started attracting attention. These were led by Iftikhar Jalib (1936–2000), Qamar Jamil (d.2000), and Mubarak Ahmed (d.2001). Some even penetrated the hitherto impregnable fortress of the hidebound *ghazal* and turned it into an avant-garde art form. They were led by Javed Shaheen (b.1932) Zafar Iqbal and Anwar Shaur (b.1943), but before they could displace the earlier generation, the 1965 war broke out.

The demands of national solidarity were catered to. Himayat Ali Shair's (b.1932) *Blood* conveyed solemnly the sentiments of the nation. Anthems were contributed by Jamiluddin Aali (b.1926) and Rais Amrohvi (d.1988).

The Tashkent Declaration (1966) was viewed as a betrayal and gave rise to protest poetry. Habib Jalib (1929–1993) led the revolutionary chorus followed by Yunus Sharar (b.1946).

The 1980s decade saw the flowering of feminist love poetry. Ada Jafri, Pervin Fana Syed, and Zahra Nigah gained respect for breaking the male monopoly over lyricism. Their poetry turned feminist only with the advent of Kishwar Naheed (b.1940), and Fehmida Riaz (b.1946). Feminist issues and grievances were amplified by Sara Shagufta and Azra Abbas.

The ingredient of glamour remained elusive till the advent of Parveen Shakir (1952–1994), a poet of exceptional sensibility and erudition, she added literary lustre to the genre of feminine poetry. Their inhibitions having diminished, a number of poets have held the field without being avowedly feminist. They are Shahida Hasan (b.1953), Tanvir Anjum (b.1956), Ishrat Afreen, Fatima Hasan (b.1952), and Fouqia Mushtaq (b.1968)

At present, Iftikhar Arif (b.1940) as an eminent poet is chairman of the Pakistan Academy of Letters. The chairman of the National Language Authority, Fateh Muhammad Malik (b.1936), represents both historians and literary critics.

Pushto

Pushto literature dates back to the eighth century AD and the legendary ruler of Ghur, Amir Karor Pehlawan is reputed to be the first poet of this language. Being a warrior, his poetry consisted of war and battle themes. There is some gap between the legendary and historical period, but the historical period had been neatly chalked out into three eras, each with its distinctive features, according to M.M. Kalim: first from the earliest times to the sixteenth century, second from the sixteenth century to the coming of the British, and finally from 1840 to the present.[5]

During the second era, the literary scene was dominated by Khushal Khan Khattak (1613–1689) contemporary and adversary of Aurangzeb. He not only immortalized his struggles, but gave a philosophical content to Pushto poetry. His poetry was noted for its realism as well. His symbol, Shaheen (Falcon), was adapted by Allama Iqbal. Among the junior contemporaries of Khushal Khan were Abdul Hamid, noted for his lyrics, and the celebrated Rahman Baba whose mystical poetry, though less appealing than Khushal Khan's still has a large number of votaries. A major influence on Pushto poets was Pir Roshan who was a pantheistically inclined mystic.[6]

In the post-Partition era, a People's Literary Society was founded by Sanober Husain, and included stalwarts like Dost Mohammad Kamil, Amir Hamza Shinwari and Samundar Khan Samundar. A major contribution was made by Abdul Wahid Thikedar of Mardan who wrote the *Jangnama-e-Pakistan* following the 1965 war. Ajmal Khattak as a poet and Abdul Ghani Khan as a scholar are writers who have a political profile. Reza Hamdani and Farigh Bukhari were poets who served as a bridge to Urdu poetry as well.

Hashim Babar, Taqi Hashmi, Fozia Anjum and others among poets, and Tahir Afridi, Gul Afzal, Abdul Kafi Adeeb and Zaitun Bano among fiction writers have made major contributions to Pushto literature.

Sindhi Literature

Sindhi is one of the oldest languages of the subcontinent. According to Shamsul Ulema Daudpota, it descended from the Virachada dialect of Prakrit.[7] Sindhi was recognized as a distinct language by many early scholars including al Beruni. It initially had many scripts according to the regions in which it was used, but came to be standardized in a script derived from Arabic. It is visible as such in the couplets of Shah Karim Bulri (1537–1623). Scholars identify a gap of about two hundred years between Shah Karim and Shah Inayat. It is possible that manuscripts dating from that era will one day be discovered and scholars will maybe be able to bridge the gap. Shah Inayat's disciple was the literary luminary Shah Abdul Latif Bhitai (1689–1752).

Shah Abdul Latif is the 'sun' in the firmament of Sindhi literature, and gave Sindhi an internationally acclaimed stature. He is credited with being the originator of *Wai* or *Kafi*. His romance *Umar–Marvi* is enchanting and well-known, and lends itself to modern interpretation. Shah Abdul Latif's poetry is multifaceted, but, in the words of Professor Daudpota; 'the poet's mind is always attuned to his Maker. His divinely inspired ecstasy, his melody and imagery have made his poetry unrivalled'. He is a classical poet who rules the hearts of the common man.

Another poet of this era was Khwaja Mohamad Zaman Lunhari (1713–74) who also had a mystical dimension to his verse, and his most illustrious contemporary was Sachal Sarmast (1730–1828). Sachal Sarmast was an original thinker and a free thinker as well. The spiritual quality of his poetry has attracted many devotees.

In the twentieth century the most famous traditional poet has been Makhdum-uz-Zaman Talibul Maula (1919–93) and among the modern poets was Shaikh Mubarak Ayaz (1922–97). Shaikh Ayaz is for the modern age what Shah Abdul Latif was for the early Sindhi era. His poetry, is in its essence, protest poetry expressing the sentiments of a deprived people. Sindhi language teaching was actively banned by the first military regime and Sindh suffered most from an effort at cultural regimentation. The other poets of this school were Tanwir Abbasi, Shamsher-ul-Haidri, Tufail Bewas, Badar Abro, Taj Baloch, Niaz Humayuni and others. Ustad Bukhari has only been recognized as a great poet since his death.

The sense of deprivation in Sindh found expression in fiction with Jamal Abro's *Pishu Pasha* and Ghulam Rabbani Agro's *Shiduldharial* potraying the travails of peasants and workers. There have emerged notable writers to comment on gender imbalance, a major social theme. Nurul Huda Shah, Samira Zarin and Mahtab Mahbub are the most prominent writers in this respect. Criticism and scholarship by the late Durre Shahwar Syed and Fehmida Husain are a lasting contribution.

PUNJABI LITERATURE

Punjabi literature, from the beginning, was attuned more to rural sensibilities than city life. It has its basic expression in folk lore.[8] This began with short poems and songs, but soon extended to what are called romances; long poems, all on love themes. There are five major romances Heer–Ranjha, Sassi–Punnoo, Sohni–Mahiwal, Mirza–Sahiban, and Puran Bhagat. Heer–Ranjha went from ballad to romance, in the hands of many poets, until finally, Waris Shah provided a version of such excellence that earlier versions were discarded. Waris Shah's version also underwent variations, until an authorized edition was presented by the historian Abdul Aziz. Waris Shah's *Heer* is also valuable as social history because it vividly portrays the ravages caused by the invasions of Ahmad Shah Abdali.

Sassi–Punnoo and *Sohni–Mahiwal* also ran a similar course. *Sassi–Punnoo* had many authors, but Hashim Shah's version was judged the best; *Sohni–Mahiwal* found its poet in Fazal Shah. The themes of these perennial romances are explained by the fact that, though on the surface they were the Romeo and Juliet type of romances, below the surface they were expressions of the mystical love for God, and the longing of lovers stood for the mystic's love of God.

According to Ahmad Salim, classical Punjabi poetry had the following traits: it was committed to the masses and aloof from royal courts, it was intelligible to both the local peasant and the university professor and it was attuned to the villages, and not to cities.[9]

Apart from the romances mentioned above, there were other forms, including the *Kafis* of Madholal Husain. Another epoch-making poet was Sultan Bahu (1631–91), the author of the *Si Harfi*. He did not use the cover of romance and presented high ethics in a straight forward manner, and because they have sincerity their appeal is direct. Another great poet, Bulleh Shah, (1680–1758), wrote poetry replete with spiritual ecstasy.

One historical figure who became the subject of romance was Dulla Bhatti. His father was killed when he defied Mughal forces over the forcible exaction of taxes. Dulla Bhatti avenged his father and began a peasants' movement. Ultimately he was overpowered, captured and executed. It is said that the Saint Madholal Husain was present at Dulla Bhatti's execution.

The Sikh period is generally considered a period of stagnation in Punjabi literature and only under the British was a revival witnessed. Post-partition Punjabi poetry was dominated by Ahmad Rahi. He wrote the most moving revolutionary poetry using folk songs. He was followed by Nawaz who wrote stories under the heading *Dohangian Shaaman*. The later generation of Punjabi writers is represented by Afzal Randhawa and Najm Husain Syed, followed by Nasrin Anjum Bhatti, Mushtaq Sufi and others. Ustad Daman, with his protest poetry, loomed large in the public eye, and today Baba Najmi has gained recognition as a representative Punjabi poet.

BALOCHI LITERATURE

The Baloch have a timeless literary lore but only a modern literary history. The Baloch have been basically a nomadic society which explains why the Balochi script is still not standardized. Balochi has its presence in three countries, Pakistan, Iran and Turkmenistan, with a lesser presence in Afghanistan and the Gulf States. The development of Balochi as a literary language is a recent phenomenon: 'Baloch literary activities have been concentrated in Pakistan and the development of Balochi as a written language is a very recent phenomenon'.[10]

Another factor retarding the development of Balochi compared to other languages of Pakistan, relates to the location of its users. In Turkmenistan, Balochi was actively suppressed, in Iran there was covert suppression and in Pakistan, because of the radical tone of Baloch poetry, it found an opportunity for development in Karachi, rather than in Balochistan itself.

'There came about a great change in Baloch society after the creation of Pakistan,' says Abdullah Jan Jamaldini.[11] Literary history was made when Maulana Khair Mohammad Nadvi launched a monthly journal, *Oman*, in 1950. Both Gul Khan Naseer (1914–83) and Mohammad Husain Anka (d.1977), the luminaries of Baloch poetry, received an impetus to publish their poetry. Gul Khan Naseer was the author of the first-ever published Baloch book *Gulbang*, (Quetta, 1952). It was closely followed by Azad Jamaldini's (1912–81) *Masteen Tawar* (1953). A new generation of poets includes Ata Shad, Malik Tooqi, Mubarak Qazi and others.

Fiction flowered in the writings of Mir Amanullah Gichki, Sher Mohammad Marri, Aziz Bugti and others. The Baloch novel made its debut with Syed Zahur Shah Hashmi's *Nazuk*. Baloch literature has always been strongly responsive to political and social crises, and though it may not have had a very illustrious past, it has a very bright future.

NOTES

1. Farman Fatehpuri, *History of the Pakistan Movement and the Language Controversy*, University of Karachi, BCCT, 2001, p. 43.
2. Tara Chand, *The Problem of Hindustani*, Allahabad, 1944, pp. 32, 33.
3. Prem Nath Bazaz, *The History of the Struggle for Freedom in Kashmir*, New Delhi: 1954, p. 348.
4. Ibid., p. 335.
5. M.M. Kalim in S.M. Ikram and Percival Spear (eds), *The Cultural Heritage of Pakistan*, Karachi: Oxford University Press, 1955, p. 145.
6. Ibid., p. 150.
7. Ibid., p. 155.
8. Ibid., p. 157.
9. S.H.M. Jafri and Ahmad Salim (eds), *Pakistan Society and Literature*, (Urdu), Karachi, Pakistan Study Centre, 1987, p. 205.
10. Carina Jahani, 'Poetry and Politics' in Paul Titus (ed.) *Marginality and Modernity*, Karachi, Oxford University Press, 1996, p. 205.
11. S.H.M. Jafri and Ahmad Salim, op. cit., p. 153.

MOHAMMAD HAFEEZ (b. Jalandhar, 14 January 1900–d. Lahore, 21 December 1982) was the national poet of Pakistan, by virtue of having written the national anthem. Iqbal is our ideological poet but it was Hafeez who lived through the literary contentions in independent Pakistan. Poetical endeavours in Pakistan have been directed towards protest and a struggle for democracy and for human rights against successive military regimes. In this struggle, progressive stalwarts like Faiz Ahmed Faiz, Habib Jalib, and Ustad Daman occupied centre-stage. In contrast, Hafeez Jalandhari became identified with the establishment, basking under the sun of patronage.

This, however, is an unfair appraisal. Literary historians by and large have turned a blind eye to Hafeez Jalandhari's struggles in his early life. In 1921, Hafeez launched a literary journal, *Ejaz*, from his native Jalandhar. To raise the capital he had to mortgage the family residence—for which his father hit him in front of his wife and child. Next, he accepted the editorship of *Shabab-i-Urdu*, Lahore. When the promised salary remained outstanding for many months, Hafeez was expelled from his house by his father-in-law.

What is not emphasized is that whilst most of the progressive stalwarts (like Josh Malihabadi, Faiz Ahmed Faiz, and Syed Sajjad Zaheer) came from aristocratic and affluent families, Hafeez came from the lower middle class. While progressive poets championed the cause of the workers and labourers; Hafeez—in order to support his family—often had to work as a common labourer, sometimes having to go to bed hungry. This struggle aroused the resentment and not the sympathy of the progressive writers. Syed Sajjad Zaheer made it a point of ideological correctness that Hafeez should be rated below Faiz Ahmed Faiz.

In the last year of his life, a controversy was created when on the death of Josh, Hafeez made reference to the former's scepticism. It was, indeed, an unfortunate utterance, but while the controversy raged, no one had cared to recall that on Fani's death, similar unkind words had been published by Josh.[1] Since the diatribe of Josh had no effect on the intrinsic worth of his poetry, the diatribe of Hafeez does not detract from his own intrinsic worth.

In 1919, while Hafeez was still in his teens, Hafeez recited a revolutionary poem in a Congress meeting at the request of Dr Saifuddin Kitchlew, and was promptly jailed. From the chronology of the events, it can be deduced that Hafeez was released the same day that the Jallianwala Bagh tragedy took place.

The critical notices of Hafeez are sparse, but they are meaningful and are reflective of the early recognition he gained. In 1925, Firaq Gorakhpuri broadcast a talk on Hafeez and focused on the euphony of his poems and lyrics. Not surprisingly, Firaq was disdainful of the *Shahnama-i-Islam*. In 1942, Hafeez received the praise of the two critics, who were acclaimed as the best in those days: Niaz and Majnun. According to Niaz: 'The basic muse of Hafeez is fixed on the ghazal, which has led him into song writing. He has simplicity and euphony imbued in equal measure...what ever he says carries weight, has insight, but in all his gravity we find not a trace of artifice.'[2] According to Majnun: 'The whole of the poetry of Hafeez, has as a permanent quality the exultation and loftiness which can be ascribed only to youth. The numbers of artistic qualities that have come together in Hafeez, are not seen in any other Urdu poet.'[3]

Hafeez had a sharp tongue, but he was also maligned. In his old age, Hafeez basked in glory, but in his youth he had to suffer a hard struggle. He has given us an inspiring anthem—let us pay him reverence.

NOTES

1. *Humayun*, Lahore, January 1942.
2. *Nigar Annual*, Lucknow, 1942.
3. *Bouquet War Publicity Mushaira*, Gorakhpur, 1942.

CHAPTER 45

HUMAN RESOURCE DEVELOPMENT AND EDUCATION

The development of education in Pakistan has been in double jeopardy. On the one side is the landlord who actively resists education for fear that education will emancipate his peasants. The peasant, on the other hand, seeing the poor quality of education, considers school a burden and is reluctant to lessen the workforce at his disposal. This situation is very bleak, but a recent survey by Shahrukh Rafi Khan has recommended that the promotion of education be made a criterion for legislative ability, just as the graduation clause was applied in the 2002 elections. For the peasants, the survey observed that the formation of Parent Teacher Associations has the potential to maximize the benefits of existing school facilities, especially if mothers, rather than fathers, are represented. This is a very small step, but a step in the right direction, and kindles hope for human resources development.

When Pakistan came into being, it was actively supported by an educational society, the All-India Muslim Educational Conference. Subsequently, however, education has been given a low priority in Pakistan. During the era of highest productivity in our history, in the Ayub Khan era, the value of imported books per person per year was limited to Rs 150; at the end of ten years the limit was raised to Rs 500. President Ayub Khan told the Raja of Mahmudabad that all the trouble in the world was caused by people who read books. Thus, the attitude which held centre stage was that of the peasant who considers that education is a burden. To regard education as a process of human development, and human development as a means of economic development seems almost to have been an after-thought.

It was a matter of some satisfaction, therefore, that in June 2002, a National Commission on Human Development (NCHD) was formed on the directive of President Pervez Musharraf, as a public-private partnership to promote development in the fields of health, education and microfinance. Under the NCHD, 481 non-formal education centres have been established where 12,900 children have achieved literacy.

THREE STREAMS OF EDUCATION

In Pakistan, there are three streams of education, one represented by schools who prepare students for Cambridge or London University 'O' and 'A' Level Examinations, the second represented by government or privately run schools which prepare students for Secondary School Certificates issued by the boards of education in the provinces, and the third are the *madrassas*, where religious and traditional education is taught.

There is a political demand to have a single, uniform system of education throughout the country. Due to a confused language policy, the general expertise in English at the time of Independence has been voluntarily foregone, and to regain expertise in English, an international language necessary for scientific progress, there is an uphill struggle to reclaim lost ground.

POLICIES

Pakistan had a number of National Education Policies beginning with the Fazlur Rahman Conference of 1947 in which all the right recommendations were made without any means of implementation. The Sharif Report of 1959 was the first to focus on vocational institutes. This Report recommended that secondary education be a distinct stage, not merely preparation for higher education. The undergraduate course was extended from two to three years, but because of student agitation, the extra year was dropped.

The Nur Khan Report of 1969 became the basis of the 1970 and 1972 education policies. It recommended nationalization of all colleges and most schools. Nationalization of educational institutions was not a part of the PPP manifesto but because of teacher lobbying it had to implement the recommendations of the Nur Khan Report.

The National Education Policy of 1978, under President Ziaul Haq, recommended the opening of mosque schools. Islamic learning and Arabic were introduced as compulsory subjects. An important feature was the establishment of a Special Education structure. Under Prime Minister Mohammad Khan Junejo (1985–88), *Nai Roshni* schools were set up in remote corners of the country but barely lasted beyond the architects' tenure.

The Education Policies of 1990–95 during the two democratic regimes, introduced the Social Action Programmes (SAP). These were intended to develop primary education and deliver crash literacy programmes aimed primarily at remote and under-developed areas.

Schools

According to the *Pakistan Economic Survey 2004–05* there are 164,970 primary schools. The enrolment figures for 2004 for primary schools is 19.795 million students. There are 28,728 middle schools with enrolment of 4.318 million students. There are 9,819 higher secondary schools with enrolment of 149,7496 students.

Colleges

Arts and Science: 939, Law: 53, Commerce: 87, Home Economics: 4, Teacher Training: 103, Engineering: 13, Agriculture: 5, Computer, Fine Arts Homeopathy and Tibb Colleges: 162, Medical: 28.

Public Sector Universities

Federal Area: 11, Punjab: 18, Sindh: 10, NWFP: 10, Balochistan: 3, Northern Areas: 1, Azad Jammu and Kashmir: 1.

Private Sector Universities

Federal Area: 3, Punjab: 11, Sindh: 21, NWFP: 8, Balochistan: 1, Azad Jammu and Kashmir: 2.

University education, which was previously regulated by the University Grants Commission, is now regulated by the Higher Education Commission of 2002.

There are three areas of education which merit special mention.

1. Computer and Information Technology

Pakistani students have adapted swiftly to computer technology. Courses in IT are offered at the most prestigious universities and institutes in both the public and private Sector: The Petroman Institutes, under the Federal Government, The Institute of Business Administration, University of Karachi, Lahore University of Management Sciences (LUMS), the University of Karachi and the NED University, Karachi have prestigious departments of computer sciences.

2. Distance Learning

The People's Open University, Islamabad, was established in 1974 (renamed Allama Iqbal Open University in 1977) as one of the earliest distance learning centres to be set up globally. It provides services to remote parts of the country where schools and colleges are not present, or are insufficient. It is complementary to formal education and allows students who have dropped out to resume education after long absences. The AIOU caters to all levels, from secondary schools to Ph.D. At present the AIOU offers 1,054 subjects in 91 programmes at 9 levels.

3. SPECIAL EDUCATION

The Ziaul Haq regime gave importance to Special Education in its 1978 Education Policy. A national policy for special education was drafted in 1985 and reviewed in 1988. Teachers Training facilities were first set up by the University of Karachi in 1988. The University of Punjab and the AIOU, Islamabad have subsequently opened facilities. The University of Karachi has granted affiliation to two special colleges, Ida Rieu College and DEWA College. At first only mental retardation, visual impairment and hearing impairment were the subjects of teacher training and instruction, but now Austism and Learning Disability are also being catered to.

At present the most notable feature is the large budget allocation to Education and the high number of national and international scholarships awarded to students and faculty members.

The most recent figures showing the Public Sector allocation for Education in 2004–05 in million rupees are:

Federal	Current	Development	Total
	16548.420	14416.464	30969.884
All Provinces	94142.970	33616.388	127759.358

CHAPTER 46

HUMAN RIGHTS IN PAKISTAN

In every political entity citizens have both rights and responsibilities, but it is more common to see duties imposed than to see rights upheld. Asian nations have struggled valiantly and successfully against colonialism, and subsequently as valiantly but less successfully to secure Human Rights. In Pakistan too, the attainment of Human Rights, which came on the trail of the struggle for democracy, has proved elusive. The struggle for freedom is itself a struggle for a Human Right, but after the attainment of freedom, unstinted delegation of Human Rights to citizens has not followed.

What are Human Rights? The United Nations defines Human Rights, as 'those rights which are inherent to our nature, and without which we cannot live as human beings'. Human Rights have been conceptualised at two levels, legal and formal articles, and social and cultural values. Legal and formal articles are necessary to save human beings from unwarranted arrests and torture, while social and cultural values are necessary to save human beings from, for example, honour killings (*karo kari*) and forced marriages.

Human Rights are such that they are valid for all, without distinction of gender, age, nationality, religion, possessions, race and/or origins. Human Rights are based on universal values of dignity, freedom, equality and justice. Since they are universal, these values can act as standards to regulate the life of all human beings. Human Rights are also specific and characterize certain activities such as enslavement, torture, and unlawful confinement of persons to be inhuman.

Human Rights are not only universal, but they are indivisible. By indivisibility is meant their inalienability. For example, economic, political and civil rights cannot be undermined for cultural and social rights of individuals and societies. It may be part of a people's culture to suppress women's or workers' rights, but it is, nevertheless, an infringement of Human Rights.

Pakistan is a signatory to the Universal Declaration of Human Rights, and its representative served on the committee that drafted the Declaration. Since 1986, Pakistan has its own Human Rights Commission (HRCP). This is an independent, voluntary, non-political, non-profit making and non-government organization registered under the Societies Registration Act. HRCP is a member-based organization, with an elected council, a number of office bearers (chairperson, four vice-chairpersons, a secretary general and a treasurer). The highest organ is the General Body comprising all HRCP members. It has its main secretariat in Lahore headed by a director. Its main affiliation is to the International Commission of Jurists (ICJ). The aims and objectives of the HRCP are:

(i) Spreading awareness of Human Rights among people.
(ii) Exposing wrongs, and disseminating knowledge about them.
(iii) Motivating communities for collective response against local wrongs.
(iv) Mobilizing public opinion against bigger or systemic ills.
(v) Intervening where important and possible for redressal of individual injustice or fear of injustice.
(vi) Information collection, in order to track incidents and tendencies on a day-to-day basis.

I.A. Rehman, director of HRCP, has traced the process of framing constitutions in Pakistan, against the standards of the Human Rights Declaration. He says that Universal Declaration of Human Rights (UDHR) were not ignored but were never wholly incorporated. Social rights like education and health, economic rights like equal pay for equal work, the right of protection against inhuman treatment or the right to participate in government were not incorporated. According to I.A. Rehman: 'Some of the reservations against total acceptance of the UDHR were plainly rooted in religious beliefs:'

> The Constitution of 1973 not only retained the provisions of the earlier Constitutions in respect of the State's name, the exclusion of non-Muslims from Presidential election, and the Islamization of laws, offered further concession to the religious lobby. A new Article 2 declared Islam to be the State religion of Pakistan, and Article 91 reserved the office of the Prime Minister for Muslims.[1]

I.A. Rehman goes on to list the Second Amendment declaring Qadianis to be non-Muslims. His comments on the implication of these constitutional provisions are most instructive:

> The title of the State (Islamic Republic of Pakistan) had no effect on fundamental rights. The Objectives Resolution was not enforceable. The exclusion of non-Muslims from the offices of the President of and Prime Minister did in theory smack of discrimination on the basis of beliefs, but in practical terms, the impossibility of a non-Muslim becoming head of state or government was generally conceded. The process of Islamization of laws through the agency of elected representatives was not considered in conflict with fundamental rights. Even the proclamation of Islam as the State religion was not seen to undermine fundamental

rights because at that time, no conflict was perceived between Islam and Socialism.[2]

According to Uzma Qureshi: 'In the modern world, guarantees regarding human rights are afforded primarily by international institutions':[3]

It was natural then, that the prime international institution, the United Nations should have highlighted the issue of Human Rights, consequently, they were included in the Charter of the United Nations on 20 June 1945. The next step was taken by a subsidiary body United Nations Economic, Social and Cultural Organization (UNESCO) while adopting its constitution on 16 November 1945. UNESCO concerned itself with peace and security. It was only expected that after the ravages and devastations of the Second World War the Universal Declaration of Human Rights was made on 10 December 1948 by the UN General Assembly.

Formally Human Rights became part of Pakistan's Constitution by virtue of its adherence to the Universal Declaration of Human Rights. In the current 1973 Constitution, there is Part II of Chapter 1 dealing with 'Fundamental Rights and the Directive Principles of State Policy'. The fundamental rights which have been spelt out are: security of person, safeguards against arrest and detention, prohibition of slavery and forced labour. Freedom of movement, of association and speech, Freedom of religion and safeguards to religious institutions were enshrined.

Education is also guaranteed under Article 37:

Unfortunately these guarantees have suffered erosion due to political exigencies. The right to private ownership was abridged due to the nationalization policy of the first PPP Government. When this policy was reversed, the labour laws suffered. More scandalous has been the violation of Women's rights and Children's rights. The HRCP, has brought to light many violations and afforded legal help to the victims. According to the HRCP report 1998: 'Women's subordination remained so routine, by custom and by tradition that much of the endemic violence against her was considered normal behaviour'. In the HRCP 2000 report it is stated that even the government accepts there is gender disparity in education.

In Pakistan, it is generally conceded that Women's Rights are Human Rights. Sadly these rights are upheld more in the breach than in the observation. The Human Rights most blatantly and most commonly trampled upon are Women's rights. They are trampled upon in unspeakable ways. It has to be realized, and, moreover, implemented, that unless women are empowered, unless their status is upheld, no values can flourish in society. Women's rights are hampered by legislation, the least of which are the divorce and *quazaf* laws. Children's Rights are trampled upon in spite of existing laws. According to Asma Jahangir, child marriages take place even though they are illegal under the Child Marriage Restraint Act 1929.[4]

One aspect of Children's Rights which has attracted international attention is child labour, which exists despite protective laws. Article 11 (3) states that: 'No child below 14 years shall be engaged in any factory or mine, or any other hazardous employment.' Article 37 (e) provides greater cover: 'The state shall make provisions for ensuring that children are not employed in vocations unsuited to their age.' Despite these provisions children are employed in carpet weaving and football manufacture. Others begin their working lives as unpaid apprentices to motor mechanics. The acts of violence against and abuse of, children and women are too numerous to be listed here. Suffice it to say that abuse is rampant and real. In a patriarchal set up women and children are the most vulnerable members of society.

Abuse offends human dignity and the greatest enemy of human dignity is 'terror'. It is terror, not greed, that principally threatens the rights of all citizens. Crime has proliferated, especially after 1981. Drug abuse and Klashinkov culture need to be controlled and prevented, since the maintenance of law and order is the basic responsibility of the state. Yet these are mostly individual (or gang) acts. 'Terror' also includes violence motivated by ethnic, religious, or sectarian prejudice. Perpetrators of crimes know and recognize that their actions are wrong. Those who spread terror in the name of race or religion, especially religion, do so because they imagine their acts to be meritorious.

The HRCP is pressurising the government to protect people held under the Blasphemy Act. This act is a relic of British Indian criminal law of 1860. The application of this law is a cause of real concern. A person has only to be accused, and his life is lost. Not only have members of the minority communities been victimized—even orthodox Muslims have been killed in custody by fellow prisoners. Judges who acquit such accused, are killed. Lawyers who defend people charged with blasphemy are constantly threatened. First individuals, mostly physicians, were targeted, now worshippers in the act of prayers are killed. To put it mildly, the government's role in protecting the rights of all its citizens has been ineffective.

The Human Rights dictum for social and economic development is 'Equal wages for equal work'. Social stratification is measured by a person's socio-economic status. It is unlikely that this standard will ever fail. The only remedy is to provide equal opportunity to all citizens to attain a socio-economic status that is in keeping with human dignity. The socialistic measures have given place to market forces. Labour laws are in place, but there is a need to offer incentives and a need to provide workers with security of service. Where these have been absent there has been a marked deterioration in economic productivity. Economic status determines social status. The role of Human Rights should be to implement workers' rights to education, to health and social welfare.

NOTES

1. I.A. Rehman, 'Human Rights' in Rafi Raza (ed) *Pakistan in Perspective,* Karachi: Oxford University Press, 1997, p. 311.
2. Ibid., p. 312.
3. Uzma Qureshi, *Human Rights*, Islamabad: Higher Education Commission, 2003, p. 4.
4. Asma Jahangir, *Newsline*, August 2002, p. 22.

Fresco
a wall painting in which colour is applied while the plaster is wet, and the colour penetrates deep into the wall.

Tempera
oil or oil based paint applied on a wall after the plaster is dry. The paint is only on the surface.

Plastic
substance easily moulded or shaped.

Terracotta
reddish brown pottery which is unglazed.

Hundi
informal instrument of payment, lying outside the formal banking system.

Riparian
occupying river banks or lakes. Upper riparian means the area from where a river flows. Lower riparian means the area to which a river flows.

Kalashnikov
an automatic rifle named after its Russian designer. It was used by Afghan refugees in large quantities.

Actonian cliche
Lord Acton had said: '*Power corrupts; absolute power corrupts absolutely*'. Cliche is a saying which is quoted again and again.

Fora
plural for forum.

KRL
Khan Research Laboratories, named after the nuclear scientist, Dr Abdul Qadeer Khan.

pargana
a measurement of land for revenue purposes (24 parganas made one district).

Afzal, M. Rafique, *Pakistan: History and Politics 1947–1971*, Karachi, Oxford University Press, 2007.

Ahmad, Aziz, *Islamic Culture in the Indian Environment*, London, Oxford University Press, 1964 reprint, OUP India, 1999.

Ahmad, Qayamuddin, *The Wahhabi Movement in India*, second edition, New Delhi, Manohar, 1994.

Akhund, Iqbal, *Memoirs of a Bystander*, Karachi, Oxford University Press, 1997.

Alam, Muzaffar and Subramanyam, Sanjay (eds.), *The Mughal State*, New Delhi, Oxford University Press, 2000.

Alavi, Seema, *The Sepoys and the Company*, New Delhi, Oxford University Press, 1999.

Arif, K. (ed.) *American–Pakistan Relations*, Lahore, Vanguard, 1984.

Arif, K.M., *Working with Zia*, Karachi, Oxford University Press, 1995.

Azad, Abul Kalam, *India Wins Freedom: The Complete Version*, London, Sangam 1988.

Aziz, K.K. (ed.), *Muslims Under Congress Rule*, Islamabad, NIHCR, 1978.

————, *The Khilafat Movement*, Karachi, Pakistan Publishers, 1972.

Aziz, Qutbuddin, *Exciting Stories to Remember*, Karachi, Islamic Media, 1995.

Bandopadhaya, Sailesh Kumar, *Quaid-i-Azam Mohammad Ali Jinnah and the Creation of Pakistan*, New Delhi, Sterling, 1991.

Bazaz, Prem Nath, *The History of the Struggle for Freedom in Kashmir*, New Delhi, Kashmir Media, 1954.

Bhargava, G.S., *Success or Surrender? The Simla Summit*, New Delhi, Sterling, 1972.

Bhutto, Zulfikar Ali, *The Great Tragedy*, Karachi, Pakistan Peoples Party, 1971.

————, *The Myth of Independence*, Dacca, Oxford University Press, 1969.

Boivin, Michel, *Jihad*, Chambery, Universite de Savoie.

Bracken, Paul, *Fire in the East*, New York, Perennial, 2002.

Brown, Percy, *Indian Architecture (The Islamic Period)*, Bombay, Taraporevalas, 1942.

Burke, S.M., and Qureshi, S.A.D., *The British Raj in India*, Karachi, Oxford University Press, 1995.

Caroe, Olaf, *The Pathans*, London, Macmillan, 1965.

Chamberlain, M.E., *Britain and India*, Devon, 1974.

Chand, Tara, *Influence of Islam on Indian Culture*, Allahabad, The Indian Press, 1946.

————, *The Problem of Hindustani*, Allahabad, The Indian Press, 1944.

Chandra, Satish, *Parties and Politics at the Mughal Court*, Aligarh, Peoples Publishing House, 1959.

Cheema, Pervaiz Iqbal, *The Armed Forces of Pakistan*, Karachi, Oxford University Press, 2003.

Chopra, Pran, *India's Second Liberation*, second edition, Cambridge, Massachusetts, MIT Press, 1976.

Choudhry, G.W., *The Last Days of United Pakistan*, Karachi, Oxford University Press, 1998.

Clarke, Peter, *The Cripp's Version*, Harmondsworth, Penguin, 2003.

Cohen, Stephen, *The Pakistan Army*, Los Angeles, University of California Press, 1984.

Dreher, Diane Sansevere, *Benazir Bhutto*, New York, Bantam-Skylark, 1991.

Eaton, Richard M., *Essays in Islam and Indian History*, New Delhi, Oxford University Press, 2000.

Eliot, T.S., *Notes Towards the Definition of Culture*, London, Faber and Faber, 1961.

Fallaci, Oriana, *Interview with History*, Boston, Houghton and Muffin, 1976.

Faruqui, Ahmad, *Rethinking the National Security of Pakistan*, Aldershot, Aldergate, 2003.

Fatehpuri, Farman, *History of the Pakistan Movement and the Language Controversy*, University of Karachi, BCCT, 2001.

Feldman, Herbert, *Pakistan: An Introduction*, Karachi, Oxford University Press, 1961.

Frankel, Joseph, *International Relations*, London, Oxford University Press, 1964.

Friedmann, Yohanan, *Shaykh Ahmad Sirhindi*, New Delhi, Oxford University Press, 2000.

Gense, James H., *A History of India*, Madras, Macmillan, 1957.

Habib, Muhammad, *Politics and Society during the Early Medieval Period*, New Delhi, Peoples Publishing House, 1981.

Haeri, Munira, *The Chishtis*, Karachi, Oxford University Press, 2000.

Hardy, Peter, *The Muslims of British India*, New Delhi, Cambridge University Press, 1998.

Hayes, Louis D., *The Struggle for Legitimacy in Pakistan*, Lahore, Vanguard, 1986.

Hodson, H.V., *The Great Divide*, second edition, Karachi, Oxford University Press, 1989.

Husain, S. Irtiza, *Compromise With Conciliation*, Karachi, Pak-American Commercial, 1997.

Husain, S. Ishtiaq, *The Life and Times of the Raja of Mahmudabad*, Karachi, Mehboob Academy, 1990.

Hunter, Shireen, *The Future of Islam and the West*, Westport, Praegar, 1998.

Irfani, Suroosh (ed.), *Fifty Years of the Kashmir Dispute*, Muzaffarabad, University of Azad Jammu and Kashmir, 1997.

Islam, Nazrul, *A Study in National Integration*, Lahore, Vanguard, 1990.

Jafri, Syed Husain Mohammad and Ahmad Saleem (eds.), *Pakistan Society and Literature*, (Urdu), University of Karachi, Pakistan Study Centre, 1987.

James, Sir Morrice, *The Pakistan Chronicle*, Karachi, Oxford University Press, 1993.

Javed, Qazi, *Barr-e-Sagheer Mein Muslim Fikr Ka Irtiqa*, (Urdu), Lahore, Nigarishat, 1986.

Jinnah, M.A., *Speeches and Statements as Governor-General*, Karachi, Oxford University Press, 2000.

Judd, Denis (ed.), *A British Tale of Indian and Foreign Service: The Memoirs of Sir Ian Scott*, London, The Radcliffe Press, 1999.

Kazimi, Muhammad Reza, *Liaquat Ali Khan. His Life and Work*, Karachi, Oxford University Press, 2003.

————, (ed.), *M.A. Jinnah: Views and Reviews*, Karachi, Oxford University Press, 2005.

Khan, M. Asghar, *The First Round*, London, Islamic Information Services, 1979.

Khan, M. Ayub, *Friends Not Masters*, Karachi, Oxford University Press, 1967.

Khan, Muin-ud-Din, *The Faraidi Movement*, Karachi, Pakistan Historical Society, 1965.

Khan, Roedad (ed.), *The American Papers*, Karachi, Oxford University Press, 1999.

————, (ed.), *The British Papers*, Karachi, Oxford University Press, 2002.

Khan, Salahuddin (ed.), *Speeches, Messages, and Statements of Mohtarma Fatima Jinnah*, Lahore, Research Society, University of the Punjab, 1976.

Kissinger, Henry, *The White House Years*, London, Weidenfeld and Nicholson, 1979.

Kux, Dennis, *Disenchanted Allies*, Karachi, Oxford University Press, 2001.

Lamb, Alastair, *Kashmir: A Disputed Legacy*, Karachi, Oxford University Press, 1992.

————, *Incomplete Partition*, Karachi, Oxford University Press, 2002.

Mahmood, Safdar, *Pakistan Divided*, Lahore, Jang Publications, 1981.

Malik, Muhammad Aslam, *The Making of the Pakistan Resolution*, Karachi, Oxford University Press, 2001.

Margolis, Eric, *War At the Top of the World*, New Delhi, Roli Books, 2001.

Martin, Richard C., (ed.) *Approaches to Islam in Religious Studies*, Tuscon, University of Arizona Press, 1985.

Matiur, Rahman, *From Consultation to Confrontation*, London, Luzac, 1970.

Minault, Gail, *The Khilafat Movement*, New Delhi, Oxford University Press, 1999.

Moon, Penderel (ed.), *Wavell: The Viceroy's Journal*, New Print, Karachi, Oxford University Press, 1997.

Moulvi, Ghulam Abbas, *Hindustani Musawwari Ka Irtiqa* (Urdu), Bombay, np. 1942.

Naim, C.M., ed. and tr. *Zikr-e-Mir*, New Delhi, Oxford University Press, 1999.

Nayar, Kuldip, *India: The Critical Years*, New Delhi, Vikas, 1971.

Nixon, Richard M., *Memoirs of Richard Nixon*, New York, Grossel and Dunlop, 1978.

Page, David, *Prelude to Partition*, Karachi, Oxford University Press, 1987.

Popatia, Mahboob A., *Pakistan's Relations with the Soviet Union*, Karachi, Pakistan Study Centre, University of Karachi, 1988.

Qanungo Kalikaranjan, *Sher Shah and his Times*, Calcutta, Orient Longman's, 1965.

Qureshi, I.H., *Muslim Community of the Indo-Pakistan Subcontinent*, Karachi, BCCT, 1999, University of Karachi, 1999.

Rabbani, Ata, *I was the Quaid's ADC*, Karachi, Oxford University Press, 1996.

Raza, Rafi, *Zulfikar Ali Bhutto and Pakistan 1971–1977*, Karachi, Oxford University Press, 1997.

Rizvi, Hasan-Askari, *The Military and Politics in Pakistan*, New Delhi, Konark, 1988.

Seervai, H.M., *Partition of India: Legend and Reality*, Karachi, Oxford University Press, 2005.

Shah, Mansoor, *The Gold Bird*, Karachi, Oxford University Press, 2002.

Shah, Mehtab Ali, *The Foreign Policy of Pakistan*, London, IB Tauris, 1997.

Siddiqi, A.R., *East Pakistan: The Endgame*, Karachi, Oxford University Press, 2004.

Singh, Khushwant, *Truth, Love and a Little Malice*, New Delhi, Viking, 2002.

Spengler, Oswald, *The Decline of the West*, New York, Vintage Books, 2006.

Symonds, Richard, *The Making of Pakistan*, second edition, Islamabad, National Book Foundation, 1976.

————, *In the Margins of Independence*, Karachi, Oxford University Press, 2001.

Syed, Anwar Husain, *China and Pakistan*, London, Oxford University Press, 1974.

Toynbee, A.J., *The Study of History*, 12 vols. London, Oxford University Press, 1934–61.

Vincent, Arthur, *The Defence of India*, Bombay, 1922.

Wolpert, Stanley, *Roots of Confrontation in South Asia*, New York, Oxford University Press, 1982.

————, *A New History of India*, 7th ed. New York, Oxford University Press, 2004.

————, *Jinnah of Pakistan*, Karachi, Oxford University Press, 1989.

————, *Zulfi Bhutto of Pakistan*, New York, Oxford University Press, 1993.

————, *Gandhi's Passion*, New York, Oxford University Press, 2001.

Zaheer, Hasan, *The Separation of East Pakistan*, Karachi, Oxford University Press, 1994.

Zia, Shakeel Ahmad, *Sindh Ka Muqaddama* (Urdu), Karachi, 1987.

Ziring, Lawrence, *Bangladesh: From Mujib to Ershad*, Karachi, Oxford University Press, 1997.

ACKNOWLEDGEMENTS

The author and the publisher would like to thank the following:

Richard Eaton and University of Arizona Press to quote from *Approaches to Islam*, Tara Chand and the Indian Press for quoting from *The Influence of Islam on Indian Culture*, I.H. Qureshi and BCCT for quoting from *The Muslim Community of the Indo Pakistan Subcontinent*, Qayamuddin Ahmad and Manohar for quoting from *The Wahabi Movement*, J.H. Gense and Macmillan for quoting from *History of India*, Peter Hardy and the Cambridge University Press for quoting from *The Muslims of British India*, Usha Sanyal and Manohar for quoting from *Muslim Communities of South Asia*, Olaf Caroe and Oxford University Press, Pakistan for quoting from *The Pathans*, Matiur Rahman and Luzac for quoting *From Consultation to Confrontation*, David Page and Oxford University Press, Pakistan for quoting from *Prelude to Partition*, Z.H. Zaidi and Oxford University Press, Pakistan for quoting from *Jinnah Papers*, Kalikaranjan Qanungo and Orient Longmans for quoting from *Sher Shah and His Times*, G.W. Choudhry and Oxford University Press, Pakistan for quoting from *The Last Days of United Pakistan*, Sultan M. Khan and the London Centre for Pakistan Studies for quoting from *Recollections and Reflections*, Hasan Zaheer and Oxford University Press, Pakistan for quoting from *The Separation of East Pakistan*, Stanley Wolpert and the Oxford University Press, Pakistan for quoting from *Jinnah of Pakistan* and *The Encyclopedia of Pakistan*, Sir Ian Scott and the Radcliffe Press for quoting from his *Memoirs*, Ahmed Faruqui and Ashgate for quoting from *Rethinking National Security of Pakistan*, Prem Nath Bazaz and the Kashmir Publishing Co. for quotes from *The Struggle for Freedom in Kashmir*, T.S. Eliot and Faber and Faber for quoting from *Notes Towards The Definition of Culture*, Nazrul Islam and Vanguard for quoting from *A Study in National Integration*, I.A. Rehman and the Oxford University Press, Pakistan for quoting from *Pakistan in Perspective*, Uzma Qureshi and the Higher Education Commission for quoting from *Human Rights*.

INDEX

114, 117, 119; 125, 135, 146, 155, 159

204-5
(1965 War Analysis)

224
(1971 Civil War)

233 (Bhutto, Z.A.)
235 (Zia's hypocracy)
240 (Saudus & UAE recognize Taliban)
241 (Nawez Shariff ousted & Gen. Musharraf steps in).
243/ (Musharraf / Shaukat Aziz)
   /4   Zia's Terrorism

⊛ 293-   Foreign Policy
  (302-4 Sino-Pak)

   337-8 BCCI

   358.61 Urdu
⊛ 366 Hafeez Jallandhari